Alfred Rambaud

History of Russia

From the Earliest Times to 1882 - Vol. II

Alfred Rambaud

History of Russia
From the Earliest Times to 1882 - Vol. II

ISBN/EAN: 9783743422322

Manufactured in Europe, USA, Canada, Australia, Japa

Cover: Foto ©ninafisch / pixelio.de

Manufactured and distributed by brebook publishing software (www.brebook.com)

Alfred Rambaud

History of Russia

HISTORY OF RUSSIA,

From the Earliest Times to 1882.

BY

ALFRED RAMBAUD,

CHIEF OF THE CABINET OF THE MINISTER OF PUBLIC INSTRUCTION AND FINE ARTS, AT PARIS;
CORRESPONDING MEMBER OF THE ACADEMY OF SCIENCES OF
ST. PETERSBURG; ETC., ETC.

THIS WORK HAS BEEN CROWNED BY THE FRENCH ACADEMY.

TRANSLATED BY L. B. LANG.

EDITED AND ENLARGED BY NATHAN HASKELL DOLE.

INCLUDING

A HISTORY OF THE TURKO-RUSSIAN WAR OF 1877-78,
FROM THE BEST AUTHORITIES, BY THE EDITOR.

IN THREE VOLUMES.

VOL. II.

BOSTON:
ESTES AND LAURIAT,
301-305 WASHINGTON STREET.

COPYRIGHT, 1880.
BY ESTES AND LAURIAT.

CONTENTS.

CHAPTER I.
PETER THE GREAT: EARLY YEARS.
1682-1709.

Regency of Sophia (1682-1689). — Peter I. — Expeditions against Azof (1695-1696). — First Journey to the West (1697). — Revolt and Destruction of the Streltsui. — Contest with the Cossacks; Revolt of the Don (1706); Mazeppa (1709) 13-50

CHAPTER II.
PETER THE GREAT: STRUGGLE WITH CHARLES THE TWELFTH.
1700-1709.

Battle of Narva (1700): Conquest of the Baltic Provinces. — Charles the Twelfth invades Russia: Battle of Poltava (1709) 51-75

CHAPTER III.
PETER THE GREAT: THE REFORMS.

General Character of the Reforms: the Collaborators of Peter the Great. — Social Reforms: the Tchin; Emancipation of Women. — Administrative, Military, and Ecclesiastical Reforms. — Economic Reforms: Manufactures. — Practical Character of the Schools founded by Peter. — Foundation of Saint Petersburg (1703) 76-105

CHAPTER IV.
PETER THE GREAT: LAST YEARS.
1709-1725.

War with Turkey: Treaty of the Pruth (1711). — Journey to Paris (1717). — Peace of Nystad (1721): Conquests on the Caspian. — Family Affairs: Evdokia; Trial of Alexis (1718); Catherine 106-126

CHAPTER V.
THE WIDOW AND GRANDSON OF PETER THE GREAT: CATHERINE THE FIRST AND PETER THE SECOND.
1725-1730.

The Work of Peter the Great continued by Catherine. — Menshikof and the Dolgorukis. — Maurice de Saxe in Kurland 127-133

CHAPTER VI.

THE TWO ANNAS: REIGN OF ANNA IVANOVNA, AND REGENCY OF ANNA LEOPOLDOVNA.
1730-1741.

Attempt at an Aristocratic Constitution (1730): the "Bironovshtchina." — Succession of the Polish Crown (1733–1735) and War with Turkey (1735–1739). — Ivan the Sixth. — Regency of Biren and Anna. — Revolution of 1741 . 134–156

CHAPTER VII.

ELISABETH PETROVNA.
1741-1762.

Reaction against the Germans: War with Sweden (1741–1743). — Austrian Succession: War against Frederic the Second (1756–1762). — Reforms under Elisabeth; French Influence 157–173

CHAPTER VIII.

PETER THE THIRD AND THE REVOLUTION OF SEVENTEEN HUNDRED AND SIXTY-TWO.

Government of Peter the Third, and the Alliance with Frederic the Second. — Revolution of Seventeen Hundred and Sixty-two: Catherine the Second . 174–182

CHAPTER IX.

CATHERINE THE SECOND: EARLY YEARS.
1762-1780.

End of the Seven Years' War: Intervention in Poland. — First Turkish War: First Partition of Poland (1772); Swedish Revolution of Seventeen Hundred and Seventy-two. — Plague at Moscow. — Pugatchef 183–202

CHAPTER X.

CATHERINE THE SECOND: GOVERNMENT AND REFORMS.
1762-1796.

The Helpers of Catherine the Second: The Great Legislative Commission (1766–1768). — Administration and Justice: Colonization. — Public Instruction. — Letters and Arts. — The French Philosophers 203–220

CHAPTER XI.

CATHERINE THE SECOND: LAST YEARS.
1780-1796.

Franco-Russian Mediation at Teschen (1779). — Armed Neutrality (1780). — Reunion of the Crimea (1783). — Second War with Turkey (1787–1792) and War with Sweden (1788–1790). — Second Partition of Poland; Diet of Grodno. — Third Partition: Kosciuszko. — Catherine the Second and the French Revolution. — War with Persia 221–247

CONTENTS.

CHAPTER XII.
PAUL THE FIRST.
1796-1801.

Peace Policy: Accession to the Second Coalition. — Campaigns of the Ionian Islands, Italy, Switzerland, Holland, and Naples. — Alliance with Bonaparte: The League of the Neutrals and the Great Scheme against India . . 248-270

CHAPTER XIII.
ALEXANDER THE FIRST: FOREIGN AFFAIRS.
1801-1825.

First War with Napoleon: Austerlitz, Eylau, Friedland, and Treaty of Tilsit. — Interview at Erfürt: Wars with England, Sweden, Austria, Turkey, and Persia. — Grand Duchy of Warsaw: Causes of the Second War with Napoleon. — The "Patriotic War": Battle of Borodino; Burning of Moscow; Destruction of the Grand Army. — Campaigns of Germany and France: Treaties of Vienna and Paris. — Kingdom of Poland: Congresses at Aix-la-Chapelle, Carlsbad, Laybach, and Verona 271-373

CHAPTER XIV.
ALEXANDER THE FIRST: INTERNAL AFFAIRS.
1801-1825.

Early Years: the Triumvirate; Liberal Measures; the Ministers; Public Instruction. — Speranski: Council of the Empire; projected Civil Code; Ideas of Social Reform. — Araktchéef: Political and University Reaction; Military Colonies. — Secret Societies: Poland. — Literary and Scientific Movement 374-399

HISTORY OF RUSSIA.

CHAPTER I.

PETER THE GREAT: EARLY YEARS.

1682-1709.

REGENCY OF SOPHIA (1682–1689). — PETER I. — EXPEDITIONS AGAINST AZOF (1695–1696). — FIRST JOURNEY TO THE WEST (1697). — REVOLT AND DESTRUCTION OF THE STRELTSUI. — CONTEST WITH THE COSSACKS: REVOLT OF THE DON (1706); MAZEPPA (1709).

REGENCY OF SOPHIA.—PETER I.

ALEXIS MIKHAÏLOVITCH had by his first wife, Maria Miloslavski, two sons, Feodor and Ivan, and six daughters; by his second wife, Natalia Naruishkin, two daughters and one son, who was afterwards the Tsar, Peter I. As he was twice married, and the kinsmen of each wife had, according to custom, surrounded the throne, there existed in the palace two factions, which were brought face to face by the death of Feodor. The Miloslavskis had on their side the claim of seniority, the number of royal children left by Maria, and, above all, the fact that Ivan was the elder of the two surviving sons; but, unluckily for them, Ivan was notoriously imbecile both in body and mind. On the side of the Naruishkins was the interest excited by Peter's precocious intelligence, and the fact that Natalia Naruishkin held the position of legal head of all the royal family, which, according to Russian law, the title of "Tsaritsa Dowager" gave her. Both factions had for some time been occupied in taking their measures and recruiting their partisans. Who should succeed Feodor? Was it to be the son of the Miloslavski, or the son of the Naruishkin? The Miloslavskis were first defeated on legal grounds. Taking the incapacity of Ivan into consideration, the boyars and the Patriarch Ioakim proclaimed the young Peter, then nine years old, Tsar. The Naruishkins triumphed: Natalia became Tsaritsa-Regent, recalled from exile her foster-father, Matvéef, and surrounded herself by her brothers and uncles.

The only means of revenge which the Miloslavskis could take lay in revolt, but they were without a head; for it was impossible for Ivan to take the lead. The eldest of his six sisters was thirty-two years of age, the youngest nineteen; the most energetic of them was Sophia, who was twenty-five. These six princesses saw themselves condemned to the dreary destiny which awaited the younger children of the Tsar; they saw that they would be obliged to renounce all hopes of marriage, to have nothing in anticipation but old age, after a life spent in the seclusion of the terem, and, to crown all, to be subjected to the authority of a step-mother. All that they in the fulness of youth had in prospect was the cloister. They, however, were longing for a life of activity; and though imperial etiquette and Byzantine manners, prejudices, and traditions forbade them to appear in public, even Byzantine traditions offered them models to follow. Had not Pulcheria, daughter of the Emperor Arcadius, reigned at Constantinople in the name of her brother, the incapable Theodosius? Had she not contracted a nominal marriage with the brave Marcian, who was her sword against the barbarians? Here was the ideal that Sophia could propose to herself, — to be a maiden emperor. To emancipate herself from the rigorous laws of the terem, to force the "twenty-seven locks," as the song expresses it, to raise the veil that covered her face, to appear in public and meet the looks of men, needed energy, cunning, and patience that could wait and be content to proceed by successive efforts. Sophia's first step was to appear at Feodor's funeral, though it was not the custom for any but the widow and the heir to be present. There her litter encountered that of Natalia Naruishkin, and her presence forced the Tsaritsa Mother to retreat. She surrounded herself with a court of educated men, who publicly praised her, encouraged and excited her to action. Simeon Polotski and Silvester Medviédef wrote verses in her honor, recalled to her the example of Pulcheria and Olga, compared her to the virgin Queen Elizabeth of England, and even to Semiramis; we might think we were listening to Voltaire addressing Catherine the Second. They played on her name Sophia, which means wisdom, and declared that she had been endowed with the quality as well as the title. Polotski dedicated to her the "Crown of Faith," and Medviédef his "Gifts of the Holy Spirit." The terem offered the strangest contrasts. There Molière's "Malade Imaginaire" was acted, and the audience was composed of the heterogeneous assembly of popes, monks, nuns, and old pensioners such as formed the courts of an ancient Tsaritsa. In this shifting crowd there were some useful instruments of intrigue. The old pensioners, while telling their rosaries, served as emissaries between the palace and the town, carried messages and presents to the turbulent streltsui, and arranged matters between the Tsarian ladies and the soldiers. Sinister rumors were skilfully disseminated through Moscow: Feodor, the eldest son of Alexis, had died, the victim of conspirators; the same lot was doubtless reserved for Ivan. What was to become of the poor princesses, in whose veins flowed the blood of kings? At last it was publicly announced that a brother of Natalia Naruishkin had seized on the crown and seated himself on the throne, and that Ivan had been strangled. Love and pity for the son of Alexis, and the indignation excited by the news of the usurpation, immediately caused the people of Moscow to revolt, and the ringleaders cleverly directed the movement. The tocsin sounded from the four hundred churches of the "holy city"; the regiments of the streltsui took up arms, and twenty thousand of them, followed by an immense crowd, marched to the Kreml, dragging cannon behind them, with drums beating and matches lighted. Natalia Naruishkin had only to show herself on the Red Staircase, accompanied by her son Peter, and Ivan, who was reported to be dead. Their mere appearance sufficed to contradict all the calumnies. The streltsui hesitated, seeing they had been deceived. A clever harangue of Matvéef, who had formerly commanded them, and the exhortations of the Patriarch shook them further. The revolt was almost appeased: the Miloslavskis had missed their aim, for they had not yet succeeded in putting to death the people of whom they were jealous. Suddenly Prince Mikhail Dolgoruki, chief of the prikaz of the streltsui, began to inveigh against the rioters in the most violent language. This ill-timed harangue awoke their fury; they seized Dolgoruki, and flung him from the top of the Red Staircase upon their pikes. They stabbed Matvéef under the eyes of the Tsaritsa; then they sacked the palace, murdering all who fell into their hands. Peter Saltuikof, whom they mistook for Afanasi Naruishkin, Natalia's brother, was thrown from a window on to the points of their lances. When they discovered their error, they brought his body to his aged father, the boyar Peter Mikhaïlovitch, who said, "It is God's will," and gave them brandy to drink. Then after a long search they discovered Afanasi himself in the Church of the Resurrection, and they dragged him out and brutally murdered him. Prince Romodanovski also, the aged conqueror of Tchigirin, found no mercy at their hands; his stern discipline was remembered against him. The following day the revolt began anew; the German quarter was visited by a band of the streltsui in search of Daniel Gaden, a baptized Jew who had been physician to the late Tsar, and whom they charged with poisoning him. Not finding him at home, they wreaked their vengeance on his son, a lad of twenty years, and also on another imperial physician, Daniel's friend. They finally found Daniel himself and put him to death. But they were not yet satisfied. The Tsaritsa's three younger brothers had luckily escaped from Moscow, disguised in peasant's clothing, but her father, Kirill, was forced by them to go into a monastery, where he took the name of Kiprian, and her eldest brother, Ivan, was torn from her arms, tortured, and cut to pieces. Historians show us Sophia interceding for the victims on her knees, but an understanding between the rebels and the Tsarévna certainly existed; the streltsui obeyed orders. The following days were consecrated to the purifying of the palace and the administration, and on the seventh day of the revolt they sent their commandant, the prince-boyar Khovanski, to declare that they would have two Tsars, — Ivan at the head and Peter as coadjutor; and if this were refused, they would again rebel. The boyars of the council deliberated on this proposal, and the greater number of them were opposed to it. In Russia the absolute power had never been shared, but the orators who spoke in Sophia's favor cited many examples both from sacred and profane history: Pharaoh and Joseph, Arcadius and Honorius, Basil the Second and Constantine the Eighth; but the best of all the arguments were the pikes of the streltsui.

Sophia had triumphed: in sixteen hundred and eighty-two she began to reign in the name of her two brothers, Ivan and Peter. She made a point of showing herself in public, at processions, solemn services, and dedications of churches. At the *Uspienski Sobor*, while her brothers occupied the place of the Tsar, she filled that of the Tsaritsa; she raised the curtains, however, and boldly allowed the Patriarch to come into her presence with the censer. When the raskolniki challenged the heads of the orthodox church to discussion, she wished to preside and hold the meeting in the open air, at the *Lobnoé Miésto* on the Red Place. There was, however, so much opposition, that she was forced to call the assembly in the Palace of Facets, and sat behind the throne of her two brothers, present though not in sight. The double-seated throne used on those occasions is still preserved at Moscow; there is an opening in the back, hidden by a veil of silk, and behind this sat Sophia. This singular piece of furniture is the symbol of a government previously unknown to Russia, composed of two visible Tsars and one invisible sovereign.

The streltsui, however, felt their prejudices against female sovereignty awaken. They were offended at the contemptuous way in which the Tsarévna treated the ancient customs. Sophia had already become in their eyes a scandalous person. Another cause of misunderstanding was the support she gave to the State Church, as reformed by Nikon, while the streltsui and the greater part of the people held to the "old faith." She had arrested certain "old believers," who, at the discussion in the Palace of Facets, had challenged the patriarchs and orthodox prelates, and she had executed the ringleader Nikita, surnamed Pustosviat or Tartuffe, who had openly called the Patriarch, bishops, and priests, wolves and servants of Antichrist, and in the heat of discussion had actually laid violent hands on the Archbishop. Khovanski, chief of the streltsui, whether from sympathy with the "heresy," or whether he wished to please his subordinates, affected to share their discontent. The Court no longer felt itself safe at Moscow, and removed to Kolomenskoé. Here it was noised abroad that Khovanski was coming with the streltsui for the purpose of destroying the imperial family, massacring the boyars, re-distributing the land among the lower classes, and making himself Tsar. Contemporary records say that this rumor was invented by Miloslavski in order to ruin Khovanski. At all events Sophia, with the Tsaritsa and the two young princes, took refuge in the fortified Monastery of Troïtsa, and sent letters to all the cities summoning the boyars and men-at-arms to aid in repressing the revolt of the streltsui and Khovanski. From all sides, from near and far, from Iaroslavl, Kolomna, Riazan, Kaluga, and other cities, came the nobles with their followers; their numbers are said to have amounted to a hundred thousand men eager to take vengeance on the hated streltsui. Khovanski and his son Andréi were deceived by flattering letters of invitation, and, accompanied by a body-guard, were on their way to join the imperial family, when they were arrested on the seventeenth of September, and brought to the village of Vozdvizhenskoé, where, without any form of trial, they were both put to death. Khovanski's younger son, Ivan, immediately incited the streltsui to rise and destroy the murderers of their beloved commander; but they, perceiving their weakness, and learning of the great army collected at Troïtsa, with the usual fickleness of a popular militia, suddenly passed from the extreme of insolence to the extreme of humility. Two or three thousand of them marched to Troïtsa, in the guise of suppliants, with cords round their necks, carrying axes and blocks for the death they expected. The Patriarch consented to intercede for them; they signed a paper acknowledging their error, and allowed themselves to be disarmed. Sophia then had thirty of the ringleaders executed, and pardoned the rest.

Sophia, having got rid of her accomplices, governed by aid of her two favorites, — Shaklovitui and Prince Vasili Galitsuin. Shaklovitui was the new commander of the streltsui, a man of great energy, who had risen from the position of a serf to be a clerk of the council, and who was completely devoted to Sophia's interests. Galitsuin has become the hero of an historic school which balances his genius with that of Peter the Great, in the same way as in France, Henry, Duke of Guise, has been exalted at the expense of Henry the Fourth. All the foreign representatives at the Court of Moscow spoke of him in terms of the highest admiration as a marvel of intelligence. He spoke Latin fluently; he did not expect his guests to drink undue quantities of brandy; in fact, he was a gentleman in the western sense of the word. He was the special favorite, the intimate friend of Sophia, the director of her foreign policy, and her right hand in military affairs. Ian Sobieski, King of Poland, and the Emperor Leopold were anxious to organize a solemn league between Russia, Poland, Venice, and Austria, against the Turks and Tatars, and in May, sixteen hundred and eighty-four, the Barons Zirovski and Von Blomberg visited Moscow to prove to the Russian Court the necessity of uniting with the rest of Christendom against their common enemy. But Galitsuin and Sophia would not come to any agreement with the envoys until the Poles had formally renounced their claims upon Smolensk and Kief. Finally, in sixteen hundred and eighty-six the arrangements were completed, and an offensive and defensive alliance between the powers was signed in the audience chamber under papal auspices, and with the greatest solemnity. In sixteen hundred and eighty-seven Iakof Dolgoruki and Iakof Muishetski disembarked at Dunkirk, as envoys to the Court of Louis the Fourteenth. They were not received very favorably : the King of France was not at all inclined to make war against the Turks ; he was, on the other hand, the ally of Mahomet the Fourth, who was about to besiege Vienna while Louis blockaded Luxemburg. Mahomet, in fact, besieged Vienna with an army of upwards of two hundred thousand men ; but his incapacity prevented him from taking advantage of his position, and the whole plan of the campaign was thrown out by the intervention of Russia and Ian Sobieski in favor of Austria. The Russian ambassadors received orders to re-embark at Havre, without going further south.

The government of the Tsarévna still persisted in its warlike projects. In return for an active co-operation against the Ottomans, Poland had consented to ratify the conditions of the Treaty of Andrusovo, and to sign a perpetual peace in sixteen hundred and eighty-six. A hundred thousand Muscovites, under the command of Prince Galitsuin, and fifty thousand

Little Russian Cossacks, under the orders of the hetman Samoïlovitch, marched against the Crimea in sixteen hundred and eighty-seven. The army suffered greatly in the southern steppes, as the Tatars had fired the grassy plains. Galitsuin was forced to return without having encountered the Turks at all. Great numbers of the horses died of starvation, and the army, fearfully reduced in numbers, finally reached the place from which it started. Starvation and disease had been arrayed on the side of their enemies. In order to direct public attention from Galitsuin, who was a skilful politician, but no general, the blame of the unsuccessful campaign was laid upon Samoïlovitch, who was accused of having set the steppes on fire, and of being in treasonable league with the Turks. Without any examination he was deprived of his command, and having been arrested in Galitsuin's tent, whither he had gone without suspicion, he was sent with his son to Moscow, and from there to Siberia, where he died. Mazeppa, who owed to Samoïlovitch his appointment as Secretary-at-war, and whose denunciations had chiefly contributed to his downfall, was appointed his successor. The army was reanimated by praise and rewards. Sophia sent chains and medals of more or less value to all the officers and even the soldiers, and the streltsui received each a gold kopek as a mark of honor. Galitsuin himself was presented with a heavy gold chain, and enjoyed even greater confidence than before. In the spring of sixteen hundred and eighty-nine the Muscovite and Ukrainian armies, commanded by Galitsuin and Mazeppa, again set out for the Crimea. The second expedition was hardly more fortunate than the first; they got as far as Perekop, and were then obliged to retreat without even having taken the fortress. This double defeat did not hinder Sophia from preparing for her favorite a triumphal entry into Moscow. In vain Peter forbade her to leave the palace; she braved his displeasure and headed the procession, accompanied by the clergy and the images and followed by the army of the Crimea, admitted the generals to kiss her hand, and distributed glasses of brandy among the officers. Peter left Moscow in anger, and retired to the village of Preobrazhenskoé, where he refused to admit Galitsuin into his presence. The foreign policy of the Tsarévna was marked by another display of weakness. By the Treaty of Nertchinsk she restored to the Chinese Empire the fertile regions of the Amur, which had been conquered by a handful of Cossacks, and razed the fortress of Albazin, where these adventurers had braved all the forces of the East. On all sides Russia seemed to retreat before the barbarians.

Meantime Peter was growing. His precocious faculties, his quick intelligence, and his strong will awakened alike the hopes of his partisans and the fears of his enemies. As a child he loved nothing so much as drums, swords, and muskets. He learned history by means of colored prints brought from Germany. Zotof, his master, a man of low condition, who had neither intellectual nor moral qualities calculated to win respect, and whom he afterwards made "the archpope of fools," taught him to read. Among the heroes held up to him as examples, we are not surprised to find Ivan the Terrible, whose character and position offer so much analogy to his own. "When the Tsarévitch was tired of reading," says M. Zabiélin, "Zotof took the book from his hand, and, to amuse him, would himself read the great deeds of his father, Alexis Mikhaïlovitch, and those of the Tsar Ivan Vasiliévitch, — their campaigns, their distant expeditions, their battles and sieges; how they endured fatigues and privations better than any common soldier; what benefits they had conferred on the empire, and how they extended the frontiers of Russia." Peter also learned Latin, German, and Dutch. He read much and widely, and learned a great deal, though without method. Like Ivan the Terrible, he was a self-taught man. He afterwards complained of not having been instructed according to rule. This was perhaps a good thing. His education, like that of Ivan the Fourth, was neglected, but at least he was not

subjected to the enervating influence of the terem,—he was
not cast in that dull mould which produced so many idiots in
the royal family. He "roamed at large, and wandered in the
streets with his comrades." The streets of Moscow at that
period were, according to M. Zabiélin, the worst school of
profligacy and debauchery that can be imagined; but they
were, on the whole, no worse for Peter than the palace. He
met there something besides mere jesters; he encountered
new elements which had as yet no place in the terem, but
contained the germ of the regeneration of Russia. He came
across Russians who, though they may have been unscrupulous, were also unprejudiced, and who could aid him in his
bold reform of the ancient society. He there became acquainted with Swiss, English, and German adventurers,—with
Lefort, with Gordon, and with Timmermann, who initiated
him into European civilization. His Court was composed of
Lvof Naruishkin; of Boris Galitsuin, Vasili's younger cousin,
who was his special director, and had undertaken never to
flatter him; of Andréi Matvéef, who had a marked taste for
everything European; and of Dolgoruki, at whose house he
first saw an instrument for taking observations from the stars
called an astrolabe. He played at soldiers with his young
friends and his grooms, and formed them into the "battalion
of playmates," who manœuvred after the European fashion, and
became the kernel of the future regular army. He learned the
elements of geometry and fortification, and constructed small
citadels, which he took or defended with his young warriors
in those fierce battles which sometimes counted their wounded
or dead, and in which the Tsar of Russia was not always
spared. Walking one day with Franz Timmermann in the
villa of Ismailof, he found, among other curiosities which had
belonged to his uncle, a foreign boat, and he became greatly
interested in it. Timmermann told him that it was an English
model, and when used with a sail would go both with and
against the wind. Peter inquired where he could find a man

who could teach him how to manage it. Timmermann suggested Brandt the Dutchman, who built the young Tsar a boat on the Iauza, and taught him the use of it. He who formerly, owing to a fright when a child, had such a horror of the water that he could not make up his mind to cross a bridge, became a determined sailor: he guided his boat first on the Iauza, then on the pond of Ismailof, and finally on the lake of Pereiaslavl. Already Peter dreamed of the sea, in spite of the terrors of his mother, Natalia, who was filled with the prejudices of her early training, and saw in his love for war and ship-building and innovation only mischief and even ruin.

"The child is amusing himself," the courtiers of Sophia affected to observe; but these amusements disquieted her. Each day added to the years of Peter seemed to bring her nearer to the cloister. In vain she proudly called herself "autocrat"; she saw her step-mother, her rival, lifting up her head. Galitsuin confined himself to regretting that they had not known better how to profit by the revolution of sixteen hundred and eighty-two; but Shaklovitui, who knew he must fall with his mistress, said aloud, "It would be wiser to put the Tsaritsa to death than to be put to death by her." Sophia could save herself only by seizing the throne,— but who would help her to take it? The streltsui? But the result of their last rising had chilled them considerably. Sophia herself, while trying to bind this formidable force, had broken it, and the streltsui had not forgotten their chiefs beheaded at Troïtsa. Now what did Shaklovitui, Sophia's emissary, propose to them? He read them a letter from the regent accusing Peter of introducing German customs, of disturbing the religion of the country, and of threatening the most faithful servants of the crown with death. He advised them again to attack the palace; to put Lvof Naruishkin, Boris Galitsuin, and other partisans of Peter to death; to arrest his mother, and to expel the Patriarch. They trusted that Peter and Natalia would perish in the tumult. The streltsui remained indifferent, and

Sophia, affecting to think her life threatened, fled to the Diévitchi Monastery, and sent them letters of entreaty. "If thy days are in peril," tranquilly replied the streltsui, "there must be an inquiry." Shaklovitui could hardly collect four hundred of them at the Kreml.

The struggle began between Moscow and Preobrazhenskoé, the village with the prophetic name which means the Transfiguration or Regeneration. Two streltsui warned Peter of his sister's plots, and, for the second time, he sought an asylum at Troïtsa. It was then seen who was the true Tsar; all men hastened to range themselves around him: his mother, his armed squires, the "battalion of playmates," the foreign officers, and even the streltsui of the regiment of Sukharef. The Patriarch also took the side of the Tsar, and brought him moral support, as the foreign soldiers had brought him material force. The partisans of Sophia were cold and irresolute; the streltsui themselves demanded that her favorite, Shaklovitui, should be surrendered to the Tsar. She had to implore the mediation of the Patriarch. Shaklovitui was first put to the torture and made to confess his plot against the Tsar, and then decapitated. Medviédef was at first only condemned to the knout, and banishment for heresy, but he acknowledged that he had intended to take the place of the Patriarch and to marry Sophia; he was dishonored by being imprisoned with two sorcerers condemned to be burned alive in a cage, and was afterwards beheaded. Vasili Galitsuin was charged with having allowed Sophia to take the title of Autocrat, and with having occasioned great losses in men and money in his Crimean campaign. It was with great difficulty that his cousin succeeded in getting the death-penalty commuted. He was deprived of his property, and exiled with his son Alexis to Pustozersk. It was a cruel misfortune that Peter was thus deprived of the services of this truly great and talented Russian. According to De la Neuville, "he caused a magnificent college to be constructed of stone; he brought from Greece a score of learned men and a multitude of valuable books; he encouraged the nobles to educate their children, and he allowed them to send them to the Latin colleges of Poland. He advised them in other instances to engage Polish tutors; he gave foreigners permission freely to come and go, which had never before been the custom in this empire. He desired also that the nobility of the country should have the advantage of travel, and should learn to wage war in distant lands. In short, he wished to people the waste places, to enrich the destitute, of savages to make men, of cowards to make heroes, and to transform cottages into marble palaces." But his treason was too deep to allow him to be pardoned, and Peter lost the greatest man that Russia had as yet produced. The young Tsar treated Sophia at first with some forbearance, but she attempted to escape into Poland, and henceforth remained in the Diévitchi Monastery, subjected to a hard captivity. Though Ivan continued, after sixteen hundred and eighty-nine, to reign conjointly with his brother, yet Peter, who was then only seventeen, governed alone, surrounded by his mother, the Naruishkins, the Dolgorukis, and Boris Galitsuin.

Sophia had freed herself from the seclusion of the terem, as Peter had emancipated himself from the seclusion of the palace to roam the streets and navigate rivers. Both had behaved scandalously, according to the ideas of the time, — the one haranguing soldiers, presiding over councils, walking with her veil raised; the other using the axe like a carpenter, plying his oars like a Cossack of the Don, brawling with foreign adventurers, and fighting with his grooms in mimic battles. But to the one her emancipation was only a means of obtaining power; to the other the emancipation of Russia, like his own emancipation, was the end. He wished the nation to shake off the old trammels from which he had freed himself. Sophia remained a Byzantine, Peter aspired to be a European. In the conflict between the Tsarévna and the Tsar, progress was not on the side of the Diévitchi Monastery.

EXPEDITIONS AGAINST AZOF.—FIRST JOURNEY TO THE WEST.

In August, sixteen hundred and ninety-three, Peter, accompanied by Lefort, Zotof, and a suite of more than a hundred persons, made a journey to Arkhangel. There, deaf to the advice and prayers of his mother, who, under the influence of the Patriarch Ioakim, tried in vain to bring him to reason, he gazed on that sea which no Tsar had ever looked on. He ate with the merchants and the officers of foreign navies; he breathed the air which had come from the West. He established a dock-yard in which the first regularly constructed Russian merchant-ship was built. This same ship was also the first to display the Russian flag in foreign ports. Peter even dared the angry waves of this unknown ocean in a voyage which lasted five days, and the following year, after the death of his mother, Natalia, when he returned to Arkhangel, in making an excursion to the Slovetski Monastery, he almost perished in a storm. Fully expecting to meet his end, he took the last sacrament, but persistently kept his place at the helm. Nothing could have saved him, had not the skipper, Antip Panof, pushed him away with the words, "I understand this better than thou," and brought the vessel in safety to the island, where Peter, in gratitude, erected a wooden cross with an inscription in Dutch. He also embraced the brave skipper, gave him a pension, and presented him with his suit of clothes, which was thoroughly soaked with the salt water. This experience did not prevent the "skipper Peter Alexiévitch" from again putting to sea, and bringing the Dutch vessels back to the Holy Cape. Unhappily, the White Sea, by which, since the time of Ivan the Fourth, the English had entered Russia, is ice-bound in winter. In order to open permanent communications with the West, with civilized countries, it was necessary for Peter to establish himself on the Baltic or the Black Sea. But the first belonged to the Swedes and the second to the Turks, while the Caspian was in the hands of the Persians. Who was first to be attacked? The treaties concluded with Poland and Austria, as well as policy and religion, urged the Tsar against the Turks, and Constantinople has always been the point of attraction for orthodox Russia. Peter shared the sentiments of his people, and had the enthusiasm of a crusader against the infidel. Notwithstanding his ardent wish to travel in the West, he took the resolution not to visit foreign lands till he could appear as a victor. Twice had Galitsuin failed in his expeditions against the Crimea; Peter determined to attack the barbarians by the Don, and besiege Azof, which had once been conquered by the Cossacks for his grandfather, the Tsar Mikhail. It was the key of the sea which bears the same name; from its walls the Turks made their plundering expeditions, and if the Russians could get it into their power, it would afford them a foothold for further operations. The army, amounting to a hundred thousand men, was divided into several sections, which were commanded by three generals, Golovin, Gordon, and Lefort, who were to act with the "bombardier of the Preobrazhenski regiment, Peter Alexiévitch." This regiment, as well as three others, had sprung from the "amusements" of Preobrazhenskoé,—the Semenovski, the Botusitski, and Lefort's regiment; the latter now amounted to upwards of twelve thousand picked men, mostly foreigners. According to Voltaire, a fourth of this regiment were Frenchmen, who were driven into exile by the revocation of the Edict of Nantes. They were the heart of the expedition. But it failed because the Tsar had no fleet with which to invest Azof by sea, because the new army and its chiefs wanted experience, and because Jansen, known as Iakushka, or Jakob, the German engineer, who had been bastinadoed by General Schein, spiked his cannon and passed over to the enemy. After two assaults the siege was raised in sixteen hundred and ninety-five. This check appeared the more grave because the Tsar himself was with the army, because the first attempt to turn from the "amusements" of Preobrazhenskoé to serious warfare had failed, and because this failure would furnish an argument against innovations, against the Germans and the heretics, against the new tactics. It might even compromise, in the eyes of the people, the work of regeneration.

Although Peter had followed the example of Galitsuin, and entered Moscow as a conqueror, he felt that he needed revenge. He engaged good officers from foreign countries. The Emperor Leopold sent among others the artillery commander, Casimir de Garga, the chief engineer, Ernest Friedrich Baron von Borgsdorf, and Laurentius Urban with six miners, and their under-officers. The Elector of Brandenburg, Friedrich the Third, afterwards Friedrich the First of Prussia, sent engineers and artillerymen. Artillerymen arrived also from Holland, engineers from Prussia, and Admiral Lima came from Venice. By means of these officers the knowledge of western modes of warfare was first introduced into Russia. Peter appointed the boyar Alexis Schein to be generalissimo of all the forces, and hastened the creation of his fleet with feverish impatience. The forests lying near Voronezh furnished oak, beech, birch, fir, and pine for his ships. He built of green wood twenty-two galleys, a hundred rafts, and seventeen hundred boats. All the small ports of the Don were metamorphosed into dock-yards; twenty-six thousand workmen were assembled there from all parts of the empire. It was like the camp of Boulogne, when Napoleon, contemplating the invasion of Great Britain, in eighteen hundred and four, was building his numberless transports. No misfortune — neither the desertion of the laborers, the burnings of the dock-yards, nor even his own illness — could lessen his activity. Peter was able to write that, "following the advice which God gave to our father Adam, in the sweat of his face he ate his bread." At last the "marine caravan," the Russian armada, descended the Don. From the slopes of Azof he wrote to his sister Natalia:

"Little sister, in obedience to thy counsels, I do not go to meet the shells and balls; it is they who come against me. Give thy orders to them that they come not." Azof was blockaded by sea and land: along the front of the city a barrier of earth was to be raised as high as the walls; ten or twelve thousand men were detailed to labor day and night upon this, and they worked with such activity that in five weeks the trench was filled, and the earth fell over the wall upon the besieged. In the middle of July the Cossacks captured two redoubts belonging to the enemy. The Tatars also attacked the Russian camp, but failed. An attempt to reinforce the garrison also proved fruitless. Preparations were being made for a general assault, when the place capitulated. The joy in Russia was great, and the jealousy that the streltsui felt at the success of foreign tactics gave place to their enthusiasm as Christians for this conquest of Islamism, which recalled the victories of Kazan and Astrakhan. The effect produced on Europe was considerable. At Warsaw the people shouted, "Long live the Tsar!" The army entered Moscow in sixteen hundred and seventy-six under triumphal arches, on which were represented Hercules trampling a pasha and two Turks under foot, and Mars throwing to the earth a murza and two Tatars. Admiral Lefort and Schein the generalissimo took part in the procession, seated on magnificent sledges; while Peter, who was determined to set an example to the nation and rise through all the grades of the service, now having been promoted to the rank of captain, followed on foot. Jansen, as a punishment for his desertion and the harm which he had caused the Russians, was taken to Moscow, where his head was put upon a stake.

Peter wished to profit by this great success to found the naval power of Russia. By the decision of the council three thousand families were established at Azof, besides four hundred Kalmuiki, or Kalmucks, and a garrison of Moscow streltsui. The city was fortified with strong bastions and a great fortress called Petropolis was built upon the other side of the Don. The Cossacks were quartered on the eastern side of the city in the islands of the Don which had been their customary habitation. The prelates and the monasteries were taxed for the construction of one vessel to every eight thousand serfs. The Patriarch Adrian and several of the wealthier princes were obliged to build twenty large frigates of fifty guns. The Tsar himself furnished nine ships of the line, carrying each sixty cannon. According to their wealth all the orders of nobility were called upon to bear a portion of the expense. The merchants also furnished seven bomb-vessels, with fourteen or eighteen cannon, and four fire-ships with eight cannon. It was proposed to unite the Don and the Volga by means of a canal. A new appeal was made to the artisans and sailors of Europe. Fifty young nobles of the Court were sent to Venice, England, and the Netherlands, to learn seamanship and ship-building. But it was necessary that the Tsar himself should be able to judge of the science of his subjects; he must counteract Russian indolence and prejudice by the force of a great example; and Peter, after having begun his career in the navy at the rank of "skipper," and in the army at that of bombardier, was to become a carpenter of Saandam. He allowed himself, as a reward for his success at Azof, the long-desired journey to the West.

But before he was able to carry out his plan he was to experience a little of the stubbornness of his people and to discover their dislike of the reforms which he was trying to effect. Discontent was on the increase among all classes, — among the streltsui because foreigners were preferred to them and because they were subjected to a discipline to which they were unused; among the nobles and gentry because the Tsar sent their children into the lands of foreigners and heretics and obliged them to learn the ignoble arts of ship-building and gunnery; and among the boyars and clergy because the cost of building and equipping a fleet of sixty-four ships of war within three years was thrown upon them. The burden of the new régime became heavier and heavier, and without exception all were complaining at the forced change in the accustomed current of their lives. Taking advantage of this universal disgust, a conspiracy was formed to overthrow the Tsar and restore the old order of things. The leading spirit of the conspiracy was Sophia, who thought that the death of Ivan, which occurred in January, would give a favorable opportunity for her to escape from the seclusion of her cloister and return to the glory of her former position.

On the second day of February, sixteen hundred and ninety-seven, as the Tsar was in company with a large number of ladies and gentlemen at the house of Lefort, and was about to sit down to supper, word was brought that some one wished to speak privately with him. Peter excused himself, and quickly took his departure in a sledge. He soon reached the house of Alexéi Sokovnin, who had assembled Alexéi Pushkin, Ivan Tsuikler, the commander of the streltsui, and a large number of other conspirators. Peter sat down to supper with them as though he were entirely ignorant of their design of setting fire to the house where he had been and of murdering him during the confusion. He waited quietly until the officer of the guard appeared with sufficient soldiery to arrest the entire company, who were immediately loaded with chains and taken to the village of Preobrazhenskoé. Peter, who, owing to the guard being an hour late through a misunderstanding, had narrowly escaped death at the hands of the drunken conspirators, immediately returned to his party, where he was so jovial and good-humored that no one suspected what had taken place until he himself related the affair. The prisoners, upon being subjected to torture, revealed the details of the plot and implicated many others. They had intended to throw the blame of the Tsar's assassination upon the foreigners, and use that as an excuse for killing them all, men, women, and children. Many of the conspirators had been concerned in the plot of

Shaklovitui and Miloslavski. Peter was urged to deal mildly with them; but judging that an example was needed, the ringleaders were first dismembered and then beheaded, and the limbs and heads were exposed in prominent parts of the city. The body of Miloslavski, who had died twelve years before, was exhumed and treated in the same way. The other conspirators were banished, but the Princess Sophia still remained in close confinement.

After this conspiracy was crushed, in March, sixteen hundred and ninety-seven, Admiral Lefort and Generals Golovin and Voznitsuin prepared to depart for the countries of the West, under the title of "the great ambassadors of the Tsar." Their suite was composed of two hundred and seventy persons, — young nobles, soldiers, interpreters, merchants, jesters, and buffoons. In the embassy was a young man who went by the name of Peter Mikhaïlof. This incognito would render the position of the Tsar easier, whether in his own personal studies or in delicate negotiations. At Riga Peter found the quarters devoted to the embassy entirely insufficient and disgraceful; moreover, the guards in that part of the city were doubled. The governor, Graf Dahlberg, avoided paying his respects to the ambassadors, excusing himself by a plea of sickness. But what most roused the indignation of the Tsar was that he himself, in taking an observation of the city and its fortifications, was rudely treated, and prevented from accomplishing his purpose. The insult was not at that time resented, but the recollection of it was laid up for future use. After spending a fortnight in Riga the Tsar went to Mitava, and finally reached Königsberg. The embassy entered the city with all possible display. First, outriders on superb steeds; then three companies of guards mounted on gray, black, and brown horses, accompanied by trumpeters, drummers, halberdiers with gilded weapons, guardsmen with silver battle-axes; and finally the ambassadors themselves in the full glory of their national costume. Some of the soldiers were dressed in

German uniform; but among them marched a small company of six Kalmucks, with all the accoutrements of Asiatic warriors. The ambassadors brought gifts of costly furs and gold and silver cloths. At Königsberg the Prussian Colonel Sternfeld delivered to M. Peter Mikhaïlof "a formal brevet of master of gunnery." They were entertained at the house of Dankelman the Minister, where the Tsar caused no little astonishment by his wild actions. Once, at dinner, he flew into such a passion with Lefort that he drew his sword upon him, and was prevented from doing serious harm only by the coolness of Lefort and another gentleman present. One time he was passing a lady on the street, when suddenly he shouted out to her, "Stop!" He then pulled out her enamelled watch, and after examining it carefully put it back. Another time he snatched the new and stylish wig from the head of the chief master of ceremonies, Besser, and after looking at it a moment threw it on the floor with utter scorn.

The great ambassadors and their travelling companion were cordially received by the Courts of Kurland, Hanover, and Brandenburg. In the Castle of Koppenbrügge, near Hanover, he was the guest of Sophia, the widow of the Elector. Both she and her daughter, Sophia Charlotte of Hanover, afterwards Queen of Prussia, have left us some curious notes about the Tsar, who was then twenty-seven years of age. He astonished them by the vivacity of his mind, and the promptitude and point of his answers, not less than by the grossness of his manners, his bad habits at table, his wild timidity (as though he were conscious of his lack of good manners), his grimaces, and a frightful twitching which at times convulsed his whole face. Peter had a beautiful brown skin, with great piercing eyes, but his features already bore traces of toil and debauchery. The Electress wrote in a letter dated August eleven: "Considering all the advantages which nature has given him, it would be well if his manners were a little less boorish." And again she says: "He is a prince endowed with very good and at the same time very bad qualities; in fact, he has all the peculiarities of his countrymen. If he had enjoyed a better education, he would be an accomplished man, for he has many good points, and an infinity of natural wit." The suite of the Tsar were not less eccentric than their master; the Muscovites danced with the Court ladies, and took the stiffening of their corsets for their bones. "The bones of these German women are devilish hard!" said the Tsar.

Leaving the great embassy on the road, Peter went down the Rhine to Utrecht, from which town he hastened to Amsterdam and departed the evening of his arrival for Saandam (or Saardam). There he took a lodging at the house of Gerrit Kist, a blacksmith, and an old fellow-workman of Peter's. He procured himself a complete outfit of clothes like those worn by the Dutch ship-carpenters, and began to wield the axe. He bargained for a boat, bought it, and drank the traditional pint of beer with its owner. He visited cutleries, rope-walks, and other manufactories, and everywhere tried his hand at the work; in a paper manufactory he made some excellent paper. However, in spite of the tradition, he remained only eight days at Saandam. On the third day after his arrival he was recognized. A sea-captain wrote from Russia that the Tsar was to visit Saandam, and described his personal appearance. The people began to trouble him, and so he sailed for Amsterdam in his own yacht. His life in that city was no less astonishing. He neither took any rest himself, nor allowed others to do so; he exhausted all his ciceroni by his insatiable curiosity. He inspected the most celebrated anatomical collections, and frequently watched the surgical operations in the Saint Peter Hospital; he visited the whaling fleet which was about to set sail from Amsterdam, in order to become familiar with all the details of the fishery; he made himself acquainted also with the different forms of religious observances; he studied into all kinds of manufactures, engaged artists, workmen, officers, engineers, and surgeons, and bought mod-

els of ships and collections of naval laws and treaties. He
entered familiarly the houses of private individuals, gained the
confidence of the Dutch by his good-nature, penetrated into
the recesses of the shops and stalls, and stood in the market-
place lost in admiration of a wandering dentist. He summoned
him to his lodgings, and, learning the use of the instruments
with great aptness, he practised his new art upon his followers. Meanwhile the news came that the ambassadors of the
Tsar of Russia were on their way to The Hague. Every preparation was made to receive them with great honor, for it was
whispered that the Tsar himself was one of their number. The
master of ceremonies, Van Dintir, went to Cleves with a throng
of courtiers and musicians, in order to receive the Russians
at the very borders of the land. Amid the thunder of cannon
they came into Nymwegen. At Amsterdam they were received by the Burgomeister, and a splendidly uniformed regiment of young men from the best families of the city. The
ambassadors rode in state; in the first coach were Lefort and
Menshikof; the Tsar took his place among the other nobles
in one of the last carriages. The nobles were dressed in long
coats, with caps of costly fur, which, as well as their weapons,
glittered with pearls and jewels. The city of Amsterdam was
filled with gay festivity. Theatrical performances and dances
were arranged for the amusement of the distinguished visitors,
and fireworks upon the river Amstel painted in colors of fire
the deeds of the Russian Tsar.

But, amidst all these distractions, he never lost sight of his
aim. "We labor," he wrote to the Patriarch Adrian, "in
order thoroughly to master the art of the sea; so that, having
once learned it, we may return to Russia and conquer the enemies of Christ, and free by His grace the Christians who are
oppressed. This is what I shall never cease to desire as long
as I live." He dwelt in Amsterdam like a common workman;
he scorned the service of lackeys; when he felt the pangs of
hunger he would kindle a fire under his kettle and cook his

own dinner. When he was dressed for work he answered only to the name of Carpenter Peter of Saandam or Master Peter; and a person who addressed him as Your Majesty, or Mynheer, would receive the cold shoulder. After the embassy had stayed two months at Amsterdam they took their departure for The Hague, where they were received with magnificence. On the journey Peter stopped to examine everything which was unfamiliar to him. Grist-mills, ferry-boats, and machines for irrigation received his most careful attention. When they arrived at the city, though a comfortable apartment was provided for the Tsar, he preferred to wander around until midnight, when finally he found a Russian servant asleep on a bear-skin at the hotel of his embassy. He woke him with a kick, and usurped his place on the floor, where he soon fell sound asleep. At the audience he dressed like a nobleman, in a blue coat trimmed with gold; he wore a great light wig and a hat with white feathers. At The Hague he had several familiar conversations with the stadtholder, King William the Third, and he made the acquaintance of many of the distinguished Dutch statesmen. From The Hague Peter went to Leyden, and studied into microscopy with the celebrated naturalist, Leeuwenhoek. He was especially delighted with the circulation of blood in the veins of a fish. From Leyden he returned to Amsterdam, and helped build a galiot, which was presented to him in the name of the city, and the next year it made its first trip to Arkhangel, laden with the Tsar's own purchases. But he was vexed at making so little progress in ship-building, for in Holland every one had to learn by personal experience. A naval captain told him that in England instruction was based on principles, and these he could learn in four months; so Peter, with Menshikof and fifteen other Russians, crossed the sea in a fleet of three ships of war and a yacht, commanded by Admiral Mitchell, which were placed at his disposal by William the Third. He spent three months in London and the neighboring towns. He took great pleasure in visiting the churches and the various sects, such as the Quakers, and he found much to study in the collections of the Tower. In April Admiral Carmarthen gave a mock naval battle at Spithead in his honor, which was carried out with magnificent detail. After taking into his service goldsmiths and gold-beaters, architects and bombardiers, astronomers and mathematicians, and buying models of all kinds, he returned to Holland. On his departure William presented him with a beautiful frigate of twenty-four guns, which had been fitted up for his own use. On the way, his ship being attacked by a violent tempest, he reassured those who trembled for his safety by the remark, "Did you ever hear of a Tsar of Russia who was drowned in the North Sea?" Though much occupied with his technical studies, he had not neglected policy. He had conversed with William the Third, but he did not visit France in this tour, for "Louis the Fourteenth," says Saint Simon, "had procured the postponement of his visit"; the fact being that his alliance with the Emperor and his wars with the Turks were looked on with disfavor at Versailles. More than six hundred skilled workmen and artists had meanwhile been engaged for him in Holland, and this number was still more increased by many who had escaped from France and were anxious to enter his service. In June the Russian ambassadors left Holland, which no doubt felt relieved at parting with so many expensive guests. Passing through Cleves and Leipsic, and delaying until June in Dresden, where he carefully studied the art galleries, Peter finally reached Vienna, where he studied the military art, and dissuaded Leopold, who was weary of the fifteen years' war, from making peace with the Sultan. Contemporaneous judgments regarding great men are always interesting and instructive. Bishop Burnet, in his "History of His Own Time," gives the following account of the Tsar's visit to England: "He is a man of a very hot temper, soon inflamed and very brutal in his passion; he raises his natural heat by drinking much brandy, which he rectifies himself with great application; he is subject to convulsive motions all over his body, and his head seems to be affected with these; he wants not capacity, and has a larger measure of knowledge than might be expected from his education, which was very indifferent. A want of judgment with an instability of temper appear in him too often and too evidently; he is mechanically turned, and seems designed by nature rather to be a ship-carpenter than a great prince: this was his chief study and exercise while he stayed here; he wrought much with his own hands, and made all about him work at the models of ships. He told me he designed a great fleet at Azuph, and with it to attack the Turkish Empire; but he did not seem capable of conducting so great a design, though his conduct in his wars since this has discovered a greater genius in him than appeared at that time. He was disposed to understand our doctrine, but he did not seem desirous to mend matters in Muscovy; he was indeed resolved to encourage learning, and to polish his people by sending some of them to travel in other countries, and to draw strangers to come and live among them. He seemed apprehensive still of his sister's intrigues. There was a mixture both of passion and severity in his temper. He is resolute, but understands little of war and seemed not at all inquisitive that way. After I had seen him often, and had conversed much with him, I could not but adore the depth of the providence of God, that had raised up such a furious man to so absolute an authority over so great a part of the world. David, considering the great things God had made for the use of man, broke out into the meditation, What is man, that thou art so mindful of him? But here there is an occasion for reversing these words, since man seems a very contemptible thing in the sight of God, while such a person as the Tsar has such multitudes put, as it were, under his feet, exposed to his resistless jealousy and savage temper." Peter was preparing to go to Venice, when vexatious intelligence reached him from Moscow.

REVOLT AND DESTRUCTION OF THE STRELTSUI.

As has been remarked, Peter's initiatory reforms, his first attempts against the national prejudices and customs, had raised him up a host of enemies. Old Russia did not allow itself quietly to be set aside by the bold innovator. There was in the interior a sullen and resolute resistance, which sometimes gave birth to bloody scenes. The revolt of the streltsui, the insurrection of Astrakhan, the rebellion of the Cossacks, and later the trial of his son and first wife, are only episodes of the great struggle. Already the priests were teaching that Antichrist was born. It had been prophesied that Antichrist should be born of an adulteress, and Peter was the son of the second wife of Alexis; therefore his mother, Natalia, was the "false virgin," the adulterous woman of the prophecies. The increasingly heavy taxes that weighed on the people were another sign that the time had come. Others, disgusted by the taste shown by the Tsar for German clothes and foreign languages and adventurers, affirmed that he was not the son of Alexis, but of Lefort the Genevan, or that his father was a German surgeon. They were scandalized to see the Tsar condescend to expose himself to blows in his military "amusements." The lower orders were indignant at the abolition of the long beards and national costume, and the raskolniki were scandalized at the authorization of "the sacrilegious smell of tobacco." The journey to the West completed the general dissatisfaction. Had any one ever before seen a Tsar of Moscow quit Holy Russia to wander in the kingdoms of foreigners? Who knew what adventures might befall him among the Turks and the Germans? for the Russian people hardly knew how to distinguish between them, and they were wholly ignorant of France and England. Under an unknown sky, at the extremity of the world, on the shores of the "ocean sea," what dangers might he not encounter? Then a singular legend was invented about the travels of the Tsar. It was said that he went to Stockholm disguised as a merchant, and that the queen had recognized him, and had tried in vain to capture him. According to another version, she had plunged him in a dungeon, and delivered him over to his enemies, who wished to put him into a cask lined with nails, and throw him into the sea. He had only been saved by one of the streltsui, who had taken his place. Some asserted that Peter was still kept there; and in seventeen hundred and five the streltsui and raskolniki of Astrakhan still gave out that it was a false Tsar who had come back to Moscow, — the true Tsar was a prisoner at Stekoln, attached to a post.

In the midst of this universal disturbance, caused by the absence of Peter, there were certain symptoms peculiarly disquieting. The Muscovite army grew more and more hostile to the new order of things. The streltsui, who had been sent to form the garrison of Azof, pined for their wives, their children, and the trades they had left in Moscow. When, in the absence of the Tsar, four regiments of them were sent from Azof to the frontiers of Poland, they again began to murmur. "What a fate is ours! It is the boyars who do all the mischief; for three years they have kept us from our homes." Two hundred deserted and returned to Moscow; but the council, fearing their presence in the already troubled capital, expelled them by force. They brought back to their regiments a letter from Sophia. "You suffer," she wrote; "later it will become worse. March on Moscow. What is it you wait for? There is no news of the Tsar." It was repeated through the army that the Tsar had died in foreign lands, and that the boyars wished to put his son Alexis to death. It was necessary to march on Moscow and exterminate the nobles. The military sedition was complicated by the religious fanaticism of the raskolniki and the demagogic passions of the popular army. Eight thousand, in spite of the efforts of their general, Prince Romodanovski, to restrain them, revolted, deposed their officers, and marched against Moscow. Generals Schein and Gordon, with their regular troops, hastened after them, came up with them near the New Jerusalem convent on the banks of the Istra, and tried to persuade them to return to their duty. The streltsui replied by a petition setting forth all their grievances: "Many of them had died during the expedition to Azof, suggested by Lefort, a German, a heretic; they had endured fatiguing marches over burning plains, their only food being bad meat; their strength had been exhausted by severe tasks, and they had been banished to distant garrisons. Moscow was now a prey to all sorts of horrors. Foreigners had introduced the custom of shaving the beard and smoking tobacco, to the entire destruction of the holy faith. It was said that these Germans meant to seize the town. On this rumor, the streltsui had arrived, and also because Romodanovski wished to disperse and put them to the sword without any one knowing why." A few cannon-shots were sufficient to scatter the rebels, who were mainly foot-soldiers. With the aid of the cavalry four thousand six hundred were arrested; torture, the gibbet, and the dungeon awaited the captives.

When Peter hastened home from Vienna, he decided that his generals and his council had been too lenient. He had old grievances against the streltsui; they had been the army of Sophia, in opposition to the army of the Tsar; he remembered the invasion of the Kreml, the massacre of his mother's family, her terrors in Troïtsa, and the conspiracies which all but prevented his journey to the West. At the very time that he was travelling in Europe for the benefit of his people, these incorrigible mutineers had forced him to renounce his dearest projects, and had stopped him on the road to Venice. He resolved to take advantage of the opportunity by completely crushing his enemies, and by making the partisans of Old Russia feel the weight of a terror that would recall the days of Ivan the Fourth. The long beards had been the standard of revolt, — they should fall. On the twenty-sixth of August, the first day after his return, the nobles presented themselves before him at Preobrazhenskoé, and fell upon their faces in accordance with the ancient customs. Peter raised them courteously to their feet, but he ordered all the gentlemen of his Court to shave themselves, and himself applied the razor to his great lords. The same day the Red Place was covered with gibbets. The Secret Chamber of Inquiry had meanwhile been holding its sessions, and hundreds of the streltsui had undergone the most terrible tortures rather than confess their guilt and reveal the names of their accomplices. The Patriarch Adrian tried in vain to appease the Tsar's anger by presenting to him the wonder-working image of the Mother of God. "Why hast thou brought out the holy ikon?" exclaimed the Tsar. "Retire, and restore it to its place. Know that I venerate God and His Mother as much as thyself, but know also that it is my duty to protect the people and punish the rebels."

On the first of October there arrived at the Red Place the first instalment of two hundred and thirty prisoners: they came in carts, with lighted torches in their hands, nearly all already broken by torture, and followed by their wives and children, who ran behind uttering mournful lamentations. Their sentence was read, and they were slain, the Tsar ordering several officers, whom he suspected of cherishing sympathy with the revolt, to help the executioner. Seven days were employed in this way; a thousand victims were executed. Some were broken on the wheel, and others died by various modes of torture. John George Korb, the Austrian agent, who as an eye-witness has left us an authentic account of the executions, heard that "five rebel heads had been sent into the dust by blows from an axe wielded by the noblest hand in Russia." The terrible carpenter of Saandam worked and obliged his boyars to work at this horrible employment. It is said that on the last day Peter himself put to death eighty-four of the streltsui. The removal of the corpses was forbidden: for five months the Muscovites had before their eyes the spectacle of the dead bodies hanging from the battlements of the Kreml and the other ramparts; and for five months three streltsui suspended to the bars of Sophia's prison presented her the petition by which they had entreated her to reign. Two of her confidants were buried alive; she herself, with Evdokia Lapukhin, Peter's wife, whom he repudiated for her obstinate attachment to the ancient customs, had their heads shaved and were confined in monasteries. After the revolt of the inhabitants of Astrakhan, who put their voïevod to death at the beginning of the next century, the old militia was completely abolished, and the way left clear for the formation of new troops. The streltsui formed an independent body or armed corporation, who were conscious of their power, and it was almost an impossibility to restrain them without using the severest measures, — in fact, without repressing the whole body of them. In August, seventeen hundred, Peter wrote the Patriarch of Jerusalem : " For the third time within nineteen years have the streltsui broken out in revolt, and they have caused us more harm than good. Since our return we have reduced them to obedience by death and other punishments. The remainder, whose number amounts to perhaps twenty thousand, we have been constrained to retain in our service as a protection against future outbreaks."

CONTEST WITH THE COSSACKS: REVOLT OF THE DON; MAZEPPA.

The streltsui did not form the only military force of ancient Russia whose existence and privileges had become incompatible with the organization of the modern State. The Voïská, or troops of Cossacks, — those republican and undisciplined warriors who had been formerly the rampart of Russia, and were its outposts against the barbarians, — had to undergo a transformation. The empire had numerous grievances against them: the Cossacks of the Ukraina or the Border and those of the Don had given birth to the first and the second of the false Dmitris, and from the army of the Don had sprung the terrible Stenko Razin.

In seventeen hundred and six the Cossacks of the Don revolted against the Tsarian government, because they were forbidden to give an asylum to the peasants who fled from their masters, or to those who took refuge from taxation in the camp. The ataman Bulavin, and his lieutenants, Nekrasof, Frolof, and Dranui, summoned them to arms. They murdered Prince Iuri Dolgoruki, defeated the Russians on the Liskovata, took Tcherkask, threatened Azof, all the while protesting their fidelity to the Tsar, and accusing the voïevodui of having acted "without orders." They soon, however, suffered defeat at the hands of Vasili Dolgoruki, brother of the man whom they had killed. Bulavin was stabbed by his own soldiers, and Nekrasof fled with two thousand men to the Kuban. The rebel camp was laid waste, and Dolgoruki was able to write: "The chief mutineers and declared traitors have been hung; of the others, one out of every ten; and all these dead malefactors have been laid on rafts and abandoned to the river, so as to strike terror into the hearts of the Dontsui, and to cause them to repent."

Since the removal of Samoïlovitch, in sixteen hundred and eighty-seven, Ivan Mazeppa had been the hetman of the Little Russian Cossacks of the Ukraina. He was a Polish gentleman of Biélaïa Tcherkov, in Volhynia. In his youth he was a page of Ian Kasimir, King of Poland, and received a thorough military training. After several years of service he went with the Polish marshal to fight the Cossacks who had revolted. Then he showed such ability that the king sent him as ambassador to the Khan of the Tatars. On his return to Poland that adventure befell him which the poem of Lord Byron and the pictures of Horace Vernet have rendered famous. After he was taken prisoner by the Zaporoshtsui, and had been loosed from the back of the unbroken horse which had carried him into the solitudes of the Ukraina, he entered the

Cossack army, and gained the good will of the hetman Ivan Samoïlovitch, who made him his secretary and confidant. He also had charge of the revenues, and thereby gained great wealth and repute. By betraying all chiefs and parties in turn, he had risen through the successive grades of military service to the highest. He owed the office of hetman to Galitsuin and Sophia, but on the banishment of Galitsuin, who had been a powerful friend to him, he found it for his interests to embrace the cause of Peter. His elevation gained him many enemies, but the Tsar, who admired his intelligence and believed in his fidelity, delivered up to him his accusers. He executed the monk Salomon, who pretended to reveal Mazeppa's intrigues with the King of Poland and Sophia; Mikhaïlof in sixteen hundred and ninety, and the secretary Suzlof in sixteen hundred and ninety-six, were likewise put to death.

All this time the Ukraina was being steadily undermined by factions. In the Cossack army there always existed a Russian party, a party who desired Polish government, and a party who wished to become vassals of the Turks. In sixteen hundred and ninety-three Petrek, one of the Turkish chiefs, invaded the Ukraina with forty thousand Tatars, but was forced to retreat. Besides this, the views of the army and those of the sedentary populations of the Ukraina were always at variance. The hetman dreamed of becoming independent, the officers disliked being responsible to any one, and the soldiers wished to live at the expense of the country, without either working or paying taxes, after the manner of the ancient nobles; but the farmers who had created the agricultural prosperity of the country, the citizens who could not work in security, in fact, all the peaceful laboring population, determined to get rid of the turbulent military oligarchy, and hailed the Tsar of Moscow as a liberator.

Mazeppa represented the military element of the Ukraina, and knew that he was hated by the more peaceful classes. The Tsar overwhelmed him with proofs of confidence: he decorated him with the cross of Saint Andrew, and tried to make him a prince of the Roman Empire; but Mazeppa, expecting to obtain more considerable titles, prerogatives, and advantages from Charles, King of Sweden, deferred paying the expenses of the diploma, and in consequence failed to obtain the dignity. Mazeppa feared the strengthening of the Russian State. He remembered how one day in an orgie the Tsar had seized him by the beard and violently shaken him. The taxes imposed on the vassal State of Little Russia became daily heavier, and in the war with Charles the Twelfth they increased still more. Everything was to be feared from Peter's imperious humor and autocratic pretensions. The invasion by the Swedes, which was now imminent, would necessarily precipitate the crisis; and either Little Russia would gain its independence by the help of the foreigners, or their defeat on its soil would give a mortal blow to its prosperity and its hopes for the future. Feeling that the hour was drawing near when he must obey the White Tsar, Mazeppa allowed himself to be drawn into communications with Stanislas Leshtchinski, the King of Poland, who in June, seventeen hundred and four, had been set up by the Swedish party, and elected by aid of the troops of Charles the Twelfth. The witty Princess Dolskaïa gave him an alphabet in cipher. Up to that time Mazeppa had delivered to the Tsar all letters tampering with his fidelity, and, in return, the Tzar surrendered to him all his accusers. When he received the communication of the princess he smiled, and said, "Wicked woman, she wants to draw me away from the Tsar." He did not give up the letter, but burned it. When the hand of Menshikof's sister was refused to one of his cousins, when Menshikof himself began to give direct orders to the commanders of the Ukrainian regiments, when the Swedish war and the march of the Muscovite troops limited his power and augmented the burdens of his territory, when the Tsar sent pressing injunctions for the equipment of the army in European style, when he felt around him the spirit of rebellion against Moscow, he wrote to Leshtchinski, saying that he did not think the Polish army sufficiently strong, but assuring him of his good will. His confidant, Orlik, was in the secret of all his intrigues. Some of his subordinates who had penetrated his designs made another attempt to denounce him to the Tsar: among these were Paleï, celebrated in the songs of the Ukraina; Kotchubey, whose daughter Mazeppa had seduced; and Colonel Iskra. The information was very exact, and revealed his secret conferences with the emissaries of the King and of Princess Dolskaïa. It failed, like former denunciations, through the blind confidence of Peter. When the denunciation was repeated, the Tsar began to suspect, not that Mazeppa was playing the traitor, but that Kotchubey and his friends were trying to overthrow the hetman and raise the Ukraina in revolt. Kotchubey and Iskra were invited to Vitepsk, where they renewed the accusation in writing. Mazeppa was charged by Kotchubey with the intention of deserting from the service of the Tsar. Iskra, on the other hand, declared that Mazeppa was planning to have the Tsar assassinated, and that he had gathered his information from Kotchubey. Kotchubey denied that he had ever spoken with Iskra on the subject. They were both tortured, forced to confess themselves false witnesses, delivered up to the hetman, and beheaded. Paleï was sent to Siberia. Mazeppa was conscious that such extraordinary good fortune could not last, and the malcontents urged him to think of their common safety. At this moment Charles the Twelfth arrived in the neighborhood of Little Russia. "The devil has brought him," cried Mazeppa; and he tried, by his skill in playing a double game with the two powers, to save the independence of his little State, without delivering himself over completely either to Charles the Twelfth or Peter the Great. When the latter invited him to join the army, he pretended that he was ill, and even received extreme unction.

But Menshikof and Charles were approaching, — a choice must be made. Mazeppa left his bed, assembled his colonels and a considerable force of Cossacks, harangued them on what they had suffered and were likely to suffer from the hard yoke of the Russians, and invited them to follow his example and join the Swedes, who with their aid would soon force the Tsar to accede to whatever condition he might see fit to impose. The Cossacks, however, declined to become traitors, and Mazeppa, with only four or five thousand, crossed the Desna to effect a junction with the Swedish army. Three days afterwards all but forty or fifty returned to their allegiance. Then Peter the Great made a proclamation denouncing the treason of Mazeppa, his alliance with the heretics, his plot to restore the Ukraina to Poland, and to fill the monasteries and temples of God with Uniates. He was cursed in all the churches of Russia. Baturin, his capital, was taken by Menshikof, with an army of twenty thousand men, who expected to find great riches; but, being disappointed, they sacked it and murdered all the inhabitants, men, women and children, and finally set fire to it. His accomplices, whom he had abandoned, died on the wheel and the gibbet; he himself fled, after the battle of Poltava, to the Turkish territory, and perished miserably at Bender. A new hetman, Skoropadski, was elected in his stead; the mass of the people and the Cossack army pronounced loudly for the Tsar, and the Swedes had to cope with the rising of the entire population of the Ukraina. In spite of this, the independence of Little Russia was past. The privileges of the Cossacks were over, and twelve hundred of them were sent to work at the Canal of Ladoga. A Muscovite official was joined to Skoropadski to govern "in concert with the advice of the hetman." Muscovite subjects were allowed to hold lands in the Ukraina by the same title as the Little Russians; Menshikof and Shafirof were given large domains there by Skoropadski, whose daughter married another Muscovite, Tolstoï, created commandant of the regiment of Niéżhin. In seventeen hundred and twenty-two Little Russia, whose affairs up to that time had been conducted by the department of Foreign Affairs, was governed by a special office founded at Moscow under the name of "Little Russian Affairs." This was clear proof that the Ukraina had ceased to be an independent State. When Skoropadski died, Peter neglected to nominate a successor, declaring that "the treasons of the preceding hetmans did not allow a decision to be made lightly in this grave matter of election, and that he needed time to find a man of assured fidelity."

From this time the institutions of the Ukraina were modified at the will of Peter the Great and his successors. The hetmanate was now abolished, now restored, till the last man who held the title, a courtier of Catherine the Second, abdicated in seventeen hundred and eighty-nine. The affairs of the Ukraina were sometimes directed by the office of Little Russia, sometimes by the office of Foreign Affairs, till the time when, under Catherine the Second, it became an integral part of the empire. As to the Zaporoshtsui, after their "sétcha" had been taken by Peter the Great, they emigrated to the Crimea, and were allowed by the Empress Anna to establish themselves on the Lower Dnieper. But they found the neighboring country already transformed; and as their existence seemed incompatible with the security of those who had become colonists, they were finally expelled in seventeen hundred and seventy-five.

From the year seventeen hundred and nine we may say that there no longer existed in the empire a single military force that could oppose its privileges to the will of the Tsar.

CHAPTER II.

PETER THE GREAT: STRUGGLE WITH CHARLES THE TWELFTH.

1700–1709.

BATTLE OF NARVA (1700): CONQUEST OF THE BALTIC PROVINCES. — CHARLES THE TWELFTH INVADES RUSSIA: BATTLE OF POLTAVA (1709).

BATTLE OF NARVA: CONQUEST OF THE BALTIC PROVINCES.

PETER THE FIRST had navigated the White Sea, and conquered a port on the Sea of Azof; but by the Baltic alone could he secure rapid and regular communication with the nations of the West. It was only by taking up a position on the Baltic that Russia could cease to be an Oriental State, and could form part of Europe. The Baltic at that time belonged to Sweden, which by its possessions, by Finland, Karelia, Ingria, Esthonia, Livonia, and Pomerania, occupied the whole extent of its coasts and made it a Swedish Mediterranean. Stockholm was situated in the centre of the monarchy of the Vasas, instead of lying, as it does at present, on its maritime frontier. For the Tsar to "open a window" into the West, it was necessary in some point to break the chain of Swedish possessions. The opportunity seemed favorable. The struggle in Sweden between the aristocracy and the crown was still in progress; the last King, Charles the Eleventh, in sixteen hundred and eighty, had made his authority absolute, and had ordered the nobles to restore to the throne all the crown lands which had been alienated since sixteen hundred and nine.

This edict of resumption, which was warranted by the peasants, citizens, and clergy, who had nothing to lose, and which was scarcely mitigated by a promise of indemnity, ruined the aristocracy. In Livonia especially, the German nobility, who were descendants of the old Order, protested strongly many times, but all their protests were either entirely neglected or were refused with expressions of open displeasure. In sixteen hundred and eighty-eight, moreover, they were commanded to restore all the lands which had ever belonged to the crown, whether they had been purchased or presented. In the following year the King ordered them to send deputies in behalf of a revision of their privileges. Accordingly they sent Gustav Budberg and John Rheinhold Patkul, who complained that if the resumption should take effect, the nobles would be deprived of all their possessions. These complaints, however, were not listened to, and the deputies left Stockholm to lay before the diet of sixteen hundred and ninety-two the result of their endeavors. Thereupon they sent a new deputation to the King, Charles the Eleventh, with Patkul at its head. He was a proud, energetic, vindictive, and intelligent man, whose free speech displeased the King; and as his colleagues supported him in all his acts, he and they were arrested, carried before a court-martial, and condemned to death on the charge of using treasonable language. Patkul, whose private property did not suffer from the resumption, but whose strong sense of the rights of the nobility had made him espouse the cause of his country, being now an outlaw, in danger of death, his riches confiscated, his conscience free from the sense of disloyalty, managed to escape, and burning with rage he sought on all sides enemies of Charles the Eleventh and his young son Charles the Twelfth. He continually was devising ways and means to free Livonia from the yoke of Sweden. For some time he remained at the Court of Brandenburg, but at the fall of the minister, Dankelmann, he succeeded in gaining the good will of Baron Flemming, the favorite of the new

King of Poland, Augustus of Saxony. Augustus, as well as the Tsar of Russia, found in him the instrument which they needed for their common plans. He proposed to the King of Poland a scheme by which Sweden was to be attacked simultaneously by all its neighbors. Poland was to take Livonia and Esthonia, Russia was to conquer Ingria and Karelia, Denmark was to invade Holstein, which belonged to a brother-in-law of Charles the Twelfth. Peter accepted the overtures of the King of Poland: he desired nothing better than to carry out the designs of Ivan the Terrible and of his father Alexis. The youth of the new King of Sweden, and his reputed incapacity, led Peter to expect speedy success. Peter the First acceded to the coalition by virtue of the Treaty of Preobrazhenskoé. In the manifesto by which he declared war, he took pains to recall his grievances, puerile though they were, against the governor of Riga.

When Peter appeared under the walls of Narva, in October, seventeen hundred, Patkul at first rejoiced, but speedily became uneasy; he had not intended that Narva should be attacked by the Russians, but advised Augustus not to raise the question. The coalition was almost immediately assailed by two unexpected blows. Frederic the Fourth, the new King of Denmark, whom Charles threatened in Copenhagen, had been forced to sign the Treaty of Traventhal, and at the approach of the Swedes the King of Poland had been forced to raise the siege of Riga. Without waiting to pursue the Poles, Charles, hearing that Peter was besieging Narva, turned against the Russians. After a severe four days' march he reached an outpost four miles from the city, which was held by General Sheremetief with six thousand cavalry. In his impatience to capture this, though it was already dusk, Charles fired a few shots, which had the effect of so frightening Sheremetief, that he fled with all his troops and reported that twenty thousand Swedes had captured the outpost and were on the way to the Russian camp.

A desire to please the victors has caused the numerical disproportion between the two armies to be exaggerated. Voltaire himself was forced to rectify, in his "History of Peter the Great," the numbers that he had given in the "History of Charles the Twelfth." The latter had hardly eight thousand four hundred and thirty men; the Russians amounted to sixty-three thousand five hundred men, of whom only forty thousand took part in the action. The army was composed of regular troops, beside streltsui, Cossacks, men-at-arms, and soldiers hastily levied. In the absence of the Tsar, who with Golovin and Menshikof had quitted the camp on the previous evening to hasten the arrival of the reinforcements which Repnin and Mazeppa were to bring, it was placed under the command of an old general of the Emperor of Germany, the Herzog von Croï, whom the troops suspected from the fact that he was a foreigner, and who had no support from the other generals. While they were besieging Narva they had at their backs the Narova, or river of Narva, and occupied a fortified line of seven versts, or nearly seven thousand five hundred meters, the whole extent of which it was impossible to defend. In some places there was only a single line of soldiers, placed about two meters apart from one another. In front, near the centre, they had erected a great battery; before the entrenchments, on the road to Revel, were outposts to the number of four thousand men.

On the thirtieth, or, according to the old style, the nineteenth of November, seventeen hundred, the battle began by a cannonade that lasted till two in the afternoon. At that time the Swedes, though thoroughly exhausted by their long march, reached the foot of the entrenchments under cover of a snow-storm, which prevented the Russians from seeing twenty paces in front. In an instant the Swedes crossed the fosse and the parapet, and the Russian camp was seized with panic. "The Germans have betrayed us," cried the soldiers, and began to massacre not only the German officers, but the women who were in the camp. The Herzog von Croï and his staff saw no refuge from their own soldiers except in surrendering themselves to the mercy of the Swedish commander, Graf Stenbock. Almost before the Swedes had struck a blow, Sheremetief, with the cavalry, abandoned the field, deserted the infantry, and hurried to the river Narova, which he succeeded in swimming just below the falls of Ioala, where the water was deep and rapid, and more than a thousand men were lost in the passage. The right wing attempted to cross the bridge which led to the island of Kamperholm, where the Tsar's headquarters were situated; but the mass of struggling soldiers broke down the bridge, and the others, seeing before them the raging stream filled with the bodies of their companions, and behind them the pitiless Swedes, betook themselves to some barracks not far from the bank, and fortified themselves as best they could, by means of the artillery and baggage wagons. Here the Preobrazhenski and Semenovski regiments, which were the favorites of Peter the Great, and had been organized after the European fashion, defended themselves with the energy of despair. Charles, hearing the tumult of battle in this direction, sent the infantry of his victorious right wing to march against this redoubt, and hastened in person to superintend the attack. But, in spite of this gallant defence, the Russian army was cut in two by the capture of the great central battery. Night came on, and increased the disorder. The wing, commanded by Dolgoruki, Golovin, Buturlin, and Alexander, Tsarévitch of Imeritia, entered into negotiations with the King; the generals signed a capitulation which insured them a free retreat with arms, standards, and baggage, but they had to abandon all their artillery except six pieces of cannon. The Preobrazhenski and Semenovski guards left their fortress of wagons, and retired in good order, and to hasten their retreat the Swedes themselves built them a bridge over the Narova. The left wing, which had caused more trouble to the King, was obliged to sign a more rigorous capitulation : it was allowed to retire, but had to lay down its arms. Charles the Twelfth then allowed the Russian army to cross the river, neither from generosity nor disdain, as has sometimes been said, but from prudence. Wrede, the Swedish general, writes : "If the Russian general, Weide, who had six thousand men under arms, had had the courage to attack us, we should have been lost; we were completely exhausted, having had neither rest nor food for many days, and our soldiers were so intoxicated with the wine that they found in the Russian camp, that it would have been impossible to restore order." The King of Sweden, by slightly straining the terms of capitulation, retained as prisoners Croï and the officers who had taken refuge in his camp. Among the more distinguished of the Russian generals who were taken were Prince Dolgoruki, Artemon Golovin, Trubretskoi, Governor of Novgorod, Buturlin, and Alexander Gordon. Many remained for twenty years in Sweden. Besides the prisoners, the Russians had lost six thousand men, the Swedes nearly a third of that number.

There are salutary defeats and fatal victories. Charles was overwhelmed by flatteries from the whole of Europe. Medals were struck in his honor, with the inscriptions, "Superant operata fidem," or again, "Tres uno contudit ictu." The young King could not entirely shake off the intoxication of his success. "He dreams of nothing but war," writes his general, Stenbock; "he no longer listens to advice; he behaves as one who thinks that God directly inspires him for what he has to do." He despised enemies who were so easily conquered, and, counting the Russian army for nothing, made great preparations for the downfall of the harmless King of Poland. During five years he did nothing but plot for his dethronement; meddling in the intrigues of the Polish diets, and trying to crush the partisans of Augustus, as if the elevation and support of Stanislas Leshtchinski had been really of vital importance to Sweden in the same way as the possession of its maritime provinces. Peter understood how much it was for his advantage that his rival should be thus occupied; he aided Augustus of Saxony with troops and money, in order to keep his own hands free in the regions of the Baltic. It was enough for him to know that the impetuous King of Sweden was for some time entangled among the marshes and intrigues of Poland.

Peter took courage after Narva. Nothing was really lost, since the greater part of his army remained intact; he had only to turn to profit this harsh lesson in the military art. He increased the fortifications of Pskof, Novgorod, and the frontier towns; every one was set to work. By terrible examples he frightened robbers of treasure and dishonest officials. Melting down the church and convent bells of Moscow, he cast several hundred cannon; he created ten new regiments, each consisting of a thousand dragoons. He sent two hundred and fifty children to the military schools.

In December, seventeen hundred and one, the year after the defeat at Narva, Sheremetief attacked the Swedish general Slipenbach, near the village of Errestfer, in Livonia. The Russians were the more numerous, but it was an advance to conquer the Swedes, even at odds of three to one. Out of seven thousand men Slipenbach lost three thousand five hundred, and only three hundred and fifty prisoners were taken, — a fact which proves the fierceness of the fighting. This "eldest of Russian victories" was celebrated at Moscow by a triumphal procession, in which the arms, guns, and banners of the vanquished were displayed. Sheremetief was created field-marshal, and was decorated with the order of Saint Andrew; and Peter wrote, "Glory be to God! we have reached so far that we can conquer the Swedes fighting two to one, but soon we shall be able to beat also with even numbers." During the winter of seventeen hundred and two the Tsar spent much time and money upon his vessels on Lake Peipus, and in the latter part of May the new Russian fleet encountered a small number of Swedish ships at the mouth of the Embach. The Russians completely surrounded the little Swedish flotilla, but a brave resistance was offered, and only after a hard fight were the Swedes conquered. In July Captain Hökeflykt was making a voyage of inspection in a yacht, when he was surrounded by two hundred Russian galleys. He defended himself for an hour, hoping in vain for aid; and then, seeing no hope, he blew his vessel up, destroying at the same time twenty Russian galleys which lay near him. The same year Sheremetief again defeated Slipenbach at Hümmelsdorff, in a four hours' battle, took from him all his artillery, and killed six thousand out of his eight thousand men. According to the Swedes, they had but six thousand men and the Russians fifty thousand; but the Russians claim to have had but twenty thousand men.

The ultimate aim of Peter was the possession of the Neva, which had belonged to the early Russian princes, and where Saint Alexander Nevski had won his glorious surname by victories over Swedish enemies. He still held his position as captain of the bombadier company of the Preobrazhenski regiment. Menshikof acted as lieutenant in the same company, and was appointed commander of this important fortress. Hastening down from Arkhangel, where he had been expecting an attack from the Swedish fleet, he assisted in the capture of Noteburg, the ancient Oréshek, or Little Nut, of the Novgorodians, which was situated on a small island and commanded the Neva where it leaves Lake Ladoga. He called it Schlüsselburg, or the fortress of the key, because the post would make him master of the river. Near the mouth of the Neva the Swedes held the small fort of Nienschantz; he captured and destroyed it, and in a neighboring island he founded the citadel around which his future capital was to cluster; the islet of Cronslot became Cronstadt, which was to close against the Scandinavians the entrance on the side of the sea. The Neva was his. The same year, seventeen hundred and three, he seized two Swedish vessels in its waters, — "an unheard-of success," as he expressed it in a letter to Moscow. Then Koporié, Iam, and Dorpat, which had once been a vassal city of Novgorod, fell into his hands, and he revenged himself for his defeat at Narva by capturing that town in seventeen hundred and four, but he protected the citizens from his own soldiers, who were thirsting for blood. Nevertheless, three thousand men were occupied for three hours in piling the bodies of the dead and dying upon wagons, and in throwing them into the Narova. During this time Livonia and Esthonia, provinces inherited by Charles the Twelfth, were given up to frightful devastation, worse than that of the Palatinate by Louis the Fourteenth. The days of Ivan the Terrible seemed to have returned. The Russians signalized the reconquest of their ancient territory by atrocities. Volmar, Venden, and Vesen were pillaged; Sheremetief spared only Riga, Pernava, and Revel, or Kobyvan, as it was called by the Tchudi. On the third of September, seventeen hundred and two, the commander of Marienburg, situated on the confines of Livonia and Ingria, found himself obliged to surrender at discretion. But as the Russians were about to enter the town the powder-magazine was exploded, destroying many both of the victors and of the vanquished. Among the three hundred and fifty-six persons who were captured was the pastor Glück and his family. Catherine, a girl who had been left an orphan at an early age, was a servant in this family. Two days before she had been married to a Swedish soldier, whom she never saw again. She became Sheremetief's mistress, and afterwards held the same position in the house of Menshikof, where the Tsar saw her and was captivated by her beauty and intelligence. In the seventeenth year of her age she became his mistress, and three years later he married her privately. One would have to search long to find a more romantic story than that of the captive waiting-maid of Marienburg, soon to be Empress of all the Russias.

The Letto-Finnish country was made a desert; the Cossacks, Kalmuicki, Bashkirs, and Tatars did not know what to do with their prisoners. The Zaporoshtsui alone carried four thousand captives — men, women, and children — back to the Lower Dnieper. This year, also, the Tsar marched in a magnificent triumphal procession through Moscow, and, considering the successes which he won during the campaign, he had even greater cause for rejoicing than the year before, when he himself was decorated by Golovin with the ribbon of the order of Saint Andrew for personal bravery. But neither the capture of the fortresses, the burning of the towns, nor the extermination of the people could distract Charles the Twelfth from the attempt to ruin Augustus. In July, seventeen hundred and five, the Polish nobility had been obliged to proceed to the election of a new king, and, notwithstanding the efforts of the Supreme Pontiff, the Cardinal Primate and the nobles elected Stanislas Leshtchinski, whom the Protestant King of Sweden caused to be acknowledged by the majority of the Poles. Three Swedish regiments met ten thousand Poles, Lithuanians, and Saxons, near Warsaw, and after a hard fight of six hours overcame them. Among the prisoners was the Saxon major-general, Paykul, a Livonian by birth, who had settled in Prussia when a boy. Nevertheless, he was sent to Stockholm as a traitor, in spite of the efforts of Patkul, his friend and countryman, who soon afterwards was to meet a worse fate.

In seventeen hundred and five the Tsar felt that it was necessary to keep an eye on the actions of the Swede in Poland, and not to allow his ally, Augustus, to be entirely crushed. It was enough to have taken from him his share of the booty, Esthonia and Livonia. The Russians crossed the Dwina, occupied Kurland and Vilna, and concentrated themselves in an entrenched camp at Grodno. Peter, like Ivan the Terrible, had to struggle not with his external enemies alone; the internal factions had not yet been subdued. At the beginning of the year seventeen hundred and five he received information that the Bashkirs and several other Tatar tribes had seized arms and were spreading death and destruction far and wide, even to the gates of Kazan. This revolt had been caused by the violent acts of the Russian commissioner, who had taken their horses and insulted their religion. In order to pacify them the commissioner was put to death; but hardly had this revolt been quelled when, just as he was preparing to give battle to the Swedes, the people of Astrakhan, who had been falsely told that Russian marriages were forbidden for seven years, during which time only foreigners would be allowed to marry their daughters, hearing that Peter had been completely defeated at the battle of Gemauers, revolted, and murdered the governor of the town. Peter was obliged to send to the Lower Volga a portion of his troops under Sheremetief, one of his best generals. It was time that Sheremetief arrived, for already the streltsui of Astrakhan had appealed for help to the Cossacks. Fear of punishment only increased their stubbornness. The city gates were barred, the walls were mounted with cannon, and the suburbs were reduced to ashes. But after Sheremetief's troops had fired the first shots their opponents fled. The field-marshal led his three thousand men boldly against the ten thousand who were in revolt, and soon reduced them to obedience. The leaders of the insurrection on the thirteenth day of March surrendered the keys of the city, and the oath of obedience was exacted from all those who had been under arms. Ninety of the guiltiest were carried to Moscow and put to death; many others were sent to distant parts of the empire. This was accomplished by Sheremetief with a loss of only twenty killed and thirty-five wounded. Meanwhile the Russian army in Lithuania found itself for an instant in great straits: Schulenburg, the general of Augustus, who afterwards became famous at Corfu in the war with the Turks, thinking to save the King at Grodno, advanced boldly toward Upper Poland, and meeting the Swedes under Rhensköld, was defeated at Fraustadt in seventeen hundred and six, and forced to fall back on Saxony. But by means of Peter's skilful generalship the Russian army, which was in the greatest danger of being captured, succeeded in retreating without opposition to Kief.

CHARLES THE TWELFTH INVADES RUSSIA: BATTLE OF POLTAVA.

In April, seventeen hundred and six, Charles the Twelfth crossed the Niemen and in slow stages marched to Volhynia, where he delayed many days with the double purpose of refreshing his men, who were suffering from bad winter-quarters, and of bringing Radzivil Tchartorniski, Lubomirski, and other powerful partisans of Augustus to terms. To punish the opposition to Stanislas Leshtchniski and the entrance of Augustus into Warsaw, he crushed the Electoral States by his extortions and requisitions, and burned and plundered far and wide. Peter was awaiting him in the Ukraina, Augustus in Lithuania, but Charles, to whom the victory of Fraustadt had given free passage, turned suddenly into Saxony and united his forces with those of Rhensköld, leaving General Mardefeld with about six thousand Swedes and fifteen thousand Poles and Lithuanians. As soon as the Tsar learned that the King of Sweden had gone into Saxony, he sent Menshikof with ten thousand Russians and a party of Cossacks to the assistance of Augustus. Meanwhile Augustus had secretly been under negotiations with Charles, whereby he agreed to acknowledge Stanislas Leshtchinski as King of Poland and to break with the Tsar. But not daring to confess this treaty to the Russians, he was obliged to allow Menshikof to engage in battle at Kalish with Mardefeld, who knew nothing of the treaty and was completely defeated. Charles remained in Saxony, levying enormous taxes upon the inhabitants and living at the expense of the land. He traversed Silesia without deigning to ask leave of the Emperor Joseph, despising the protestations of the diet of Ratisbon; he received the complaints of the Protestants of this province who were persecuted by Austria, and appeared before the malcontents of Hungary as the great redresser of wrongs. This happened at the most critical moment in the war of the Spanish Succession. France, defeated at Hochstadt, Ramillies, and Turin, was looking for help from victorious Sweden. England, Holland, Austria, Brandenburg, Hanover, all the powers concerned in the attack on the French frontiers, trembled lest the Swedish army should assail the coalition in the rear. Had not Sweden been the ally of France since the time of Gustavus Adolphus and of Oxenstiern? Had not the Swedes been the companions of the French in their days of glory? Did they not owe to France their great influence in Germany? Had they not to fear lest they might suffer from the defeat of France? Was not Charles the Twelfth at this moment receiving subsidies from the Grand Monarque? Was not his help entreated by the French envoys? The fate of the world seemed to lie in the hands of the young victor. If he turned to the West, if he revenged his own grievances and those of Protestantism against Austria, France was saved, and Sweden, for whom fearful misfortunes were in store on the plains of Russia, was saved also. There was a pause of anxious and solemn expectation, all the greater because the proud and silent monarch had allowed no hint of his projects to escape him. The situation appeared so grave that in April, seventeen hundred and seven, Marlborough resolved to seek him in his camp. Few words were exchanged between these two great generals, whose characters were so unlike, but the clever Englishman was able to guess Charles's hatred and jealousy of France; he saw that his eyes glittered at the mention of the Tsar; he noticed a map of Russia spread out on the table. Marlborough retired full of hope. Those who feared Charles agreed to whatever he proposed to them;

Augustus accepted the humiliating treaty which his plenipotentiaries had signed at Altranstädt, by which he abdicated the throne and delivered up Patkul, whom the Tsar had accredited to him as ambassador. The Emperor relinquished a hundred churches to the Protestants of Silesia, dismissed a chamberlain of whom the King had reason to complain, surrendered fifteen hundred Russian refugees, and recalled four hundred German officers who had taken service with the Tsar. The Elector of Brandenburg signed a perpetual peace. Charles the Twelfth might now break up his camp at Leipsic; he saw only one enemy, the Tsar of Russia.

Before, however, we enter upon the details of the latter part of the Northern war, it seems worth while to pay more particular attention to the extraordinary man whose misfortune it was to fall into the hands of the son of Charles the Eleventh. Envy at his success and jealousy of his position as ambassador of the Tsar caused Patkul to gain many enemies. Augustus, though he openly flattered him and appeared to be on terms of the greatest familiarity, was secretly angry with him, because he had complained that the Polish government was considered corrupt by all the courts of Europe. The wise advice which Patkul freely offered the King was worse than wasted. The Saxon government, full of anger and hatred of him, had long been seeking a pretext to get rid of so dangerous a person. His position as General-in-Chief of the Russian army sent to the King's aid made him personally responsible to Augustus. But he found himself without the means to support his troops, who complained bitterly of their winter-quarters. After pawning his jewels, and reducing himself to the greatest straits, in order to prevent his forces from starving, he found himself obliged to sign an agreement with Graf von Stratmann, minister plenipotentiary of the Court of Vienna, by which his seven thousand men entered the service of the Emperor. The loss of that number was of no serious consequence, but the manner in which the troops left the service of the King was so derogatory to the honor of the latter, that it seemed likely to cause a rupture between him and the Tsar. In order to prevent the Russian troops from taking their departure, the Secret Council determined to arrest Patkul. Accordingly, on the nineteenth of December, seventeen hundred and five, Colonel Brown, with an escort of twenty men, proceeded to Patkul's lodgings. It was ten o'clock at night. The house was perfectly quiet. Colonel Brown, on being admitted, roughly woke the sleeping minister, and seizing him by the hand, said, " I arrest you in the name of the King." Patkul, astonished at such an unexpected summons, asked where he was to be taken, and was assured: " To the Secret Council." He was then carried in a Sedan-chair to the city gate, where, after waiting an hour, a coach appeared which brought him to the dungeon of Sonnenstein. He was anxious to know whether the King had knowledge of the indignity offered to the Tsar's minister, and then, thinking of his newly married bride, Anna Sophia von Einsiedel, he became very sad. He was put in the dungeon and treated with the greatest brutality; he was allowed no servant, no bed was furnished him, his private papers were taken from him, and he dared not eat the food set before him for fear that it was poisoned. The arrest and imprisonment of the Tsar's plenipotentiary was a direct violation of the law of nations, and created great surprise throughout Europe. Graf von Stratmann demanded of the council security for his personal safety. The Prince Galitsuin, though he was considered to be a man without resolution, expressed his indignation in the strongest terms. The Secret Council tried to exculpate themselves by bringing the severest accusations against Patkul. In order to pacify the Court of Vienna, it was even felt necessary to spread the rumor that the Tsar had himself ordered his arrest. The King approved the action of the Secret Council, and Peter refused to confirm the agreement with Stratmann, but insisted that Patkul should be handed over to him as the condition on which Augustus should retain the reinforcements. Patkul, however, was still kept in prison, and in order to make him appear guilty, every possible form of slander was heaped upon him. He was charged with being the cause of the misunderstanding between the Saxon and Prussian Courts, and the loss of the battle of Fraustadt was attributed to him. In June the Tsar wrote that he saw no proof of his treason, and promised him his protection and favor. But three months later the Swedes were in Saxony, and on the twenty-eighth of March, seventeen hundred and seven, Patkul was delivered over to Charles. He was accused of high treason, and condemned to be broken on the wheel and beheaded. The Tsar wrote a letter to the different Powers complaining of this insult to his majesty; but Charles had the double satisfaction of wounding Peter and of revenging himself on his former vassal. He well knew that he had no enemy more dangerous than Patkul. His courage, his unbending will, his talents, his thorough knowledge of internal and external affairs, and his skill in statesmanship made him one of the most remarkable men of the century. It was he who saw with the greatest clearness the destiny of Russia, and his highest ambition was to be the leader of diplomacy in the growing State. That part he played with consummate ability as long as he remained in the service of the Tsar.

The adversary of Peter the Great was an admirable knight-errant rather than a sovereign. The absolute power of which he became possessed at an early age left without counterpoise his fiery temper and obstinate character, — his "iron head," as the Turks said at Bender. Voltaire observes that he carried all his virtues to such an excess that they became as dangerous as the opposite vices. His dominant virtue and vice was a passion for glory. Glory, and glory alone, was to him the end of war. He appears not to have understood that it was possible to acquire it by practising the arts of peace. Up to the moment when the news of the coalition of Poland, Denmark, and Russia revealed to him his military vocation, he seemed the most insignificant of all the European princes. His conduct appeared to be regulated, not by the political principles current in the eighteenth century, but by some strange and archaic point of honor. He knew Alexander the Great only as the romantic hero of Quintus Curtius, and this phantom he took for his ideal. He was nourished on the old Scandinavian sagas, and we may truly say that the soul and spirit of the old vikings revived in him: he had their wonderful deeds forever before his eyes, and the versified maxims of the Scalds forever present to his memory. Charles the Twelfth was a hero of the Edda set down by mistake in a matter-of-fact century. A Russian historian, M. Guerrier, calls him "the last of the Variagi"; he was the last of those Scandinavian adventurers who marched over the Russian plains from Novgorod to Kief, but to whom henceforth the road to the south remained forever shut. Pitiless to others as well as to himself, we find him undergoing useless dangers and fatigues seeking adventures like a sea-king who had only his head to risk; considering a war as a single combat between two champions, which could only end, if not with the death, at least with the dethronement, of the vanquished; fighting not to gain crowns, but to distribute them; giving largesses to his soldiers as if he had always the treasures of pillage, the "red gold of Fafnir's heath," at his disposal; despising all the luxuries of life, like the Northmen who boasted of never having slept beneath a roof; flying from women, "whose silken hairs," says the sagas, "are nets of perfidy"; regarding a backward movement as dishonor, and considering prudent advice an evidence of weakness; ready to face water, as in the marshes of Lithuania, or fire, as in the conflagration of Bender. He had his own guard of halberdiers, as the kings of heroic times had their drujina, as Alexander had his companions. His comrades also are heroes of sagas, and legend has embellished their exploits. The story is current in Sweden that Hinstersfelt carried off the enemy's guns on his shoulders, and that, passing through a vaulted gateway, from which hung a ring, he put his little finger through it and pulled himself up by it, and with him the horse which he pressed between his knees. "When I have nine of my halberdiers with me," said Charles, "nothing can hinder me from going where I will." He was thus impelled to seek adventures in distant lands, and, like the warriors of old, to "win the world by the force of his arm." He sent officers even into Asia and Egypt to reconnoitre and to collect information.

Pushkin, in his poem "Poltava," puts into the mouth of the disappointed Mazeppa the following remark: "I have been mistaken about this Charles: no doubt he is a bold and audacious youth; two or three battles he can gain; he can fall suddenly on the enemy after supper, reply to a bomb with a burst of laughter; like a Russian sharpshooter, he can steal by night into the camp of the foe, overthrow the Cossack as he has done to-day, give blow for blow and wound for wound: but it is not for him to cope with the giant autocrat; he wishes to make Fortune manœuvre like a regiment at the sound of the drum. He is blind, obstinate, impatient, and thoughtless and presumptuous; he trusts in God knows what star. The new forces of his enemy he measures by his past success. The horn of his strength is broken. I am ashamed to have been seduced in my old age by a military vagabond. Like a timid girl, I was dazzled by his boldness and the rapid success of his victories." Herrmann says: "Of the four princes who took the leading parts in the Northern war, Peter alone proved himself to be the statesman who kept ever in sight a great and useful end. Augustus the Magnificent and the weak Frederick the Fourth were the slaves of the contemptible false god of idle show and brutal pleasure. The temperate, hard-headed hero, Charles the Twelfth, in his restless pursuit of a purposeless design, became a mere Don Quixote."

The two adversaries were to meet at last. In January, seventeen hundred and eight, Charles quitted Saxony with forty-three thousand men, enriched with the spoils of the country; he left ten thousand of them behind to support Stanislas on the throne, and marched towards the Niemen. Peter also started from Moscow to join his army at Grodno. There he learned that Charles had crossed the frozen Weichsel, or Vistula, which was guarded by Mühlenfeldt. But Mühlenfeldt deserted to the enemy, and the Tsar had scarcely time to leave the city, together with Menshikof, on the evening of the sixth of February, when the Swedes made their appearance. Charles led the way into Grodno with but six hundred men, and only the prodigies of valor which he performed prevented his being captured by the Russian rear-guard. The Tsar, in pursuance of a system which was again to be followed in eighteen hundred and twelve, fell back on Russia, laying waste Lithuania as he went. The Swedish name was still a universal terror. Besides the thirty-three thousand men who followed Charles, Lewenhaupt was to bring up eighteen thousand from Poland. No Russian force seemed fit to cope with this the most experienced army in Europe. The internal affairs of Russia were also causing Peter anxiety; it was at this decisive moment that the revolt of Bulavin, in the camp of the Don, occurred, and the first agitation among the Cossacks of the Dnieper. Before risking the safety of his empire, within which terrible disorders were still fermenting, before exposing his new creations to the horrors of an invasion, Peter tried to negotiate with his enemy; he offered to be content with a single port on the Baltic. "I will treat with the Tsar in Moscow," was Charles's answer. But Peter said, "My brother Charles is going to be Alexander, but in me he will not find Darius."

Three routes now lay open for Charles to invade Russia, — through Novgorod, through Smolensk, or through the Ukraina. He delayed thirteen weeks in the vicinity of Minsk, uncertain which way to turn. Had he by a bold stroke captured the city of Pskof, which he might easily have done, neither the skill nor the wisdom nor the power of the Tsar could have prevented him from invading Russia. He could have brought Peter to submit to the most humiliating treaty.

From the Niemen, across the forest of Minsk, where the Swedes were obliged to cut a passage with their axes, Charles the Twelfth reached the Berezina, which he crossed at the head of a body of three thousand men. At Golovtchin, on the fifteenth of July, he came up with twenty thousand Russians, whose steadiness should have caused him to consider, for they yielded only at the seventh charge of the King. He reached the Dnieper at Mohilef, and followed its course up as far as Mstislaf. At Dobroë, south of Smolensk, on the twenty-ninth of August, he attacked a body of ten thousand Russians and six thousand Kalmuicki. This time he had a horse killed under him, two aides-de-camp killed at his side, and, finding himself alone with five men, slew twelve of the enemy with his own hand, and escaped only by a miracle. Russia was not going to allow itself to be conquered so easily. He was now three hundred miles from the Russian capital, on the road to Moscow, which Napoleon was afterwards to take. It was already the end of September; winter was coming on, and showed signs of being severe; provisions were scarce, and Charles was advised to retreat from Mstislaf to Mohilef, and there await Lewenhaupt, who would bring up between ten and twenty thousand men and plenty of food. Charles, however, allowed himself to be tempted by the offers of the aged Mazeppa, who promised him a reinforcement of thirty thousand Cossacks, and by the hopes of abundance in the fertile plains of the south. Besides, as he confessed to Gyllenkruk, who was horrified by this announcement, he had no plan. So he turned towards the Ukraina, followed by Sheremetief. Then the Tsar and his generals hung like wolves on the flank of Lewenhaupt, who found himself isolated and without support on the plains of the Dnieper. On the ninth of October, at Liesna, by the Sozha, they fought a battle which raged for three days, and where, this time, the numbers were equal. The Swedish general saved only six thousand seven hundred men, and was forced to spike his cannon and burn a thousand wagon-loads of provisions, besides which six thousand were captured by the Russians. All the convoy, which was the sole hope of the royal army, was destroyed. Lewenhaupt, however, by a masterly piece of manœuvring brought to Charles the fragments that were left after the disaster. Peter, on the thirteenth of October, withdrew to Smolensk, which he entered amid the thunder of artillery, displaying his prisoners and the cannon and banners which had been taken. His joy was redoubled when a few days later he learned from his cousin, Admiral Apraxin, that the Swedish attempt upon Ingria had failed, as well as the meditated destruction of Saint Petersburg and Cronstadt.

By this time winter had come, — the terrible winter of seventeen hundred and nine. In the forced marches which the King of Sweden had the imprudence to impose on his army, the men, who lacked winter clothing, and the starving horses perished by thousands; the guns were thrown into the river for want of beasts to transport them. The very crows fell dead from the cold, and the doctors were employed in amputating frost-bitten fingers and toes. Charles continued his march, ascertained the distance which separated him from Asia, and consoled his half-naked soldiers with the assurance that he would conduct them so far that they could receive news of Sweden only three times a year. A soldier showed him the horrible mouldy bread on which the army was fed. Charles took it, tasted it, and observed quietly, "It is not good, but it may be eaten."

The arrival of spring did not put an end to the sufferings of the army. Prince Menshikof sacked Baturin, the capital of the fugitive hetman, and razed the fort of the Zaporoshtsui, in May, seventeen hundred and nine. Charles reached the walls of Poltava, and halted there to wait for the Turks and the Poles of Leshtchinski, who were never to arrive. While awaiting them he determined to attack the town "for a diversion." It was in vain that the uselessness of the enterprise and the impossibility of success were represented to him. What was the good of wasting powder and the munitions of war, which had now become rare in the camp? "Yes," replied the Iron-head to Gyllenkruk, "we are obliged to do extraordinary things to gain honor and glory"; and to Piper, "An angel would have to descend from heaven with orders for me to go before I stirred from this place." When had his favorite heroes of the Eddas ever been seen to retreat? He made Gutman, his servant, recite the saga of Rolf Ericsen, who "vanquished the Russian sorcerer in the isle of Retusari, and conquered all Russia and Denmark, so that his name is honored and glorified throughout the North." Menshikof then came up, and showed that he had profited by the lessons of the Swedes by making a feint which enabled him to throw some troops into Poltava.

The Tsar arrived on the fourth (or, by modern reckoning, the fifteenth) of June, seventeen hundred and nine, with sixty thousand men, whom he protected by an intrenchment raised during a single night. Charles's army was now reduced to twenty-nine thousand men, who lacked everything, suffered as much from the extreme heat as they had formerly done from the extreme cold, and were exhausted by suffering and privations. He had only four field-pieces against the seventy-two guns of the Tsar. In one of his nightly sallies, when he was trying to harass the enemy's vanguard, Charles received a wound in his heel which necessitated a cruel operation, and on the day of the famous battle, twenty-seventh of June (or eighth of July), seventeen hundred and nine, he had to be carried in a litter. The generals on whom the responsibility of command fell could not agree; he himself thwarted the dispositions of Rhensköld, who was nominated general-in-chief.

Peter had confided the centre to Sheremetief, the right to Renne, the left to Menshikof, and the artillery to Bruce. He then harangued his troops. "The moment is come," he said; "the fate of our country is to be decided. You must not think, 'It is for Peter we fight'; no, it is for the empire confided to Peter, it is for the country, it is for our orthodox faith, for the Church of God. As for Peter, know that he is ready to sacrifice his life for a prosperous and glorious future for Russia."

The Swedes took the offensive. "All those who have served in the Swedish army," says Voltaire, "know that it was impossible to resist their first shock." They saw in victory an end of their sufferings, and fought like the wild Bersarkers of the legends. They charged with fury the cavalry placed at the right of the Russians, wounded Renne, who had to yield his command to Bauer, and took two redoubts. Peter, in trying to rally his cavalry, received a ball in his hat. Menshikof had three horses killed under him.

Unluckily for Charles, the corps of Kreutz, which ought to have made a détour and fallen on the enemy's flank, was lost, and never appeared. The superior artillery of the Russians arrested the charge of the Swedes. Menshikof marched boldly on their rear, and thus separated the body of the army from the camp under Poltava, which he finally reached. The Russian fire on the front of the Swedes was so violent that the horses harnessed to Charles's litter were killed; his halberdiers then took it in turns to carry him, but twenty-one out of the twenty-four were left where they fell. The Russian cavalry rallied, and the Russian infantry, which was now put in motion, broke the Swedish line. Attacked in front by Peter and in the rear by Menshikof, the Swedes were speedily thrown into disorder. They fled, and Charles was placed on horseback by his guards, and obliged to go with the stream. He hardly escaped being taken. Accompanied by Mazeppa and by the Pole Poniatovski, he arrived after two days' flight at the banks of the celebrated Borysthenes, the Dnieper, down which in the tenth century so many Scandinavian fleets had sailed. He crossed the Dnieper in a little boat with Mazeppa, and continued his route to Otchakof. It was thus that "the last of the Variagi and the last of the free Cossacks entered the land of the Sultan as fugitives." The Swedes had lost about ten thousand men, — three thousand were taken on the field of battle ; the bulk of the army, which had continued, under Lewenhaupt, its march to the Dnieper, had to pause on its banks. Menshikof, sent there hastily by the Tsar, obliged sixteen thousand more Swedes to lay down their arms. This was called the Capitulation of Perevolotchna. Of the magnificent army which at Leipsic had made all Europe tremble, not a battalion escaped.

The evening after the battle the Tsar received in his tent Rhensköld, Prince Maximilian Emanuel von Würtemberg, Stackelberg, Hamilton, Kruse, — those Swedish generals whose names had been cited among the first captains of the age. He treated these glorious prisoners courteously, and invited the minister, Graf Piper, and the generals to dinner. He praised Rhensköld's bravery, and even gave him his own sword as a mark of personal esteem. When a Russian officer spoke disrespectfully of Charles, the Tsar chided him with the words : "Am I too not a king? And who was to assure me that Charles's fate would not be mine?" Then he drank to the health of his master in the art of war. The Russian generals were rewarded with landed possessions and ribbons of the various orders; the lower officers, with gold and silver badges. Menshikof became second field-marshal, and Peter himself accepted the grades of lieutenant-general and vice-admiral; the Russian churches resounded with songs of triumph ; the Tsar was exalted in eloquent sermons; and Kurbatof wrote to him : "Rejoice, because, obedient to the Word of God, thou hast exposed thy life for thy servants ; rejoice, because thou hast forged thine army by thy courage, as men heat gold in a furnace; rejoice, because thou mayest hope for the realization of thy dearest wish, — the domination of the sea of the Variagi." Peter after Poltava, like Charles after Narva, tasted in his turn the sweets of glory. But the success of Poltava differed from the success of Narva. Narva had been only a victory; Poltava marks a new era in universal history. Sweden, which under Gustavus Adolphus, and again under Charles the Eleventh, had played in Europe the part of a great Power, which had even obtained an importance out of all proportion to its actual resources, was suddenly relegated to the third rank among States. The place it had left vacant in the North was taken by a nation which had at its disposal far larger resources, besides a greater power of expansion. The shores of the Baltic were to pass into its hands. Already Russia declared itself, not only a Power of the North, but a Power of Europe. Muscovy, which had been formerly held in check by little Sweden, by anarchic Poland, by decrepit Turkey, or even by the Khan of the Tatars, was destined to become formidable to France, to England, and to the house of Austria. With Russia, the Slav race, so long humiliated, made a triumphal entry into the stage of the world. Finally, Poltava was not only a victory, it was the proof of the regeneration of Russia; it justified the Tsar, his foreign auxiliaries, his regular army; it left his hands free to reform, gave to the empire a new capital, and promised to Europe a new civilized people. "Now," he wrote to Apraxin from the field of battle, " the fate of Phaethon has come upon our adversary, and the first stone for the foundation of Saint Petersburg is laid by the help of God."

CHAPTER III.

PETER THE GREAT: THE REFORMS.

GENERAL CHARACTER OF THE REFORMS: THE COLLABORATORS OF PETER THE GREAT. — SOCIAL REFORMS: THE TCHIN; EMANCIPATION OF WOMEN. — ADMINISTRATIVE, MILITARY, AND ECCLESIASITCAL REFORMS. — ECONOMIC REFORMS: MANUFACTURES. — PRACTICAL CHARACTER OF THE SCHOOLS FOUNDED BY PETER. — FOUNDATION OF SAINT PETERSBURG (1703).

GENERAL CHARACTER OF THE REFORMS: THE COLLABORATORS OF PETER THE GREAT.

THE way for the reforms of Peter the Great had been made smooth by those of Alexis, and by all the movement of the seventeenth century. Under the Ivans, under Boris, under the early Romanofs, Russia had been little by little thrown open to strangers. It by no means followed, however, that the whole country was disposed to support Peter the Great in his innovations. Opposed to him were those who had refused to accept the reforms of Nikon, and many who, while accepting them, had no idea of going further. Those who belonged to the party of the dissenters, and certain members of the State Church, were his enemies. The Russian people were more averse to innovation than any in Europe; as their proverb says, "Novelty brings calamity"; the nobles also were hostile to everything that could contribute to autocratic centralization.

Peter the Great found, then, a steady resistance among the majority of the nation; to conquer it, where persuasion and his own example did not suffice he employed the energy of his semi-barbarous character, and the terrible resources of absolute power. By main force he dragged the nation in the path of progress; at every page of his reforming edicts we find the knout and the penalty of death.

These innovations effected by the prince were not intended to prejudice his own authority; on the contrary, they had, we may say, for their sole end the transformation of a patriarchal into a modern despotism. The force of the government was to be increased without any essential change in its character. The Tsar remained as much an autocrat as Ivan the Terrible, but his authority was to be exercised by means of more perfect instruments, and by agents subjected to the discipline and rules of the West.

The mass of the people still remained serfs and attached to the soil; twenty millions of human beings were the property of the territorial oligarchy; but, in spite of this fact, the Russian nation was to be furnished with the means necessary to enter into regular communications with the free people of Europe. Russia was to give the idea of a state centralized and civilized like the France of Louis the Fourteenth, yet the patriarchal and Asiatic principle, which, confounding paternal and territorial authority with political rule, presided over the relations of the father with his children, of the Tsar with his subjects, of the proprietor with his slaves, of the superior with his inferiors, was still unimpaired. On the basis of a social organization, which seemed to date from the eleventh century, were to be constructed a system of diplomacy, a regular army, a complete order of administrative officers, together with schools and academies, and the trade and manufactures of a luxurious civilization.

A fourth characteristic of the reforms of Peter the Great was that, in order to make a thorough introduction of European civilization into Russia, he was obliged to borrow everything abroad, without always having the time to choose the institutions best suited to his purpose. What is meant by civilization was then, and is still, the civilization of the West;

therefore Peter surrounded himself with Dutchmen, Englishmen, Scotchmen, Swiss, and Germans. For the same reason he indiscriminately imported manufactures, trades, and artisans; he had Western books translated, and sprinkled his administrative terminology with words borrowed from Sweden or Germany. That he might introduce Western ideas, he made himself a Dutchman and a German, forbade his subjects to wear the long garments peculiar to Asia, and obliged them to adopt the European costume, including the short trousers, the cocked hat, and the buckled shoes.

There was nothing servile, however, in this imitation; it was the method of a man of genius, who wished to outstrip time and hasten reforms by a hundred years. He intended that the Russians should be the pupils and not the subjects of the Germans; and as under his German dress he remained a Russian patriot, he reserved the first posts in the army and state for the natives. To be sure, we may cite among his fellow-workers his admiral, the Genevese Lefort, who until his early death, in March, sixteen hundred and ninety-nine, by his genial manners and great fund of experience gathered in all parts of Europe, had the greatest influence upon him; the Scotch Gordon, whom he made general; Bruce, a Scotchman born in Westphalia, who organized the artillery, directed the diplomacy, and after the publication of the almanac, in seventeen hundred, by which the beginning of the year was changed from September to January, passed with the people for a sorcerer and a magician, who could alter the course of the sun; Ostermann, son of a pastor in the county of La Marck, a skilful negotiator, of whom Peter said that he never committed faults in diplomacy; and a native of the county of Oldenburg, Münnich, a good engineer, who constructed for Peter the canal of the Ladoga, and afterwards became field-marshal. But among the chosen companions of Peter the Great, in the nest of "Peter's eaglets," as Pushkin calls them, we find many Russians, and in the highest post among these men Alexander Menshikof, a "new man," who rose from the position of a pastry-cook's boy to become prince, field-marshal, admiral, and conqueror, but whose probity did not stand as high as his talents. Another was Boris Sheremetief, a great noble, whose name and exploits are still preserved in the songs of the people, who travelled in the West before Peter, and came back to Russia in German clothes, a man as honest as he was brave, first in date of the Russian marshals. There were also Dmitri Mikhaïlovitch, head of the princely family of Galitsuin, who devoted himself to the reformer, though detesting "new men"; his brother, Mikhail Galitsuin, who when he became field-marshal continued to show to his elder brother an old-fashioned deference, and refused to sit at the same table with him; Iakof Dolgoruki, who could brave the wrath of Peter and force him to hear the truth; Golovin, high-admiral and diplomatist; Apraxin, admiral, conqueror on the Swedish seas; the diplomatist Golovkin, grand chancellor; Shafirof, vice-chancellor of the empire; Gregory and Vasili Dolgoruki; Andrei Matvéef; the Kurakins, ambassadors, father and son, to the courts of the West. Not to be forgotten are the intelligent and quick-tempered Iaguzhinski, afterwards procurator-general of the senate; Tolstoï, an accomplice of Sophia, pardoned on account of his high intelligence, who was an excellent negotiator and administrator of justice; Romodanovski, the cruel director of the State inquisition; Kurbatof, the financier of the new régime; besides three Little Russians who had been brilliant pupils of the Academy of Kief, — Saint Dmitri, metropolitan of Rostof, who wrote the lives of saints, and a treatise against heresy; Stephan Iavorski, metropolitan of Riazan, a man of great ability, full of zeal for Church and State; and his enemy, Feofan Prokopovitch, chief ecclesiastic of Novgorod, a distinguished preacher and writer, — to whom we must add the bishop Feofilakt Lopatinski. Such were the Russian men of the vrémia of Peter the Great.

SOCIAL REFORMS: THE "TCHIN"; EMANCIPATION OF WOMEN.

The most numerous class in Russia was the rural population, on which the reform made the State to press with a daily increasing weight, and which paid by its enforced labor for the cost of the change. It was subdivided into the peasants, who had sprung from the settlers in the south of Russia, with whom there had become mixed many of the impoverished lower nobility; into the farmers on the *métayer* system, who cultivated the land of the nobles and handed over to them half the products, but who had retained their personal liberty; into peasants of the crown, of the monasteries and of proprietors, who were attached to the soil. The edicts of Peter confounded all these classes, and subjected all the cultivators to a capitation tax and a fixed residence: this was equivalent to serfage. The reasons which had caused Godunof to legalize their attachment to the soil still subsisted in all their original force, and were likely to cause even more severe legislation. The tax on the fires was changed into a tax upon individuals, and the proprietors, by a considerable increase of their seignorial authority, were intrusted with the collection of it. A proprietor who concealed a single soul in order to avoid paying the tax was fined a ruble; and the crime of concealing the tenth part of the population of a village was punished by the galleys. Peter the Great merely promulgated an edict which had for an object the regulation of the sale of slaves. "If the sale cannot be abolished completely, slaves must be sold by families without separating husbands from wives, parents from children, and no longer like cattle, a thing unheard of in the whole world." This act, at least in its philanthropic clauses, never received any sanction. Anna Ivanovna later legalized this shameful abuse by collecting her dues on the sale of slaves.

The inhabitants of the towns were divided into three categories. To the first belonged bankers, manufacturers, rich traders, physicians, chemists, capitalists, merchants, jewellers, workers in metal, and artists; to the second, small traders and masters of crafts; to the third, the lowest class of journeymen and artisans. The first two of these divisions took the name of first and second guilds, chose their starosta or mayor and his assistant, and were invested with certain privileges.

Foreigners obtained the right of freely engaging in trade or commerce, of acquiring real property, of intermarrying with Russians, of entering the service of the State, of practising their respective modes of worship, and of leaving the empire at will, on condition of giving up the tenth of their goods.

The Russian nobility assumed the character of a nobility based on service. In the reign of Feodor Alexiévitch an important reform had already been effected. Until that time the nobles had preserved with scrupulous exactness the books which contained their pedigree, and the posts and offices which their ancestors had held. The consequence was that nobles were unwilling to accept any position in government employ subordinate to a person any of whose ancestors had ever stood in a position inferior to his own. Questions of precedence had become so complicated that Feodor, by the advice of Prince Vasili Galitsuin, determined to put an end to such quarrels. Accordingly he called in the service-rolls of all the noble families, with the pretended object of correcting certain errors that had been discovered in them. Then he made an assembly of the great men of the empire, and the Patriarch delivered an address, in which he attacked the custom of consulting prerogatives. The nobles seemed to assent, and Feodor immediately had the titles burnt. The Patriarch cursed those who should dare to rebel, and the assembly ratified the proceeding. Feodor had new books of nobility made out, which preserved the record of the ancestry and kinship of the families. But now, under Peter the Great, the two ideas of nobility and service of the Tsar became correlative. By an ukas of seventeen hundred and twenty-two the department of Heraldry had the supervision of the nobility and the books of pedigree, which were divided into two classes, one for the old nobility, the other for those who had gained rank by service. Every noble was obliged to serve, and whoever, Russian or foreigner, entered the service of the State became a gentleman. Peter the Great was as inexorable as Louvois in exacting service from the aristocracy: every individual with a title was at the disposal of the government till his death. Thus was the distinction finally effaced between the two kinds of lands possessed by the nobles, — the fiefs, held from the crown, and the freeholds or allods; both were henceforward held only as fiefs of the Tsar, on condition of military service. Up to this time the civil, military, naval, and ecclesiastical hierarchies had no common standard. Peter established in each hierarchy corresponding grades, confounded hereditary nobility and the nobility of service, and distributed the officers of the State among the fourteen degrees of the Tchin, or Order of Rank. These extended, in the civil order, from the registrar of the college to the chancellor of the empire; in the military order, from the cornet or ensign to the field-marshal; in the fleet, from the midshipman to the high admiral; in the Court, from the tafeldecker to the grand chamberlain; in the Church, from the deacon to the metropolitan.

Peter, desirous of imitating the English precedent of primogeniture, borrowed a custom which was entirely at variance with the Russian laws, which insisted on equality in the division of property. He passed a decree in accordance with which the property passed to the heir together with the title. In virtue of this new law the land of a noble belonged exclusively to the eldest, or to the son nominated heir by his father. Peter saw in this practice, which was destined to survive him but a short time, the following advantages: the noble families could no longer ruin and impoverish themselves by repeated partitions of the property; the peasants would be happier under the rule of one rich proprietor than under that of his needy co-heirs; the younger branches, no longer reckoning on the paternal estate, would be obliged to seek their livelihood in commerce or in the service of the State, for he felt that "idleness was the mother of all the vices." The younger members of the nobility were, besides, to be admitted into the service only under certain conditions of elementary or special instruction and technical preparation. Even marriage was forbidden to an uneducated gentleman. The destruction of the barrier of caste was finished by the foundation of the orders of Saint Andrew and Saint Catherine, the latter of which was instituted on Catherine's birthday, twenty-fifth of November (old style), seventeen hundred and fourteen, as a memorial of the battle with the Turks at the Pruth, and Catherine's bravery.

The seclusion of women was an Asiatic custom with which Peter waged fierce war. He was determined to abolish the terem locked "with twenty-seven bolts," the veil over the face, and litters with closed curtains. Six weeks before every marriage the betrothal was to take place, and from that moment the bridal pair might freely see each other, and might even break off the engagement if they were not satisfied on further acquaintance. Fathers and guardians had to take an oath that they would not marry young people against their will; and masters, that they would not force the consent of their slaves. Midwives were forbidden to put to death misshapen infants. Peter the Great took wives and daughters from their domestic cloisters, and brought them into the life of European salons. He instituted assemblies, free meetings which might take place in any house, to which all persons of respectability might go without invitation, where men and women appeared in European dress, where they partook together of light refreshments, danced Polish or German dances, and where French or Swedish prisoners served as models in manners. The assemblies of Peter the Great were at first only a parody of those of Versailles. Bergholtz, a German who came in the train of the Duke of Holstein in seventeen hundred and twenty-one, complains that men allowed themselves to smoke in the presence of the ladies; that the ladies sat apart, embarrassed in their unwonted attire, silently watching each other; that the nobles were often carried away in a state of drunkenness by their drunken lackeys. Did not Peter himself institute as a punishment for any breach of good behavior the emptying of the "great eagle," a huge goblet filled with brandy? To amuse the new society and give life to his capital, he instituted masquerades, cavalcades of disguised lords and ladies, the feast of fools, the Great Conclave, presided over by the "Prince-pope," his former tutor, the aged Zotof, who was dressed in crimson velvet trimmed with ermine. At his feet sat a Bacchus riding on a cask, with a rummer in one hand and a drinking vessel in the other. He was surrounded by intoxicated Cardinals, among whom were to be found noblemen, princes, acting-governors, and sometimes the Tsar himself. The procession would pass along the street followed by a sledge harnessed to four huge hogs driven by a gentleman of rank. Then a court jester, dressed as Neptune, with crown, long white beard, and trident, would come sitting in a sort of mussel shell, accompanied by two sirens. Then a throng of sledges arranged with sails like boats, and commanded by the Admiral or the Tsar. Bergholtz describes the launching of a ship which took place in July, seventeen hundred and twenty-one. The Tsar, the Prince-pope and all his Cardinals, the senators, and a large number of the first men of the empire were present. No one was allowed to leave the ship until word was given. "Almost all were drunk, and yet they desired still more, until their powers were exhausted. The great Admiral was so full that he wept like a child, which is said to be a habit of his when he takes too much. The Prince, Menshikof, was so intoxicated that he fell dead drunk," and was taken home by his servants. "The Prince of Moldavia was quarrelling with the oberpolitsci-meister; here a couple were fighting, there another couple were drinking, and swearing everlasting brotherhood and fidelity." Peter forbade the use of servile diminutives and prostrations before the Tsar, and by blows with his cane he taught his nobility to feel themselves free men and Europeans.

ADMINISTRATIVE, MILITARY, AND ECCLESIASTICAL REFORMS.

The ancient duma of the boyars was replaced in February, seventeen hundred and eleven, by the "directing senate," composed of eight members, which at first never acted save in the absence of the Prince. The number was afterwards increased, and it became permanently the great council of government, high committee of finance, and supreme court of justice. Peter commanded the senate to be obeyed like himself, but on all important questions the senate made its report to the Tsar. He appointed, in connection with this body, a procurator-general, charged with superintending the execution of the laws. Peter often reproached the new senators with conducting affairs "after the old fashion," with dragging out deliberations, and taking bribes. He had to make a new rule, in virtue of which senators were forbidden, under different penalties, to cry out, to beat each other, or to call each other thieves.

Peter suppressed the ancient Muscovite prikazui. By the advice of Leibnitz he created instead, after the German model, "colleges" of government similar to those by which the regent Orleans replaced the ministers of Louis the Fourteenth. There were ten of these colleges: those of foreign affairs, war, admiralty, treasury, revenue, justice, property of the nobles, manufactures, mines, and commerce. A collection of Swedish edicts was translated for their use. As they had few capable men, foreigners were employed, in the proportion of one for each college, and often they were obliged to resort to interpreters to enable them to understand each other. Captive Swedish officers and dragoons might be seen administering the empire. Peter sent for Slavs from Bohemia, Silesia, and Moravia, as being quicker at learning the Russian language. He despatched forty young men to Königsberg to study the elements of administration and finance. This autocrat permitted his colleges to elect their presidents. In seventeen hundred and twenty-two, the office of president of the college of justice being vacant, he assembled at the palace the senators, generals, officers, and a hundred members of the nobility, and after having taken their oaths made them proceed to the election in his presence.

Before the time of Peter the Great the provincial governments were in hopeless confusion. The governors of provinces and the voïevodui had at one and the same time the direction of war, finance, justice, and superintendence of buildings. In December, seventeen hundred and eight, Peter divided the empire into eight governments, subdivided into thirty-nine provinces, which were afterwards increased to twelve governments and forty-three provinces; the former were administered by governors and vice-governors, the latter by voïevodui. These representatives of the sovereign were assisted by a council, or landrath, elected by the nobles. The towns were divided into classes according to the number of inhabitants, and received an autonomous and municipal government; the citizens elected burgomasters, and these a president or mayor. The larger cities had four burgomasters, assisted by eight councillors. These, with the mayor, formed the rathhaus, or corporation of the city. In special cases the citizens of the first and second guilds were summoned to the council. All the city governments of Russia were subject to a superior board or council, chosen from the municipal council of Saint Petersburg, of which one half was composed of foreigners. This superior council watched over the prosperity of commerce and manufactures, sanctioned the sentences of death pronounced by the corporations of the province, decided disputes between the rathhaus and the citizens, confirmed the municipal elections, and sent in reports to the senate. The presiding officer was nominated by the Tsar. The towns had their own militia. The patriarchal and socialistic constitution of the rural communes was not touched.

Ignorance, inexperience, and corruption were the vices of the new administration. The functionaries had always present to their minds the advice of the ancient Tsars, — " Live upon thy office, and satisfy thyself." Peter attacked with fury this deeply rooted abuse, practised by the chief personages of the empire, headed by Menshikof. The exactions of the governor provoked a revolt at Astrakhan. Another governor of the same city was condemned by Peter to be torn by pigs. In seventeen hundred and eighteen Gagarin, Governor of Siberia, against whom many complaints had come, was brought from Tobolsk, and though he offered to give up a part of his spoils, was put to death, and his young son, Shafirof's son-in-law, was reduced to a common sailor and deprived of his property. Shafirof, the son of one of the translators in the department of foreign affairs, whom the Tsar had made a baron, was pardoned on the scaffold. Nesterof, after having made the denunciation of thieves a profession, was himself broken on the wheel as a thief. One day Peter made one of his nobles show him the accounts of his expenditure, and proved to him that he was robbing the State, and was himself robbed in turn by his steward. The Tsar beat him with his own hand, and said to him, " Now go and find your steward, and settle accounts with him." Menshikof himself was convicted of misuse of funds, and was condemned to lose his sword and put on probation. Admiral Apraxin was stripped of his possessions and titles, and kept in strict confinement. Afterwards the Tsar relented, and Menshikof paid a fine of five hundred thousand and Apraxin three hundred thousand rubles, and both drank a health to the forgetfulness of the past at Peter's table.

The recruits were the chief sufferers from extortions. These unhappy men, who were torn from their native villages and chained like galley-slaves, were thrown into prison on arriving at their halting-place, were fed with mushrooms, upon which their captains made them graze in the forests, and, as a natural consequence, died by hundreds before reaching their regiments. Peter was obliged to invite his subjects to denounce the thieves by promising to give the accusers the rank and the fortune of the person found guilty.

The Ulozhenie, the code of Alexis Mikhaïlovitch, was no longer suitable to the Russia of Peter the Great. At the beginning of his reign, therefore, Peter had commanded his boyars to insert in the proper places the various supplementary clauses and decrees which had been enacted since the time of Alexis. The boyars worked several years without bringing the new edition to completion. In seventeen hundred and fourteen he intrusted to his Senate the work which had been begun by the boyars fourteen years before, and in seventeen hundred and eighteen a new edition was published, with the title of the Revised Ulozhenie. But Peter was not satisfied with this: he wished an entirely new code of laws, and determined to select the Swedish as a basis, modifying what was inapplicable in it to the Russians by means of ancient Muscovite laws or new legislation. This project, however, could not be realized. But, nevertheless, some of the most important enactments of Peter's reign were borrowed from the Swedish code, more especially those relating to the regulation of the army and navy. In criminal cases he still employed torture, though with mitigations. He punished various crimes by sending the guilty to labor in the public works or the galleys. Those condemned to such punishment had their nostrils slit. Witches were condemned to be burnt. Blasphemers had their tongues torn out, and were tortured to death. The form of procedure he introduced had all the faults of an inquisition. Justice was administered in various districts, sometimes by tribunals properly so called, sometimes by the voïevodui, the commissioners, or by the magistrates of the towns. At Petersburg sat the supreme court, consisting of delegates from the senate.

The Petersburg police was controlled by the general politseimeister, that of Moscow by the oberpolitsei-meister. In the large towns there was an inspector of police for every ten houses; all the citizens over twenty years of age had to enter the service of the watch. The governors, voïevodui, commissioners of the country, and all who held authority, were responsible for the public safety; for the Russia of that day needed strict superintendence. People were afraid to go at night without lanterns, although the streets were ordered to be furnished with lamps. Moscow, whose streets were common sewers, began to be paved with wood. Servants, under penalty of fines, stripes, or the knout, were enjoined to keep the house-front clean. Owing to the long duration of the war and the increase in the taxes, beggars multiplied; well-to-do citizens were not ashamed to ask for alms, or to send their children to beg in the streets; they were in future to be arrested and taken before the police. People who pretended to be in the public service and were furnished with false credentials, and imposed on the credulity of the peasants, were sought out and punished. Hospitals were established for the sick, workhouses for vagabonds, the insane were housed together, usurers, coiners, and forgers either suffered corporal punishment or were banished. Most difficult of all to deal with were the brigands. Brigandage was habitual in Russia, and was favored by the vast and vacant wilds, the deep forests, the passive temper of the peasants, who did not dare to arm for the defence of one of their members, and would allow him to be despoiled by a few bandits, and tortured in presence of the whole village. The brigands formed themselves into great troops, armed and disciplined in the European manner, furnished with cavalry and artillery; they pillaged the crown taverns, burned the villages, invaded the dwellings of the nobles, and took the small towns by assault. Their recruits were Cossacks, fugitive peasants, soldiers who had deserted, and unfrocked priests; gentlemen, and even noble ladies, were seen riding at their head, thus augmenting their revenues by robbery. Battles had to be fought before security could be restored.

The open or sullen opposition with which his reforms were met caused Peter to create a State inquisition. This opposition came to light on all occasions. The ladies of honor, who wore the European costume when the Tsar was present, threw it off with contempt when he went away. Insulting placards were affixed to the walls. Even in the bosom of his own family the Tsar met with hostility. The Preobrazhenskaia Kantseliaria, or secret court of police, had originally been founded by Ivan the Terrible. Peter revived it, and gave it the jurisdiction of crimes against the majesty of the Tsar and murders committed in the capital. This bureau has left a terrible memory. To ruin his enemy a man had only to hint treason to one of the secret police, and immediately the accuser and accused were arrested and conducted to the "hall of the question," which the latter seldom left unconvicted.

The increased expenditure caused by the new army and navy, and the change in administration, obliged Peter to increase his revenues. The poll or capitation tax has already been mentioned. Ecclesiastics and their children, nobles, soldiers released from service, foreigners, the inhabitants of the Baltic provinces, Bashkirs, and Lapps were alone exempted from it. Even free peasants were liable. Every person who lived in a city paid one hundred and twenty kopeks, but the crown and church peasants paid only forty. If a peasant died, or became a recruit, in the time between one census and the following, his tax must be paid; but, on the other hand, no account was taken of those born in the same period. Kurbatof introduced the tax of the stamped paper. But in the midst of the terrible necessities of war Peter had recourse to other expedients. The coinage was several times debased. After the battle of Narva the value of the kopek was diminished. The ruble, in seventeen hundred and eighteen, was worth less than half as much as it had been in sixteen hundred and thirty-three. The officials were often deprived of part of their pay. The raskolniki were doubly taxed. Those who wore beards had to pay from thirty to one hundred rubles, according to their fortune. The peasants were taxed two dengi, or half-kopeks, for their beards when they entered the towns. Baths, mills, huts, and bees were taxed. All treasure-troves or new mines became the property of the crown.

One day Peter ordered all oak coffins at the makers' to be seized and sold for his profit. In seventeen hundred and eighteen the Tsar renounced all the monopolies which for a long time had been the possession of the crown, except those on tar, potash, caviare, and isinglass. Some of the more uncertain occupations, such as the whale-fisheries, were let out to companies on payment of a fixed impost. The crown leased to taverns the right of selling mead, beer, and brandy, and it also controlled the price of salt. The revenues of the State, in fifteen years alone, from seventeen hundred and ten to seventeen hundred and twenty-five, rose from three to ten million rubles.

After the dissolution of the streltsui the regular army was composed of infantry and dragoons, dressed in European uniforms, and raised to two hundred and ten thousand men. The peasantry were subjected to a system of conscription, which was long to be a source of despotism and tyranny. At this period was formed a whole popular literature of "lamentations of recruits." The irregular troops of the Cossacks and the tribes of the east furnished endless numbers of soldiers.

A maritime conscription was established along the banks of lakes, rivers, and the sea. The Tsar established also naval academies, especially for young Russians. Soon the Russian fleet numbered forty-eight ships of the line, eight hundred vessels of a lower class, and twenty-eight thousand sailors.

In seventeen hundred, upon the death of the Patriarch Adrian, who had little sympathy with the reforms, Peter conferred on Stephan Iavorski the title of "Superintendent of the Patriarchal Throne." Peter had resolved to abolish this institution, which was due to Godunof, and to give to the Church itself the collegiate organization with which he was at that time so fascinated. The preamble of the edict instituting the Holy Synod, which was compiled by Feofan Prokopovitch, is very curious: "The collegiate organization will not cause the country to fear the troubles and seditions that may arise when only one man finds himself at the head of the Church. The simple people are not quick to seize the distinction between the spiritual and imperial power; struck with the virtue and the splendor of the supreme pastor of the Church, they imagine that he is a second sovereign, equal and even superior in power to the autocrat. If a dispute takes place between the Patriarch and the Tsar, they are disposed to take the side of the former, believing that they thus embrace the cause of God." This mistrust of the spiritual power is again found in the Ukas, in which bishops are recommended to avoid pride and show, never to allow themselves to be supported under the arm in walking, unless they are ill, and to permit no prostrations before them. In the same manner as Peter had suppressed the hetmanate and established the College of Little Russia, he suppressed the patriarchate and founded the Holy Synod. He wished to be sole emperor in Moscow, as in the Ukraina.

The Holy Synod was composed of a certain number of bishops, among whom a procurator-general, often a soldier, represented the Tsar. The Holy Synod was to be the instrument of reform in the Church. Each bishop was ordered to keep a school in his diocese, which was to be supported by the revenues of the churches and cloisters; the sons of the popes who refused to be educated were to be taken as soldiers. The grave question of monasteries was reopened, but Peter did not yet dare to undertake the liquidation of their property. As Russia needed to be peopled, no Russian was allowed to become a monk till he was thirty. No servant of the State might enter a cloister without leave. As the monks showed themselves more and more hostile to reform, they were forbidden to shut themselves up to write, or to have ink or pens in their cells. They were, however, compelled to work at some trade. Hospitals and schools were given into their charge, and also broken-down soldiers, who found in the monastery an honorable asylum. The bishops, on the contrary, were encouraged by Peter to write. Stephan Iavorski published his book called "The Signs of the Coming of Antichrist," to refute Talitski, who had seen in the reforms of Peter the omens of the end of the world. As Voltaire relates, Talitski was put to death and Iavorski rewarded. "Peter, the Corner-Stone of the Faith," another of his works, was directed against Protestantism, but was not published until seventeen hundred and twenty-eight, after his death. Saint Dmitri of Rostof wrote his "Investigation of the Raskolnik Church of Bruinsk."

Assailed at once by the religions of the West and by the raskol sects, the orthodox Church was forced to defend itself. The dissenters were about this time divided into communities with priests and communities without priests. The most fanatical raskolniki fled into the deep forests, and there founded hermitages and even centres of population, which escaped for a long while the knowledge of government. Tracked and driven to extremity, certain enthusiasts burned themselves in a sort of auto-da-fé. Many of these shepherds of the desert, like Daniel Vikulof and the brothers Denisof, made themselves famous by polemical works. Peter wished to relax the systems of preceding régimes, and protected all peaceable subjects who did not interfere with politics. Passing through the deserts of the Vuiga, he found there a colony of industrious raskolniki, ordered them to be left in peace, and begged them to pray for him. "God," he said, "has given the Tsar power over the nations, but Christ alone has power over the conscience of men." He contented himself with doubling the taxes, and imposing a peculiar dress on the raskolniki of Moscow. Being, however, a true believer, he regarded the faith of the raskol as an error, and did not wish it to spread. Penalties were enforced against its propagators, and precautions taken with regard to their listeners. The proper attendance every Sunday at church and at Easter Communion became a matter of obligation.

He followed the same policy with regard to Western religions, allowed foreigners to have their churches in Saint Petersburg, and himself attended the French church, where his chair is still preserved. The Nevski Prospekt, bordered with dissenting churches, was the "prospect of tolerance." He protected the Capuchins established at Astrakhan, and even tried to live on good terms with the Jesuits; but as they continued to work at their propaganda, they were banished in sixteen hundred and eighty-nine, then recalled, then again definitely expelled in seventeen hundred and ten. "He endured the Capuchins," says Voltaire, "as being monks of no consequence, but regarded the Jesuits as dangerous political enemies." The friend of the Dutch and the English persecuted the foreign Protestants who insulted the orthodox faith by word or deed. A Russian woman, Nastasia Zima, having spread the principles of Luther, was conducted, with her husband and six other neophytes, before the terrible secret chamber, and was cruelly tortured.

ECONOMIC REFORMS: MANUFACTURES.

Peter the Great had toiled hard to establish himself on the Baltic, because he felt that the White Sea, frozen over for so many months in the year, was insufficient to secure to Russia uninterrupted communication with the West. When Saint Petersburg was founded, he wished to suppress Arkhangel for the benefit of the new port, and forbade the merchants to carry their merchandise down the Dwina. This project met with the most lively opposition. Apraxin assured him that such a measure would be the ruin of Russian commerce. The Dutch traders and the Hanse towns represented that the money they had spent in establishing themselves at Arkhangel would be lost, that it would be necessary to build vessels for the Baltic on an entirely different model, that they were obliged to pay for the privilege of passing through the Sound, and that in case of a war the smallest merchant-ship would there need a convoy. The Russians who were accustomed to go to Arkhangel showed great repugnance to the journey to Saint Petersburg, across a wide space without provender, and where they would find no inns such as had been established for centuries on the route to the White Sea. It was necessary to make a complete revolution in the habits of Russian commerce, in the distribution of the centres of industry and of the market towns. The conductors of the caravan, in despair at the length of the voyage, often deserted, abandoning the wagons or pillaging the merchandise. Peter the Great yielded, leaving time to justify his preference for the new city. He authorized trade both by way of Arkhangel and Saint Petersburg, contenting himself with raising by a fourth the tariff of customs of the former town. Above all, he resolved to connect the city of the Neva with the great river artery of Russia, the Volga. To this end he created the canal of the Ladoga, which has a length of sixty-three versts, laid plans to bring the White Sea into communication with the Gulf of Finland, and to unite the Black Sea with the Caspian by means of a canal between the Don and the Volga.

Peter negotiated treaties of commerce with many European States, stirred up the national agriculture, whose progress had been hindered by the slavery of the people, promulgated an edict which forced them to reap with scythes instead of the old hooks, encouraged the cultivation of the vine and the mulberry in the regions of the southeast, ordered tobacco to be planted, introduced new kinds of cattle into Kholmogorui and other central provinces, stimulated sheep-raising, which was necessary for his wool factories, sent for Silesian shepherds, and made Russians go to learn the trade in Silesia; moreover, he created the imperial stud. He took measures to preserve the forests, and caused his whole empire to be searched for coal-beds. To counteract the indolence of such nobles as might have mines upon their lands, he declared that, in the case of their remaining unworked, strangers should have leave to work them, paying only a small premium to the proprietor. He decreed stripes and the penalty of death against any one who should dare to interfere with the mining labors and researches. Under him began the fortunes of the Demidofs, the great mine-owners, as in the reign of Ivan the Fourth began the fortunes of the Strogonofs. Peter, passing one day through Tula, inquired if there was a workman skilful enough to manufacture a musket like a foreign one which he had with him. Demid was recommended as a good gunsmith, and presented himself before the Tsar, who said, "That man would make a fine grenadier for my guards." But the man begged him to spare the father of four children. Peter was so well satisfied with the musket which Demid made, that he ordered several more, and finally gave him iron-mines in the Ural Mountains for the manufacture of cannon. The Demidofs finally became immensely rich, and Pavel Demidof founded at Moscow the Hospital for Foundlings. Peter established and encouraged his courtiers to establish, manufactures of chemical productions; of cloth, from the managers of which he purchased the materials which he wanted for the uniforms of the army; of sail-cloth, for which the navy would furnish a ready market. The French were specially skilled in making use of the Russian wool. The Russians owe them the first manufactories of tapestries; a Frenchman named Manvriou opened a stocking manufactory at Moscow. The Englishman Humphrey introduced an improvement in the fabrication of Russia leather; the Tsar required every town to send a certain number of shoemakers to take lessons in their art at Moscow, threatening them, if they continued to work in their old way, with confiscation and the galleys. The admiral Apraxin manufactured silk brocades. A muzhik invented a lacquer superior to anything in Europe except that of Venice. Considering the versatility of the national genius, economic progress would have immensely developed if the Tsar had been able to secure the Russian merchants against the cupidity of the great and the exactions of the officials, — a danger already noted by Fletcher in the sixteenth century. Nothwithstanding this drawback, more than two hundred mills were opened in this reign.

PRACTICAL CHARACTER OF THE SCHOOLS FOUNDED BY PETER.

Peter the Great took great pains with the education of his people. He felt that the surest way of obtaining those who would help him and would continue his work was gradually to initiate the nation into his new ideas, and little by little to reconcile them to reform. He especially insisted on the education of the sons of nobles and priests; and it was decreed that a noble who could not read, write, nor express himself in a foreign tongue, should lose this birthright. But it was to be many years before the masses of the people were to have the means of instruction. A certain number of elementary schools to which all the children of officials, from the age of ten to fifteen, were obliged to be sent, were, however, founded in all the provinces, and the pupils of the mathematical schools of Saint Petersburg were sent there as masters. These schools of Peter's had all a practical character and were of immediate utility. Classical studies were neglected, and he did not trouble himself to create branch establishments to the Greco-Latin academy at Moscow. In his fierce struggle with the forces of the past he hastened to throw Russia open to his natural auxiliaries, the ideas and sciences of the West. The schools he multiplied were special schools, — a naval academy, a school of engineers, a school of book-keeping. The literature he encouraged was a literature of translation, by means of which a huge mass of European ideas could be introduced all at once. He also encouraged polemic writings, to plead the cause of reform before the tribunal of Russian and foreign opinion. It was for this reason that he had an enormous number of technical books translated, employing for the purpose the professors of the Greco-Latin academy, the brothers Likhudi, who had retired to Novgorod, and even the members of the synod. Some of the books were translated at Moscow, and some were caused to be translated abroad, many at first into Tchek, so that the Muscovites might more easily reproduce them in their own tongue. History, geography, jurisprudence, political economy, navigation, military sciences, agriculture, and philology were soon represented in Russia by numerous books, translated from Western languages. Peter himself gave his brigade of writers advice which shows his practical sense, and even his instinctive literary taste. He said to Zotof: "You must beware of translating word for word without knowing the complete meaning of the text. You must read with care, become penetrated with the sense of your author, must be able to think his thoughts in Russian, and only after that try to reproduce them." He also recommended them to refrain from long dissertations and useless digressions, with which the Germans fill their books to make them appear thicker, and which only serve to waste time and to disgust the reader." On the other hand, he forbade the suppression of some passages in Puffendorf, where Russian barbarism is denounced. His subjects must learn to blush for their rudeness before they could cure themselves of it. He caused books to be printed in Holland, in which he attempted to teach the Europeans what Russia was, and to appreciate his reforms; while he published others in Russia to make his subjects acquainted with Europe. He had recourse to Saint Dmitri, Feofan, and Feofilakt, who by their polemical writings combated superstitions and sects hostile to the State. Other writers turned into ridicule on the stage, by means of operettas, all the enemies of reform, fanatical raskolniki, the deacon who wept because his son was torn from him and sent to school, the employés who fished in troubled waters, the partisans of the ancient customs, who regretted the "good old times," when German garments were unknown, and men wore long beards. Natalia, Peter's sister, associated herself in his work by composing Russian plays. The merchant Passoshkof wrote his book on "Poverty and Riches," a sort of domostroï, in which all the changes in manners since the time of the priest Silvester can be followed. Passoshkof dared to lift up his voice in favor of the oppressed peasant, to demand the establishment of a tribunal before which all Russian subjects should be equal, a regular organization of justice and administration, which should protect the people against those who rob in public, the brigands and thieves, and those who steal in secret, the employés and officials. He expected great things of Peter. "Unhappily," he says, "our great monarch is almost alone, with ten others, in pulling upwards, while millions of individuals pull downwards. How then can we hope for a good result?"

Peter needed means of rapid publication. But Russian

printing had made little progress since the sixteenth century; it had tried specially to imitate the ancient Slavonic manuscripts, and its method was extremely slow. Peter abandoned the Slavonic alphabet, no longer in use except for the Church books; he was the creator of the Russian alphabet properly so called, the civil alphabet, which is merely a modification of the Greek alphabet. He improved the machines and the types, imported Dutch printers, and made printing the instrument of a powerful and rapid propaganda. In his reign there were two printing-presses instead of one at Moscow, four at Saint Petersburg, and others at Tchernigof, Novgorod the Great, and Novgorod-Severski. He founded the Gazette of Saint Petersburg, the first public newspaper in Russia.

A prince who had studied medicine and surgery in the West, who sometimes practised on his courtiers, took out a tooth or lanced an abscess, could not neglect an art so necessary to his vast empire, where the mortality of infants was a bar to the increase of population. He intrusted to Doctor Bidloo the management of the hospitals and the instruction of fifty young men. In seventeen hundred and eighteen he put forth an edict enjoining the collection of valuable minerals, of extraordinary bones that might be found in the fields, of antique inscriptions on stone or metal, of any monstrosities of birth occurring among men or animals. "There are certain to be some of these births," says the ordinance, "but ignorant people make mysteries of them, believing that the birth of these monsters is due to some diabolic influence. This is impossible, for it is God and not the devil who is the creator of all things." Peter had a taste for geography; in seventeen hundred and nineteen he fitted out an expedition to Kamtchatka, to solve the question asked by Leibnitz: Is Asia united to America? In seventeen hundred and twenty he opened a school for the improvement of maps. The science of history also has deep obligations to him; in seventeen hundred and twenty-two he ordered a collection to be made in the archives of the monasteries, of the chronicles and letters of the Tsars, and had copies taken of them. Polykarpof wrote a History of Russia from the sixteenth century, for which the Tsar gave him a reward of two hundred rubles. Finally, in seventeen hundred and twenty-four, Peter the Great, who was at the time corresponding member of the Academy of Sciences in Paris, founded that of Saint Petersburg with a gift of two hundred thousand rubles, and assigned it a revenue of twenty-four thousand nine hundred and twelve rubles drawn from the revenues of the customs of Narva, Dorpat, and Pernava, desiring it, above all, to devote itself to translations, and to teach its pupils practical sciences and languages. The utilitarian character of Peter's creations is found even in his Academy. As it was not possible at that time to count on the Russians to form a learned body, the first academicians were necessarily foreigners. Germany furnished Wolff and Hermann; France, Daniel Bernouilli, the famous mathematician, philosopher, and physiologist, and Joseph De l'Isle, who was summoned to found the department of astronomy. Thus a country which as yet had neither secondary schools nor universities was given an academy.

FOUNDATION OF SAINT PETERSBURG.

Saint Petersburg was now fairly founded. Its situation, as Goethe remarks, "recalls that of Amsterdam or of Venice, the Italian Amsterdam." The wide and majestic Neva, which issues from the great lakes of the north, there divides into four arms, the great and little Neva, and the great and little Nevka. If we add to these its numerous affluents, the Fontanka, the Okhta, and the two Tchernaïas, we shall at present find fourteen water-courses, a lake, eight canals, and nineteen islands. It is distinctively the aquatic city, and is exposed to terrible inundations when the vast reservoirs of the Ladoga and Onega overflow, or when the west winds force the waters of the Baltic back toward the Neva. No building is ever erected there without first strengthening the foundation by driving in many wooden piles. When Peter the Great first cast his eyes over the country, after the capture of Nienschantz, there were only dark forests, vast marshes, dreary wastes, where, according to the poet, "a Tchud fisherman, a sorrowful son of his step-mother Nature, might occasionally be seen alone on the marshy shore, casting his worn-out line into these nameless waters." The Finnish names then borne by the islands, on which palaces were afterwards to rise, are very significant; there were the Isle of Brushwood, the Isle of Birches, the Isle of Goats, the Isle of Hares, the Isle of Buffaloes, Isle Michael, a name for the bear, and the Wild Isle. In Enisary, or "the Isle of Hares," Peter built in seventeen hundred and three the new fortress of Saint Peter and Saint Paul. There he assembled regular soldiers, Cossacks, Tatars, Kalmuicki, Ingrian or Karelian natives, and peasants of the interior, in all more than forty thousand men. No tools were provided for their first labors; the muzhik dug the soil with sticks or his nails, and carried the earth in his caftan. He had to sleep in the open air among the marshes; he often lacked food, and the workmen died by thousands. Afterwards the service was made more regular. Peter installed himself in the celebrated little wooden house on the right bank, watching the building, sometimes piloting with his own hand the first Dutch ships which ventured into these waters, sometimes giving chase to Swedish vessels, which came to insult the infant capital. In November, seventeen hundred and three, he himself piloted the first merchant-ship into his new port. Peter granted the captain freedom from tolls for his cargo of wine and salt, and presented him with five hundred ducats, and each of the sailors with two hundred reichsthaler. The same favors were shown to the next ship, which was English. On the Isle of Buffaloes, afterwards called the Vasili-Ostrof, situated on the northern bank of the Neva, numerous edifices rose; the southern bank, which became the real site of the town, seemed to be at that time neglected. It contained only the Admiralty, to which Anna Ivanovna added a spire; the cathedral of Saint Isaac, then built of wood, now of marble and bronze; the church of Saint Alexander Nevski, where Peter the Great deposited the remains of the first conqueror of the Swedes; the house of Apraxin, on the site of which Elisabeth built the Winter Palace, and the already splendid mansions of the Millionaïa. Through it the Nevski Prospekt, the most magnificent boulevard in Europe, was to run. The city was built and settled by dint of edicts. Finns, Esthonians, Tatars, Kalmuicki, Swedish prisoners, and merchants of Novgorod were transplanted thither; and in seventeen hundred and seven they were aided by thirty thousand day laborers from the country. To attract all the masons of the empire, it was forbidden on pain of exile and confiscation to construct stone houses anywhere but at Saint Petersburg. Every proprietor owning five hundred peasants was obliged to raise a stone house of two stories; those who were poor clubbed together to build one among themselves. Every boat that wanted to enter had to bring a certain number of unhewn stones, for stone was lacking in these wastes. Provender was also wanting, and to save it Peter proscribed the use of carriages, and encouraged navigation by the river and canals; every inhabitant was obliged to have his boat, and only by water could the Court be approached.

In seventeen hundred and six Peter wrote to Menshikof that all was going on wonderfully, and that "he seemed here in paradise." He decorated the church of the fortress with carvings in ivory, the work of his own hands, and hung it with flags conquered from the Swedes; he there in August, seventeen hundred and twenty-three, made a great festival in honor of the founding of his fleet, and consecrated, amid the thunders of artillery, the little boat which the English government had given Ivan the Fourth. It was named "the little grandfather of many large grandchildren." Breaking through the tradition which insisted that the princes should be buried at Saint Michael at Moscow, he selected a place in the Peter-Paul Church for his own tomb and that of his successors. "Before the new capital," says Pushkin, "Moscow bowed her head, as an imperial widow bows before a young Tsaritsa."

Saint Petersburg had another enemy besides the Swedes, — the inundations. The soil was not yet raised by the incessant heaping up of materials; the granite quays did not yet confine the formidable river. In seventeen hundred and five nearly the whole town was flooded; in seventeen hundred and twenty-one all the streets were navigable, and Peter was nearly drowned in the Nevski Prospekt. The enemies of reform, exasperated by the desertion of Moscow, rejoiced over these disasters, and predicted that this German town, built by foreign hands and soiled by the presence of heretic temples, would disappear beneath the floods, that some day the place of this cursed city should be sought in vain. Even at the end of Peter's reign it was the general opinion that after his death the Court and the nobility would return to Moscow, and that the city and the fleet created by the Tsar would be abandoned. They were mistaken; the town that he had flung like a forlorn hope on the newly conquered soil remained the seat of the empire. Russia is almost the only State that has built its capital on its very frontiers. Saint Petersburg was not only to be the "window" open to the West, but it was to be also the centre of the Russian regeneration. More freely, more completely than at Moscow the Holy, where everything recalled the traditions and recollections of the past, Peter could enthrone at Saint Petersburg the sentiments of toleration for the Protestant and Catholic religions, and sympathy for foreigners, who were always detested at Moscow. He could more easily persuade the nobles to adopt German fashions, to speak Western languages, to cultivate sciences and useful arts, to discard with the national caftan the old Russian prejudices. At Moscow, the City of the Tsars, foreigners were confined in the German Sloboda; at Saint Petersburg, the City of the Emperors, the Russian and the stranger were to meet and receive mutual impressions.

CHAPTER IV.

PETER THE GREAT: LAST YEARS.

1709-1725.

WAR WITH TURKEY: TREATY OF THE PRUTH (1711). — JOURNEY TO PARIS (1717). — PEACE OF NYSTAD (1721): CONQUESTS ON THE CASPIAN. — FAMILY AFFAIRS: EVDOKIA; TRIAL OF ALEXIS (1718); CATHERINE.

WAR WITH TURKEY: THE TREATY OF THE PRUTH.

CHARLES THE TWELFTH, who had allowed himself to be detained in Poland during the five years that followed Narva, proceeded after the battle of Poltava, in seventeen hundred and nine, to idle away five years more at Bender. Peter turned this new delay to advantage with as much energy as the former. Charles's Polish king, Leshtchinski, was obliged to retire into Pomerania, having been deserted by his most powerful friends, who had heard that Augustus was about to come with a Saxon army of fourteen thousand men, and that the Tsar himself was on his way to Poland. Augustus of Saxony re-entered Warsaw after making a reconciliation with Peter the Great. In the North Peter again attempted the capture of Vuiborg, the most important city of Karelia, situated on the Gulf of Finland. On the thirteenth of June the Swedish commander was forced to surrender, and the garrison, together with nearly all the inhabitants, was transplanted to Saint Petersburg. In September the whole province, including the important city of Kexholm, had submitted to the Tsar. On the fourth of July Riga capitulated after a long and costly siege in which both armies suffered from the plague, which had broken out. After the loss of Riga the other cities of Livonia were unable to make a long resistance. Pernava surrendered on the fourteenth of August, and on the twenty-ninth of September Revel, the capital of Esthonia. Thus by the conquest of Livonia, Esthonia, and a part of Finland, Peter gained a stronger hold on the Baltic. Owing to the fact that Kurland was a State subject to Poland, he was unable to make a conquest of it; but he paved the way for its union with Russia by marrying the young Duke, Friedrich Wilhelm, nephew of the King of Prussia, to Anna Ivanovna, daughter of his brother Ivan. The Duke died a few days after the wedding. Nevertheless, his widow took up her residence in Mitava, where she lived until she ascended the throne of Russia.

The agents of Sweden, generals Poniatovski and Pototski, the friends of Stanislas and Charles, Désaleurs, ambassador of France, and the warlike Khan of the Tatars, were all urging the Divan to go to war. Akhmet the Third was anxious to recapture Azof. In August, seventeen hundred and ten, the grand vizier gave the command for the army and fleet to be put on a war basis. On the twenty-first of November war was declared, and the Russian ambassador, Tolstoi, was thrown in the Seven Towers. As soon as Peter learned that this rupture of the peace had taken place, and that Baltazhi-Mahomet was assembling an immense army in the plains of Adrianople, he ordered Prince Mikhail Galitsuin to go to the boundaries of Moldavia with ten regiments of dragoons in order to watch the movements of the Turks and Tatars. Sheremetief was commanded to report from Riga in Livonia, with twenty-two regiments of infantry, while Dmitri Galitsuin kept an eye on the Zaporoshtsui and Prince Romodonovski drew near Putivl with the forces at his command. On the eighth of March service was said in the Uspienski Sobor at Moscow, and public declaration of the war was made from the altar. The Tsar received this declaration of war almost with joy; the whole of

Russia trembled with gladness at the thought of treading in the steps of its ancient princes, of marching to Tsargrad, the "Sovereign City," of freeing the Christians of the East, of exterminating the old enemies of the Slav race, and of eclipsing the glory of Ivan the Terrible.

On the seventeenth of March Peter took his departure for Poland together with Catherine, whom he had secretly married in seventeen hundred and seven, and whom now he acknowledged as his wife. He had an interview with Augustus, who promised him aid against the Turks; but without waiting for the Polish contingent of thirty thousand men, he hastened to the scene of action, depending more upon the Princes of Moldavia and Valakhia than on the King. Konstantin Bessaraba, Count of Brankovan, had been for twenty-two years hospodar of Valakhia, and with the hope of securing the princedom to his family he promised Peter to furnish him provisions and men, and to stir up a revolt among the Christians in the Turkish dominions. Peter expected still more valuable aid from Moldavia, which was separated from Poland only by the Dniester. Dmitri Kantemir, whose father had been hospodar of Moldavia, just before the declaration of war had been appointed by the grand vizier to the same position, with a promise of freedom from paying tribute and the customary gift to the divan. But hardly had he reached the capital when the gift was demanded from him. He then resolved to unite with the Russians, whose star seemed to be in the ascendant. Accordingly, on the twenty-fourth of April he agreed to place Moldavia under Russian protection and join his army to Peter's, on the condition of being kept in his princely rights. As soon as Sheremetief, with his army of fifteen thousand men, had crossed the Dniester, Kantemir judged it a favorable time to throw off the mask. By a printed proclamation he announced his treaty with the Tsar, and threatened his boyars with death and confiscation if they did not attach themselves to the Tsar's army. But the fear of the Turks had greater influence on his subjects than his threats and promises, and a majority of the nobles hastened to join the Turks, carrying with them the larger part of the provisions of the country. The Russian army, contrary to their usual custom, had neglected to bring supplies, and not more than a week's rations were at their command.

Peter drew near the Dniester and held a council of war. It was the opinion of the German generals that they should secure their position on the river, where they had easy access into Poland, and if possible capture Bender, where Charles the Twelfth was staying, which would furnish a stronghold and magazine for the army. They reminded Peter of the mistake made by Charles the Twelfth in seventeen hundred and nine, and showed him the danger of counting on the doubtful help of these barbarous and thinly peopled countries. But the brave General Rönne of Kurland, in whom Peter had the fullest confidence, thought that the only step worthy of the Tsar was to press on through the deserts of Moldavia. The Russian generals and ministers seconded Rönne, and Peter decided to follow the advice of the majority. On the twenty-seventh of June he crossed the river. After a seven days' march through a desert lacking water and trees and without a habitation, they reached the Pruth, where Kantemir joined them with his little army. Here they learned of Brankovan's defection. Peter was so incensed that he was prevented only by the greatest difficulty from killing the Valakhian messenger on the spot. Meanwhile the Turkish army was approaching, and had succeeded in throwing two bridges across the Danube. General Rönne, in attempting to attack these bridges, was cut off from the main division of the Russians. Peter's position became more and more hazardous. Provisions were scarce, as well as provender for the horses. The locusts had eaten the grass to the very roots. It was decided to beat a retreat, and the shortest way was chosen between the mountains and the river. But this was found to be impassable, owing to a morass that occupied the width of the plain. The whole army came together again on the night of the nineteenth of July, and it was found that out of the thirty-eight thousand which had crossed the Dniester, only twenty-four thousand answered the muster-roll. The march was directed to a clump of woodland on a hill which would give the army a little protection. But the Tatar Khan managed to invest the hill before the Russians reached it. The next morning the Tatars attacked the Russian rear, which was guarded by the Preobrazhenski regiment. In steady conflict they marched until noon, when they were obliged to stop and recover from the effects of the intense heat and their weariness. Meanwhile the whole Turkish and Tatar army, amounting to over two hundred thousand, had assembled in the plain of Horste Guesti. The grand vizier, Baltazhi-Mahomet, was a poor soldier, but he had able assistants in the Swedish general, Sparre, and in Count Poniatovski. Charles had kept away from the Turkish camp through his dislike at holding a subordinate position. On the evening of the twentieth of July, just before sunset, the battle was renewed. The Russians thrice repulsed the ferocious attacks of the Janissaries, and more than seven thousand Turks perished. Night came on and offered little consolation to the weary Russians. Poniatovski advised the vizier to throw up an embankment and post upon it all the cannon. Five hundred would have sufficed to annihilate the Russians. Peter seemed irretrievably lost. Sick in his tent and alone, he gave himself up to the most melancholy forebodings. A moment was sufficient to overthrow the work of his life. To retreat was impossible. It was equally impossible to remain without provisions. A council of war was held in Shafirof's tent. Catherine was present. It was determined to tempt the well-known avarice of the grand vizier. Two hundred thousand rubles were collected, and Catherine added her jewels. Then she went to Peter's tent and told him the determination of the council.

He consented against his will, and the ambassadors, Shafirof at their head, proceeded to the Turkish camp. Baltazhi, attracted by the sight of the money and the glittering jewels, seemed inclined to yield. Peter wrote to Shafirof to accede to any terms, to make any sacrifice demanded by the Turks; to restore Azof, Livonia, even Esthonia and Karelia, but to hold fast upon Ingria, the loss of which would involve that of the new capital. He commanded the envoys rather to sacrifice even Pskof, and besought them to let him know that very day, so that they might try the "desperate way" if negotiations failed. He was determined under those circumstances to force a passage, and to fight to the last man. He had already written to the senate announcing his perilous condition, and commanding them, in case he met with disaster, to choose from their number the one most worthy to be his successor. But the vizier acceded to the treaty, and his demands were smaller than were anticipated: he contented himself with the restitution of Azof, the destruction of the fortresses of Taganrog, Kamennov, Saton, and others erected on the Turkish territory, and the promise that Charles the Twelfth should not be hindered in his return to Sweden, and that he should be left in peace when he returned to his own kingdom; he also demanded that Kantemir should be given into his hands. But this demand Peter managed not to satisfy. Such was the celebrated Treaty of the Pruth, or of Hush, as it was called from the little city near by. It caused universal joy in the Russian army, for few had expected such a result. The Count de Lion wrote: "If in the morning any one had told us that peace would come about in such a manner, everybody would have considered him a visionary, a lunatic, a scatterbrain, who had the audacity to encourage us with a hope in which there was certainly not the least reason to indulge. And I remember that after General Janus's flag of truce had departed with the marshal's letter, this general said to us, as we were returning to our places, that the man who had induced his Tsarian majesty to undertake this business ought to be considered the most ridiculous, the most foolish person on earth; but that if the grand vizier accepted the offer made him, in the situation in which we were, he would give the grand vizier the precedence. God granted that the general of that infidel army was blinded by the glitter of two hundred thousand ducats, so that so large a number of excellent people in this army were saved when they were actually at the mercy of the Turks." Peter the Great never recovered from the sadness which the reverses in this war caused him,— to have come as deliverer of the Christian world and to be forced to capitulate; to surrender Azof, his first conquest; to annihilate his fleet on the Black Sea, which had cost him so many efforts! But he wrote to the senate that, although the loss of the cities which had cost so much labor and treasure was, indeed, grievous to him, yet he could see wherein advantage might be the ultimate result. He waited, and took his revenge on another side.

JOURNEY TO PARIS.—PEACE OF NYSTAD.—CONQUESTS ON THE CASPIAN.

In seventeen hundred and twelve and seventeen hundred and thirteen, while France was passing through a supreme crisis in the war of the Spanish Succession, the Russians, with their Danish and Saxon allies, were expelling the Swedes from Pomerania. In May, seventeen hundred and thirteen, a fleet of two hundred Russian ships, commanded by Apraxin, with Peter for vice-admiral, left the Neva, took Helsingfors and Abo, capital of Finland, the library of which was sent to Saint Petersburg, and disembarked troops who defeated the Swedes at Tammersfors. The following year the Russians again defeated the enemy's fleet at Hankül, and occupied the isles of Aland. Even Stockholm was threatened, the Russians not being more than fifteen miles from the Swedish capital. The capture of Nyslott completed the conquest of Finland, and Charles the Twelfth, who hastened from Bender, could save neither Stralsund nor Vismar. After long hesitation the King of Prussia had joined his enemies, and the last Swedish fortresses in Pomerania had fallen. The Elector of Hanover, King of England, also turned against him, and took Verden, a possession of Charles on the Weser. With Sweden deprived of its provinces in the German Empire, the results of the Treaty of Westphalia were imperilled. The war in the North, formerly localized in the eastern Baltic, became a European war, and threatened the equilibrium of the Continent. Russian armies, for the first time, poured into Northern Germany. Peter, who had married one of his nieces to the Duke of Kurland, found a husband for the other, Ekaterina Ivanovna, in the Duke of Mecklenburg, and lent his support to help this prince to reduce his nobility to obedience. North Germany seemed ready to fall under the Muscovite yoke, as in the seventeenth century it had passed under the Swedish rule. The allies of the Tsar began to fear his ambition. The Mecklenburg nobles took their revenge by everywhere stirring up enemies against him. Bernsdorff induced George of Hanover to break off his alliance with the Tsar, and two other Mecklenburgers obtained the promise of the King of Denmark to close the gates of Vismar on Peter. Peter felt that he also must find support, and, as the question had now become European, must seek European allies. It was at this juncture that Baron Görtz undertook to reconcile him with Charles the Twelfth, whose courage was to be used to overthrow the King of England, and to replace the Stuart dynasty on the throne. Peter wished, moreover, to enter into relations with France. In seventeen hundred and eleven he had sent Gregory Volkof to Louis the Fourteenth, to ask his mediation, but the Grand Monarque thought himself too deeply involved with Sweden, though Charles had but scantily fulfilled his own obligations. After the death of Louis the Fourteenth the Duke of Orleans became Regent. Peter decided to visit Versailles, and Prince Kurakin, his agent at the Court of France, assured him of the good-will of the Duke. The Tsar had, therefore, grounds to hope for the conclusion of a close alliance with a powerful kingdom, and perhaps to look forward to the marriage of his daughter Elisabeth with the young King Louis the Fifteenth. The circumstances under which Peter made his second journey to the West were all unlike those of his former tour. He was no longer the young prince, only half civilized, master of a nearly unknown State in Eastern Europe, but the conqueror of Poltava and of Hankül, the master of the Baltic and Northern Germany, the reformer of a numerous people, the founder of a new capital and a new empire, the head of a great European nation.

"This monarch," says Saint Simon, "astonished Paris by his extreme curiosity on all points of government, commerce, education, and police, — a curiosity which disdained nothing, but probed everything. All his conduct displayed the breadth of his views and the acuteness of his reasoning. His manner was at once the most majestic, the proudest, the most sustained, and at the same time the least embarrassing. He had the sort of familiarity that springs from boundless liberty, but he was not exempt from a trace of the old-world barbarism of his country, which made him abrupt and even uncourteous, and with nothing certain about his wishes but the fact that not one of them was to be contradicted. His habits at meals were rough; the revelry that followed was even more indecent. He seldom tried to hide in his establishment the freedom and the self-will of a king. His love of unrestrained sight-seeing, his dislike of being made a spectacle, his habit of liberty for which he was accountable to none, made him prefer hired carriages, even fiacres. He would jump into the first carriage he met with, without caring to whom it belonged, and have himself driven about the town or beyond the walls. He was a very tall man, well made, though rather thin, his face somewhat round, with a high forehead, beautiful eyebrows, a short nose, thick at the end; his lips were rather thick, his skin brown and ruddy. He had splendid eyes, large, black, piercing, and wide-awake; his expression was dignified and gracious when he liked, but often wild and stern; his eyes and his whole face were distorted by an occasional twitch that was very unpleasant. It lasted only a moment, and gave him a haggard and terrible look till he was himself again. His air expressed intellect, thoughtfulness, and greatness, and had a certain grace about it. He wore a linen collar, a round peruke, brown and unpowdered, which did not reach his shoulders; a brown, close-fitting coat, with gold buttons, a vest, breeches, stockings, and neither gloves nor cuffs; the star of his order on his coat, and the ribbon underneath it; his coat was often entirely unbuttoned, his hat lay on the table, and never on his head, even out of doors. In this simplicity, however shabby might be his carriage or scanty his retinue, his natural air of greatness could not be mistaken."

Peter visited both the Regent and the King, took Louis the Fifteenth in his arms, to the great consternation of the courtiers, and wrote to his wife Catherine, who this time did not accompany him: "The little king is scarcely taller than our dwarf Loaki; his face and figure are distinguished, and he is tolerably intelligent for his age." The Tsar despised all that was merely fashionable and unproductive luxury, and occupied himself entirely with government, commerce, science, and military affairs. He neglected to call on the princes of the blood, but entered the shops of coach-builders and goldsmiths. He tasted the soup of the Invalides, drank their health, struck them on the shoulder, and treated them as comrades. The Gobelins, the Observatory, the King's garden, the collection of plans in relief of fortified places, the works of the Pont Tournant, and the machine at Marly, for carrying water across the Seine to Versailles, captivated his attention. A gold medal was struck for him at the Mint with his own effigy and the motto "Vires acquirit eundo." He was present at a meeting of the Academy of Sciences, which elected him a member, and he corrected with his own hand a map of his dominions which was shown to him. He embraced a bust of Richelieu at the Sorbonne, and went to see Madame de Maintenon as a relic of the great reign of Louis the Fourteenth. She was confined to her bed, but Peter pulled aside the curtains and stood gazing at her for some time. Neither said a word, and Madame de Maintenon was very indignant, but unable to have her revenge.

Things did not run quite as smoothly as he wished in the matter which had chiefly brought him to France. He was in search of an ally against George the First; but the English alliance was then the corner-stone of the French foreign policy. "The Tsar," says Saint Simon, " had an intense desire to unite himself with France. Nothing could have been better for our commerce, or for our position with regard to Germany, the North, and the whole of Europe. Peter held England in check by its fears for its commerce, and King George by his fears for his German territories. He made Holland treat him with respect, and kept the Emperor in great order. . . . . No one can deny that he made a grand figure both in Europe and Asia, and that France would have gained enormously by an alliance with him. . . . . We repented long ago of our fatal infatuation for England, and our silly contempt for Russia."

Notwithstanding the mad confidence of the Regent in the Abbé Dubois, the plenipotentiaries of Peter the Great concluded at Amsterdam, in seventeen hundred and seventeen, after the return of the Tsar to his dominions, a treaty of commerce with France. The two Powers, now joined by Prussia, declared that they specially united to guarantee the Treaty of Utrecht, and the eventual peace of the North; they laid down the basis of a defensive alliance, the ways and means of which were afterwards to be considered. Peter, later in the same year, found himself somewhat compromised in the plans of

Görtz and Cardinal Alberoni of Spain, which caused a coolness between them. A regular communication between the two countries was, however, inaugurated. First Kurakin and then Dolgoruki were nominated ambassadors at Paris, while Campredon represented France at Saint Petersburg. More than once negotiations were set on foot for Elisabeth's marriage, sometimes with Louis the Fifteenth, sometimes with the Duke of Bourbon, or some other French prince. France lent its good offices to Russia, in the matter of peace with Sweden.

Görtz was on the point of reconciling Peter with Charles, and a congress had already opened in May in the isles of Aland, between Bruce and Ostermann on the one hand and Görtz and Gyllenburg on the other, when the King of Sweden was killed in Norway, in December, seventeen hundred and eighteen. An aristocratic reaction broke out at Stockholm: Charles Frederic of Holstein-Gottorp, nephew of Charles the Twelfth, was excluded from the throne, and the crown was offered to the youngest sister of the late king, Ulrica-Eleonora, wife of Frederic of Hesse-Cassel, who was regarded as more pliable. An aristocratic constitution was established which deprived the crown of nearly all its prerogatives, and left Sweden a prey for fifty-three years to anarchy and insignificance. Authority passed into the hands of a diet composed of the deputies of the four orders, the nobles, clergy, citizens, and peasants, but in which the nobles had a decided majority. Görtz was recalled to Stockholm and condemned to death, and his policy was abandoned. The Diet revived, on the contrary, the alliance with Hanover, and resolved to continue the war with Russia, with the probable support of the English fleet. Peter accepted the challenge, and waged with his enemies a war of extermination. In seventeen hundred and nineteen his army landed on the shores of Sweden itself, and burned two towns and a hundred and twenty-nine villages. Apraxin extended his ravages to within seven miles of Stockholm. The booty he collected was estimated at one million rubles, and twelve times as much was destroyed. When they withdrew, a piece of forest forty miles long was set on fire, by the burning of which the copper and iron mines situated in it became useless for many years. In seventeen hundred and twenty the devastation recommenced, in the very presence of the English fleet, which did not dare to pursue the Russians into the recesses of the Swedish coast. In seventeen hundred and twenty-one the Diet decided to treat. Peter kept Livonia, Esthonia, Ingria, part of Finland, and Karelia. Such was the Peace of Nystad, which avenged Ivan the Terrible and Alexis Mikhaïlovitch.

When the Tsar felt the weight of this twenty-two years' war lifted from his shoulders, he returned to Saint Petersburg to announce the happy news of peace to his people, and, mounted on a platform, he drank to the health of his subjects. A whole week was given up to fêtes and masquerades. Peter, in his joy, burned twelve thousand rubles' worth of powder, put on a fancy dress, danced on the table, and sang songs. The senate united with the Holy Synod in a great council, decreed to the Tsar the titles of " Great, of the Father of his Country, and of Emperor of all the Russias," and throughout the whole city thousands of voices cried, " Long live the Father of his Country, the Emperor, Peter the Great ! " It was thus that the son of Alexis became, according to the expression of the popular songs, " the first emperor of the country." Feofan Prokopovitch preached one of his most beautiful sermons on this occasion.

Peter's great desire was to make Russia the centre of communication between Asia and Europe. He had conquered the shores of the Baltic, but it was necessary that he should find an equivalent for Azof and throw open at least one of the seas of the East. Persia, mistress of the Caspian, was then a prey to anarchy under a weak prince, who was attacked by rebels on all sides. Russian merchants had been robbed, and Peter took advantage of this pretext for war to seize Derbend, the key of Persia, and he himself commanded the expedition which descended the Volga, from Nijni to Astrakhan, in seventeen hundred and twenty-two. The operations still continued after his departure: the Russians took Baku, the principal city of Shirvan, interfered in the internal affairs of Persia, promised help to the Shah against his enemies, and occupied Daghestan, Ghilan, and Mazanderan, with Resht and Asterabad.

FAMILY AFFAIRS: EVDOKIA; TRIAL OF ALEXIS; CATHERINE.

The last years of Peter the Great were saddened by terrible domestic tragedies. He had been married, at the age of seventeen, to Evdokia Lapukhin, the daughter of a very conservative family. As she shared the views of her relations, Peter soon began to hate her. After the capture of Azof he signified that he did not wish on his return to find her at the palace, and she was obliged to retire to the Pokrovski Monastery at Susdal. Soon afterwards he obtained a divorce, in order to marry Catherine. Banished and divorced, Evdokia still retained power. In the eyes of the people, and of a large part of the clergy, she remained the Tsar's only lawful wife; she was the mother of the Tsar's only son, Alexis, over whose mind and character she had, during the Tsar's frequent absences, exercised the most fatal influence. After the dismissal of Evdokia, Peter paid more attention to the education of his heir, who was then eight years old, and gave him foreign masters. It was too late; Alexis was already a young man. Narrow-minded, indolent, lazy, feeble, and obstinate, the son of the reformer was only a Lapukhin. While Peter was exposing himself on battle-fields in Finland, Lithuania, and the Ukraina, Alexis was surrounded by monks, devotees, and visionaries, and reading his Bible and theological works over and over again. His Court was formed of those who disparaged and abused the reforms and the new laws. Against his own wishes, he was forced in October, seventeen hundred and eleven, to marry Charlotte of Brunswick at Torgau, but consoled himself with the idea that he would one day have the heads of the authors of the marriage. He hated her because she was a foreigner and a heretic. When his confidant tried to make him fear that he would only alienate the nobles, "I spit upon them," he replied; "the people are on my side. When my father dies, I shall have only to say a word in the ear of the archbishops, who will tell their priests, who will whisper it to their parishioners, and I shall be made Tsar, even were it in spite of myself." During his travels in Germany he would learn nothing, he wounded his hand that he might not be obliged to draw, and alleged his feeble health as an excuse for living in idleness. Peter tried to bring him to reason. "Disquiet for the future destroys the joy caused by our present successes, for I see that you despise all that can make you worthy to reign after me. Your incapacity I call rebellion, for you cannot excuse yourself on the ground of feebleness of mind and weakness of health. We have struggled from our former obscurity only through the toils of war, which has taught other nations to know and respect us, and yet you will not even hear of military exercises. I, a man, am subject to death; to whom shall I leave what I have established and accomplished? If you do not alter your conduct, know that I shall deprive you of my succession. I have not spared, and I shall not spare, my own life for my country and my people; do you think that I shall spare yours? Better a worthy stranger than a good-for-nothing relation." Alexis still persisted that he had neither health nor memory, and would prefer to become a monk. Peter then gave him six months' time in which to decide whether he would obey him or go into a convent. His confidant, Kikin, advised him to dissemble, and to allow himself to be shut up in a convent. "You can come out of it," he said; "they do not nail the cowl to your head." During his father's travels in the West the Tsarévitch fled to Germany with his mistress, the Finland serf Afrosinia. He went to the court of Vienna, which promised to provide him with a secret and secure asylum. It was in this manner that he was successively confined in the castle of Ehrenberg, in the Tyrol, and of Sant' Elmo, near Naples. His father's agents, who had instantly started in pursuit, finally succeeded in tracing him, and Tolstoï obtained an interview with Alexis, who was assured of pardon, and persuaded to return to Moscow. The Tsar immediately assembled the three orders at the Kreml, arraigned the prisoner before it, and obliged him to sign a formal renunciation of the crown. Alexis had also to denounce his accomplices, and in the course of the interrogation some terrible disclosures were made to Peter. His son was the centre of a permanent conspiracy against his reforms, and was the hope of all who after his death would seek to destroy his work. If Alexis had consented to enter the cloister, it was in the expectation of one day leaving it ; in the same way his renunciation of the throne could not have been sincere : he did not belong to himself, he belonged to the enemies of his father, who would understand how to absolve him from his vows. Peter learned, among other things, that Alexis had solicited at Vienna the armed protection of the Emperor, that he had intrigued with Sweden, and that, on the occasion of a sedition in the Russian army of Mecklenburg, he entered into relations with the leaders, and only awaited a letter to hasten to the camp. He had longed for the death of his father, and his confessor, Varlaam, had said, " We all desire it." The threads of the plot between the palace of the Tsarévitch and the convent of the divorced Tsaritsa were soon grasped. Evdokia was treated, not as a nun, but as a Tsaritsa ; she had her court of malcontents, wore a secular costume, was mentioned in the prayers like a sovereign. Dosifeï, Archbishop of Rostof, had predicted to her the approaching death of the Tsar, and to hasten it the Archimandrite Peter made hundreds of prostrations before the holy images. General Glebof, who had established a correspondence in cipher with the Tsaritsa, avowed that he was her lover, and that he was to marry her after the death of the Tsar. Her relations, her brother Avraam Lapukhin among others, were concerned in these intrigues and hopes. Peter crushed with cruel penalties this nest of conspirators. Glebof was impaled, Dosifeï broken on the wheel, Lapukhin tortured and beheaded; thirty people were put to death or exiled; Evdokia was whipped and confined in New Ladoga. Peter's own sister Maria, who was also implicated, was imprisoned in Schlüsselburg. The affair of the Tsarévitch had changed its character after all these revelations; there could now be no question of clemency. Peter had no longer to deal with a lazy and disobedient son, but with a traitor who had become the chief of his enemies within and the ally of those without, and who had sought foreign aid. Peter had to choose between his son and his reforms, for Alexis had openly promised to abandon Saint Petersburg, the navy, the Swedish conquests, and to return to Moscow. There was no hope now of putting him in a condition where he would be harmless after the death of his father. Alexis knew they could not "nail the cowl on his head," and the seclusion of a convent had not prevented Evdokia from indulging in secular hopes. Henceforth Alexis found in his father only an inexorable judge. Twice he suffered the knout; and a tribunal composed of the highest officials of the State condemned him to death. The difficulty seemed to lie in the execution of the sentence; but two days after the sentence was passed it became known that he had ceased to live. Divers rumors as to the manner of his death were circulated in the Memoirs of the time: some say it was caused by a sudden apoplexy, or a disease of the bowels, arising from deep emotion; some that he was beheaded with an axe, struck down with a club, suffocated under cushions, strangled with his cravat; some that he was put to death by poison; others that his veins were opened. All that is certain is, that on the morning of the twenty-seventh of June, seventeen hundred and eighteen the Tsar compelled his son to appear before a commission of nine of the greatest men of the State. About what then took place these nine men were forever silent; but it seems now to have been ascertained that in order to wring fresh confessions from the Tsarévitch the knout was again applied to him, and that he died from the consequences of the torture.

Peter had already another family. In seventeen hundred and two, at the sack of Marienburg, the Russians had made prisoner a young girl, about whose condition, origin, and nationality original authorities differ. It seems most probable that she was a Livonian, the natural daughter of a gentleman named Von Rosen, whose mother afterwards married a serf, Skavronski; that she was a privileged servant at the house of the pastor Glück, and that she had been betrothed to a Swedish dragoon. It was thus that in obscurity and dishonor her imperial destiny began. Though ignorant and completely illiterate, she fascinated the Tsar by the vivacity of her mind, the correctness of her judgment, and something free and adventurous about her which contrasted with the manners of the Russian terem, and marked out this Lutheran slave as the future Empress of Russia. Their marriage, secretly contracted, received a final consecration under the fire of the Ottoman batteries on the Pruth. In memory of the services then rendered by Catherine to the Tsar and to the country, Peter founded the Order "for love and fidelity," and solemnly married her in seventeen hundred and twelve. He did not, however, dare to take her with him in his journey to France. The contrast would have been too obvious at Versailles between the ladies of the proud French nobility and this foreign slave; between the cultivated wit of a Sévigné and a Deffand and this empress who could not sign her name; between the refinements of the French fine ladies and the awkward wench described by the Margravine of Baireuth.

"The Tsaritsa," says the German princess, "was small and

clumsily made, very much tanned, and without either grace
or an air of distinction. You had only to see her to know
that she was low-born. From her usual costume you would
have taken her for a German comedian. Her dress had been
bought at a second-hand shop; it was very old-fashioned, and
covered with silver and dirt. She had a dozen orders, and as
many portraits of saints or reliquaries, fastened down all her
dress, in such a way that when she walked you would have
thought by the jingling that a mule was passing." In seventeen
hundred and twenty-one Peter promulgated the celebrated
edict which recognized the right of the Russian sovereign
to nominate his successor, thus derogating from the
hereditary principle which seems the very essence of the monarchy.
Peter invoked the precedent of Ivan the Great, and
the "Absalom revolt" of Alexis. To justify this measure of
the Tsar, Feofan Prokopovitch wrote his book, called *Pravda
voli monarsheï*, or "The Law of the Monarch's Will." By
Catherine Peter had had two sons, Peter and Pavel, who died
when children, and two daughters,—Anna, married to the
Duke of Holstein, and Elisabeth, who became Tsaritsa. Besides
these, Alexis had left a son by Charlotte of Brunswick, who
was then named last in the public prayers, and afterwards became
Peter the Second. In May, seventeen hundred and
twenty-four, Peter the Great published a manifesto, recalling
the services Catherine had rendered, and solemnly crowned
her Empress. This was the culmination of her strange destiny.
Soon it began to change; the Emperor thought that he
had discovered proofs of her infidelity, and spoke of repudiating
her. At all events, he had not as yet exercised the right
of naming his successor, claimed two years before. His health
was broken by his toils and his excesses, and he no longer
took any care of himself. On the twenty-seventh of October,
seventeen hundred and twenty-four, he flung himself into icy
water up to his waist to save a boat in distress; he began to
feel the first symptoms of illness, but he recovered, and in Jan-

uary he again instituted the election of a Prince-pope. Buturlin, who had taken the place of Zotof in this office, had just died, and a new Conclave of Cardinals was assembled. Peter, as usual, drank to excess. In the " benediction of the waters " he caught a fresh cold, and died on the twenty-eighth of January, seventeen hundred and twenty-five, without being able either to speak or write his last wishes. He was then only fifty-three years of age.

He was, above all, a man of war, marked as such by his tall figure, his robust limbs, his nervous and sanguine temperament, and his arm as strong as a blacksmith's. His life was a struggle with the forces of the past, with the ignorant nobles, with the fanatical clergy, with the people who plumed themselves on their barbarism and national isolation, with the Cossack and Strelits, representatives of the old army, and with the raskol, the representative of the old superstition. This combat, which shook Russia and the world, he found repeated in his own family. It began with his sister Sophia, and continued with his wife Evdokia and his son Alexis. Entirely given up to his terrible task, Peter all his life disdained pomp, luxury, and every kind of display. The first Emperor of Russia, the founder of Saint Petersburg, forgot to build himself a palace ; his favorite residence of Peterhof is like the villa of a well-to-do citizen of Saandam. His table was frugal, and what he sought in his orgies of beer or brandy was a stimulant or a distraction. The people have preserved his memory in their songs or popular traditions ; they delight in repeating, " He worked harder than a burlak." This well-filled life was like a fever of perpetual activity, in which Peter, with Russia, panted and exhausted himself. Is it wonderful that he roughly hurled all obstacles out of his way? His movement was prompt and his hand heavy ; the staff of Ivan the Fourth seems to have passed into his grasp. We have seen him strike with his cane the greatest lords, Prince Menshikof among the number. To his will he bent men, things, nature, and time ; he realized his end by despotic blows. For a long while yet Russian and foreign historians will either hesitate to pass a final judgment on him, or will advance contradictory opinions. The truth will probably be found not in the fulsome adulations of Voltaire, nor in the bitter criticism of Prince Augustin Galitsuin, but in a reasonable estimate which, while recognizing his faults, sees his virtues and the real greatness of his character.

CHAPTER V.

THE WIDOW AND GRANDSON OF PETER THE GREAT: CATHERINE THE FIRST AND PETER THE SECOND.

1725-1730.

THE WORK OF PETER THE GREAT CONTINUED BY CATHERINE. — MENSHIKOF AND THE DOLGORUKIS. — MAURICE DE SAXE IN KURLAND.

THE WORK OF PETER THE GREAT CONTINUED BY CATHERINE.

AT the death of Peter the Great the nation was divided into two parties : one supported his grandson, Peter Alexiévitch, then twelve years old, the other wished to proclaim Catherine the Livonian. The Galitsuins, the Dolgorukis, Repnin, and all Old Russia desired to place the crown on the head of Peter Alexiévitch; but those who owed their elevation to Peter the First, those who were involved in the trial of his son, — Prince Menshikof, Admiral Apraxin, Buturlin, Colonel of the Guard, the Chancellor Golovkin, Iaguzhinski, Procurator-General of the Senate, the German Ostermann, Tolstoï, who had induced Alexis to quit the Castle of Sant' Elmo, the Bishop Feofan, author of the *Pravda voli monarshéi*, and the members of the tribunal which had condemned the Tsarévitch, — all felt that their only hope of salvation lay in Catherine. They were the more capable and the more enlightened ; they held the power actually in their hands, — directed the administration and commanded the army. Their adversaries felt that they must be content with a compromise. Dmitri Galitsuin proposed to proclaim Peter the Second, but only under the guardianship of the Empress-widow. Tolstoï opposed this, on the ground that it was the most certain means of arming one party against the other, of giving birth to troubles, of offering hostile factions a pretext for raising the people against the regent. He proved that, in the absence of all testamentary disposition, Catherine had the best right to succeed Peter the First. She had been solemnly crowned, and had received the oaths of her subjects; she was initiated into all the State secrets, and had learned from her husband how to govern. The officers and regiments of Guards loudly declared in favor of the heroine of the Pruth. It was at last decided that she should reign alone, and absolute, by the same title as the dead Tsar. To be sure, it was a novelty in Russia, — a novelty even greater than the regency of Sophia. Catherine was not only a woman, but a foreigner, a captive, a second wife, hardly considered as a wife at all. There was more than one protest against a decision which excluded the grandson of Peter the Great from the throne, and many raskolniki suffered torture rather than take the oath of allegiance to a woman.

Menshikof, one of Catherine's early lovers, found himself all-powerful. He was able to stop the trial for maladministration which had been brought against him by the late Tsar, and obtained the gift of Baturin, Mazeppa's ancient capital, which was equivalent to the whole principality of the Ukraina. His despotic temper and his bad character made him hated by his companions. Discord broke out among the "eaglets" of Peter the Great. Iaguzhinski, angry because he did not enjoy as much authority as under Peter, and feeling that he had been insulted by Catherine, went to weep publicly over the tomb of the Tsar, and tried to open the coffin with his teeth and nails, crying out : "Come forth, O my master, from thy tomb, to avenge me, and behold how Russia is governed now that thou art dead!" Tolstoï was afterwards sent to Siberia. Catherine succeeded, however, in bridling the ambition of her favorite, and refused to sacrifice her other councillors to him.

This régime was the continuation of that of Peter. It disappointed the pessimist predictions which announced the abandonment of Saint Petersburg and the fleet, and the return to Moscow. Most of the schemes which had been devised by the reforming Tsar were carried out. The Academy of Sciences was inaugurated in seventeen hundred and twenty-six; the publication of the *Gazette* was carefully watched over; the Order of Alexander Nevski, which Peter had originated after the Peace of Nystad, was founded; Behring, the Danish captain, was placed at the head of the scientific expedition to Kamtchatka; Shafirof, recalled from banishment, was ordered to write the History of Peter the Great; Anna Petrovna was solemnly married on the first of June, seventeen hundred and twenty-five, to the Duke of Holstein, to whom she had been betrothed by her father. On the other hand, the senate and and the Holy Synod lost their title of "directing," and affairs of State had to be conducted in the Secret High Council, which met under the presidency of the Empress, and was composed of Menshikof, of the Admiral Apraxin, of the Chancellor Golovkin, Tolstoï, Dmitri Galitsuin, and of the Vice-Chancellor Ostermann.

On her death-bed, Catherine nominated Peter Alexiévitch, her husband's grandson, as her successor, and, in default of Peter, her two daughters Anna of Holstein and Elisabeth. During the young Emperor's minority, the regency was to be exercised by the High Council, in which Anna and Elisabeth were to hold precedence. The Duke of Holstein, Menshikof, Apraxin, Golovkin, Ostermann, Dmitri Galitsuin, and Vasili Dolgoruki were the other members of this Council; but in reality it met only once, Menshikof taking upon himself the duties of regent.

The Empress died on the seventeenth of May, seventeen hundred and twenty-seven, and on the following morning the nobility and clergy of the empire assembled in the great hall of the palace, to hear the reading of the will. Peter was declared Emperor of all the Russias. Menshikof took measures to keep his high appointment under the new reign, and even to increase his power. Those whom he felt would limit his influence, he took pains to send on distant commissions or to banish. Iaguzhinski was sent to the Ukraina. Makarof was detailed to inspect the mines of Siberia. Apraxin was removed from the Court. Menshikof had obtained from Catherine the promise that she would consent to the young prince's betrothal to his own daughter, though she was the elder by two years. He assigned his own palace on the right bank of the river as the Emperor's residence, and surrounded him by men devoted to his own interests. He caused himself to be made Generalissimo, and signed his letters to his sovereign with the words, "Your father." He had the members of his own family inscribed in the almanac with those of the imperial house, and his daughter mentioned in the public prayers. He even planned to marry Peter's sister, Natalia Alexiévna, to his son at the same time that his daughter became the wife of the Emperor. Peter the Second soon began to be impatient of the government of the Generalissimo. Menshikof had given him as tutor the Vice-Chancellor Ostermann, but the young prince detested study, and preferred to hunt with his favorite, Ivan Dolgoruki. The clever Ostermann took care to make Menshikof responsible for the odium of his appointment as tutor, and to excuse himself as best he could to the prince. One day in September, seventeen hundred and twenty-one, the Emperor sent a present of nine thousand ducats to his sister Natalia. Menshikof had the insolence to take them from the princess, saying that "the Emperor was young, and did not yet know how to use money properly." This time Peter rebelled, and the prince appeased him with great difficulty. Another enemy of the Generalissimo, who managed playfully to undermine his popularity, was Elisabeth, the young aunt of Peter the Second, and the daughter of Peter the Great. She was then seventeen years old, bright, gay, and careless, with a pink-and-white complexion and blue eyes; and she laughed the intolerable guardian out of power. An attack of illness which happened to Menshikof, by keeping him away from Court, led to his fall. Peter the Second became accustomed to the idea of getting rid of him. When the prince recovered and began as usual to oppose his wishes, Peter quitted Menshikof's palace, caused the furniture belonging to the Crown to be removed from it and placed in the imperial palace, treated his bride elect with marked coldness, and finally commanded the guards to take no orders but from their colonels. This was the prelude to an overwhelming public disgrace. In September, seventeen hundred and twenty-seven, Menshikof was arrested, despoiled of all his dignities and decorations, and banished to his own lands.

The Dolgorukis profited by the revolution they had prepared, but immediately committed the same fault as Menshikof, and surrounded Peter with the same officious attentions. Like Menshikof, they banished all who offended them, even Ostermann, to whom the Emperor began to be attached; and the old Tsaritsa, Evdokia Lapukhin, who had been recalled from the prison in Ladoga. Using as a pretext some insulting placards recalling the services of Menshikof, they exiled him to Berezof in Siberia, where he died in seventeen hundred and twenty-nine. Unwarned by his example, they imposed on the prince a new bride, — Ekaterina Dolgoruki, the sister of his favorite Ivan. Their administration then assumed the character of a reaction against the reforms of Peter the Great. In January, seventeen hundred and twenty-eight, the young Emperor went to Moscow for his coronation. He was received with the warmest expression of affection by the people. But Ostermann and all the faithful servants, foreign or Russian, of the "Giant Tsar," saw with sorrow the return of the Court to Moscow, and its indifference to all European affairs. In order the better to keep their master to themselves, the Dolgorukis flattered his tastes for frivolity and dissipation, and organized great hunting-parties which lasted for whole weeks. Peter would have wearied of them in the end as he did of Menshikof. He had already replied to his aunt Elisabeth, who complained that she was left without money, "It is not my fault; they never execute my orders, but I shall find means of breaking my fetters." The crisis happened, but not as had been expected. His marriage was to have taken place in January, seventeen hundred and thirty; but the young Emperor caught cold at the ceremony of the "benediction of the waters," and died suddenly of small-pox. He was fourteen years and about four months old.

The two reigns of Catherine and Peter the Second, which lasted in all only five years, were peaceful.

In seventeen hundred and twenty-six Russia had concluded a treaty of alliance with the Court of Vienna, and found itself involved, in seventeen hundred and twenty-seven, in the war of the quadruple alliance. Notwithstanding the efforts of Kurakin and of Campredon, the failure of the projected marriage of Louis the Fifteenth and Elisabeth had produced a coldness between France and Russia. The most curious episode in the foreign relations was the attempt of Maurice de Saxe, illegitimate son of King Augustus, to get possession of the Duchy of Kurland. The offer of his hand had been accepted by the Duchess Anna Ivanovna, now a widow; he had been elected at Mitava by the deputies of the nobility. Neglecting the protest of the Polish diet and the remonstrances of France and Russia, he raised troops with the money produced by the sale of the diamonds belonging to an abbess of Quedlimburg, and a French comedian, his mother Aurora von Königsmark, and his mistress Adrienne Lecouvreur, and began to put the duchy in a state of defence. He was disavowed by his father, and Cardinal Fleury did not dare to support him even indirectly. Menshikof, left more free since the death of Catherine the First, was himself a candidate for the duchy. He sent Lascy, at the head of eight thousand men, to expel the Saxon adventurers; and the future victor of Fontenoy could collect only two hundred and forty-seven men in the isle of Usmaüs, and was obliged, in his retreat, to swim across an arm of the sea. His election was annulled, his father publicly called him a galopin, or scullion, and Kurland once more fell back under Russian influence.

A treaty with Prussia was signed under Peter the Second, in virtue of which the two Powers engaged at the death of Augustus to support the candidate whom they might choose for Poland. The Emperor Charles the Sixth and the "sergeant-king" sounded Russia about an eventual dismemberment of the republic of Poland. This is the first time that the question of partition was mooted.

In Asia, Iaguzhinski concluded on the Bura a treaty of commerce with the Celestial Empire, in the name of Peter the Second. Every three years Russian caravans might go to Pekin and trade without paying dues. Russia might keep four priests at Pekin, and six young men to learn Chinese. Kiakhta, on the Russian territory, and Maimaitchin, on the Chinese territory, were the authorized depôts.

CHAPTER VI.

THE TWO ANNAS: REIGN OF ANNA IVANOVNA, AND REGENCY OF ANNA LEOPOLDOVNA.

1730-1741.

ATTEMPT AT AN ARISTOCRATIC CONSTITUTION (1730): THE "BIRONOVSHTCHINA." — SUCCESSION OF THE POLISH CROWN (1733-1735) AND WAR WITH TURKEY (1735-1739). — IVAN THE SIXTH. — REGENCY OF BIREN AND ANNA. — REVOLUTION OF 1741.

ATTEMPT AT AN ARISTOCRATIC CONSTITUTION: THE "BIRONOVSHTCHINA."

THE untimely death of the last male heir of Peter the First had taken everybody by surprise. It was so sudden that no party had been formed to determine the succession. Peter had left two daughters, Elisabeth and Anna, Duchess of Holstein, who died in seventeen hundred and twenty-eight, and was represented by her son, afterwards Peter the Third. The Tsar's brother, Ivan Alexiévitch the Fifth, had also left two daughters, Anna Ivanovna, Duchess of Kurland, and Catherine Ivanovna, Duchess of Mecklenburg. The wishes of some even turned towards the late Emperor's grandmother, the Tsaritsa Lapukhin. Alexis Dolgoruki, father of Ivan, the friend of Peter the Second, had a yet bolder idea; he claimed the throne for his daughter Ekaterina, although she was not even Peter's wife, but only his betrothed, and he had the audacity to speak of a certain will of the sovereign, instituting her his heir. This proposal naturally found little favor in the Secret High Council, and was rejected with contempt, even by a part of the house of Dolgoruki, whose chiefs did not relish the notion of being the subjects of their niece. It was decided to take another step. In the absence of the prudent Ostermann, who used the pretext of a feigned illness, and the fact that he was a foreigner, the Secret High Council, after the addition of the marshals Dolgoruki and Galitsuin, was entirely composed of the great Russian nobility. It found itself, as the principal organ of government, invested with the chief power, and master of the position. It resolved to profit by these circumstances to limit the supreme authority, to give to the Russian aristocracy a sort of constitutional charter, and to impose on the sovereign who might be elected a kind of pacta conventa, such as existed in the republic of Poland. Elisabeth and the Duchess of Holstein, being the nearest to the throne, would no doubt manifest the greatest reluctance to accept these conditions. Thus it was necessary to turn to another branch of the family of Romanof, to the line of Ivan, and offer the crown to a princess who, having little hope of gaining the throne, would be ready to accede to all the Council wished. The Council then resolved to open negotiations with Anna Ivanovna, and to propose to her the following terms: That the High Council should always be composed of eight members, to be consulted by the Tsaritsa in all affairs of government; that without the consent of the Council she should make neither peace nor war, impose no taxes, alienate no crown lands, nominate to no post nor any rank above that of colonel; that she should put to death no member of the nobility, nor confiscate the property of any noble, without a regular trial; that she was neither to marry nor to choose a successor without the consent of the Council. "And," adds the draught of the letter laid before her for signature, and containing the points indicated, "in case of my ceasing to fulfil my engagements, I shall forfeit the crown of Russia." This was the *si non non* of the Cortes of Aragon. If this constitution had been carried out, Russia would have become an oligarchic republic instead of an autocratic empire, a sort of *pospolit*, where nothing would have remained of the work of the Ivans and Peter the Great. The High Council likewise proposed to fix the seat of government at Moscow.

This constitution, which assured to the Russian nobles the inviolability of their persons and property, the English " habeas corpus " and self-imposed taxation, raised, however, a general outcry. What! give Russia the same anarchic institutions that the three Northern powers were trying to maintain in Poland? All the prerogatives, all the rights, all the authority, were reserved to the members of the High Council. Instead of one Tsar they would have eight. And who were these eight? With the exception of Golovkin and Ostermann, they were all Galitsuins and Dolgorukis, — two Galitsuins and four Dolgorukis ; the empire was to be the property of two families. While the monarchical instincts of the greater number, and the aristocratic jealousy of many others, were excited, the partisans of reform were troubled at finding in the supreme council only the members of the old nobility who were the upholders of the ancient order of things. The discontent broke forth in murmurs and turmoils ; the High Council was obliged to take severe measures against meetings, — a singular inauguration of the reign of liberty, which showed how little sympathy the nation felt with the attempt of the nobles.

A few days later the High Council convoked the general assembly to listen to the letter in which Anna Ivanovna announced her acceptance of all the conditions. " There was no one present," says Archbishop Feofan, " who heard the letter who did not tremble in all his limbs. Even those who had hoped much from this reunion lowered their ears like poor asses: there was a ' whispering' and a general murmur, but none dared to speak or cry out." The five hundred people present silently affixed their signatures. However, on the twenty-first of February, seventeen hundred and thirty, the new Empress made her solemn entrance into Moscow. While Vasili Lukitch Dolgoruki and his party constituted themselves the guards of the Empress, surrounded her jealously, and saw that no enemy of the constitution came near her, the malcontents, with Feofan at their head, were agitating the clergy and the people. They found means to pass some notes to the Empress, acquainting her with the situation, and imploring her to act energetically. Children or ladies-in-waiting served as go-betweens. On the eighth of March the members of the Council were deliberating, when they were suddenly summoned before the Empress. They were much astonished to find an assembly composed of eight hundred persons, belonging to the senate, the clergy, the nobility, and to the different administrations, who laid before Anna a petition that she would examine the complaints addressed to the High Council about the new constitution. At the lower end of the hall the officers of the guard cried out in excitement, " We do not want them to lay down the law to the Empress. Let her be an autocrat like her predecessors ! " Others offered to lay at her feet the heads of her enemies. She calmed the tumult, and prorogued the sitting till the afternoon, when the deputies presented a formal request for the re-establishment of autocracy. The Empress was astonished, and exclaimed, " What ! the conditions sent me at Mitava, were they not the will of the whole nation ? " " No, no," they cried. " Then," she said, turning to Vasili Lukitch Dolgoruki, " you have deceived me."

Such was the check received by the first liberal constitution that had ever been tried in Russia. " The table was prepared," said Prince Dmitri Galitsuin, " but the guests were not worthy. I know that I shall pay for the failure of this enterprise ; so be it. I shall suffer for my country, I have not long to live, and those who cause me to weep will one day weep themselves." The Galitsuins and Dolgorukis did indeed expiate this generous attempt, in which unhappily they had taken no thought of the time nor the country. Anna's vengeance was cunning, refined, and gradual. She began by banishing them to their estates; then, seeing that no one protested, she exiled them to Siberia. Finally, encouraged by the universal silence, she crowned her revenge. The marshals Dolgoruki and Galitsuin died in prison; Vasili Lukitch and two other Dolgorukis were beheaded; Ivan, the former favorite, was broken on the wheel to Novgorod. With these sufferings is associated the touching and tragic history of Natalia Sheremetief, betrothed wife of Ivan Dolgoruki, who, having accepted his hand in the days of his prosperity, persisted in sharing his misfortunes.

Anna Ivanovna was then thirty-five years of age. In her youth she had lived in the dreary court of Mitava, a bride sought for her duchy, the political plaything of the four Northern courts, despised by Menshikof, and receiving orders and reproaches from Moscow. The bitterness of her regrets and her disappointments was painted in her severe countenance, and reflected in her soured and coldly cruel character. A head taller than the gentlemen of her court, with a hard and masculine beauty, and the deep voice of a man, she was imposing, and even terrible. The aristocratic attempt of seventeen hundred and thirty made her mistrust the Russians, and she felt that a project less exclusive and more clever than that of the High Council would perhaps have had a chance with the Russian nation. By way of precaution, and from taste, she surrounded herself with Germans, Ernest Biren, or Biron, her lover, at the head of them, a Kurlander, who in the reign of Peter the Great had desired to enter the Russian service, but was refused because of his low birth. The nobility of the duchy had at first refused to admit him among them; but, gaining Anna's affection by his many amiable qualities and agreeable manners, she caused him to be elected Duke of Kurland. He now became Lord Chamberlain, and was created by the Emperor, Charles the Sixth, a Prince of the Holy Roman Empire. She made Lewenwold manager of court affairs, Ostermann chief of the foreign administration, Korff and Kayserling directors of the embassies; Lascy, Münnich, Bismark, and Gustaf Biren, Ernest's brother, general of the army. It was in Germany that she afterwards chose to seek for her successor, — Ivan the Sixth, the son of her niece Anna, and grandson of Catherine Ivanovna, Princess of Mecklenburg, who was married to the Duke of Brunswick-Bevern. The Russians henceforth held only secondary positions in the government. Biren, insolent and brutal, boasted in their presence of his being a foreigner, of his holding the title of Duke of Kurland. The Germans ruled in Russia, just as the Tatars had formerly done; and a new word, *Bironovshtchina*, expressive of the new régime, was coined on the model of the old *Tatarshtchina*. But if the Germans were triumphant, was it not the fault of the Russians themselves? The "eaglets" of Peter the Great had torn each other to pieces. Menshikof had ruined Tolstoï and Iaguzhinski, and was in his turn destroyed by the Dolgorukis, themselves victims, with the Galitsuins, of the national hate. Besides all this, the strangers who took their posts and filled the place they had left vacant were far more laborious and more exact than the natives. The Russians had still to pass through a hard school to acquire the qualities they lacked.

The new government was pitiless towards the Russians: Feofilakt Lopatinski was deposed and imprisoned in Vuiborg, for having edited Stephan Iavorski's book against the Protestants, "Peter, the Corner-Stone of the Faith." Thousands of executions and banishments decimated the upper classes, and a merciless collection of arrears of taxes, which Russian indolence had allowed to accumulate, desolated the country; the peasants beheld their last head of cattle, their last tool, seized by the government for payment. The new despotism methodically organized its means of oppression. To be sure, it suppressed the High Council, in order to restore the epithet of "directing" to the senate, but in reality it was the cabinet, presided over by the Empress, and composed of

Golovkin, Ostermann, and Prince Alexis Tcherkaski, that
regulated all affairs. The old "Prikaz of Reformation" was
re-established under the name of the "Secret Court of Police,"
and the cruel Ushakof placed at the head. As the Empress
had confidence only in her guards, two new regiments, the
Ismaïlovski, and the horse guards, were created. Foreign
officers were everywhere, and the brothers of the German
favorites distributed among themselves the ranks of colonel
and lieutenant-colonel.

Reassured as to the solidity of her throne, Anna thought
only how to make up for the time she had wasted in ennui
and regret. A few passages from the Memoirs of Manstein
Münnich's Adjutant will give an amusing picture of the life
and manners of the Empress and her Court: "The Duke of
Kurland was extraordinarily fond of pomp and display. For
this reason Anna felt that she must make her Court the most
brilliant in Europe. But she fell short in the accomplishment
of her purpose. There was often a want of harmony between
the most gorgeous apparel and an ill-combed wig; the most
beautiful fabrics were ruined by an unskilful tailor; or, if no
exception could be taken to the coat, the equipage was apt
to be in bad condition. A superbly dressed man would arrive
in a shabby coach drawn by villanous old nags. In mansions where everything glittered with gold and silver one
would nevertheless find the reign of untidiness. The ladies
showed no better taste than the men. Where there was one
lady clad becomingly you could count on finding ten sorry
toilets. The lack of arrangement was noticeable throughout
the whole domestic economy, and there were only a few
houses, at least in the earlier years, where everything was in
complete harmony. In the mean time the example of a better
style began to find imitators.

"The excess of display was a source of immoderate expense
to the Court. A courtier who spent only two or three thousand rubles for his wardrobe could scarcely provide what was

indispensable. Very many ruined themselves in order to cut a figure at Court. A fashion merchant coming to Petersburg, who was obliged to get his goods on credit, could become a rich man in two or three years.

"The manner of life led by the Empress was very regular. She always arose about eight o'clock. At nine she began her work with her secretary and ministers. At noon she dined in her chamber with Biron's family. Only on great occasions did she keep open table. Then she was accustomed to sit under a canopy together with the two princesses, Elisabeth Petrovna and Anna of Mecklenburg. On such occasions the Lord Chamberlain waited upon her. Usually there was a very large table laid in the same hall for the nobles and the officials, the clergy and the representatives of foreign courts. In her last years she gave up the habit of dining in public, and the foreign ministers were entertained by Ostermann. In summer she walked much for exercise, in winter she played billiards. She ate little in the evening. She went to bed regularly between eleven o'clock and midnight.

"A large portion of the pleasant season the Court spent at the Peterhof, a mansion seven miles from Petersburg; the remainder of the summer Anna lived in the city at the summer palace, a somewhat ill-constructed house on the bank of the Neva. Play was carried very high at Court. Very many won fortunes by gambling, — very many more were ruined by it. Not infrequently twenty thousand rubles were lost at a single game of faro or quinze. The Empress herself did not win much in play, and when she played it was on purpose to lose. She then would keep the bank, and only those whom she summoned were permitted to punt; the winner was immediately paid, and as they played only with masks, she never took money from the loser. She was fond of the theatre and music, and she had everything that pertained thereto imported from Italy. Italian and German comedies gave her extraordinary satisfaction, because they generally ended in blows with canes. In seventeen hundred and thirty-six the first opera was performed in Petersburg; but though it was well given, the Empress found it less to her taste than the comedy and the Italian intermezzo.

"The habit of much drinking, which had been characteristic of the Court in the time of Peter the First and his successors, Anna could not endure; she would not allow a drunken person in her sight. Prince Kurakin alone had permission to drink as much as he wished. But in order not to do away entirely with such a pretty custom, the twenty-ninth of January (old style), the Empress's coronation day, was devoted to Bacchus. On this day every courtier was expected to kneel before the Empress and drain a monstrous glass filled with Hungarian wine."

Manstein speaks also of the grossness of the buffoonery which pleased Anna. In former times every household of any consequence would have at least one fool, or jester. Peter the Great usually had a dozen. Anna of Mecklenburg, when she became regent, was the first to dispense with them at Court; but the Empress had six: Lakosta, a Portuguese Jew; Pedrillo, an Italian who had been a court violinist; Prince Galitsuin, who was thus punished for becoming a Roman Catholic; Volkonski, brother-in-law of Alexis Bestuzhef, the next Lord Chancellor; Apraxin; and Balakef. They were beaten if they refused to amuse the Court in any way desired. Anna forced Nastasia and Anisia, two Russian princesses, to gulp balls of pastry, and crouch in bark pails, and cackle like hens sitting on eggs. The wife of Prince Galitsuin having died, Anna obliged him to marry a girl of common birth, a Kalmuik named Buzhenina, after her favorite dish of pork, and she herself defrayed the cost of the ceremony. The governors of all the provinces sent to Saint Petersburg representatives of every nation belonging to the empire to take part in the festival. Toward the end of the cold winter of seventeen hundred and thirty-nine Anna had a palace built entirely of ice, all the furniture, the chairs, the mirrors, and even the bridal couch being made of the same. Ice cannon and ice mortars guarded the doors, and were fired without bursting. Manstein gives a picture of the procession starting out from Voluinski's palace. The newly married couple were enclosed in a cage carried on the back of an elephant. Then the guests followed in sledges drawn by reindeers, dogs, oxen, and swine. The dinner was served in Biren's riding-school, and was followed by a ball, each nation dancing its peculiar dances to its own music. The bride and bridegroom were obliged to spend the night in their ice palace, guards being stationed to prevent their escape.

In the luxury with which Anna's Court dazzled Russia there was a mixture of antique barbarism and bad German taste which moved the mirth of Western travellers. "The favorite, Biren," relates Prince Dolgorukof, "loved bright colors, therefore black coats were forbidden at Court, and every one appeared in brilliant raiment; nothing was seen but light blue, pale green, yellow, and pink. Old men, like Prince Tcherkaski or the Vice-Chancellor Ostermann, came to the palace in delicate rose-color costumes. But this was of slight consequence. Russian taste would be formed in time, especially by the help of another school. The Germans were preparing the way for the French. From the point of view of dress and domestic economy, the Bironovshtchina marks an important revolution in Russia.

It is an important fact that the German masters of Russia were sufficiently enlightened to follow in the steps of Peter the Great and maintain his reforms. In the first months of their rule Ostermann had impressed upon the mind of the Empress the necessity of returning to Saint Petersburg. This was accomplished in the beginning of the year seventeen hundred and thirty-two, and immediately greater safety was found to have been secured. Lefort wrote from the capital in February: "No one dares here to utter a murmur against the will of the Empress, and the evil-minded have been so effectually put out of the way, that now scarce a trace can be found of the Russian whose unfriendly designs are to be feared."

Anna abolished entail, which Peter the Great had unfortunately borrowed from Western nations, and which had produced such sad results in Russia. The fathers of families wrung the last drop of blood from their peasants in order to give a portion to the younger sons; if they bequeathed the land to the eldest, they gave the cattle to the other sons. On the other hand, the time devoted to the education and the military service of the young nobles was more clearly defined. From the age of seven to that of twenty the young noble was to study, and from twenty to forty-five he was to serve the State. Examinations were established to test the progress of the boys; from twelve to sixteen they had to appear before a board, and whoever after the second examination was found ignorant of the catechism, arithmetic, and geometry, was forced to become a sailor. These rigorous measures prove how indifferent the mass of the nobles then were to the advantages of education. It cannot be denied that the rule of the Germans, rough instructors though they were, had a salutary influence on Russian civilization. On the suggestion of Münnich, the "corps of cadets," for three hundred and sixty young nobles, was founded at Saint Petersburg. General education held a larger place in the programme of this school than purely military instruction. Boys were prepared for the civil service as well as for the army. Orthography, style, rhetoric, jurisprudence, ethics, heraldry, arithmetic, the art of fortification, artillery, geography, general history, and the history of Germany, though not of Russia, were all taught. The most industrious and the most distinguished pupils might, after they had finished the preliminary courses, follow those of the Academy of Sciences.

SUCCESSION OF THE POLISH CROWN AND WAR WITH TURKEY.

With regard to the East, the government of Anna Ivanovna resolved to abandon the Persian provinces conquered by Peter the Great, where the climate had proved fatal to the Russian armies.

In seventeen hundred and thirty-three, after the death of Augustus the Second, the question of the succession of the Polish Crown was reopened. Prussia, which desired to weaken Poland, did not wish to support either the French candidate, Leshtchinski, or the Saxon candidate, Augustus the Third. Austria, on the contrary, which would gladly have beheld Poland sufficiently strong to co-operate against the Turks, declared for Augustus. Russia, whose object it was to remain mistress in Poland and Kurland, cared little who was elected, provided it was neither a powerful prince nor a client of France. But Louis the Fifteenth thought himself bound in honor to maintain the cause of his father-in-law, Stanislas Leshtchinski, the former protégé of Charles the Twelfth. The Power whose interests in this affair most nearly corresponded with those of Russia was therefore the house of Austria. The Austro-Russian alliance, inaugurated in the reign of Catherine the First, was re-established under Anna Ivanóvna. Prussia, whose project of partition had been set aside, remained neutral. The struggle between France and Russia began by a diplomatic rivalry. We find at Berlin La Chétardie pitted against Iaguzhinski; at Stockholm, Saint Sévérin against Mikhail Bestuzhef; at Copenhagen, Plélo against Alexis Bestuzhef; at Constantinople, Villeneuve against Nepluief; at Warsaw, Monti against Lewenwold. France hoped to support its candidate by Swedish and Turkish diversions, and to render the neutrality of Prussia more favorable; in Poland, the French worked as hard to persuade as Russia to intimidate.

Even at Saint Petersburg, the French ambassador, Magnan,

neglected nothing to gain over the Empress and her favorite to a more peaceful policy; but the struggle was inevitable. While a false Leshtchinski, the Chevalier de Thiange, was ostentatiously embarking at Brest, the real Stanislas, disguised as a commercial traveller, crossed Europe, and entered Warsaw at night. Sixty thousand nobles declared in his favor on the field of election, and there were only four thousand dissidents. He was therefore legitimate King of Poland, yet the Russian army was invading the territory of the republic. Then Stanislas called the pospolit to arms, and retired into the maritime fortress of Dantzig to await aid from France. After his departure the malcontents, under the protection of twenty thousand Russian bayonets, proclaimed Augustus the Third. Stanislas found himself besieged in Dantzig by Marshal Münnich, who, without waiting for the artillery, took the suburbs of Schotlandia by assault. The King of Prussia refused the Russian guns passage through his territory, and the French frigates were watching the sea; but notwithstanding the blockade, Münnich received his cannon, and by the capture of Sommerschantz cut off the communications of Dantzig with the fortress of Weichselmünde and the mouth of the Vistula; he then threw fifteen hundred bombs into the town. He failed, however, in a bloody midnight attack on the fort of Hagelsberg. The French troops came up, led by Count de Plélo and Lamothe de la Peyrouse, but they numbered only two thousand men. Plélo was killed, and the Count de Lamothe, who had taken refuge in Weichselmünde, was forced to capitulate. Dantzig opened its gates. But Stanislas had already fled, disguised as a peasant. Such was the first contest between the French and the Russians. Lady Rondeau gives an account of the presentation of the Count de Lamothe and his officers to the Tsaritsa; the soldiers were quartered in the camp of Koporić, in Ingria; and Anna did all she could to make them desert and to draw them into her service. Monti, the French ambassador at Warsaw, was taken prisoner at Dantzig, and in spite of his diplomatic character was retained in captivity.

The war of the Polish Succession was ended in Poland; it now began on the Rhine and in Italy, and the cost of it was paid by the house of Austria, against which the French excited the electors of Cologne, Mayence, Bavaria, and the Palatinate; they took Kehl and Philippsburg, and deprived it of the Duchy of Parma and the Kingdom of Naples. In virtue of the treaty of alliance of seventeen hundred and twenty-six, the Emperor demanded help of the Tsaritsa. Lascy, at the head of twenty thousand men, crossed Silesia, Bohemia, and Franconia, displaying a Russian army for the first time before the eyes of Western Germany; and on the fifteenth of August, seventeen hundred and thirty-five, formed a junction with the Austrian troops between Heidelberg and Ladenberg, two miles from the French outposts. The Peace of Vienna, however, put an end to hostilities. The French had revenged themselves on Austria, which ceded Lorraine and part of Italy, but not on Russia, which had taken Dantzig under their very eyes. The French ambassador Villeneuve, his former countryman, the renegade Bonneval, who had become Pasha of Bosnia, and the Hungarian Ragotski, were raising heaven and earth to induce the Turks to declare war, although they had every reason to avoid a collision with the Russians. The long struggle with Persia, the disturbances in Constantinople, and the emptiness of the treasury, made the Porte hesitate long before it took the decisive step. But the result of the war with Poland was a war in the East, which narrowly escaped being complicated by a Swedish war.

In the East also Russia had Austria for an ally. Campaigns against the Turks, across the desert steppes of the South, offered the same difficulties as in seventeen hundred and eleven, as everything had to be carried with the army, even wood and water. In spite of all Münnich's efforts, the Russian cavalry was second-rate. The army, encumbered with baggage, moved slowly over the interminable plains; it seemed lost amid the vastness of its accompanying train. A simple sergeant had as many as ten chariots, an officer thirty, the general, Gustaf Biren, three hundred beasts of burden. There were always ten thousand sick men in the army, which, in spite of the dispensation of the Holy Synod, was becoming exhausted by a rigorous observance of fasts and days of abstinence.

In May, seventeen hundred and thirty-six, Münnich forced the lines of Perekop, and pressing farther into the Crimea on the twenty-eighth of June pillaged Bakhtchi-Séraï, the capital of the khans, and laid waste the Western Crimea in such a way that the prosperity of the country has never recovered from it. But the lack of drinking-water and fodder for the horses obliged him to evacuate the peninsula, and on the twenty-eighth of August the walls of Perekop were blown up, and the army took its departure. Meanwhile Lascy had forced Azof to surrender, and went into winter-quarters in the Eastern Ukraina. The next year, while Lascy was devastating the eastern part of the peninsula, Münnich marched against the strong fortress of Otchakof. The accidental blowing up of the great powder-magazine with six thousand Turks reduced the garrison to submission, and the Russian army, which had been in a precarious situation, was saved. In seventeen hundred and thirty-nine Münnich gained a splendid victory at Stavutchani, captured Khotin, crossed the Pruth, with the boast that he had avenged the defeat of Peter the Great, and entered the capital of Moldavia. During this time the Austrians were constantly beaten. Besides, they feared the Russians as neighbors of their orthodox provinces of Transylvania and Illyria more than they did the Turks. They insisted on the conclusion of peace, and at Belgrade, or Bielgorod (the White City), in seventeen hundred and thirty-nine, they ceded to Turkey all Servia, with Orsova and Austrian Valakhia; the Russians obtained as a new boundary line only a tongue of land between the Bug and the Dnieper, and contented themselves with the demolition of Perekop, and surrendered all their conquests except Azof. This war had cost them more than a hundred thousand men. The King of France had succeeded in proving that he knew how to reach his enemies, even though separated from him by vast spaces. Anna Ivanovna found herself obliged to ask his mediation to prevent a war with Sweden, which was greatly irritated by the murder of Sinclair, the Swedish ambassador to Constantinople. Sinclair had a bitter hatred against Russia, and on his way through Poland had spoken with too great freedom of the Empress. Münnich, hearing of this, determined to destroy him, and in June, seventeen hundred and thirty-nine, he was waylaid and shot, and his papers were taken from him. Although Anna disclaimed all knowledge of the crime, there was a strong demand in Sweden for a declaration of war. At the instance of Ostermann, and by orders of Louis the Fifteenth, Saint Sévérin negotiated at Stockholm, and the danger was averted. The French also brought about a conclusion of peace with the Turks by means of Villeneuve. The Empress showed her gratitude to the latter by offering him fifteen thousand thalers. He, however, would accept only the cross of Saint Andrew. Kantemir, the Russian ambassador at Paris, still continued to warn his court that "Russia being the only Power which could counterbalance that of France, the latter would lose no opportunity of diminishing its strength."

IVAN THE SIXTH. — REGENCY OF BIREN AND ANNA. — REVOLUTION OF SEVENTEEN HUNDRED AND FORTY-ONE.

But while danger from without seemed to be averted, affairs within the empire showed that the old Russian party was not yet brought to terms. In seventeen hundred and thirty-three the Governor of Smolensk, Prince Tcherkaski, a cousin of the cabinet-minister, was arrested for plotting to raise the young Duke of Holstein to the throne, and three years later the aged

Prince Dmitri Galitsuin who was considered one of the wisest men in Russia, was sentenced to death. Popular discontent against the Duke of Kurland grew more and more pronounced. His insolence toward the nobles, the avarice of his favorites, the enormous sums spent upon pleasures and magnificent buildings, the cost of the fleet and the losses in the army, all caused great uneasiness throughout the country. Taking advantage of the immense drain upon the available forces by the campaign of seventeen hundred and thirty-eight, the discontented party, with the Dolgorukis at their head, made overtures to Sweden and France. On the supposition that Münnich would be obliged to capitulate at Stavutchani, the Swedes were invited to land thirty thousand men in Russia, and raise the standard of revolt. The Empress was to be confined in a monastery, Biren removed, Anna of Mecklenburg and her husband, the Duke of Brunswick, were to be sent back to Germany, and after all the foreigners were exiled, Naruishkin and Elisabeth were to be raised to the throne. But Münnich's good fortune saved him, and the Court got wind of the conspiracy. The Dolgorukis were punished, as was described at the beginning of this chapter.

The minister who was most strenuous for the severity of the sentence against the conspirators was Artemi Voluinski, who was himself preparing for a still more extensive revolution. Voluinski belonged to the ancient family of the Naruishkins, and was related to the younger branch of the Romanof line. He had begun his career, during the reign of Peter the Great as a common soldier, and attracting Shafirof's attention, he rapidly rose. Peter appointed him Governor of Astrakhan while he was yet a very young man. Solovief says : "Voluinski was distinguished for his great intellect and intolerable disposition. Turbulent, ostentatious, proud, constantly making advances, insolent to his equals, ready for any act of crying injustice toward the poor, he drew upon himself the hatred of all. When he became governor, his distinguishing characteristics were avarice, extortion, and his treatment of those subordinate, which was worthy of the barbarism of Middle Ages."

By means of many spies he found out those who were opposed to him. A merchant in Astrakhan spoke uncivilly of his wife. Voluinski invited him to dinner, and then set his dogs upon him, and sent him out, stripped naked, into the snow. He plundered the convents of their jewels. He ruined the rich manufacturer, Turtsinof, and finally poisoned him. His exactions knew no bounds. Finally he gained the good-will of the Duke of Kurland, and in seventeen hundred and thirty-eight entered the cabinet of the ministry. He immediately began to plan the downfall of those who stood in his way. His greatest enemy was Ostermann, whom he tried to traduce by means of an anonymous letter. His hatred was directed not alone against the Germans. A young Russian who was secretary in the Academy of Sciences gained his ill-will. He had him bastinadoed so severely that he nearly died. The secretary was Trediakovski, who was the first to compose Russian poetry according to the rules of prosody.

Had it not been for Voluinski's unpopularity, he might have succeeded in his designs. But his fall was partly brought about by the wit of Kurakin, who was a privileged character in Court. He was one day complimenting Anna on her reign, but said that there was one of Peter's plans which she had not yet accomplished. On being asked which it was, Kurakin replied that Peter had put the halter around Voluinski's neck, but it was left for her to draw it tight. The reply was received with shouts of laughter, but two days afterward the minister was put under arrest. Unfortunately he had offended Biren, who said to Anna, "One of us must go." When his papers, which he had neglected to burn, were examined, besides the proofs of his unlimited peculations, there were found undoubted evidences of his conspiracy to put himself upon the throne. He designed to throw Anna into a convent if she refused his hand. The great conflagrations which had broken out successively in Moscow, Petersburg, Vuiborg, and Iaroslaf were also laid to him. He was condemned to have his tongue cut out and to be put to death, and his children were sent to Siberia. The son was obliged to become a common soldier and serve without a term. His accomplices were also punished. Though he was so hated during his lifetime, Voluinski had the fame of a patriot and a martyr after his death, because of the universal dislike of Biren, who was rewarded with his confiscated estates.

The weight of the taxes, the rigor with which they were collected, and the frequent conscriptions maddened the peasants, whilst the disgrace of Feofilakt, of Tatishtchef, of Rumantsof and Makarof, who were old servants of Peter the Great, as well as the sacrifice of Voluinski, of Galitsuin and the Dolgorukis, seemed to threaten the whole nation. Soon the echoes of the general discontent reached the Secret Court of Police. The people attributed all their misfortunes to the reign of a woman, and repeated the proverb, " Cities governed by women do not endure; the walls built by women are never high." Others said the corn did not grow because a woman ruled. They began to regret the iron despotism of Peter the First, and a popular song exhorts him to leave his tomb and chastise " Biren, the cursed German." The raskolniki had predicted that in seventeen hundred and thirty-three the wrath of God would fall on men, and that Anna would be taken and judged at Moscow. She reigned, however, till seventeen hundred and forty, at which time her health began to give way. Biren's scheme was to obtain from Anna Ivanovna the investiture of the regency during the minority of the little Emperor Ivan of Brunswick. Alexis Bestuzhef, who owed his fortune to Biren, assured him of the support of Münnich and of the cabinet-minister Tcherkaski. The Germans of the Court said, with Mengden, " If the Duke of Kurland is not appointed regent, the rest of us Germans are lost." The Empress signed the nomination of Biren, and died the next day. Her last words to her favorite were, " Ne boïs " (fear nothing).

Biren, however, had his own reasons for feeling uncomfortable. The Russians were indignant at having a master imposed on them who was a foreigner and a heretic, without morality and without talent, and whose only claim was a criminal union which dishonored the memory of their Empress. If a foreign regent was necessary, why not have the father of the Emperor? The long minority of a child who was only three months old at the death of Anna alarmed every one, and the thoughts of many turned towards the daughter of Peter the Great, and her grandson Peter of Holstein. The reign of the Germans still continued; besides Biren, the empire had to obey Prince Anton of Brunswick-Bevern, and his wife Anna Leopoldovna of Mecklenburg, governed in their turn by Anna's lover, the Saxon Lynar, and the prince's mistress, Julia von Mengden, Anna's lady of honor. Happily, however, these foreign masters never thought of combining. The parents of the Emperor bore Biren's authority with impatience; and the latter, discontented with their conduct, spoke of sending for Peter of Holstein, giving him his daughter in marriage, and marrying his son to Elisabeth. The fate of Menshikof and the Dolgorukis was lost on him. His clumsy nonenity embarrassed Ostermann and Münnich; and the latter, in an interview with Anna Leopoldovna, promised her to get rid of the tyrant. His aide-de-camp, Manstein, has given us a graphic account of this coup d'état. On the night of the thirtieth of November, Biren, who suspected nothing, and who in the evening had dined in company with Münnich, was taken from his bed, and wounded in more than twenty places in his struggles to escape, the Duchess of Kurland was thrust almost naked from the palace, all his friends were arrested, and he was sent to Pelim, in Siberia, where he, with his wife and three children, lived on an allowance of sixteen rubles a day.

Münnich had given liberty and power to the parents of the Emperor; how could they reward him? Like Menshikof, he wished to be Generalissimo, but Anton of Brunswick coveted the place. Münnich then contented himself with the title of First Minister; and Ostermann was recompensed by being nominated High Admiral. Anton, Anna, and Ostermann soon united against their liberator; and Münnich, filled with disgust, sent in his resignation. The Germans, when they attained the supreme power, conducted themselves exactly like the "eaglets" of Peter the Great: they mutually banished and exterminated each other. The father and mother of the Emperor, left in possession of the field, continued to dispute the authority, and to reproach each other with their mutual infidelities. Ostermann supported Anton against Anna. The incapacity of the regent was beyond belief. Not having the energy to dress herself, nor attend to the most important State papers, Anna Leopoldovna would lie for whole days on a couch, her head covered with a handkerchief, conversing with her intimate friends. The divisions and indifference of the government threw open the way to its numerous enemies; all they wanted was a chief who would attack the Brunswickers as they had successfully attacked Biren.

Elisabeth, daughter of Peter the Great, who had been narrowly watched under the hard rule of Anna Ivanovna and Biren, raised her head under this weak government. Twenty-eight years old, tall and very pretty, with great quickness of mind though extremely ignorant, lively and joyous, a bold rider and fearless on the water, with soldier-like manners, she had all the qualities necessary to a party leader. Her confidants were the brothers Alexander and Peter Shuvalof, Mikhail Vorontsof, Razumovski, Schwartz, and her private physician, Lestocq. Schwartz was an adventurer from Saxony, who had been a musician in her service, and afterwards went with a caravan to China. On his return he was promoted to a position in the geographical department of the Academy of Sciences, and had become a favorite of the princess. All these men, who were able and unscrupulous, were urging her to action. The regent feared her, but did not have the energy to act on the advice of Ostermann, who besought her to put Elisabeth under arrest. It was known at the palace that after the downfall of Biren three regiments of guards had hastened to swear fealty to her, believing the next step would be the proclamation of Peter the Great's daughter; and that at Kronstadt the soldiers had said, "Will no one put himself at our head in favor of Elisabeth Petrovna?" She accepted the office of godmother to their children, visited the guards in their barracks, and invited them to her house. When she passed through the streets in her sledge, the common grenadiers climbed on the back of the carriage and whispered familiarly in her ear. The French ambassador, La Chétardie, had orders to favor any revolution in Russia that would destroy the influence of the Germans and break the alliance with Austria. He aided Elisabeth with advice and money, and hoped to obtain for her the support of a Swedish diversion. The Swedes had repented of their quiescence during the late wars with Poland and Turkey, and were disposed to take their own grievances and those of Elisabeth as a pretext for declaring war against the Regent. The Swedish ambassador, Nolken, stipulated only that at her accession the Tzarévna should promise to restore part of the conquests of Peter the Great. This she declined to do; but the Swedes, nevertheless, began hostilities, and issued a manifesto to the "glorious Russian nation," which they wished to deliver from German ministers, and from the "heavy oppression and cruel foreign tyranny," so as to enable it freely to elect "a legitimate and just government." This diversion precipitated the crisis. The Court was by this time too well accustomed to plots for the conspirators to delay; and, besides, the regiments upon whom Elisabeth counted had orders to proceed to the frontier. She had only the choice between the throne and the convent. In the night of the sixth of December, seventeen hundred and forty-one, she went with Lestocq and Vorontsof to the quarters of the Preobrazhenski. "My children," she said to them, "you know whose daughter I am." " Mother, we are ready; we will kill *them* all." She forbade bloodshed, and added, "I swear to die for you; will you swear to die for me?" They all swore. Anna Leopoldovna, Prince Anton, the young Emperor in his cradle, Münnich, Ostermann, Lewenwold, and the Mengdens were arrested during the night. Elisabeth was proclaimed absolute Empress, and the nobles of the empire hastened to give in their adhesion to the new order of things. Ivan the Sixth was confined at Schlüsselburg; Anna, with her husband and children, at Kholmogory, where she died in seventeen hundred and forty-six. A tribunal was held, and the Dolgorukis were among the judges. Ostermann was condemned to be broken on the wheel, Münnich to be quartered, and the others to decapitation. The Empress, however, spared their lives. Ostermann was exiled to Berezof, where he died five years later, and Münnich to Pelim, where he lived in the house he had planned for Biren. Many of the exiles of the preceding reign were recalled, and the Birens were allowed to reside in Iaroslavl. One of the brothers of the Duke of Kurland returned to his estates in Livonia, where he died in seventeen hundred and forty-six. Gustaf Biren died the same year in Saint Petersburg. General von Bismark was appointed commander of the troops in the Ukraina in seventeen hundred and forty-seven.

CHAPTER VII.

ELISABETH PETROVNA.

1741-1762.

REACTION AGAINST THE GERMANS: WAR WITH SWEDEN (1741-1743).—AUSTRIAN SUCCESSION: WAR AGAINST FREDERIC THE SECOND (1756-1762).—REFORMS UNDER ELISABETH: FRENCH INFLUENCE.

REACTION AGAINST THE GERMANS: WAR WITH SWEDEN.

IN sixteen hundred and forty-two, at the time when Elisabeth was crowned at Moscow, she sent to Holstein for the son of her sister, Anna Petrovna, and of the Duke Karl Friedrich. The grandson of Peter the Great embraced orthodoxy, took the name of Peter Feodorovitch, was proclaimed heir to the throne, and in seventeen hundred and forty-four the Empress married him to the Princess Sophia of Anhalt-Zerbst, afterwards Catherine the Second. Thus the power which had been diverted to the Ivanian branch of the Romanof dynasty, to Anna of Kurland and her great-nephew of Brunswick, returned to the immediate family of Peter the Great in the person of Elisabeth as Empress, and of her nephew of Holstein as heir to the throne.

The revolution of seventeen hundred and forty-one meant much more than the substitution of the Petrovian for the Ivanian branch; it signified the triumph of the national over the German party, the reaction of the Russian element against the hard rule of the foreigners, and thus it was understood by the people. The orthodox clergy, persecuted by the heretics, took its revenge in the sermons of Amvrosi Iushkévitch, Archbishop of Novgorod, against the "emissaries of the devil," and against "Beelzebub and his angels." The poet Lomonosof hails in Elisabeth the Astræa who had "brought back the golden age," the Moses who "had snatched Russia in one night from her Egyptian slavery," the Noah "who had saved her from the foreign deluge." Citizens and soldiers rose against the Germans; there were revolts at Saint Petersburg, and in the army of Finland, against the foreign officers, on whom the men wished to inflict the punishment of Ostermann and Münnich. At Court, Finch, the English ambassador, Botta, the Austrian ambassador, and Lynar, the Saxon ambassador, had compromised themselves under the preceding dynasty; therefore all the sympathies of the nation and the Tsaritsa were for Mardefeld, ambassador of Prussia, and especially for La Chétardie, whom they looked on as one of the authors of the revolution, and whose hands the officers of the guard came to kiss, addressing him as "their father." The Austro-Russian alliance, consolidated under Catherine the First and Anna Ivanovna, seemed broken.

This good understanding between the courts of France and Russia was imperilled by the affairs of Sweden. The cabinet of Versailles had only been able to persuade its Scandinavian ally into war, by hinting that the new Empress would cede back certain territory, but Elisabeth, daughter of Peter the Great, could not renounce the conquests of her father, which even Anna Leopoldovna, a foreign princess, had maintained at the cost of war. The Swedes, who pretended to have taken up arms in favor of Elisabeth, continued the war against their former protégée. This war had no result except to show the weakness of the Sweden of Charles the Twelfth when pitted against the new Russia. The Scandinavian armies proved themselves very unworthy of their former reputation. Elisabeth's generals, Lascy and Keith, subdued all the strongholds in Finland. At Helsingfors seventeen thousand Swedes laid down their arms before a hardly more numerous Russian force. The Swedes then offered the crown to Elisabeth's nephew Peter, but it was refused. Elisabeth had other plans for him. By the treaty of Abo, in August, seventeen hundred and forty-three, the Empress acquired South Finland as far as the river Kiümen, and caused Adolph Friedrich, Bishop of Lübeck, administrator of the duchy of Holstein, and one of her allies, to be elected Prince Royal of Sweden, in place of the Prince Royal of Denmark, in whose favor the Swedish peasantry had risen.

AUSTRIAN SUCCESSION: WAR AGAINST FREDERIC THE SECOND.

The war of the Austrian Succession had broken out in Europe. For whom would Russia declare, — for Maria Theresa, or for France and its allies? Bestuzhef-Riumin, who had been disgraced by Biren, but had returned under the protection of Lestocq, and was now Vice-Chancellor of the empire, was on the side of Austria. Vorontsof, associated with him as Vice-Chancellor, trimmed between both parties; La Chétardie and Mardefeld, ambassadors of Louis the Fifteenth and Frederic the Second, in order to draw Elisabeth into the Franco-Prussian Alliance and overthrow Bestuzhef, were intriguing with the Court physician, Lestocq, and the Princess of Zerbst, mother of Sophia of Anhalt, who in July, seventeen hundred and forty-four, became the Tsesarevna, or Grand Duchess Catherine. Lestocq, on his side, left no stone unturned to discover some political plot in which he might involve his rivals, the Bestuzhefs. At last his opportunity arrived. A lieutenant by the name of Berger, on service at Saint Petersburg, was detailed to Soliamsk, in Permia, to guard Count Lewenwold, who was there in banishment. When Madame Lapukhin learned of Berger's intended departure, she sent by him an assurance of her undying affection for the Count, and bade him hope for better things. Berger informed Lestocq of the message, which had been delivered by Madame Lapukhin's son, formerly one of Anna's chamberlains. Madame Lapukhin and her son were arrested on the night of the fourth of August, seventeen hundred and forty-three. The Empress, who was always on the watch for conspiracies, summoned a commission composed of the terrible Utchakof, General Trubetskoï, Lestocq, and Demidof, all unfriendly to Bestuzhef. Though nothing worse than certain hasty speeches could be proved against those who were implicated, the Council felt that they had gone too far to retreat in safety. The confidential relationship which Madame Bestuzhef, the Vice-Chancellor's sister-in-law, and Madame Lapukhin held with the Austrian ambassador, Marquis Botta d'Adorno, was taken as a pretext for an investigation. Botta had left Saint Petersburg eight months before, and was now accredited to Berlin. It was claimed that Botta had expressed his opinion that there would soon be a change in Russia, and he was also charged with trying to induce the King of Prussia to bring the unfortunate Brunswick family again to the throne. Bestuzhef's private papers were searched, but nothing whatsoever was found to implicate him. The persons arrested, however, in order to shield themselves, accused Botta of spending money to further the plot, and they declared that the only reason for which he had left Russia was to win Frederic to support Anna. At last a grand council was assembled, under a pledge of secrecy, to judge those who had been arrested. One senator thought that a simple death-penalty was sufficient, since the accused had not as yet proceeded to take extreme measures. But the Prince of Homburg sprang to his feet, and claimed that the guilty must be dealt with to the full extent of the law. In this he was seconded by Trubetskoï and Lestocq. The Empress, however, pardoned all but seven, who suffered the punishment of the knout and exile. In addition, Madame Lapukhin, her husband and son, together with Madame Bestuzhef, were horribly mutilated.

Frederic, in order to show complaisance to the Empress, forbade Botta the Court, and advised her to send the young

Ivan far into the interior, where he would never be heard from again. This was actually done the following year, when the prisoner was taken to the vicinity of Arkhangel. Although the Queen of Hungary was firmly convinced of the innocence of her ambassador, yet as she felt that it was of the greatest importance to preserve the favor of Elisabeth, she confined Botta in one of her castles; but the following year, when Bestuzhef had triumphed over Lestocq, he was set at liberty and thoroughly indemnified for the punishment he had endured. The efforts of Lestocq to ruin Bestuzhef had failed; but, on the other hand, the Chancellor neglected no means to destroy his enemies. He had his black cabinet, where he looked over the despatches of the foreign ambassadors; he found himself able to place under the sovereign's eyes extracts from the cipher letters of La Chétardie, proving that Lestocq was a pensioner of France, and that La Chétardie had spoken insultingly of Elisabeth in his political correspondence. As soon as Elisabeth read the very free criticism which La Chétardie had passed upon her abilities, her modes of conducting business, and her amours, the extraordinary friendliness which she had before shown him was changed to corresponding hatred. She also showed her displeasure with the Princess of Zerbst. She declared that she would never again take a drop of Lestocq's medicine. On the seventeenth of June, seventeen hundred and forty-four, the French ambassador received orders to quit the capital within twenty-four hours, and Russia within eight days, and the Grand Duchess's mother was sent back to Germany. As a reward for his great services, Bestuzhef was raised to the Chancellorship with great ceremonies, on the fifteenth of July. Later, in seventeen hundred and forty-nine, Lestocq was summoned before a commission, put to the torture, and banished to Uglitch, and afterwards to Ustiug Viliki, near Arkhangel, where his wife accompanied him. There he remained until seventeen hundred and sixty-two. Bestuzhef triumphed; it seemed as if Russia were going to interfere on behalf of Maria

Theresa. But time passed on. Russia, satisfied with the sort of intimidation that it exercised over all the European courts, did not care to go into action. Bestuzhef and the Vice-Chancellor Vorontsof played with the various courts, the one holding out hopes to Austria, the other allowing himself to be cajoled by D'Allion, La Chétardie's successor.

France, abandoned by its allies, had transported the war into the Low Countries, where Maurice de Saxe, the former Duke of Kurland, gained a series of victories. In seventeen hundred and forty-six an Austro-Russian treaty of alliance was concluded; England promised subsidies to Elisabeth, but it was not till seventeen hundred and forty-eight that thirty thousand Russians, under Repnin, crossed Germany and took up a position on the Rhine. They served only to hasten the Peace of Aix-la-Chapelle, which was signed in seventeen hundred and forty-eight, and returned to Russia without having fired a shot or risked the prestige of the empire.

D'Allion had been recalled in seventeen hundred and forty-seven, and had no successor at Saint Petersburg. However, the same Bestuzhef who had caused La Chétardie to be expelled, and concluded the Austrian alliance, had proclaimed, as far back as seventeen hundred and forty-four, that Prussia was more dangerous than France, "because of its near neighborhood and its late accession of strength." Elisabeth hated Frederic. "The King of Prussia," she said to Lord Hyndford, " is certainly a bad prince, who has no fear of God before his eyes; he turns holy things into ridicule, he never goes to church, he is the Nadir-Shah of Prussia." He had no religion, he had not been consecrated, he did not spare epigrams about the Empress. The "overweening neighbor" had shown off his importance at Aix-la-Chapelle, and had opposed the admission of a Russian plenipotentiary to the congress. Other things led to a sort of diplomatic rupture. Finally, on the seventeenth of May, seventeen hundred and fifty-six, the Chancellor read to the Empress a statement of foreign affairs. He reminded her that the new growth of the Prussian power was unfavorable to Russia, and pointed out how Frederic the Second, who had raised his army from eighty thousand to two hundred thousand soldiers, who had deprived Austria of Silesia, who from the "large revenues" of the latter province and the "millions levied on Saxony" had constituted a great war-fund for himself, who coveted Hanover and Kurland, and hoped for the dismemberment of Poland, had consequently become "the most dangerous of neighbors." He concluded by proving the necessity of reducing the forces of the King of Prussia, and of supporting the States menaced by him. This patriotic anxiety, this wholesome mistrust which Bestuzhef felt, might well have seemed worthy to become the traditional policy of Russia.

At this moment it was still believed at Saint Petersburg that in this war, as in the last, Prussia would be the ally of France, against Austria and England. The reversal of French policy had not been expected. Bestuzhef was in too great haste to conclude a treaty of subsidies with England. Vorontsof warned the Empress to beware lest the Russian troops should be employed in favor of that very Prussia whom she wished to fight. The event justified his prediction, confounded the plans and the provisions of Bestuzhef, and brought about his fall. When Prussia became the ally of England, and Austria of France, Russia found itself indirectly also allied to the latter power. Diplomatic relations between the courts were renewed. It was then that the secret missions of Valcroissant, of the Scotch Douglas, and the mysterious Chevalier d'Eon took place; that L'Hôpital became the French ambassador in Russia; and that a private correspondence was exchanged between Louis the Fifteenth and the Empress Elisabeth.

Frederic was alarmed on hearing the decision Russia had made; he feared nothing so much as the invasion of its "undisciplined hordes." It was to secure the friendship of "these barbarians" that he had arranged in seventeen hundred and forty-four the marriage of Peter Feodorovitch with Sophia of Anhalt. His invasion of Saxony put the Russian army in motion. In seventeen hundred and fifty-seven, the year of Rosbach, eighty-three thousand Muscovites, under the Generalissimo Apraxin, crossed the frontier of Prussia, occupied the province of Eastern Prussia, slowly advanced in the direction of the Oder, committing the most horrible excesses, and crushed the corps of Lewald at Gross-Jägersdorff. The Prussian loss was four thousand six hundred killed, six hundred taken prisoners, and twenty-nine guns. But, to the astonishment of all Europe, instead of following up his advantages, Apraxin retraced his steps and recrossed the Niemen. The ambassadors of France and Austria suspected treachery, and clamored for his dismissal from the chief command. His papers were examined, and were found gravely to compromise the Grand Duchess Catherine and the Chancellor Bestuzhef-Riumin, who, expecting Elisabeth's immediate death, and knowing that Peter would have little favor to show him, was planning to have the young son of Catherine appointed Tsar, with his mother as regent. The latter was deprived of his office and dignities, and exiled to one of his estates, one hundred and twenty versts from Moscow, whither his wife and son followed him. His place was filled by Vorontsof. Catherine threw herself at the Empress's feet, assuring her of her innocence, and begged her permission to quit Russia and return to her mother. The Empress finally forgave her and restored her to favor.

In January, seventeen hundred and fifty-eight, Fermor, who after Apraxin's dismissal had taken the command of the Russian army, again invaded the Prussian states, took Königsberg, and in August bombarded Küstrin on the Oder. Frederic the Second hastened to Silesia, made a junction with Graf Dohna, and thus found himself at the head of thirty-two thousand men, in presence of eighty-nine thousand Russians, near the village of Zorndorff, which lies a short distance from Küstrin. In spite of the stoical bravery of the Muscovites, and the defeat of the Prussian left wing, their inexperience, the weakness of their commander, and the superiority of the cavalry of General Seidlitz caused them to be beaten. They lost five generals, nine hundred and thirty-five other officers, twenty thousand five hundred and ninety men, one hundred cannon, and thirty flags. The Prussians lost three hundred and twenty-four officers and eleven thousand men. But Frederic the Second had not yet reached his aim, as his enemies were by no means annihilated, and were able to make an imposing retreat.

In seventeen hundred and fifty-nine Soltuikof, Fermor's successor, returned to the Oder, defeated the Prussians at Paltzig, near Züllichau, and made his entry into Frankfort. Frederic again came to the help of his lieutenants, and encountered the Russians near Künersdorff. This time his army was simply crushed under the enormous weight of the Muscovite masses. He lost eight thousand men and one hundred and seventy-two guns. He himself escaped with great difficulty from the field of battle, with forty hussars. From the battlefield he wrote to his minister, Finkenstein : " Only three thousand men now remain to me of my army of forty-eight thousand. All are in flight ; it is a cruel blow. The consequences of the battle will be worse than the losses which it has already caused. I no longer have any resource, and I think all is lost. I shall not survive the fall of my fatherland. I bid you farewell forever." But the disagreement between the Austrians and the Russians saved him. He was allowed time to collect his scattered forces, and soon he saw himself at the head of twenty thousand men. At this moment he thought of suicide. The disaster of Künersdorff weighed on him during the remainder of the war. Henceforth he could only hold himself on the defensive, without daring to descend into the plain.

The allies were not less exhausted than Frederic. Elisabeth alone declined to speak of peace till she had "reduced the forces" of Frederic, and secured the annexation of Eastern Prussia. Soltuikof was made field-marshal, and Prince Galitsuin, general-in-chief. All the lieutenant-generals received the order of Saint Andrew, and each soldier was munificently rewarded. In seventeen hundred and sixty the Russians entered Berlin after a short resistance, pillaged the State coffers and the arsenals, and destroyed the manufactories of arms and powder. The following year they conquered Pomerania, and Rumantsof took Kolberg. This was the last disaster that Frederic suffered at the hands of the Russians. He would have been lost if this terrible war had continued; he was saved by Elisabeth's sudden death, which took place on the twenty-fifth of December (old style), seventeen hundred and sixty-one. Still his power was much weakened. The Empress had left Prussia less dangerous and threatening than she had found it.

REFORMS UNDER ELISABETH: FRENCH INFLUENCE.

The reign of Elisabeth was marked by an increase of orthodox zeal. In spite of her dissolute manners, she was much influenced by the priests, though she still clung to her old superstitions. In seventeen hundred and forty-two the Holy Synod ordered the suppression of the Armenian churches in the two capitals, and hoped likewise to suppress the dissenting churches on the Nevski Prospekt. In the Tatar regions some of the mosques were closed, and the erection of new ones forbidden. The intolerance of the bishops and missionaries caused the Pagan or Mussulman tribes of the Mordva, the Tcheremisa, the Tchuvashi, and the Meshtchera to revolt. Thirty-five thousand Jews were expelled on the ground that they were "the enemies of Christ our Saviour, and did much evil to our subjects." To the observation of the senate that she was ruining commerce and the empire, Elisabeth replied.

"I desire no gain from the foes of Christ." The fanaticism of the raskolniki rose by contact with the fanaticism of the officials. Fifty-three men burned themselves at once near Ustiug, and one hundred and seventy-two near Tomsk in Siberia.

On the other hand, the morals of the clergy were corrected, and attention paid to their education. The monasteries were enjoined to send pupils to the Ecclesiastical Academy of Moscow, which complained that at present its number consisted of only five. Rebellion and drunkenness were repressed by stripes and chains. The fair of the priests was put down, and all popes who hired themselves out in public were whipped. The laws of Peter the First against persons who walked about and talked in church were revived. The tobacco pouches of those who used snuff in church were confiscated. Inspectors nominated by the bishops obliged the peasants to clean their holy images, the dirtiness of which was shocking to strangers. Catechisms were distributed in the churches, and a new corrected edition of the Bible was exposed for sale. Theological studies, when they were not absolutely neglected, were still very puerile. At the Ecclesiastical Academy of Moscow they discussed whether the angels think by analysis or by synthesis, and what is the nature of the light of glory in the future life.

The senate was re-established, with the functions given it by Peter the Great, of which it had been deprived by the High Council of Catherine the First, or the Cabinet of Anna Ivanovna. Trade was encouraged. The tchin, or rank, of assessor, of secretary of colleges, and of councillor of state, was given to manufacturers of cloth, linen, silk, and cotton. In seventeen hundred and fifty-three the custom-houses of the interior were suppressed, as well as many toll-duties. Agricultural banks were founded which loaned money to landholders at six per cent; while private individuals were raising usurious interest to fifteen or even twenty per cent. Sons of merchants were sent to study trade and book-keeping in Holland. New mines were discovered, and the commerce with the far East increased rapidly. Siberia began to be peopled. Attempts were made to colonize Southern Russia, now freed from the prospect of Tatar incursions, with Slavs who had fled from the Turkish or Tatar provinces. On the territory acquired by Anna Ivanovna, between the Bug and the Oder, the agricultural and military colony of Novaia Serbia, or New Servia, was founded, which furnished four regiments of light cavalry.

Legislation became less severe. Elisabeth imagined that she had abolished the penalty of death, but the knout of her executioners killed as well as the axe. Those who survived flagellation were sent, with their nose or ears cut, to the public works. Torture was employed only in the gravest cases. It is estimated that during her reign more than eighty thousand were knouted or sent to Siberia. But if the civil code did not advance, a code of procedure and a code of criminal investigation were completed. The police had hard work to maintain even a show of order in this rude society. The government was powerless to stop brigandage on the great highways, pirates still captured ships on the Volga, and armed bands gave battle to regular troops. Moscow and Saint Petersburg were like woods of ill-fame. Thieves had lost none of their audacity, and one of them, Vanka Kaïn, the Russian Cartouche, is the hero of a whole cycle of songs. Edicts were promulgated to prevent the keeping of bears in both capitals, and to hinder them from being allowed to roam at night through the towns of the provinces. Public baths common to both men and women were forbidden in the large towns.

Under the reign of Elisabeth the real minister of literature and the fine arts was her young favorite, Count Ivan Shuvalof. He founded, in seventeen hundred and fifty-five, at the centre of the empire, the University of Moscow, whose small beginnings have excited the contempt of German historians, but of which Nikolai Turgénief was able to say in eighteen hundred and forty-four, that "never in any country has any institution been more useful and more fruitful in good results; even to-day it is rare to find a man who writes his own language correctly, a well-educated and enlightened official, an upright and firm magistrate, who has not been at the University of Moscow." Shuvalof desired that every student, whatever his origin, should carry a sword, and bear the rank of the tenth degree of the tchin, corresponding to major in the army; doctors were given the eighth degree. Ten professors taught the three branches of jurisprudence, medicine, and philosophy. He likewise planned to open two universities, at Saint Petersburg and at Baturin, and gymnasia and schools in all the governments; he established schools on the military frontier of the south, and one at Orenburg for the children of the exiles. He sent young men abroad to finish their studies in medicine. In seventeen hundred and fifty-eight he endowed the Academy of Fine Arts at Saint Petersburg, and over it he set French masters. The painter Louis Joseph de Lorraine, the sculptor Gilet, the architect Valois, and later Dévely and Louis Jean François Lagrenée, chief painter to the Court, were among them.

Saint Petersburg, which in seventeen hundred and fifty contained only seventy-four thousand inhabitants, began to look like a capital. The Italian Rastrelli built the Winter Palace, the Monastery of Smolna, which became under Catherine the Second an institution for the daughters of the aristocracy, and the Palace of the Academy of Sciences, and traced the plan of Tsarskoe-Selo, the Russian Versailles.

Under the presidency of Kirill Razumovski, the brother of Elisabeth's morganatic husband, the Academy of Sciences, which had been founded by Peter the Great and Catherine the First, began to make itself known. In spite of the interminable contests excited by Lomonosof between its German and Russian professors, it continued to publish both books and translations.

The Academicians Bauer and Müller devoted themselves to the origin of Russia. Tatishtchef, formerly governor of Astrakhan, wrote the first history of the monarchy. Lomonosof, Professor of Physic, made himself the Vaugelas and the Malherbe of his country. The son of a fisher in the neighborhood of Arkhangel, he had the colossal frame of the ancient *bogatuir*, and many of the vices of the people. His real name was Doroféef. He was sent abroad to complete his studies, and there became the hero of a hundred adventures. He married the daughter of a Magdeburg tailor, was kidnapped for the King of Prussia, and imprisoned. Even in Russia his drunkenness and turbulence would have drawn him into many scrapes, but for the intervention of his protectors. He published a grammar, a book of rhetoric and poetics, and labored to free the modern Russian language from the Slavonic of the Church. His "panegyrics" of Peter and Elisabeth, and, above all, his Odes, are the masterpieces of the time. Sumarokof wrote dramas, comedies, and satires, and published the first Russian review, "The Busy Bee." Kniazhnin was very successful in comedy, though his tragedies were poor. Prince Kantemir, son of the Hospodar of Moldavia, ambassador at Paris and London, published letters and satires. Trediakovski, author of the tragedy of "Deidamia" and of another inferior epic poem, called the "Telemakhid," imitated from Fénelon, is chiefly known as a reformer of the language, and an indefatigable translator. He translated all Rollin's "Ancient History," Boileau's "Art Poétique," the libretti of Italian operas, and works of science and politics. His biography proves the small estimation in which a poet was then held. Anna Ivanovna had employed him to make rhymes for her masquerades, and we have seen how brutally he was treated by Voluinski.

Elisabeth, like Anna Ivanovna, loved the theatre. The Italian company of Locatelli acted ballets and comic operas.

Sérigny, director of a French theatre, made twenty-five thousand rubles a year. The Empress furnished spectators, willing or reluctant, sending lackeys to beat up the laggards, and imposing a fine of fifty rubles on all who would not come. The Russian theatre had already begun to exist. Sumarokof led his actors, who were members of the corps of cadets, into the apartments of the Empress. Volkof, the son of a merchant, and a protégé of the voïevod Mussin-Pushkin, was at once author, actor, manager, decorator, and scene-painter, and having seen the German company at Saint Petersburg, he started a company at Iaroslavl. The Empress, hearing of it, invited him to come to the capital, where he founded the first public Russian theatre in seventeen hundred and fifty-six. Three years later he was sent to Moscow for the same purpose. Sumarokof afterwards became the manager of it, and wrote twenty-six pieces for it, among which were "Khorev," "Sineus and Truvor," "Dmitri the Impostor," and some translations of Shakespeare and of French pieces.

The characteristic feature of the reign of Elisabeth is the establishment of direct relations with France, which had been, since the seventeenth century, the highest representative of European civilization. Up to this time French civilization had been only known at second hand in Russia. The people were Dutch under Peter the First, German under Anna Ivanovna. The Russians had made themselves the pupils of those who were themselves but pupils of the French. Now the barriers were thrown down. Learned Frenchmen were members of the Academy of Sciences, French artists of the Academy of Fine Arts. Sérigny's French theatre was thronged; Sumarokof caused Russian translations from French works to be put on the stage, and the Russians learned to know Corneille, Racine, and Molière. The writings of Vauban on Fortifications, and of Saint Rémy on Artillery, were translated. The favorite, Ivan Shuvalof, had his furniture brought from France, his dresses from Paris, loved everything French, and caused

Elisabeth, who had once been betrothed to Louis the Fifteenth, to share his tastes. Elisabeth herself dressed most expensively in the French fashion. When she died more than fifteen thousand rich dresses were found in her wardrobe, none of which had ever been worn more than once. Several thousand pairs of shoes and slippers and two great chests of silk stockings also bore witness to her extravagance. La Chétardie and L'Hôpital made the manners of Versailles fashionable. The Russians perceived that they had more affinity with the French than with the Germans. Trediakovski and Kirill Razumovski went to perfect themselves in Paris, where the Russian students were sufficiently numerous to have a chapel of their own, under the protection of the ambassador. A Vorontsof entered the service of Louis the Fifteenth, and in the uniform of the light cavalry stood on guard in the galleries of Versailles. The ambassador Kantemir was a friend of Montesquieu. A generation of French in ideas and culture grew up at Elisabeth's Court. Catherine the Second, Princess Dashkof, and the Vorontsofs wrote French as easily as their own language. In seventeen hundred and forty-six De l'Isle communicated to the Academy of Sciences the wish expressed by Voltaire to become a corresponding member. The following year, by means of D'Allion and Kirill Razumovski, Voltaire entered into relations with Shuvalof, who furnished him with documents, as well as with advice and criticism, for his "History of Russia under Peter the Great."

In her internal policy, then, Elisabeth continued the traditions of the great Emperor. She developed the material prosperity of the country, reformed the legislation, and created new centres of population; she gave an energetic impulse to science and the national literature; she prepared the way for the alliance of France and Russia, now emancipated from the German yoke; while in foreign affairs she put a stop to the threatening advance of Prussia, vanquished and reduced to despair the first general of the age, and concluded the first

Franco-Russian alliance against the military monarchy of the Hohenzollerns. Better appreciated by the light of later discoveries, Elisabeth will hold an honorable place in history, even when compared to Peter the Great and Catherine the Second.

CHAPTER VIII.

PETER THE THIRD AND THE REVOLUTION OF SEVENTEEN HUNDRED AND SIXTY-TWO.

GOVERNMENT OF PETER THE THIRD, AND THE ALLIANCE WITH FREDERIC THE SECOND. — REVOLUTION OF SEVENTEEN HUNDRED AND SIXTY-TWO: CATHERINE THE SECOND.

GOVERNMENT OF PETER THE THIRD, AND THE ALLIANCE WITH FREDERIC THE SECOND.

THE successor of Elisabeth was her nephew, the grandson of Peter the Great, son of Anna Petrovna and of Karl Friedrich, Duke of Holstein-Gottorp; at the time he was thirty-four years of age. His accession was looked forward to with feelings of mistrust, because he affected to think himself a stranger in Russia, and to act more as the Duke of Holstein than as heir to the imperial throne. Without education and without training, his youth had been passed in puerile amusements; he seemed to care only for minute military details, occupied himself in drilling his battalion of Holsteiners, — known by the name of "long-suffering," — and showed himself the fanatical admirer of Frederic the Second and of the Prussian tactics. His aunt suspected him of communicating to Frederic the secret deliberations of her government, and thought herself obliged to exclude him from conferences which were concerned with affairs of war and administration.

The first measures of Peter the Third caused, however, a delightful surprise. In February, seventeen hundred and sixty-two, he published a manifesto which freed the nobility from the obligation imposed on them by Peter the Great, of devoting themselves to the service of the State. He reminded them that this law of his grandfather had produced most salutary effects, by forcing the nobles to educate themselves and take an interest in the public welfare, by giving birth to an enlightened generation, and by furnishing the State with distinguished generals and administrators. But now that the love of the sovereign and zeal for his service was spread abroad, he thought it no longer necessary to maintain the law. The Russian nobles, overcome with gratitude, thought of raising a statue of gold to him. Peter the Third answered that they could put the gold to a better use, and he hoped by his reign to raise a more enduring memorial in the hearts of his people. Another reform was the abolition of the Secret Court of Police, — "an abominable tribunal," writes the English ambassador, "as bad, and in some respects worse than the Spanish Inquisition." Peter the Third respected the raskolniki; they had been so cruelly persecuted during the preceding reign, that their number had fallen from forty thousand to five thousand in the government of Novgorod alone; and thousands of these unhappy creatures had fled to the deserts, or emigrated into the neighboring countries. He commanded that they should be brought back to Russia, offering them at the same time lands in Siberia; "for," says the ukaz, "the Mahometans and even idolaters are tolerated in the empire. But the raskolniki are Christians." He took up his grandfather's project of the resumption of conventual property, allowing the monks a pension in its stead. He even thought of the peasants, on whom the modern State founded by Peter the Great weighed so heavily, and proclaimed a pardon to those who, misled by false intelligence, thought they were able to rise against their masters. The greater part of these acts were inspired by his Secretary of State, Volkof. The culprits of the last reign — the Mengdens, Madame Lapukhin, old Marshal Münnich and his son, Lestocq, the Duke of Kurland, and all the Birens — were recalled.

Unhappily, the Emperor's personal conduct almost neutralized any wisdom in his laws. Not only did he plunder the clergy, but he did not hide his contempt for the national religion, which he had been forced to embrace instead of Lutheranism. The people were scandalized by his attitude in the funeral chamber where the corpse of his aunt was exposed. "He was seen," says Princess Dashkof, "whispering and laughing with the ladies-in-waiting, turning the priests into ridicule, picking quarrels with the officers, or even with the sentinels, about the way their cravats were folded, the length of their curls, or the cut of their uniforms." The reforms that he introduced into the dress and drill, so as to assimilate them to those of Prussia, irritated the army; the guards were jealous of the favor shown the battalions of Holstein, which he wished to raise to eighteen thousand men, and proposed as models for the national troops. The suppression of the body-guard of grenadiers, formed by Elisabeth in seventeen hundred and forty-one, announced to the regiments of Preobrazhenski, Semenovski, and Ismaïlovski the lot that awaited them. The Emperor had already observed that "the guards were dangerous, and held the palace in a state of siege."

The court was discontented with the foolish innovations he introduced into etiquette, obliging the ladies to courtesy in the German fashion. He seemed to have taken an aversion to all the tastes of his aunt, and one of his first cares was to dismiss the French company of actors. The manners of the upper classes had become sufficiently refined to look upon Peter's gross habits with disgust. "The life led by the Emperor," writes the French ambassador, De Breteuil, "is shameful." He smokes and drinks beer for hours together, and only ceases from these amusements at five or six in the morning, when he is dead drunk. . . . . He has redoubled his attentions towards Mademoiselle Vorontsof. One must allow that it is a strange taste: she has no wit; and as to her face, it is impossible to imagine anything uglier: she resembles in every way a servant at a low inn."

The foreign policy of Peter the Third only widened the breach between himself and his subjects. Frederic the Second, since the battle of Künersdorff, was brought to the greatest straits; the slow movements of Buturlin in the campaign of seventeen hundred and sixty-one had indeed procured him a little respite, but if the war with Russia was prolonged, he was ruined. We may imagine with what joy and hope he hailed the accession of Peter the Third. He addressed his congratulations to the new Emperor through the English ambassador in Russia, and the friendship between the great king and his admirer was soon renewed. The king sent him the brevet of major-general in the Prussian service, and Peter is said to have boasted that his surest title to glory was in his subordination to Frederic. Tchernishef received orders to detach himself from the Austrians in Silesia, and the King of Prussia sent Goltz to make proposals of peace to the Tsar. He authorized his envoy even to cede Eastern Prussia if it was exacted by Peter, merely reserving to himself an indemnity. On his arrival Goltz found a prince who swore only by Frederic the Second, wore his portrait in a ring, and remembered all that he had suffered for him in the reign of Elisabeth, when he had been dismissed from the "Conference." There was no longer any question of annexing Eastern Prussia, as the late Tsaritsa had so ardently wished; Peter the Third restored to his "old friend" all the Russian conquests, and formed an offensive and defensive alliance with him. The two princes promised each other help to the amount of twelve thousand infantry and eight thousand horses, and the Prussians, who had till that moment been fighting the Russians, now joined them against Austria. Frederic guaranteed to the Emperor his States of Holstein, and confirmed Peter's uncle in the duchy of Kurland, undertaking to come to an understanding with him on the subject of Poland. Such a sudden change in State policy had never before been seen. Breteuil and Mercy d'Argenteau, the French and Austrian ambassadors, found themselves all at once in disfavor. The envoy of Frederic the Second was not only a favorite, he was really the chief minister of the Emperor of Russia, pointing out suspicious characters, banishing his enemies, accusing Vorontsof and the Shuvalofs of French sympathies. The treaty being concluded, Peter the Third, at a grand dinner, proposed the health of the King of Prussia, amidst the thunders of the guns of the fortress. He carried his extravagances, by which he testified his admiration for the great man, to such a point as to disquiet Goltz himself. "Let us drink to the health of the king our master," he cried in one of his orgies; "he has done me the honor to confide to me one of his regiments. I hope he will not dismiss me; you may be assured that if he should order it, I would make war on hell with all my empire."

REVOLUTION OF SEVENTEEN HUNDRED AND SIXTY-TWO: CATHERINE THE SECOND.

The Russians would have hailed with pleasure the end of a tedious war, though they regretted the abandonment of the conquests of Elisabeth, but a new war succeeded the old one; the empire was to be exhausted anew, combating its allies of yesterday, and to fight against Denmark for the pretensions of the house of Holstein. The hearts of the people softened towards the Empress Catherine on account of the harsh treatment she had received, her intelligence and her demonstrations of piety throwing into relief the incapacity and extravagances of her husband. Peter the Third wished to divorce her and to marry Elisabeth Vorontsof; he was said to meditate disinheriting his son Pavel, or Paul, in favor of Ivan the Sixth; once he gave an order, which was not executed, to arrest his wife, and to confine her in a convent.

Sophia of Anhalt, now the Empress Catherine, was not a woman to pardon these threats, nor to wait till they were carried into effect. As Breteuil remarks, "All this, joined to daily humiliations, fermented in a brain like hers, and wanted only an occasion to break out." She bided her time and acted.

Numerous contemporary documents exist about the revolution of June, seventeen hundred and sixty-two. It must be remembered, however, that all of these accounts were written by Peter's enemies. The accounts best known are those of Rulhière, of Princess Dashkof in her Memoirs, of Keith and Bretcuil in their despatches, and of Catherine the Second herself in her letter to Poniatovski. The order given to the guards to leave for Holstein precipitated the revolution of seventeen hundred and sixty-two, as a similar order precipitated that of seventeen hundred and forty-one. Peter the Third had no idea of his danger, although he was frequently warned by Frederic to be on his guard; he did not see that conspirators were silently increasing and multiplying in the senate, in the court, and in the army. The number of them was great, and their aims often different. Some wished to proclaim Paul the First, under the guardianship of his mother; others desired to crown Catherine herself. The group which had then all the confidence of the Empress was composed of young officers: Gregory Orlof, her lover, Alexis Orlof, and three other brothers, Bibikof, and Passek. The Orlofs were acquainted with all the details of the affair, and concealed it with care from the other conspirators, among them Princess Dashkof, the sister of the Emperor's favorite mistress, whom they considered wanting in discretion. Put on her guard by the arrest of Lieutenant Passek on the eighth of June, Catherine resolved to act. Peter the Third was then at Oranienbaum, about twenty miles from Saint Petersburg, with his Holsteiners, and Catherine at Peterhof, between Oranienbaum and Saint Petersburg. She abruptly quitted her residence, accompanied by Gregory and Alexis Orlof and two servants. On her arrival in the capital the three regiments of Foot Guards rose and took the oaths to her at the hands of their priests. Peter's uncle, George of Holstein, was arrested by his own regiment of Horse Guards. From Our Lady of Kazan, Catherine went to the Winter Palace, whence Admiral Taluizin was sent to secure the allegiance of Kronstadt, and whence proclamations were issued to the people and the army. Then, at the head of nearly twenty thousand men, besides artillery, she marched on Oranienbaum.

Peter the Third, suddenly aroused from his tranquil repose, embarked for Kronstadt to put himself at the head of the garrison. "I am the Emperor," he cried to Taluizin. "There is no longer any Emperor," replied the admiral, and, menaced by the artillery of the fortress, Peter had to return to his residence. There, in spite of the counsels of the warlike old Münnich and the presence of his fifteen hundred Holsteiners, he quietly abdicated, — " like a child being sent to sleep," as Frederic the Second remarked. He visited his wife with his mistress and his most intimate friends : "after which," relates the Empress, "I sent the deposed Emperor, under the command of Alexis Orlof, accompanied by four officers and a detachment of gentle and reasonable men, to a place named Ropsha, fifteen miles from Peterhof, a secluded spot, but very pleasant." Here he died in four days, of a hæmorrhoidal colic," his wife assures us, which was complicated by " flying to the brain." This was the version officially adopted. The English ambassador relates that he received the following note from the Russian Cabinet : " The imperial minister of Russia thinks it his duty to inform the foreign ministers that the late Emperor having been taken ill with a violent colic, to which he was subject, died yesterday."

Capefique, in his history of Catherine the Second, which always takes the best view of her character, thus describes the death of Peter: " Six days after his abdication the three Orlofs came to visit him in his prison. What was the design of this dark mission ? Was a new abdication or was exile the question at issue ? Was the prison the portal of the tomb ? The only explanation which has any certainty is, that a hand-to-hand struggle ensued in the cell. Peter was of great muscular activity. Alexis Orlof was in no respect his inferior; the Tsar was overcome by the grasp of his adversary. The fingers of Orlof's colossal hand left a black and blue mark around his neck; the Tsar was choked to death in a brutal and savage conflict. It is said that the Empress had no desire for this melancholy catastrophe; the Orlofs of their own free will assassinated the prince, who some day might be able to avenge himself for so many insults. Oftentimes when such revolutions occur we find accidents, catastrophes which at first were not premeditated. The bloody demon of political exigency arises to command these State crimes which save empires; and it is perhaps with a sad and bitter thought that Voltaire celebrates Catherine as the Semiramis of the North."

The unhappy son of Anna Leopoldovna and of Anton, the great-grandson of the Tsar Ivan the Fifth, the Emperor, imprisoned since his childhood by Elisabeth and confined at Schlüsselburg, had been brought by Peter the Third to Saint Petersburg. He was now twenty-one years old, and had lost his reason. Catherine the Second imprisoned him anew at Schlüsselburg. He was no dangerous character, but merely a name. A memorandum of the Empress on the subject still exists. "It is my opinion that he should not be allowed to escape, so as to place him beyond the power of doing harm. It would be best to tonsure him, and to transfer him to some monastery, neither too near nor too far off; it will suffice if it does not become a shrine."

Revolutions are almost invariably followed by revolts. The frequency of these military coups-de-main encouraged audacious spirits; and only two years after Catherine's usurpation, Mirovitch, lieutenant of the guards, conceived the project of delivering Ivan the Sixth. His warders, seeing no other means of preventing his escape, put him to death at the moment that Mirovitch entered his chamber, and the conspirator found nothing but his corpse. He was himself arrested and condemned to death. The day of the execution, the people, who during the twenty years' reign of Elisabeth had seen no one beheaded, uttered such a cry, and were seized with such emotion, that when the executioner held up the head of Mirovitch the bridge over the Neva almost gave way under the pressure of the crowd, and the balustrades broke. Catherine had now no rival for the throne of Russia except her own son.

"I know," writes Voltaire some years later, speaking of Catherine, — "I know that she is reproached with some trifles about her husband, but these are family affairs with which I do not meddle. And, after all, it is often as well to have a fault to repair; it obliges people to make greater efforts to wrest esteem and admiration from the public." We shall see what efforts were used by Catherine the Second to force the Russians to forget the means by which she had gained the throne.

CHAPTER IX.

CATHERINE II.: EARLY YEARS.

1762-1780.

END OF THE SEVEN YEARS' WAR: INTERVENTION IN POLAND — FIRST TURKISH WAR: FIRST PARTITION OF POLAND (1772): SWEDISH REVOLUTION OF SEVENTEEN HUNDRED AND SEVENTY-TWO. — PLAGUE AT MOSCOW. — PUGATCHEF.

END OF THE SEVEN YEARS' WAR: INTERVENTION IN POLAND.

IN the first moments that followed her triumph, Catherine the Second published a manifesto in which Frederic was treated as "perturber of the public peace," and "perfidious enemy of Russia." She soon, however, changed her mind. This princess, who had punished Peter the Third for his alliance with Prussia and his designs upon the Church property, was herself destined to realize, both in her foreign and domestic policy, the plans of her husband. Tchernishef had received the order to detach himself from the Prussians, as he had formerly received the order to detach himself from the Austrians. Frederic managed to retard the departure of the general for three days, and Tchernishef consented to occupy with grounded arms a position which covered the Prussian army. Frederic profited by this to defeat Daun at Burkersdorff and Leutmannsdorff. The final withdrawal of Russia from the Seven Years' War hastened the conclusion of peace. During all the early part of her reign, Catherine's policy consisted in what is known as the "system of the North"; that is, a close alliance with Prussia, England, and

Denmark, against the two great powers of the South, the house of Bourbon and the house of Austria. The diplomatic struggle with France especially was very lively in the secondary courts; that is to say, at Warsaw, at Stockholm, and at Constantinople.

The duchy of Kurland, legally a dependency of the Polish crown, but in reality annexed to the Russian Empire, found itself at that time without a sovereign. Anna Leopoldovna had exiled the Duke Biren; Peter the Third had intended that George of Holstein should have the crown; Augustus the Third had coveted it for his son Charles of Saxony; Catherine put an end to the competition by re-establishing Biren. It was a union in disguise of Kurland and the empire.

A more important event soon absorbed all her attention: this was the approaching death of the King of Poland, and the consequent opening of the whole question of succession. Two parties were then disputing the power at Warsaw: the court party, with the minister Brühl and his son-in-law Mnishek, and the party supported by Russia, headed by the Tchartoruiski. The former wished to secure the succession for the Prince of Saxony, which was also the policy of France and Austria; the latter intended to elect a piast, that is, a native noble of their own party, and their choice had fallen on Stanislas Poniatovski, a nephew of the Tchartoruiski. Thus France, which in seventeen hundred and thirty-three had made war for a piast against the Saxon candidate, now supported the Saxon candidate against Poniatovski. Circumstances had changed, and the kingdom of Poland, becoming every day more feeble, could be sustained at all only by the forces of a German state, Saxony. But Frederic the Second feared an increase of power for Saxony quite as much as for Poland; Saxony was the old rival of Prussia in the empire, as Poland had been in the country of the Vistula. Russia, on its side, which, by fighting Stanislas Leshtchinski, had fought the father-in-law of Louis the Fifteenth, now fought for the

Saxon, the client of France and Austria. Further, it had
no intention that a Polish noble should become too powerful,
and meant to get rid of the Tchartoruiski. The candida-
ture of Stanislas Poniatovski, a man without any personal
power, therefore satisfied the desires of Frederic the Second,
the interests of the Russian Empire, and the sentiments of
Catherine, who was glad to be able to crown one of her early
lovers. When Augustus the Third really died, the country
was violently agitated by the diets of convocation and election.
Power was fiercely disputed by the two parties. The Tchartoruiski called in the Russian arms to put down their enemies,
and under the protection of foreign bayonets Poniatovski inaugurated his fatal reign, in which Poland was thrice dismembered, and erased from the list of the nations.

Three principal causes led to the ruin of the ancient royal
republic. The first was the national movement of Russia,
which tended to complete itself on the Western side, and, to
use the expression of its historians, to "recover" the provinces
which had formed part of the territory of Saint Vladimir;
that is, White Russia, Black Russia, and Little Russia. The
national question was complicated by the same religious question which had led, under Alexis Mikhaïlovitch, to a first
dismemberment of the Polish State. The complaints of the
agitations of the Uniates were on the increase in Lithuania,
and Russia had often tried to interfere diplomatically. In
seventeen hundred and eighteen and seventeen hundred and
twenty Peter the Great wrote to Augustus the Second to
inform him of the ill-treatment suffered by his brethren of
the Greek Church. Augustus published an edict which
insured the free exercise of the orthodox religion, but which
remained unexecuted, as the king was never sufficiently strong
to restrain the zeal of the clergy and the Jesuits, to repress
the abuses of power on the part of his officers, and to protect
the peasants belonging to the Greek Church against their
lords. In seventeen hundred and twenty-three Peter wrote to

the Pope to entreat his interference, threatening reprisals against the Roman Church in his dominions. The Pope declined the proposals of Peter, and the annoyances continued.

The second cause of the ruin of Poland was the insatiable greed of Prussia. Poland possessed Western Prussia, that is, the lower Vistula between Thorn and Dantzig, separating Eastern Prussia from the rest of the Brandenburg monarchy. It thus spoilt the construction of the latter State by dividing it into two parts. Poland also occupied the side of the country where German colonization had greatly developed, especially in the towns. Moreover, the government of Warsaw was so foolish as to annoy the Protestant dissenters in the same way as it did those of the Greek Church.

In the third place, Poland could not escape the spirit of reform which was the spirit of the eighteenth century. Poniatovski and the more enlightened Poles were well aware of the contrast between the national anarchy and the order that existed in the neighboring States. While Prussia, Russia, and Austria tried to constitute themselves into modern States, to build up the central powers on the ruins of the forces of the Middle Ages, to realize the reforms proclaimed by French philosophers and political economists, Poland had, up to that time, followed the opposite plan, despoiling the kingly power at each accession, weakening the national strength, persisting in the traditions of feudalism. In the midst of European monarchies which attained, on its very frontiers, the maximum of their power, Poland remained a state of the eleventh century. It had allowed them to get such a start, that even the effort for reform hastened its dissolution.

From a social point of view it was a nation of agricultural serfs, under the power of a numerous class of small nobility, themselves subject to a few great families, against which the king was absolutely powerless. There was no middle class at all, unless we give that name to some thousands of Catholic citizens, and to a million of Jews, who had no interest in maintaining a state of things which condemned them to eternal opprobrium. Economically, it had a primitive system of agriculture worked by a serf population, little commerce, no retail trade, no public finances. From a political point of view the country was legally composed of nobles only. The rivalry of the great families, the anarchy of the diets, the weakness of the king, the pacta conventa, the liberum veto, the confederations or diets under the shield, the inveterate habit of invoking the intervention of foreign powers, or of selling them their votes, had extinguished in Poland the very idea of law and a state. From a military point of view the Polish soldiers were merely the lawless soldiers of the Middle Ages; the only cavalry was that of the nobility; there was no infantry, little artillery, and scarcely any fortresses on the frontiers, which were everywhere exposed. Maurice de Saxe affirms, in his "Reveries," that it needed only forty-eight thousand men to conquer Poland. What could this State do, divided against itself, long ago corrupted by the gold of its enemies, enclosed by three powerful monarchies, which occupied its territory with never a thought that they were violating its frontiers, and whose ambassadors had more power in its diets than the king?

Catherine and Frederic had come to an understanding on two essential points: to vindicate the rights of the dissenters, and to prevent all reform of the anarchic constitution, which was giving Poland into their hands. While affecting to espouse the cause of tolerance, they made Europe forget that it was to be gained at the price of the independence and integrity of the country. The noisy fanaticism of the Poles helped them to conceal their object.

In seventeen hundred and sixty-five Konisski, the orthodox bishop of White Russia, presented a petition to the King of Poland, recalling all the vexations to which the Greek Church in the kingdom was subject. Two hundred churches had been taken away from them and given to the Uniates; they were forbidden to rebuild those which had fallen into ruin, or to construct new ones; their priests were ill-treated, sometimes put to death. "The Missionary Fathers," says the petition, "are specially distinguished for their zeal: seconded by the secular authority when they are engaged on a mission, they assemble the Greco-Russian people of all the neighboring villages, as if they were a flock of sheep, keep them for six weeks together, force them to confess to them, and, to frighten those that resist, raise impaling poles, display rods, thorny branches, erect scaffolds, separate children from their parents, women from their husbands, and seek to astound them by imaginary miracles. In cases of stout resistance men are beaten with rods or with thorny branches, their hands are burned, and they are kept in prison for months together."

Russia supported the complaints of the dissenters before the Polish Diet, and Stanislas promised to sustain them. It was necessary to secure to the people the free exercise of their religion, and to the orthodox nobles the political rights of which they had been deprived by former legislatures. The Diet of seventeen hundred and sixty-six made a frantic opposition to this proposal; the deputy Gurovski, who attempted to speak in favor of the dissenters, narrowly escaped being put to death.

Repnin, Catherine's ambassador, got the dissenters to promise that they would resort to the legal means of confederations. The orthodox assembled at Slutsk, the Protestants under the patronage of the Russian ambassador at Thorn; there was also at Radom a confederation of Catholics, who were enemies of the Tchartoruiski, and of those who feared a reform of the constitution, and the abolition of the liberum veto. Russia, which with Prussia had guaranteed the maintenance of this absurd constitution, likewise took them under its protection. Eighty thousand Muscovites were ready, at a sign from Repnin, to enter Poland. Under these auspices opened the Diet of seventeen hundred and sixty-seven: the Poles did not appear to feel the insult to their independence, and only exerted themselves to support the system of intolerance. Soltuik, bishop of Krakof, Zalutski, bishop of Kief, and two other nuncios showed themselves most warm in their opposition to the project. Repnin caused them to be violently removed and taken to Russia, and the Poles had done so much themselves that Europe applauded this violation of the law of nations, as it seemed to secure liberty of conscience. The Diet yielded, and consented that the dissident nobles should have political rights equal to those of the Catholics; but Romanism remained the religion of the State, and that which the king must always profess. In seventeen hundred and sixty-eight a treaty was made between Poland and Russia, in virtue of which the constitution could never be modified without the consent of the latter power. This was to legalize foreign intervention, and to condemn Poland to perish by reason of its abuses. The Russian troops evacuated Warsaw, and the Confederates sent deputies to thank the Empress.

In spite of this, the Confederation of Radom, the most considerable of the three, which had taken up arms to hinder the reform of the constitution, and in no wise to support reforms in favor of the dissenters, was much discontented with the result. When it was dissolved, there sprang from its remains the Confederation of Bar, in Podolia, which was more numerous still, and had adopted as its programme not only the maintenance of the liberum veto, but also that of the exclusive privileges of the Catholics. In Gallicia and Lublin two other confederations were formed with the same objects in view. The insurgents took for their motto, "Religion and liberty"; but the word "liberty" was heard with indifference by the mass of the people, who saw in the "liberty" of the Poles only that of the nobles. The Confederates of Bar sent deputies to the courts of Dresden, Vienna, and Versailles, to interest them in their cause. In the West opinion might well be perplexed. On which side, men asked, was the nation ranged?

Whither did the forces of the future tend? Were right and justice at Warsaw with the king and the senate, and all the men who had voted for the enfranchisement of the dissenters, and who meditated in secret the reform of the constitution and the revival of Poland, or were they at Bar, where turbulent nobles, guided by fanatical priests, revolted in the name of the liberum veto and religious intolerance? Voltaire and the greater part of the French philosophers declared in favor of King Stanislas; but the Duke de Choiseul, minister of Louis the Fifteenth, supported the Confederates. It did not strike him that by weakening the authority of the Polish king he was weakening Poland itself. The Polish government, in presence of the insurrection, found itself forced to commit a fresh blunder. The royal army did not amount to nine thousand effective men, and, according to the treaty of alliance with Russia, they appealed to Catherine for troops. The Muscovite columns wrested Bar, Berditchef, and Krakof from the Confederates. The orthodox monks replied by their sermons to those of the Catholic priests. Hontaï and Zheliczniak called to arms the Cossacks of the Ukraina, the Zaporoshtsui, and the haïdamaki, or brigands, who in a few days amounted to twenty thousand men, and went plundering from estate to estate. Prince Kaspar Liubomirski, to his own harm, out of hatred to the Confederates, gave fresh inducements to the peasants. A savage war, at once national, religious, and social, desolated the provinces of the Dnieper; the land-owners saw the return of the bloody days of Khmelnitski. No Catholic priest, no Jew, no noble, was safe. One of each of these classes was seen, hanging upon a tree in company with a dog. The farther they spread the more their strength increased, and the more brutal they became. The massacre of Uman, a town of Count Pototski's, horrified the Ukraina. All the residences within forty miles were burned to the ground, and at the least calculation ten thousand Jews and Catholics were put to death.

The Confederates, repulsed by the Russian columns, obtained some support from the Court of Vienna. They had established the council of the Confederation at Teshen, their headquarters at Eperies in Hungary, and still held three places in Poland. Choiseul sent them money, and sent also the Chevalier de Taulès, Dumouriez, and the Baron de Viomesnil, to organize them. In the Memoirs of Dumouriez we find that the forces of the Confederation, scattered through the whole extent of Poland, did not exceed sixteen or seventeen thousand horsemen, without infantry, and divided into five or six bands, each with its independent chief. Zaremba, in Great Poland, the Cossack Sava, Miatchinski, Valevski, and many others, usually acted without combination. Pulavski was the open enemy of Pototski; Dumouriez, with his undisciplined troops, was beaten at Landskron in seventeen hundred and seventy-one; but Viomesnil, Dussaillans, and Choisy, three French officers, surprised the Castle of Krakof in seventeen hundred and seventy-two; it was shortly afterwards recaptured by Suvorof. On the third of November, seventeen hundred and seventy-one, an attempt was made by some of the Confederates to secure the person of the king. As he was about to leave the house of his uncle, the Chancellor of Lithuania, at ten o'clock at night, he was suddenly surrounded by twelve or fifteen men. His escort was overpowered. A bullet grazed his skin. He was dragged out of the carriage by his feet. His orders and decorations were torn from him, and he was severely wounded in the head by a sabre-cut. Two horsemen then hurried away with him before the spectators could make any plan of rescue. In a few moments he was set upon a horse which, fortunately, stumbled and broke a leg. Those who were intrusted with guarding him missed their way in a wood, and, thinking that they heard the voices of Russians, they forsook him and fled. About five o'clock in the morning the king returned to Warsaw, wounded and bleeding. This deed of the Confederates placed them in a very bad light, excited the ostentatious and insincere indignation of the European courts, and increased Voltaire's dislike of them.

FIRST TURKISH WAR: FIRST PARTITION OF POLAND: SWEDISH REVOLUTION OF SEVENTEEN HUNDRED AND SEVENTY-TWO.

Choiseul imagined that the best way of aiding the Confederates was to induce the Turks to declare war against Russia. Vergennes, the French ambassador at Constantinople, set to work energetically to bring it to pass; but unhappily France greatly exaggerated the power of Turkey, and was ignorant how far its strength had diminished since its last war with Austria. The mistake made by Choiseul when he linked the fate of his ally on the Vistula with the success of the Ottoman arms only rendered the partition of Poland inevitable. On the news of the violation of the frontier at Balta, not by the Russian troops but by the haïdamaki, or brigands, who were pursued by the former, the Sublime Porte declared war on Russia. The Baron de Tott had been sent by Vergennes to Kruim-Girai, Khan of the Crimea, to persuade him to second the Turks. In the winter of seventeen hundred and sixty-eight the Tatars devastated Novaïa Serbia, one of the new centres which had been founded by Elisabeth. Catherine, whose forces were occupied in Poland, had only a feeble army to oppose to the Turco-Tatar invasion. "The Romans," she writes to her generals, "did not concern themselves with the number of their enemies; they only asked, 'Where are they?'" Alexander Galitsuin, with thirty thousand men, was therefore ordered to check the Grand Vizier at the head of one hundred thousand, who was on the point of entering Podolia to join the Polish Confederates; Rumiantsof was to occupy the Ukraina and watch the Crimean Tatars and the Kalmuicki. Galitsuin took the initiative, defeated the Grand Vizier on the Dnieper, near Khotin, which capitulated in September, seventeen hundred and sixty-nine, and took up a position in Valakhia and Moldavia, to the great joy of the orthodox populations of the Danube. The following year his successor, Rumiantsof, defeated the Khan of the Tatars, although the latter had one hundred thousand men, and was intrenched on the banks of the Larga. He then gained over the Grand Vizier in person the victory of Kahul in seventeen hundred and seventy, where seventeen thousand Russians defeated one hundred and fifty thousand Mussulmans. In seventeen hundred and seventy-one Prince Dolgoruki forced the lines of Perekop, ravaged the Crimea, took Kaffa, Kertch, and Ienikale, and put an end forever to the Turkish rule in the peninsula. During this time the army of Valakhia captured the fortresses on the Danube, successfully completed the conquest of Bessarabia by taking Bender, and penetrated into Bulgaria.

Catherine the Second prepared a yet more terrible surprise for the Turkish Empire, disturbed as it was by the revolt of the Pasha of Egypt. A Russian fleet left the Baltic under the orders of Alexis Orlof, and, after having put in at the English ports and made the tour of Europe, suddenly appeared on the coast of Greece. The Christian populations of the Western Morea and the Maïnotes, the inhabitants of the ancient Lacedæmon, revolted; Voltaire was already singing the regeneration of Athens and the resurrection of Sparta; but Orlof abandoned the Greeks after he had compromised them, and hastened away in search of the Turkish fleet. With the help of his lieutenants, Spiridof and Greig, he defeated it at the harbor of Chios, and totally annihilated it in the port of Tchesmé, aided by fire-ships started by the English lieutenant, Dugdale. At this news the terror of Constantinople exceeded all bounds; they pictured the Russians arriving in the Bosphorus. Admiral Elphinstone, to whom nearly the whole credit of this great victory was due, advised Orlof to sail immediately for Constantinople. But Orlof wasted his time in the conquest of the islands, while Baron de Tott rallied the courage of the Sultan and the Turkish people, drilled the Ottoman soldiers, cast cannon, and put the Dardanelles in a state of defence. When the Russians at last, in seventeen hundred and seventy, presented themselves at the entrance of the Straits, they were too late. Elphinstone, in disgust, resigned his position, and, being received with great coolness at Saint Petersburg, he returned to England unrewarded. Orlof, on the other hand, whose folly and stupidity had prevented any use being made of the victory, was received as a conquering hero.

Russia, however, had none the less conquered Azof, the Crimea, the shore of the Black Sea between the Dnieper and the Dniester, Bessarabia, Valakhia, Moldavia, a part of Bulgaria, and of the islands of the Archipelago, and would willingly have kept its conquests, but Austria took fright at Russia's close neighborhood and at the disturbance in the equilibrium of the East. It was at this time that the Turkish and Polish questions became involved in each other: Poland was to serve as the ransom of Turkey.

Of the three Northern States, Prussia was the most interested in the dismemberment of Poland; it was a geographical necessity that it should lay hands on Western Prussia, and, if possible, on the cities of the Vistula. Its king, Frederic the Second, denounced to Catherine the projects of the Tchartoruiski for the reform of the constitution, and brought to light the wrongs of the dissenters; in a word, he created the Polish question. In the interviews of Neiss in Silesia, and of Neustadt in Moravia, he had disquieted Joseph the Second and Kaunitz on the subject of Russian ambition in the East, and had suggested the idea of a partition of Poland; and he also sent his brother, Prince Henry, to Saint Petersburg, to gain over Catherine the Second. Prince Henry made her clearly comprehend that her pretensions in the East would cause Austria and France to side against her; that her ally, his brother, the King of Prussia, weakened by the Seven Years' War, would be unable to stand a war against united Europe; that no doubt she had a right to an equivalent for the expenses of the double war, but that it could matter little to her whether she procured this indemnity from the Vistula or from the Danube; that she could therefore aggrandize herself at the expense of Poland, and that to re-establish equilibrium in the North she must suffer Prussia and Austria to aggrandize themselves also.

Catherine the Second, who had already on her hands the wars with Poland and Turkey, could not dream of fighting also both Austria and Prussia. Although she would have preferred to maintain the integrity of Poland, on condition of holding a preponderating influence over its affairs, she was forced to submit to the proposal of Frederic the Second. The King of Prussia knew how to play off Russia and Austria against each other. Even now he was acting as master in Great Poland, taking away the wheat for his own subjects, and the inhabitants for his own army. Once he occupied Dantzig. Austria in turn, in order to vindicate its ancient rights, invaded the county of Zips. The partition was almost completed, when it was legalized by the treaty of February seventeen, seventeen hundred and seventy-one, between Prussia and Russia, accepted by Austria in April, and signified to the King of Poland on the eighteenth of September in that same year. Russia obtained White Russia, including Polotsk, Vitepsk, Orsha, Mohilef, Mstislavl, Gomel, with one million six hundred thousand inhabitants; Austria had Western Gallicia and Red Russia, with two million five hundred thousand people; while Prussia got possession of the long-coveted Western Prussia, with a population of nine hundred thousand souls.

Russia had still to treat with the Porte. After the rupture of the Congress of Fokshany, in seventeen hundred and seventy-two, the war again broke out. The Russians had been forced to raise the siege of Silistria, but they had surrounded the Grand Vizier in his camp of Shumla, and a single victory might open to them the way to Constantinople. Sultan Abdul Hamid consented to sign the Peace of Kutchuk-Kaïrnadji in seventeen hundred and seventy-four. He undertook to recognize the independence of the Tatars of the Bug, of the Crimea, and of Kuban; to cede Azof on the Don, Kinburn at the mouth of the Dnieper, and all the strong places in the Crimea; to open the Straits of the Bosphorus and the Dardanelles to the merchant ships of Russia; to treat the Russian merchants in the same way as the French, who were then the most favored nation; to grant an amnesty to all the Christian populations engaged in the last insurrection; to allow the Russian ambassadors to interfere in favor of their subjects in the Danubian principalities; to pay a war indemnity of four million five hundred thousand rubles, and to recognize the imperial title of the Russian sovereign. Not only did Russia acquire important territories and numerous strategical points, but it established a sort of protectorate over the Christian subjects of the Sultan, and prepared the way for the annexation of the Crimea, of the Kuban, and of all the northern shore of the Black Sea.

France, indirectly defeated in Poland and Turkey, had lately obtained a great diplomatic success in Sweden. Frederic the Second and Catherine the Second were under a tacit understanding to guarantee in the latter country the maintenance of the oligarchic constitution, which was practically the maintenance of anarchy. This was in order to reserve to themselves a pretext for interference, and even to prepare for a dismemberment, which would have given Finland to Russia, and Swedish Pomerania to Prussia; the rôle of third partitioner, played by Austria in the Polish question, would have been here assigned to Denmark. Gustavus the Third, who had grown up amidst the clamors and intrigues of the Diet, was determined to re-establish the royal power, as being the only hope for the independence of the country. In seventeen hundred and seventy-one, while he was still prince royal, he went to France, visited the philosophers, frequented the fashionable salons, amongst others that of Madame Géoffrin, and received encouragement and promises of help from the French government. The spectacle of the anticipated partition of Poland strengthened him in his patriotic resolutions, and a favorable opportunity seemed offered by the embarrassing situation of both Russia and Prussia. Recalled to Sweden by the death of his father, he prepared his coup-d'état with the utmost secrecy, having previously gained over the army and the nation. On the nineteenth of August, seventeen hundred and seventy-two, he assembled the guard, dismissed the senators, made the people of Stockholm rise in revolt, and imposed on the Diet a constitution of fifty-seven articles, which guaranteed the public liberties, at the same time that it restored to the Crown its essential prerogatives. He then abolished torture and the State inquisition, shut up the "cave of roses," a hole full of reptiles used for "the question," and set on foot useful reforms which placed Sweden, already impregnated with French ideas, in the current of the eighteenth century. The success of this bloodless revolution, which doubled the real power of Sweden, and put it beyond the pale of foreign intrigue, caused great mortification to Frederic the Second and Catherine; but the affairs of Poland deprived them of the power or will to interfere.

PLAGUE AT MOSCOW.—PUGATCHEF.

Catherine the Second, victorious in Poland and in Turkey, found herself face to face with terrible difficulties in her own empire. In seventeen hundred and seventy-one the plague broke out at Moscow, and during the months of July and August the deaths amounted to a thousand a day. The people, wild with fright, and bringing costly offerings and jewels, thronged to the feet of the holy image the Mother of God at Bogoliubovo, and many died of suffocation in the crowd. Archbishop Amvrosi, an enlightened and educated man, sent five men to remove the image. This was the signal for a terrible insurrection. "The archbishop is an infidel," cried the people;

"he would deprive us of our protectress; he is in a conspiracy with the doctors to make us die. It is wrong for the orthodox to suffer injustice from those above them. If they had not smoked up the streets and the hospitals, then surely the plague would have long ago ceased. To the Kreml! to the Kreml! Let us demand of Amvrosi why he forbids us to pray to the Mother of God!" Amvrosi was put to death, and his palace pillaged. It was necessary to use muskets and cannons to disperse the crowd, which was ready to commit new deeds of violence. Catherine in October sent Gregory Orlof with the skilful Dr. Todte to appease the revolt, and to reassure the people. At last the plague ceased, and peace was restored. On his return Orlof was received with a triumphal arch with an inscription: "To the man who freed Moscow from the plague."

The insurrection of Moscow proved in what gross darkness the lower classes of the capital, the domestic serfs, lackeys, small tradesmen, and workingmen then lived. The revolt of Pugatchef shows what elements of disorder were fermenting in the distant provinces of the capital. The peasants, on whom were laid the burden of all the State expenses, all the needs of the proprietors, and all the exactions of the officials, were forever dreaming of impossible changes. In their profound ignorance they were ever ready to follow any impostors, and there were now plenty; false Peters the Third, Ivans the Sixth, and even a Paul the First, who took advantage of these debased classes, prejudiced as they always were against "the rule of women." The raskolniki, made wild and fanatical by many persecutions, remained in their forests or in the scattered villages of the Volga, irreconcilable enemies of this second Roman Empire, stained with the blood of the martyrs. The Cossacks of the Iaïk and the Don, and the Zaporoshtsui of the Dnieper, chafed under the yoke of authority to which they were unused. The tribes of the Volga, Pagan, Mussulman, or converted to Christianity in spite of themselves, awaited only a pretext to recover their lawless liberty, or to reclaim the lands which the Russian colonists had usurped.

How little these ungovernable elements accommodated themselves to the laws of a modern State was seen when, in seventeen hundred and seventy, the Kalmuik-Torgauts, men, women, and children, to the number of about three hundred thousand, with their cattle, their tents, and their chariots, abandoned their encampments. Ravaging everything in their road, they crossed the Volga, and retired to the terrritory of the empire of China. Catherine demanded of the Chinese Emperor their return, but he replied that they had simply come back to their ancient dwelling-place and were now under his protection. When we add to these malcontents the vagabonds of all kinds, the ruined nobles, the disfrocked monks, the military deserters, fugitive serfs, highwaymen, and Volga pirates, we shall see that Russia, especially in its Oriental part, contained all the materials necessary for an immense Jacquerie, like that which the false Dmitri or Stenko Razin had let loose. The Iaïk, whose Cossacks had risen in seventeen hundred and sixty-six, and had been cruelly repressed in seventeen hundred and seventy-one, was destined to furnish the chief to this servile war. Emilian Pugatchef, a Cossack deserter and a raskolnik, who had been already confined as a dangerous character in the prison of Kazan, and had found means to escape into the steppes of the Iaïk, gave himself out as Peter the Third, and asserted that he was saved under the very hands of the executioner. Displaying the banner of Holstein, he proclaimed that he would march to Saint Petersburg to punish his wife and to crown his son. He besieged the small fortress of Iaïtsk with only three hundred men. This in itself was an insignificant affair, but all the troops sent against him passed over to his side and delivered up their chiefs. It was his custom to hang the officers, and cut the hair of the soldiers in the Cossack style. In the villages the nobles were also hung. All who resisted him were punished as rebels, convicted of the crime of high treason. He thus gained possession of many little fortresses on the Steppe. Whilst his intimate friends who knew his origin treated him when alone as a simple Cossack, the people began to receive him with bells, and the priests to present him bread and salt. Some of the Polish Confederates, captives in those regions, organized his artillery. For almost a year he made Kazan and Orenburg tremble, and defeated all the generals sent against him. Everywhere proprietors fled, and the barbarous tribes hastened to his headquarters. The peasants rose against the nobles, the Tatars and Tchuvashi against the Russians: a war of race, a social war, a servile war, was let loose in the basin of the Volga. Moscow, with its one hundred thousand serfs, was agitated : the lower orders, seeing the frightened land-owners pour in from Eastern Russia, began openly to speak of liberty and the extermination of the masters. Catherine the Second charged Alexander Bibikof to check the progress of the scourge. Bibikof, on his arrival at Kazan, was alarmed at the universal demoralization, but he rallied his courage, reassured and armed the nobles, restrained the people, and affected the greatest confidence, while he wrote to his wife, "The evil is great — it is frightful! Alas! it is ugly!" He thoroughly comprehended that all this disorder was not the work of a single man. "Pugatchef," he said, "is only a bugbear worked by the Cossack thieves; it is not Pugatchef that is important, but the general discontent." Although very uncertain of his own troops, he attacked the impostor, defeated him both at Tatishtcheva and at Kargula, dispersed his army and took his guns. Bibikof died in the midst of his victories, but his lieutenants, Michelson, de Collonges, and Galitsuin, gave chase to Pugatchef. Tracked to the Lower Volga, he suddenly ascended the river, threw himself into Kazan, which he pillaged and burned, received a check before its Kreml, and was beaten on the Kazanka. Then he returned down the river, boldly entered Saransk, Samara, and

Tsaritsuin, and, though closely followed by his enemies, had time to hang the imperialists, and to establish new municipalities. During his retreat to the south the people awaited him on the road to Moscow, and, in order not to disappoint them, false Peters the Third and false Pugatchefs sprang up on all sides, and at the head of savage bands put proprietors to death and burned castles. Moscow was nearer revolt than ever. It was time that Pugatchef was arrested. Shut in between the Volga and the Iaïk, by Michelson and the indefatigable Suvorof, he was pinioned and surrendered by his own accomplices, at the very moment when he intended flying into Persia. He was brought to Moscow, so that the people might witness his punishment. There he was quartered in January, seventeen hundred and seventy-five. Many declined to believe in the death of the false Peter the Third, and if the revolt was put down the spirit of revolt existed some time longer.

It was a warning for Catherine the Second, and she remembered it when in seventeen hundred and seventy-five she extinguished the Zaporozh republic. This brave tribe, expelled by Peter the Great and recalled by Anna Ivanovna, no longer recognized their former territory in the Ukraina. Southern Russia, freed from Tatar incursions, was being rapidly colonized; cities were in process of construction everywhere, the boundaries of property were fixed, and the vast herbaceous steppes, through which their ancestors had roamed as freely as the Arabs in the desert, were transformed into cultivated fields with a beautiful black soil. The Zaporoshtsui were much discontented with this transformation; they intended to reclaim their lands, and re-establish the desert; they protected the haïdamaki, who ill-treated the colonists. Potemkin, the creator of New Russia, became weary of these inconvenient neighbors. By order of the Empress he occupied the sétcha and destroyed it. The malcontents fled to the territory of the Sultan; the rest were organized like the Black

Sea Cossacks, and in seventeen hundred and ninety-two the Isle of Phanagoria and the eastern shore of the Sea of Azof were assigned them. Such was the end of the great Cossack power. It no longer existed save in the songs of the kobzarui or mandolin-players.

CHAPTER X.

CATHERINE THE SECOND: GOVERNMENT AND REFORMS.

1762-1796.

The Helpers of Catherine the Second: the Great Legislative Commission (1766-1768).— Administration and Justice: Colonization. — Public Instruction. — Letters and Arts. — The French Philosophers.

THE HELPERS OF CATHERINE THE SECOND: THE GREAT LEGISLATIVE COMMISSION.

CATHERINE THE SECOND surrounded herself with distinguished fellow-workers, some of whom were her lovers. In the early part of her reign, the influence of the Orlofs was predominant: these were Gregory Orlof, the favorite above all others, grand master of the artillery, by whom she had a recognized son, Alexis, created Count Bobrinski; Alexis Orlof, the admiral, who received the name of Tchesmenski after the expedition to the Archipelago, and was involved in the tragic history of the Princess Tarankof; Feodor Orlof, who became procurator-general of the senate; Vladimir Orlof, who was director of the Academy of Sciences at the age of twenty-one. A Russian writer asserts that from seventeen hundred and sixty-two to seventeen hundred and eighty-three they received forty-five thousand serfs and seventeen million rubles in money from the Empress. Later, the favor of the Orlofs was outweighed by that of Potemkin, or Patiomkin, creator of New Russia, organizer of the Crimea, conqueror of the Ottomans in the second war with Turkey, and who, as Prince of the Taurid, displayed his Asiatic luxury in his palace of the same name at Saint Petersburg. During the two years of his influence he received thirty-seven thousand serfs and nine million rubles, and his income in seventeen hundred and eighty-five was calculated at four hundred thousand rubles. At one of his feasts seventy thousand rubles worth of wax candles were burnt. Of all the favorites who, in the latter part of the reign, succeeded each other so rapidly, only one had any real influence over affairs. This was Platon Zubof, whose brother Valerian conducted the war with Persia. In the direction of foreign affairs were distinguished Nikita Panin, and later Bezborodko, Ostermann, Markof, and Vorontsof. Repnin and Sievers in Poland, Budberg at Stockholm, Semen Vorontsof in London, and Dmitri Galitsuin at Paris, made themselves a name in diplomacy. The army was commanded by Alexander Galitsuin, Dolgoruki, Rumiantsof, and Suvorof; the fleet by Greig, Spiridof, and Tchitchagof; Ivan Betski had charge of the fine arts and of benevolent institutions.

From seventeen hundred and sixty-six to seventeen hundred and sixty-eight, Catherine the Second assembled, first at Moscow and afterwards at Saint Petersburg, the commission for the compilation of the new code. This commission was composed of deputies from all the services of the State, from all the orders and all the races of the empire. Besides the delegates from the senate, the synod, and the colleges and the courts of police, the nobles elected a representative for each district, the citizens one for every city, the free colonists one for every province, the soldiers, militia, and other fighting men also one for each province; the Crown peasants, the fixed tribes, whether Christians or not, equally elected one for each province; the deputation of the Cossack armies was fixed by their atamans.

Six hundred and fifty-two deputies assembled at Moscow; officials, nobles, citizens, peasants, Tatars, Kalmuiki, Lapps,

Samoyedui, and many others. Each man was to be furnished with full powers, and with instructions compiled by at least five of the electors. Each received a medal with Catherine's effigy, and the motto, "For the happiness of each and of all, December fourteen, seventeen hundred and sixty-six." They were exempted forever from all corporal punishments, and were declared inviolable during the session. In the "Instructions for the arrangement of the New Code" Catherine the Second, according to her own expression, "pillaged" the philosophers of the West, especially Montesquieu and Beccaria. "It contained," says the prudent Panin, "axioms that would knock a wall down." Catherine the Second assures Voltaire that her "Book of Instructions" was interdicted at Paris. Among the ideas of which she boasted, we meet with the following, which were certainly calculated to enrage Louis the Fifteenth: "The nation is not made for the sovereign, but the sovereign for the nation. Equality consists in the obedience of the citizens to the law alone; liberty is the right to do everything that is not forbidden by law. It is better to spare ten guilty men than to put one innocent man to death. Torture is an admirable means for convicting an innocent but weakly man, and for saving a stout fellow even when he is guilty." Other maxims loudly condemned intolerance, religious persecutions, and cruel punishments.

The assembly nominated many committees, and held more than two hundred sittings. The most vexed questions were openly discussed. Nobles of the Baltic claimed their provincial rights, merchants brought forward municipal organization and all sorts of economical questions, gentlemen proposed to restrain the rights of masters, and to pronounce the pregnant words, "enfranchisement of the peasants." An assembly so numerous, so divided by the interests of classes, and of such various races, was not one, however, that could arrange a new code. It was a work almost impossible in the Russia of that period, which contained within itself so many conflicting forces. The Empress, forced by the Turkish war to break up the assembly, expressed herself satisfied with her experiment. "The Commission for the Code has given me light and knowledge for all the empire. I know now what is necessary, and with what I should occupy myself. It has elaborated all parts of the legislation, and has distributed the affairs under heads. I should have done more had it not been for the war with Turkey, but a unity hitherto unknown in the principles and methods of discussion has been introduced." These States-general of Russia influenced the laws of Catherine the Second, as the French States-general of thirteen hundred and fifty-six, of fourteen hundred and thirteen, or of the sixteenth century, influenced the laws of Charles the Fifth, Charles the Seventh, and the later Valois.

In the course of the discussions the deputy noble Korobin proposed to suppress the rights of property over the serfs, and to leave the masters only the right of superintendence. Protasof, another deputy, then observed that "in that case nothing would remain but to set the peasant free, but that, if this was the intention of the Empress, it was necessary to proceed gradually." The Economical Society, founded, under the auspices of Catherine the Second, by the care of Gregory Orlof and other "patriots," proposed the question for public competition. A paper, dated from Aix-la-Chapelle, pronouncing for emancipation, obtained the prize, but other influences were at work to efface the recollection of this essay from the mind of the Empress. The Russian aristocracy were then little disposed to abdicate their rights, as is shown by the conversations of Princess Dashkof with Diderot, and the correspondence of Dmitri Galitsuin. Catherine confined herself to repressing the most crying abuses. The trial of Daria Saltuidof, convicted of having caused the death of forty of her servants by torture, shows to what a point slavery, which degrades the serf, could demoralize the masters. She was condemned in seventeen hundred and sixty-eight to be publicly pilloried, and to perpetual imprisonment; her memory still lives in the legends of the people. The same reasons which had caused the establishment of serfage in the time of Boris Godunof seemed to operate in favor of its continuance. Catherine the Second, in spite of a few generous impulses, finally aggravated the existing state of things. More than one hundred and fifty thousand Crown peasants were transformed into serfs of nobles, by being distributed among her favorites. In seventeen hundred and sixty-seven an edict forbade peasants to complain of their masters, who were authorized to send them at will to Siberia, or to force them to become recruits. Moreover, Catherine the Second established serfage in Little Russia, where it had hitherto had no legal existence.

ADMINISTRATION AND JUSTICE: COLONIZATION.

The Empress's "Council" deprived the Senate of part of its political importance; but the latter, divided into six departments, had under its jurisdiction all the branches of the public administration. Catherine the Second attacked the custom of exactions and peculations, which was the most inveterate evil of this administration. "We consider it," says a ukas of seventeen hundred and sixty-two, "as our essential and necessary duty to declare to the people, with true bitterness of heart, that we for a long time have heard, and to-day, by manifest deeds, see to what a degree corruption has progressed in our empire, so that there is hardly an office in the government in which that divine action, justice, is not attacked by the infection of this pest. If any one asks for a place, he must pay for it; if a man has to defend himself against calumny, it is with money; if any one wishes falsely to accuse his neighbor, he can by gifts insure the success of his wicked designs. Many judges have transformed into a market the sacred place where they should administer justice in the name of the Almighty, using the position of judge, to which we appointed them, expecting impartiality and disinterestedness, in such a manner as to divert to their own use the revenues accruing, and build up their own houses, and not for the service of God, the Empress, and the State. Our heart trembled when we learned that a registrar of the Government Court of Police at Novgorod found an opportunity, while receiving the oath of allegiance from my subjects, to accept from each a piece of money."

One way of securing the administration of the laws was, perhaps, to diminish the extent of the governments, which placed the seat of justice too far from the people governed. By an edict of seventeen hundred and seventy-five Catherine modified all the territorial divisions of the empire. Instead of fifteen provinces she created fifty governments, each with a population of from three hundred thousand to four hundred thousand souls, and subdivided into districts of twenty thousand to thirty thousand inhabitants. Every province had its governor and its vice-governor; the governor-generals, or namiéstniki, were invested with authority over two or three governments. Thus Livonia, Esthonia, and Kurland had each a governor, while a governor-general had jurisdiction over the three provinces. Administration was definitely separated from justice; each governor was aided by a council of regency for administration and the police, by a chamber of finance for taxes, property, mines, the census, and by a college of provision for hospitals and public charity.

The judicial system increased the profound separation of classes. There were, in each district, district tribunals for gentlemen, civil magistrates for the townspeople, inferior justices for the free colonists and for the Crown peasants. There was nothing for the serfs of the nobles. No text of law positively authorized the repression of the most cruel seigniorial abuses; the sense of two articles of the military code had to be wrested before even the lives of agricultural slaves could be protected. To serve as courts of appeal, a supreme tribunal, a government magistracy, and a superior court of justice were to be found in the principal city of each division of government. All this hierarchy led to a court of final appeal in the senate. In the towns of the government there were for certain criminal causes juries which acted as justices of the peace in civil actions.

The nobility received a sort of provincial organization. In each government there existed an assembly of the nobles, which elected a marshal and other dignitaries; and as Catherine the Second could not revoke the law of Peter the Third, she obliged gentlemen to join the army by depriving those nobles of the right of suffrage in the elections who had not obtained the rank of officers, and also refused them certain prerogatives of their own order.

Special privileges were accorded to the merchants and citizens of the towns; among them were the election of their magistrates, and individual jurisdiction, and a kind of municipal self-government. The merchants were divided into three guilds: to the first belonged men with a capital of not less than ten thousand rubles; to the second, those who had at least one thousand; to the third, those with a property worth more than five hundred rubles. Below this, all the citizens were confounded in the appellation of miéshtchané, or townsmen. In the matter of commerce and trade Catherine renounced the system of protection and surveillance adopted by Peter the Great, except in the case of cereals, the consumption of which she tried to regulate by establishing granaries for surplus stores. She finally suppressed the three colleges of mines, manufactures, and commerce.

To people the uninhabited though fertile lands of the Volga and the Ukraina, Catherine called in foreign colonists; she offered them capital to aid in their settlement, for which no interest was to be asked for the space of ten years, and exempted them from all taxes for thirty years. These colonists were chiefly Germans, the greater part from the Palatinate. Like Frederic the Second, she offered an asylum to the Moravians, and to all persecuted religious sects. In the province of Saratof alone she induced twelve thousand families to take up their abode, and their descendants, now very numerous, still inhabit the country, and preserve unbroken the German language and customs. In the single year of seventeen hundred and seventy-one as many as twenty-six thousand people answered her appeal. The suppression of the hetmanate of Little Russia in seventeen hundred and sixty-two, and the extinction of the sétcha of the Zaporoshtsui, favored colonization. The Empress founded nearly two hundred new towns, many of which, as Ekaterinburg and Ekaterinoslaf, "Glory of Catherine," bore her name. They have not all prospered, but in seventeen hundred and ninety-three Pallas reckoned a population of thirty-three thousand at Saratof.

One reform projected by Peter the First and clumsily pushed forward by Peter the Third was accomplished by Catherine the Second: this was the secularization of the Church property. The number of peasants belonging to the clergy, regular as well as secular, amounted to nearly a million. The monastery of Saint Cyril, on the White Lake, possessed thirty-five thousand; that of Saint Sergius, at Troitsa, one hundred and twenty thousand. The abbots of these monasteries may be compared to the sovereign prelates, to the priest-kings on the banks of the Rhine. Catherine the Second, who was afterwards to protest so loudly against the resumption of Church property during the French Revolution, effected this important change with the greatest quietness. She formed a commission of churchmen and functionaries, who managed to carry out the operation. The property of the Church was placed under the administration of an "economical commission," charged with the collection of the revenues, in the proportion of a ruble and a half for every male peasant. The monasteries, thus converted from proprietors to Crown-pensioners, were indemnified according to their importance, and were divided into three classes. Their surplus revenues were applied to the foundation of ecclesiastical schools, homes for invalids, and hospitals.

Catherine the Second wrote to Voltaire an account of the work of the commission in compiling the code. "I think you will be pleased by this assembly, where the orthodox man is to be found seated between the heretic and the Mussulman, all three listening to the voice of an idolater, and all four consulting how to render their conclusion palatable to all." This was the restoration of religious tolerance in Russia, after the reign of the pious Elisabeth. In the provinces taken from Poland, a natural reaction from the Polish system obtained many converts to orthodoxy; in the latter years of the reign they amounted to one million five hundred thousand souls. Catherine the Second was so far from persecuting the Catholics, that she allowed the Jesuits, notwithstanding the suppression of their order by Pope Clement the Fourteenth, to purchase the right of existence in White Russia. She authorized the Volga Tatars to rebuild their mosques, and thus checked the Mussulman emigration which had been provoked by Elisabeth's severity. The raskolniki were protected, reassured, and freed from the double tax imposed on them by Peter the Great, and the "bureau" of the raskolniki was suppressed.

The population of the empire increased during this reign to forty millions, but it was still far too small to cultivate the vast plains. One great obstacle to the multiplication of inhabitants has always been the want of hygiene, the lack of doctors, the absence of all assistance from science, and the mortality of children, which offsets the fruitfulness of marriages. Catherine the Second did everything that could be done at that period. She encouraged the study of medicine, sent for foreign physicians, founded a "department of the College of Pharmacy" at Moscow, and helped to build manufactories of surgical instruments. In seventeen hundred and sixty-nine, when she was forty years old, she introduced inoculation into Moscow, and vanquished the popular outcry by being herself the first subject. She desired Dimsdale, the Englishman, to inoculate her as well as her son by Gregory Orlof. The senate presented her with twelve gold medals in honor of the occasion, and the hall of the senate-house at Moscow was ornamented with a bas-relief, with the inscription, "She saved others to the danger of herself." "Dr. Dimsdale," says Andreif, "received a fee of ten thousand pounds for the operation, an annual pension of five hundred pounds, and the title of Baron. The little boy, Markof, who furnished the matter, was made an hereditary noble." This was at the time that small-pox carried off Louis the Fifteenth and the children of the King of Spain. "That is very strange," writes Catherine to Voltaire; and again, "More people have been inoculated here in one month than have been inoculated in Vienna in a year." Even the natives of Siberia recognized the benefits of the new invention, but the Mussulmans, the raskolniki, and part of the Russian people energetically held themselves aloof from it.

PUBLIC INSTRUCTION.—LETTERS AND ARTS.—THE FRENCH PHILOSOPHERS.

The Empress displayed the greatest eagerness to instruct the upper and middle classes, if she did not seek to touch the people, properly speaking, the mass of whom could not be penetrated by a culture that was still superficial. "To triumph over the superstitions of ages," were the words she dictated to Betski, "to give a new education, and so to speak a new life to one's people, is a work demanding incredible toil, and of which posterity alone will reap the fruits." From the lack of a national education, "Russia wanted the class of men known in other countries as the third estate." Ivan Betski, one of those truly disinterested friends of humanity who so rarely appear in history, and who had cultivated his natural talents by study in the European universities, thought it necessary that the children should be taught by Russians, as foreigners would fail to understand how much in their pupils belonged to the religion, habits, and manners of the country. The moment had not yet come when Russia could do without foreign teachers. The scheme of national education for children of all classes, presented by Betski, could only partially be realized; secondary schools were founded in the great cities alone. Catherine the Second also interested herself in the instruction of women. At the monastery or institute of Smolna she assembled four hundred and eighty young girls, under the direction of a Frenchwoman, Madame Lafond. "We want them to be neither prudes nor coquettes," she writes to Voltaire. French and other foreign languages and accomplishments were taught there; but the line between the pupils of noble birth and tradesmen's daughters was sharply drawn. A splendid foundation of Catherine's was the "Vospitatelnui Dom," or house of education for foundlings, at Moscow, in seventeen hundred and sixty-three,—a large establishment, which afterwards was the admiration of Napoleon the First, and where nearly forty thousand children in need of assistance, or girl-pupils, were received in Catherine's reign. The serf who married one of these orphans became free.

The influence of French genius over Russian civilization greatly increased during the reign of Catherine the Second. The national poets translated and imitated the French classics of the seventeenth century. The great Russian nobles, the Vorontsofs and the Galitsuins, esteemed it an honor, as did also the French nobility, to correspond with the writers and thinkers of the West. This French influence was beneficial, although it was exercised only upon the upper classes of society, and often stopped at the exterior without modifying very essentially either the character or the manners. It was this that introduced or strengthened in the Russian nobility those ideas of religious tolerance, of moral dignity, of respect for the human body, even in the person of a slave, — those habits of courtesy and politeness, those aspirations after social justice and political liberty, which must, in the long run, perform their work, soften the hardness of the old boyars, prepare for the emancipation of the agricultural classes, and bring about the regeneration of Russia. We shall, however, see the Russian nobility, who had apparently followed the French philosophers into their most audacious deductions, suddenly frightened at the most moderate reforms of seventeen hundred and eighty-nine, and declaring loudly against revolutionary France. We shall find characters in which a slight varnish of Parisian civilization scarcely hides the ancient barbarism, but it was not in vain that Catherine's contemporaries had been fascinated by Montesquieu, by Voltaire, and by the American revolution. The social state of Russia, divided into an aristocracy of proprietors and a people of serfs, prevented the country from advancing with the same rapidity as France, but French ideas certainly did not delay its progress.

Catherine the Second was not less eager than her nobles in seeking the sympathy of French writers; her correspondence with philosophers added not a little to her prestige in the Europe of the eighteenth century, and to her fame with posterity. She attracted Grimm, once a friend of Rousseau, to her service, and he sent her regular letters from Paris on the affairs of France. She affected a gracious familiarity towards the Prince de Ligne, and the French ambassador, Count de Ségur, both men distinguished for wit and literary talents; admitted them into her travelling-carriage during a long journey to the South, and was able to respond to their ingenious flatteries and to their lively sallies. She wished to employ Mercier de la Rivière, and to secure the services of Beccaria, author of the "Treatise on Crimes and Penalties"; she declared herself the "good friend" of Madame Géoffrin, whose Parisian salon was one of the intellectual powers of that epoch. She offered to D'Alembert, who refused it, the superintendence of the education of the Grand Duke Paul, heir to the throne; later, she placed the Swiss Laharpe, celebrated for his republican opinions, with her grandsons Alexander and Konstantin. She thanked Marmontel for sending her his "Belisarius," "a book which deserves to be translated into all languages," caused a translation of it to be made by her friends during a voyage down the Volga, and even undertook the ninth chapter herself. She bought Diderot's library, yet allowed him to enjoy it; subscribed to the "Encyclopædia," which was forbidden to appear in Paris; admired the "Pensées Philosophiques," a book which was condemned by the Parliament to be burned, and the "Lettre sur les Aveugles," which had consigned the philosopher to the Bastile. She sent for the author to come to Saint Petersburg, and entertained him for a month with the most brilliant hospitality. The great sculptor Falconet, the friend of Diderot and the Encyclopædists, was already there, working at the statue of Peter the Great, which he represents as riding a horse in the act of springing, and with the fore feet in the air. His hind feet tread on a serpent of brass, the symbol of envy, and the serpent biting the flowing tail of the horse secures his equilibrium. The whole was mounted on an immense boulder brought from a morass in Karelia eleven versts from Saint Petersburg. This boulder represented emblematically the rude obstacles which Peter the Great had to overcome.

It was with Voltaire, above all, that Catherine kept up a close correspondence, beginning in seventeen hundred and sixty-three, and continuing to the death of the great man in seventeen hundred and seventy-eight. She herself endeavored to keep him informed, not only of her victories, but of her reforms, her efforts at legislation and labors for the colonization of Russia, knowing that the hermit of Ferney had fame in his gift. She gave money to his protégés, the families of Sirven and Calas, victims of the judicial abuses of the eighteenth century; and, after the expedition of Alexis Orlof to the Archipelago, caused him to hope for the resurrection of Greece. In a single year she spent one million of rubles to acquire the pictures and works of art of the most celebrated painters of the Italian and Flemish schools, and endowed the capital of Peter the Great with artistic splendors hitherto unknown.

In spite of her devotion to the arts and letters of the West, Catherine piqued herself on being, above everything, a Russian Empress; and jestingly bade her doctor to bleed her of her last drop of German blood. She has a place of her own in Russian literature of the eighteenth century, having compiled for the use of her grandsons Alexander and Konstantin the "Grandmother's A B C," stories from Russian history, and the "Library of the Grand Dukes Alexander and Konstantin," which had the honor to be printed in Germany. The prefaces to her laws, her correspondence in Russian, French, and German with her ministers, her governors, and friends in France and Germany, prove her literary activity. She also worked for the new-born Russian theatre, and ridiculed hypocrisy, avarice, prejudice against education, the discontent caused by government decrees, the use of French words, the frivolous intrigues of the nobles, and the extravagance of the Russians abroad: in her lyric drama called "Oleg," the first expedition of the Russians against Constantinople is celebrated; in her comedy of *Horé Bogatuir*, or "Misfortune, the Knight," she turns into ridicule her enemy, the adventurous Gustavus the Third; in those of "The Charlatan" and "The Mystified Man" she chastises Cagliostro, who sought for dupes even in Russia; while "The Birthday of Madame Vortchalkina," "O Time," and many others are satires on contemporary manners. In the palace of the Hermitage she had a theatre constructed somewhat after the model of that at Mycenæ, where the plays of the Prince de Ligne, the Count de Ségur, Strogonof, and her own were performed. Most of the pieces which the Empress composed have been collected and published. They were written in French. Against the French Abbé Chappe d'Auteroche, and his voyage to Siberia, she published an amusing pamphlet, called "The Antidote." Finally, she has left in French some curious memoirs about her arrival in Russia and her life as a Grand Duchess.

The Russian Academy, modelled in some degree after the French, was founded in seventeen hundred and eighty-three, on the suggestion of Princess Dashkof, then President of the Academy of Sciences. It was intrusted with the task of "fixing the rules of the orthography, grammar, and prosody of the Russian language, and of encouraging the study of Russian history." It then undertook the publication of a dictionary which appeared from seventeen hundred and eighty-nine to seventeen hundred and ninety-nine. It included in its six volumes forty-three thousand two hundred and fifty-seven words, and was re-edited from eighteen hundred and forty to eighteen hundred and fifty. Indeed, the Russian Academy was so much in fashion that the most illustrious men of letters and the highest ladies of rank — Princess Dashkof, the poets Derzhavin, Fon-Vizin, Kniazhnin, and Count Ivan Shuvalof — insisted on working at the dictionary. Catherine herself compiled "Complementary Notes" for the first volume. In eighteen hundred and thirty-five the minister Uvarof amalgamated the Russian Academy with the Academy of Sciences, under the title of "Second Class."

Catherine made herself the patroness of Russian men of letters. If she imposed the recital of a certain number of lines from the "Telemakhid" of Trediakovski as a penance on her friends of Tsarkoe-Selo, or the Hermitage, she encouraged Fon-Vizin, the comic author, the Russian Molière, who in his comedy of "The Brigadier" derided those whose only source of information was the French romances, and who ridiculed in his *Niédorosl*, or "The Spoilt Child," the indolence and frivolity of the young Russian nobles, the foolish infatuation of their parents, and the strange choice of their preceptors. The principal characters of "The Brigadier" are Ivanushka, who is studying in Paris and hates everything Russian, and a councillor who is the type of an absurd official. Both pieces are found to be faulty when examined critically. The dialogue is not connected; the persons represented are mere caricatures, but they are full of wit and end wholly in the French fashion. The taste for the pleasures of wit was spread by the theatre of Sumarokof, whose plays were often acted by the corps of cadets, at the court and in public places. In many ways it was an imitation of the French theatre. Ablesimof wrote "The Miller," a comedy which was performed twenty-seven times in Moscow and has kept its place on the stage, "The Boaster," "The Originals," "The Fatal Carriage," and attempted an historical drama in "Vadim of Novgorod." Imitations of Voltaire's Henriade were much in vogue. Of these the most popular were the "Russiad," by Kheraskof, an epic poem which celebrated the capture of Kazan, and "Vladimir, or the Conversion of the Russians." But neither had much merit. Bogdanovitch imitated La Fontaine in a light piece of verse called "Dushenka," which treated the antique subject of Psyche. Khemnitser translated the fables of Gellert, and composed others in Russian which are remarkable for the simplicity and natural grace of the style. Khemnitser, like Lessing, looked upon morals as the essential foundation of fables. His works reflect his thoughts and his peculiarities. The prevailing moral is that success is always gained by fearless men, and that a great inheritance is better than a good education. His fables are usually melancholy and affecting in tone. He is the natural predecessor of Kruilof. In lyric poetry Derzhavin holds the principal place. The school of Lomonosof was falling into disrepute, owing to its pompous style. Derzhavin's distinguishing characteristics are indicated by himself when he says that he was the first to praise the merits of Catherine in a pleasing style, to speak of God with simplicity, and to tell truth to the Tsar with a smile. His poems usually celebrate his own time, but he is superficial in his brilliancy, and hence unsatisfactory. He recognizes the dignity of the true man, and exalts a pure conscience and virtue. Like Horace and Anakreon, he is the poet of liberty, peace, and love. He brought the Russian language to a high state of perfection. His patriotic odes, "The Capture of Ismail," "The Great Noble," "The Cascade," "My Idol," "To Fortune," are remarkable for a certain sublimity mingled with a shade of satire. The second part of "Felitsa" is a lively attack on high society, full of malicious allusions to different people of the Court; and though it might have cost him dear in preceding reigns, the poem gained him a gold snuff-box and a rich gift from the Empress, who took care to send copies of it to all who were satirized, underlining the passages applied to them. Derzhavin's religious odes are inferior to those of Lomonosof. Some are philosophical, and directed against the French Encyclopædists. The best is the one entitled "On the Death of Prince Meshtcherski." Perhaps the most famous is the "Ode to God," which the Emperor of China had printed in letters of gold and hung up in a temple. Derzhavin, having made a thorough study of German poetry, was enabled to use a greater variety of metres than his predecessors. He had considerable merit as a versifier; his faults were the faults of his day, — turgidity, inequality, and inconsistency. Beautiful and sublime thoughts are often spoiled by his extravagant and inflated rhetoric. Although a poet, Derzhavin was Minister of Justice.

The ardent and laborious Novikof, in order that the new culture might penetrate to the silent masses concerned with the smaller trades, and also to the people, took up the "Moscow Gazette," secured for it four thousand subscribers (an enormous number for the time), perfected the Russian typography, created new libraries, and published a series of reviews and magazines for home readings for the young and for workmen, who were almost destitute of literature. Among these were "The Pilgrim's Staff," "The Painter," "The Purse,"

"The Ancient Library of Russia," "The Courier of Russian Antiquities," "The Morning Aurora," "The Evening Aurora," the "Edition of Moscow," and "The Worker's Rest." He founded several philanthropical societies, and that of the Friends of Instruction, and took in hand the cause of national education. He was sent to Moscow, and made director of the precious archives of the foreign department.

The aged Müller edited the first "National History of Russia," by Tatishtchef; and the "Compendium of Russian History," by Mankief. Pallas of Berlin, who was made president of the Academy of Sciences at only thirty years of age, was commanded to make an observation of the passage of Venus over the sun. He then made his celebrated travels in the Crimea, in Siberia, and on the frontiers of China, and was given by the Empress an estate in the Taurid. Golikof, pardoned by Catherine on the occasion of the inauguration of Falconet's bronze, vowed at the feet of Peter's statue to raise an historical monument to the glory of the Russian hero, and published in twelve volumes "The Actions of Peter the Great." Prince Shtcherbatof wrote the "History of Russia from the Earliest Times." He was well educated, careful, and diligent, but not a man of much talent or depth. His work, however, holds an honorable place in Russian historical literature. General Boltin, a man of remarkable gifts, found great fault with the recent history of Old and New Russia, written by the French Leclerc in seventeen hundred and eighty-four, but he also severely criticised the work of Prince Shtcherbatof, which led to a great dispute between them. Mussin-Pushkin discovered the unique manuscript of the "Song of Igor." Khrapovitski, Catherine's confidential secretary, Poroshin, one of the tutors of the Grand Duke Paul; Nikita Panin, the diplomatist, the great nobles, Semen and Alexander Vorontsof, their sister Catherine Dashkof, and the old soldier Bolotof, collected or prepared valuable memoirs on the reigns of Elisabeth and Catherine. The historian Karamzin, and the dramatic poet Ozerof, who glorified the following reigns, were as yet only boys.

CHAPTER XI.

CATHERINE THE SECOND: LAST YEARS.

1780 – 1796.

FRANCO-RUSSIAN MEDIATION AT TESCHEN (1779).—ARMED NEUTRALITY (1780).—REUNION OF THE CRIMEA (1783).—SECOND WAR WITH TURKEY (1787–1792) AND WAR WITH SWEDEN (1788–1790).—SECOND PARTITION OF POLAND: DIET OF GRODNO.—THIRD PARTITION: KOSCIUSZKO.—CATHERINE THE SECOND AND THE FRENCH REVOLUTION.—WAR WITH PERSIA.

FRANCO-RUSSIAN MEDIATION AT TESCHEN.—ARMED NEUTRALITY.—REUNION OF THE CRIMEA.

THE second part of the reign of Catherine the Second is characterized by the abandonment of the "System of the North," that is, of the English and Prussian alliance, and by a marked reconciliation, first with Austria, and then with France. After the death of Nikita Panin, who had been especially influential in foreign affairs, Count Alexander Bezborodko was advanced to the head of the diplomatic service. Bezborodko was the son of a Little Russian official, and was early distinguished for his rare endowments and his extraordinary memory, which attracted the attention of Field-Marshal Rumiantsof, who introduced him to the Empress. He took an important part in the treaty of Kaïradji, and received the office of Catherine's first secretary. He soon gained her entire confidence by his eloquence and brilliancy, and assisted her in the composition of many important ordinances. In seventeen hundred and eighty he presented a memorial on foreign relations, and was immediately made a member of that

College of which he soon became the head. About this same time the influence of Potemkin became all-powerful. The French ambassadors, the Marquis de Juigné, Bourée de Corberon, the Marquis de Vérac, and above all the Comte de Ségur, who represented France from seventeen hundred and eighty-five until seventeen hundred and eighty-nine, were again taken into favor in Russia.

In seventeen hundred and seventy-seven, Maximilian-Joseph, the Elector of Bavaria, being dead, his succession occasioned a conflict between the house of Austria and Frederic the Second. In order to stop this war, which had already begun in Bohemia, the Courts of France and Russia agreed to offer their mediation, and in seventeen hundred and seventy-nine assembled a Congress at Teschen, in which Louis the Sixteenth was represented by M. Breteuil, and Catherine the Second by Prince Repnin. Peace was signed on the tenth of May. Bavaria passed to the Elector Palatine, and Austria acquired only some districts upon the Danube, the Inn, and the Salza.

In seventeen hundred and eighty, during the American War, the Empress, moved to indignation by the wrongs committed by the English Admiralty against foreign merchantmen, joined with Sweden, Denmark, Prussia, Austria, and Portugal to proclaim an armed neutrality. The celebrated act embodied the principles of a new maritime law, agreeing with the French code of seventeen hundred and seventy-eight. It was settled that neutral ships could freely navigate the coasts of the nations which were at war; that the goods belonging to the subjects of the belligerent powers should be safe in neutral vessels, except in the case of contraband merchandise; that "contraband goods" included only arms and munition; that a port should be considered in a state of blockade only when the blockade was effectual, — that is, when the vessels attacking it should be so near as to render it dangerous to pass out; and lastly that these principles should serve as a rule in trials and judgments on the legality of captures.

These principles were opposed at all points to those which the English Admiralty wished to see prevail. The latter held the theory that the blockade exists from the moment that it is declared by an act of the Admiralty, and considered as contraband even grain, and all that could be, however indirectly, of use to the belligerents. France, which had at first laid down these principles, and to which the armed neutrality brought a moral support in its struggle with Great Britain, adhered to this declaration. Its allies, Spain and the Two Sicilies, followed the example. Holland even began a war with England to maintain the rights of the neutral powers.

The Crimea had been declared independent by the treaty of Kaïrnadji; and since seventeen hundred and seventy-four anarchy had been the normal state of the peninsula. The Sultan, deprived by this treaty of his temporal sovereignty, continued, as successor of the Khalifs, to claim the religious supremacy. The Tatar nobles, abandoned to themselves, were divided into two factions, the Russian party and the Turkish party, which in turn made and then deposed a Khan of the Crimea. Nearly thirty-five thousand Christians, Greeks, Armenians, and Catholics, disturbed by these civil discords, quitted the ravine of Tchufut-Kalé and the wonder-working sanctuary of the Assumption, which was dug out of the hard rock, and emigrated in a body to the territory of Russia. In seventeen hundred and seventy-five the Khan Sahib-Girei, who was devoted to Russia, was overthrown and replaced by Devlet-Girei. He in his turn was dethroned by Catherine, and Shahin-Girei, whom Catherine made a captain of the Preobrazhenski regiment, reigned in his stead, but, by his attempts at European reforms, caused a general revolt. Shahin-Girei's own brothers put themselves at the head of the revolt, and he was obliged to take refuge at Taganrog. Russia interfered; it proclaimed the union of the empire and the peninsula, which had been since the thirteenth century the home of banditti, and whose ravines had so often sent forth

Tatar squadrons to bring fire and flame to Moscow. Thus Catherine finished the work of the conqueror of Kazan, of Astrakhan, and of Siberia, by the extinction of the last kingdom that recalled the Mongol yoke.

The two military States which formerly disputed the steppes of the South, the Tatar khanate and the equally warlike republic of the Zaporoshtsui, succumbed almost at the same time. In the face of the advent of civilization these old enemies were alike condemned to total ruin. Representatives of the ancient anarchy, children of the desert and the steppe, knights of pillage and of prey, they constituted a dangerous anachronism and an intolerable anomaly on the frontier of a prosperous Russia. The Porte protested against the annexation of the Crimea, and threatened a rupture; but France, which had formerly excited the war, tried this time to smooth matters. Catherine the Second recognized the good offices of the ambassador Saint-Priest, and addressed her thanks to Louis the Sixteenth. The Sultan acknowledged the cession of the Crimea and of the Kuban by the Treaty of Constantinople in seventeen hundred and eighty-three. Catherine gave great rewards to those who had had a share in bringing about this treaty. Potemkin was made general field-marshal and president of the college of war, and received a present of one hundred thousand rubles. Bezborodko received the order of Saint Andrew and a gift of three thousand serfs and forty thousand rubles. And the Austrian internuncio was presented with twenty thousand rubles and other valuable gifts.

In seventeen hundred and eighty-four the Grand Duke Paul and his wife, under the names of the Count and Countess du Nord, made a tour in the West, and received a brilliant reception in Paris. In seventeen hundred and eighty-seven the Comte de Ségur, taking advantage of the good terms on which he stood with Potemkin, and the latter's desire to hasten the development of Odessa, by trading with the French ports on the Mediterranean, concluded a treaty of commerce, an important negotiation in which all his predecessors had hitherto failed.

SECOND WAR WITH TURKEY AND WAR WITH SWEDEN.

All this time Russia maintained a close alliance with Joseph the Second, whom Catherine had gained over to her ambitious projects in the East. The Cabinet of Saint Petersburg proposed to that of Vienna a plan for the dismemberment of Turkey. "There ought to exist between the Russian, Austrian, and Turkish monarchies an intermediate State, forever independent of each, which, under the name of Dacia, should comprehend Moldavia, Valakhia, and Bessarabia, and have a sovereign who should belong to the Greek Church. Russia is to acquire Otchakof and the seaboard between the Bug and the Dnieper, besides one or two isles in the Archipelago. Austria is to annex the Turkish provinces on its frontiers. If the war is crowned with such success that the Turks are expelled from Constantinople, the Greek Empire is to be reestablished in complete independence, and the throne is to be filled by the grandson of the Empress, the Grand Duke Konstantin Pavlovitch, who is to renounce all claims to the throne of Russia, so that the two kingdoms may never be united under the same sceptre." Joseph the Second accepted these propositions, but further stipulated that besides Servia, Bosnia, and the Herzegovina, the Slav provinces of the Turkish Empire, he should have the Venetian possessions in Dalmatia. Venice was to receive in exchange the Morea, Candia, and Cyprus. England, France, and Spain might share the spoils of Turkey. Such was the celebrated scheme of partition, known under the name of the "Greek project," which would have fulfilled all the wishes of Voltaire, who had died five years previously.

The attitude of Russia became each day more threatening

to the Porte. The second son of Paul the First bore the significant name of Konstantin, and had been given a Greek nurse. The Taurid, annexed by Catherine the Second, who had alleged the security of the empire as the reason of her act, was becoming, in the hands of Potemkin, a menace to the Turks. Already Kherson had a formidable arsenal; Sevastopol was being built; there was a Russian fleet on the Black Sea, and in two days it might cast anchor under the walls of the Seraglio. Catherine's agents continued to agitate in the Rumanian, Slav, and Greek provinces, and even in Egypt; she was preparing to incorporate the Caucasus, and had taken the Tsar of Georgia under her protection. The triumphal journey made by the Empress in seventeen hundred and eighty-seven to the governments of the South and the newly conquered provinces; her interviews with the King of Poland and Joseph the Second; the military equipment arrayed by Potemkin, prince of the Taurid; the arches with the famous Greek inscription, "The Way to Byzantium," still further alarmed and irritated the Porte. France, which too well knew the weakness of its former ally, tried to use a restraining influence; but England, and even Prussia, acted in the contrary way, in order to spite Russia. Sweden, which the French ambassador also tried to moderate, promised to aid the Sublime Porte.

On the twenty-sixth of July, seventeen hundred and eighty-seven, Bulgakof, the Russian envoy, received the ultimatum of Turkey. It demanded the extradition of Maurokordato, hospodar of Moldavia, who had taken refuge in Russia; the recall of the Russian consuls of Iassy, Bukarest, and Alexandria, on the ground that they were disturbing the peace; the abandonment of the protectorate over Irakli the Second, Tsar of Georgia, the vassal of the Sultan; the right of the Turks to inspect all Russian vessels navigating the Straits; and the admission of Turkish consuls or commissaries into the ports of the Russian territory. Bulgakof refused to agree to these conditions.

He was then confined in the Seven Towers, and on the sixteenth of August the Porte declared war.

Russia was taken by surprise. Potemkin had not finished his preparations, and the fleet at Sevastopol had suffered severely from a recent tempest. "The child of fortune began to despair when he saw that he was beginning to be unfortunate." His letters to Catherine show how deeply he was discouraged; and he even spoke of evacuating the Crimea. The Empress shows in her replies a masculine and dauntless soul; she managed to prove to her favorite that the evacuation of the Peninsula would be the certain ruin of the great port of Sevastopol and the infant fleet which had been created at such cost. Without waiting for the enemy, it was necessary to assume the offensive, and march on Otchakof or Bender. "I implore you to take courage and reflect," she writes; "the brave soul can repair even a disaster."

But Catherine had more than one enemy to cope with. While Turkey menaced her on the south, Prussia was scheming to force Poland to cede Dantzig and Thorn, and to oblige the two other co-partitioners to give up Gallicia. Finally Gustavus the Third declared his designs, abruptly laid claim to South Finland, demanded that he should be allowed to mediate between Russia and Turkey, and, without awaiting a reply to his ultimatum, laid siege to Nyslot and Frederikshamn. If he had acted promptly, instead of wasting the ardor of his troops against the fortresses, he might have conquered Livonia, then defended by only two regiments, or surprised Saint Petersburg, which was deprived of its troops. Although the roar of the Swedish cannon could be heard in the Winter Palace, Catherine showed the courage that she enjoined on Potemkin. Nevertheless, horses were kept in readiness to transport the Court to Moscow if worse came to worst. She refused to desert her capital, and assembled in a few days twelve thousand men for its defence. She sent to Potemkin for re-inforcements which he refused to grant, saying that he himself needed them more, and that the Swedish war was an old woman's war, which required only a few troops. The Swedish fleet was arrested on its way by the indecisive battle of Hogland, which took place July seventeen, seventeen hundred and eighty-eight. The Russian fleet suffered more severely than the Swedish; but the Swedish ammunition gave out, and had the battle been renewed the following day, it would have been completely disastrous to the Swedes. The Russians lost their able commander, Admiral Greig, who had served with such honor in the naval engagement with the Turks. A revolt broke out even in the camp of the Swedish king, who was accused by his officers of violating his own constitution by declaring war without consulting the senate. Gustavus the Third was obliged to return to Stockholm, where he punished the conspirators, and by a new coup-d'état obliged the assembly to give to the constitution a still more monarchical character. A diversion of the Danes in Sweden forbade his assuming the offensive, but in seventeen hundred and eighty-nine he got rid of them through the threatened intervention of England and Prussia, and took up arms against Russia; his fleet, however, suffered considerable loss. Though he gained the naval battle of Svenska-Sund, where he captured thirty vessels, six hundred cannon, and six thousand men, on the ninth of July, seventeen hundred and ninety, he found himself unable to pursue his advantage, which was compromised by a second battle on the same seas. The affairs of France gave another direction to the ideas of this strange prince. He hastened to sign the Peace of Verelä, on the basis of statu quo ante bellum, and passed from open hostilities to propositions of an alliance with Russia against the Revolution.

In the South, Catherine had ready, in seventeen hundred and eighty-eight, an army of eighteen thousand men to protect the Caucasus, eighty thousand under Potemkin to capture Otchakof and to defend the Crimea, and thirty-seven thousand under Rumiantsof to operate on the Dniester and in Moldavia; while two hundred thousand Austrians under Joseph the Second, who had declared war against Abdul-Hamid on the ninth of February, threatened the line of the Danube and the Save. The Emperor was unfortunate in this war. He was forced to fall back beyond the Save. In the fall, feeling the growing discontent of Hungary, where the people had been irritated by his religious innovations and the nobles by encroachments on their privileges, he resigned his command to the aged Laudon. Two little fortresses were captured, but the main army before Belgrad operated with such stupidity that the Grand Vizier penetrated into Hungary as far as Temesvar, where the Emperor met them with forty thousand men and was defeated. The Austrian left wing, amounting to eighteen thousand men under the Prince of Koburg, being joined by thirteen thousand Russians under Soltuikof, had better success, and on the seventeenth of September captured Khotin, the key of Moldavia. During this time Suvorof defended Kinburn against superior forces, and was wounded in a sortie. Potemkin, with his large army, was wasting his time and opportunity, instead of attacking Otchakof. Had he followed Suvorof's advice or appointed him to lead the Russians, this important place could easily have been taken in the spring. But Potemkin saw fit to despise the advice of others. A pasha came to the assistance of the city with half the Turkish fleet; but in a naval battle with the Russians, who were commanded by the "so-called" Prince of Nassau-Siegen and Rear-Admiral John Paul Jones, he was defeated, with a loss of three thousand five hundred men. In trying to escape to his fleet in the Black Sea his remaining vessels were almost annihilated by a battery placed by Suvorof at Kinburn. While the Russian fleet was thus victorious, Potemkin began his work of beleaguering the city, threw up a few redoubts at a considerable distance from the walls, and waited for the Turks to be starved out; but the Russians suffered far more severely. The summer and the fall had passed, and the bitter winter was at hand. There was no firewood, and the soldiers were scantily clad. On the sixteenth of December there was only bread enough for one day. Potemkin, therefore, brought to a decision by the necessity of the situation, commanded an assault to be made. On the seventeenth, the morning of Saint Nicholas's day, the attack was begun. In order to give the men animation, they were furnished with brandy seasoned with Spanish pepper. Four columns under Prince Repnin stormed the west side of the great intrenchment, two attacked the east side and the city itself. The fearful cross-fire of the enemy, though it nearly destroyed one column of two thousand men, did not dismay the desperate Russians. In a few hours, after a fearful struggle, they mastered the city, making an entrance, some by ladders, some by breaches in the walls, some by crossing the frozen river and clambering over the lower fortifications on that side. The loss of the Turks was eight thousand, and the Russians lost even more. Among them were one hundred and seventy officers. In the massacre that followed, men and women were butchered with the most horrible cruelty. The treasure captured was enormous, gold, silver, and precious stones. Lieutenant Bauer undertook to carry the news of the victory to the Empress, and accomplished the distance, more than two thousand versts, in the short space of nine days. Potemkin was rewarded with the great band of the Order of George, and a sword set with diamonds and bearing the inscription, "For Bravery." But according to the common belief he was distinguished rather for the opposite quality. During this campaign the Russians lost sixty thousand men, while the Austrians suffered still more severely. Catherine the Second, who had been in previous years accustomed to see French volunteers in the enemy's camp, now had the opportunity to applaud the prowess of the Baron de Damas and Count de Bombelles, who fought under her own standard.

In seventeen hundred and eighty-nine Selim the Third, a man of great character, spirit, and knowledge, became Sultan at Constantinople, and Potemkin's intrigues finally succeeded in getting Count Rumiantsof recalled. The first action of this campaign took place on the twenty-seventh of April, and resulted in a victory for the Russians. On the thirty-first of July the Turks, thirty thousand strong, endeavored to attack the Prince of Koburg. Suvorof, with wonderful rapidity, marched with seven thousand of his troops through narrow passes over rough mountains, and in thirty-six hours joined his men with those of the Prince, who was at Fokshani, thirty-six miles away. The Turks lost ten cannon, sixteen flags, and their whole camp. Six weeks later the Austrians were again threatened by an overwhelming Turkish force amounting to one hundred thousand men. Again Suvorof saved the Prince of Koburg. At the battle of the Ruimnik, near Martinestie, on September twenty-second, the victory was won by twenty-five thousand Christians. The Grand Vizier, Kutchuk-Hassan, did not long survive this defeat. Suvorof earned by this victory the surname of Ruimnikski, and was made a count of the Roman and Russian empires, and the Prince of Koburg was appointed field-marshal. Each of the generals received also a sword adorned with precious stones valued at sixty thousand rubles. On the west Laudon took Belgrad in October, and conquered Servia; while on the east Potemkin, on the sixteenth of November, successfully besieged Bender and subdued Bessarabia. Potemkin was again rewarded by the Empress. She presented him with one hundred thousand rubles in gold, and a laurel wreath of emeralds and diamonds worth one hundred and fifty thousand rubles.

Freed from the war with Sweden, Catherine the Second carried on hostilities with the Turks with greater vigor in seventeen hundred and ninety. Ismail, on the northern side of the Danube, was formidable from its position, and was defended besides by forty thousand men. Kutuzof had abandoned all hope of taking it, and Potemkin entreated the impetuous Suvorof to be prudent. Suvorof, however, carried it by assault, with a loss of ten thousand men on the Russian and thirty thousand on the Turkish side. "Never," he writes to Potemkin, "was a fortress stronger than Ismail, and never was a defence more desperate! But Ismail is taken." His exploits were sung by Derzhavin.

In seventeen hundred and ninety Joseph the Second died; and his successor, Leopold the Second, signed a peace at Sistova, in August, seventeen hundred and ninety-one, which gave him only the old town of Orsova and the territory of the Unna. Catherine still continued the war for some months. The fall of Akkerman and Kilia made her mistress of the mouths of the Danube. Repnin, with forty thousand men, defeated the Grand Vizier with one hundred thousand at Matchin, while Ushakof dispersed the Turkish fleet and surrounded Varna, so as to cut off the Grand Vizier's communications with Constantinople, and the Sultan, in alarm, implored peace; and, as Catherine's attention was claimed by the affairs of France and Poland, she was not disinclined. By the separate Peace of Iassy, which was signed in January, seventeen hundred and ninety-two, she retained only Otchakof and the seaboard between the Bug and the Dniester, and stipulated for guarantees in favor of the Danubian Principalities. This war was more severe than the preceding one had been, and the success more disputed. The Turks, thinking themselves on the eve of being driven into Asia, managed to make a better fight than in the struggle of seventeen hundred and sixty-seven.

SECOND PARTITION OF POLAND: DIET OF GRODNO. — THIRD PARTITION: KOSCIUSZKO.

The years between seventeen hundred and seventy-three and seventeen hundred and ninety-one had been, for Poland, years of valiant efforts and needful reforms. Tyzenhaus had founded a school of medicine in Warsaw, the old universities of Vilna and Cracow had been reorganized, and a number of secondary schools created, for which the French philosopher Condillac had compiled a manual of logic. Stanislas Poniatovski, the correspondent of Voltaire, the friend, the "dear son" of Madame Géoffrin, had induced French and Italian artists to visit the country. National historians and poets adorned with their talents the last years of independence. It was a real Polish renaissance, under the salutary influence of the universal French genius. "Progress was rapid," says Lélével; "in a few years no more was seen of those sombre superstitious practices, of that hideous bigotry, which had stained with blood the piety of the faithful; charlatanism could no longer seduce them; they spoke with a smile of the ancient faith in sorcery; the phenomena of nature were explained in a reasonable way; hatred gave place to fraternity among the worshippers at different shrines." The characters of the people, degraded for centuries by a fatal education, became elevated by the rational instruction given them at the new schools. A generation of men grew up strangers to the fanaticism and corruption of the preceding age, possessed with a passion for liberty and the country, whose crowning glory they were to be. To give an idea of the work accomplished, we have only to compare the Zamoïskis, the Kosciuszkos, the Niemtsevitches, and the Dombrovskis with the men of the first partition. Poland wished to live, and made a last effort for its regeneration.

It was necessary first to reform the hateful and anarchic constitution, which had been perfidiously guaranteed by the foreign powers, and had made Poland the laughing-stock and prey of its enemies. In seventeen hundred and eighty-eight the Diet of Warsaw established a committee for this purpose, raised the number of the army to sixty thousand men, and imposed new taxes. Circumstances seemed favorable to the boldest measures; if France, occupied with its revolution, could not come to the aid of Poland, England appeared openly hostile to Russia; Turkey and Sweden declared war against Catherine, while Prussia was seeking the friendship of the Poles, and had persuaded Poniatovski to despise the Russian guarantee, and negotiated a treaty of alliance offensive and defensive. The Diet of seventeen hundred and ninety-one was formed into a confederation, and, deciding this time by a majority, undertook the reform of the constitution. It declared the throne hereditary, and nominated the house of Saxony heirs to Poniatovski; it abolished the liberum veto, which was legal anarchy and organized venality; it shared the legislative power between the king, the senate, and the Chamber of Nuncios; it centred the executive power in the king, assisted by six ministers, responsible to the Chambers, and invested him with the command of the armies and the appointment of the officials. The towns obtained the right of electing their judges, and of sending deputies to the Diet. None dared touch the rights of nobles over their peasants, for the nobles were then the fighting part of the nation, the "legal country"; and it was owing, in fact, to their patriotism that the revolution was accomplished. All that the Diet could do was to sanction beforehand individual compacts made between the owners and their serfs, to the advantage of the latter. Such was the memorable constitution of the third of May, seventeen hundred and ninety-one. A similar transformation which took place in Sweden at the royal coup-d'état of seventeen hundred and seventy-two had saved the monarchy of the Vasas from dismemberment, — would the parliamentary coup-d'état of seventeen hundred ninety-one save Poland? Would the Northern courts, which thought it a crime on the part of the French liberals to weaken, by the constitution of the same year, the powers of the Bourbon kings, permit the Polish patriots to restore to their sovereign the essential prerogatives of royalty, the force necessary to subdue anarchy within, and cause the nation to be respected without?

Catherine the Second feared to protest as long as she had

the Turkish war on her hands; but when the Peace of Iassy was signed, she received at Saint Petersburg a deputation of Polish malcontents, who were disposed to cling to the liberum veto, and were alarmed at the promises made to the peasants. Amongst these unworthy citizens we may remark Felix Pototski, the hetman Branitski, Rzhevutski, and the two brothers Kazakovski. Catherine the Second authorized them to form the Confederation of Targovitsa. In her manifesto of the eighteenth of May, seventeen hundred and ninety-two, she reminded men that Russia had guaranteed the Polish constitution, and signalized the reformers of the third of May as accomplices of the Jacobins. Enlightened Russians were indignant at the perfidious language used by their ministers. Semen Vorontsof, ambassador in London, writes, " The manifesto had no right to enter into ridiculous eulogies on the ancient form of government, under which the Republic has flourished and prospered for so many centuries. That has an air of stupidity, if it is said in good faith, or of insulting contempt, if they believe, like the rest of the world, that it is the most absurd and detestable of all governments." The epithet " Jacobin " was, besides, singularly inapplicable to the Poles, who wished to strengthen the royal power.

At the request of the Confederates of Targovitsa, eighty thousand Russians and twenty thousand Cossacks entered the Ukraina. Poniatovski turned to Prussia, and recalled the promises of help which had been given. Frederic William the Second replied that he had not been consulted about the change of the constitution, and that he considered himself absolved from all engagements. He was already arranging with Russia a second treaty of partition, from which Austria was to be excluded. Austria would have to content itself with any provinces it might wrest from revolutionary France. Russia likewise promised to help it to acquire Bavaria, in exchange for the Low Countries. The Poles, deserted by all, tried in vain to resist the Russian invasion. Their army of

Lithuania retreated without fighting, while the Polish army, properly so-called, gave battle at Ziélentsé, under Prince Iosiph Poniatovski; and at Dubienka, on the Bug, under Thaddeus Kosciuzko, or Kostsiushko. Then King Stanislas pronounced himself ready to accede to the Confederation of Targovitsa, thus disavowing his glorious work of the third of May. The reformers Ignati Pototski, Kolontaï, and Malakhovski had to withdraw, and their places in the council of the king were taken by Confederates of Targovitsa, who abolished the constitution. The liberum veto was re-established.

The Polish patriots, remaining in ignorance of the treaty of partition, were unconscious of half their misfortunes. The King of Prussia in his turn crossed the western frontier, announcing in his manifesto that the troubles of Poland compromised the safety of his own States, that Dantzig had sent corn to the French revolutionaries, and that Great Poland was infested by Jacobin clubs, whose intrigues were rendered doubly dangerous by the continuation of the war with France. The King of Prussia affected to see Jacobins whenever it was his interest to find them. The share which each of the powers should have was marked out in advance. Russia was to seize the eastern provinces with a population of three millions, as far as a line drawn from the eastern frontier of Kurland, which, passing Pinsk, ended in Gallicia, and included Borisof, Minsk, Slutsk, Volhynia, Podolia, and Little Russia. Prussia would take the long-coveted cities of Thorn and Dantzig, as well as Great Poland, Posnania, Gniezen, Kalish, and Tchenstokhovo. If Russia still only annexed Russian or Lithuanian territory, Prussia for the second time cut Poland to the quick, and another million and a half of Slavs passed under the yoke of the Germans.

It was not enough to despoil Poland, now reduced to a territory less extensive than that which was now taken possession of by Russia; it was necessary that it should consent to the spoliation, — that it should legalize the partition. A diet was convoked at Grodno, under the pressure of the Russian bayonets. This same pressure, enforced by pecuniary corruption, had been exercised in the elections, and the King was in some sense dragged to Grodno to preside over the ruin of his country. Sivers, Catherine's ambassador, displayed all the resources of an unscrupulous diplomacy which had seduction, intimidation, and violence at its service. In spite of the support of bought deputies and Targovitsan traitors, he gained nothing for a long time. At last the Diet, in the deceitful hope of dividing its enemies, consented that the treaty of cession to Russia should be ratified, but showed itself more stubborn with regard to Prussia. Sivers was forced to surround the Hall of Session by two battalions of grenadiers, point four pieces of cannon, and install General Rautenfels in a chair beside the King. Twenty days passed without his being able to extract a word of assent from the defenceless assembly. The Poles hated the Prussians above everything. Catherine might have delivered Great Poland from a hated yoke, and united all the kingdom under her authority, which would have been almost gratefully accepted. Like Semen Vorontsof, Sivers felt the enormous fault that was committed by aggrandizing Prussia at the expense of a Slav country. Unhappily his instructions were positive. In order to triumph over this stubbornness he had four deputies carried off by his dragoons, and closely blockaded the assembly in the hall of deliberations. The day of September twenty-third, seventeen hundred and ninety-three, and the following night, were occupied by a "silent session," while the King sat on his throne, and the deputies on their benches, gloomy and dumb. At three in the morning Rautenfels left to fetch his grenadiers; then the Marshal of the Diet, Bielinski, put the question. Ankić-vitch proposed to the nuncios a compromise which would give satisfaction to Prussia, while leaving to a "more happy posterity" the task of raising up the country. Bielinski asked three times, without taking breath, if the Diet authorized the delegate to sign the treaty. No one replied; then a voice was heard declaring the silence to be equivalent to consent. It was four o'clock in the morning, — the nuncios left the hall in profound grief, with streaming eyes.

On the sixteenth of October the Diet concluded with Russia a treaty of alliance, or rather a compact of slavery, by which Catherine the Second guaranteed "the liberty of the republic"; that is, all the abuses of the old constitution. The Polish troops who were encamped on the provinces ceded to the Empress received orders to swear allegiance to her; the army belonging to the republic was to be reduced to only fifteen thousand men.

By its fanaticism and electoral corruption Poland had merited its misfortunes in seventeen hundred and seventy-two; it did not merit those of seventeen ninety-three. History will not forget the generous efforts of the Tchartoruiski, of the greater part of the nobility, and of the patriotic "third estate," for the reform of the country.

The citizens of the large towns, inspired by French ideas, were indignant at this new attempt against their country. The army, still twenty-five thousand men strong, had received with fury the order to disband. Part of the noblemen shared these sentiments, while the others, through fear of new taxes or social reforms, resigned themselves to foreign rule. The country proper remained apathetic and indifferent. Poland was cruelly expiating the harsh servitude that her pospolit, in the full current of eighteenth-century civilization, had allowed to weigh on the rural classes. George Forster writes in seventeen hundred and ninety-one, "The Polish nobles alone in Europe have pushed ignorance and barbarism so far that they have almost extinguished in their serfs the last lingering sparks of thought." This is one of the extenuating circumstances invoked by Russian or German historians to excuse the dismemberment; the lot of the peasants was not to grow worse under Russian domination, and was to improve under German rule.

The Polish patriots had, however, placed all their hopes on Thaddeus Kosciuszko, the hero of Dubienka. He was born in seventeen hundred and fifty-two, and admitted in seventeen hundred and sixty-four to the military school, founded by the Tchartoruiski, where he had distinguished himself by unceasing labor. In Poland he received hard lessons in equality; he saw his father assassinated by exasperated peasants, and he himself had been put to shame by the powerful noble Sosnovski, whose daughter he, a simple portionless gentleman, dared to ask in marriage.

He fought in the American War, and returned invested with the republican decoration of the Cincinnati. After the second partition he quitted Warsaw and retired into Saxony, where he found the men of the third of May, — Malakhovski, Ignati Pototski, the ex-Chancellor Kolontaï, Niemtsevitch, and all of Poland that was honorably devoted to liberty. He was then sent into France, and received promises of help from the Committee of Public Safety, and now he was working in Dresden to organize in Poland a vast conspiracy. He was soon able to reckon thousands of nobles, priests, citizens, and disbanded soldiers; but in spite of the number of the conspirators, General Igelstrom, who commanded in Warsaw for Catherine the Second, failed to seize the principal threads of the plot.

The order to disband the army hastened the explosion. Madalinski refused to allow the brigade that he commanded to be disarmed, crossed the Bug, threw himself on the Prussian provinces, and then fell back on Krakof. At his approach this city, the second in Poland, the capital of the ancient kings, rose and expelled the Russian garrison. Kosciuszko hastened to the scene of action, and put forth the "act of insurrection," in which the hateful conduct of the co-partitioners was branded, and the population called to arms. Five thousand scythes were made for the peasants, the voluntary offerings of patriots were collected, and those of obstinate and lukewarm people were extracted by force. Igelstrom, who was very uneasy in Warsaw, detached, nevertheless, Tormasof and Denisof against Krakof · Deserted by Denisof, Tormasof came up near Ratslavitsa with Kosciuszko and Madalinski, the number of whose troops — four thousand men, one half of whom were peasants — was almost equal to his own. The cavalry of the nobles gave way at the first shock, and fled, announcing everywhere that Kosciuszko was defeated and captured; but the steadiness of the peasants preserved the Polish army, and twelve guns were taken from the Russians. To punish the cowardice of the cavalry officers, the dictator took off the dress of the gentleman and assumed that of a peasant.

The news of this success soon reached Warsaw, and the representation of the "Krakovians," which seemed an allusion to the events in Gallicia, still further increased the excitement. Igelstrom had posted his regiments so injudiciously that their communication could easily be cut off by the Polish regiments in the town. The arsenal had not yet been delivered to the Russians, and remained in the hands of the patriots.

On the seventeenth of April, at three o'clock in the morning, the tocsin sounded in all the churches, and the insurrection broke out. The people, excited by the shoemaker Kilinski and the merchant Kapostas, fell everywhere on the isolated detachments of Russians. Igelstrom found himself blockaded in his palace, unable to communicate with the scattered regiments, and assailed at once by the citizens and the Polish troops. On the eighteenth he left the town with great difficulty, abandoning twelve cannons, four thousand killed and wounded, and two thousand prisoners. Vilna, capital of Lithuania, followed the example of Warsaw, and expelled General Arsenief.

A provisional government installed itself at Warsaw, and sent a courier to Kosciuszko. It was composed of men of the third of May, amongst whom Ignati Pototski represented the moderate and Kilinski the extreme party. King Stanislas remained in his palace, treated with respect but watched, and taking no active part in public affairs, of which he was kept informed only by the courtesy of the government. To sum up, the revolution of the seventeenth of April, seventeen hundred and ninety-four, had a national and monarchic character, like the Constitution of the third of May, seventeen hundred and ninety-one. It sought the support of France, without following all the advice of the Convention. A special tribunal gave some satisfaction to the public conscience by seeking out the wretches who had betrayed their country, and whose connection with foreigners had been proved by the papers seized at the Russian embassy. Ankiévitch, the hetmans Zabiello and Ozarovski, and Kazakovski, bishop of Livonia, were hung; the brother of the latter, Kazakovski, hetman of Lithuania, had been punished at Vilna.

In spite of the agitation caused by Kolontaï and the democrats, Kosciuszko dared not settle the question about the peasants, and his manifesto of the seventh of May, seventeen hundred and ninety-four, was not put in force. He feared to risk the alienation of the military class, without gaining the rural masses, brutalized by centuries of oppression; still he tried to win the clergy and the orthodox populations, by proclaiming liberty of conscience, and the equality of different religions in the eye of the law.

The Prussians, however, managed to take Krakof, which was only feebly defended by its commander. The government of Warsaw declared war against Frederic William the Second. The people, attributing the loss of Krakof to treason, rushed to the prisons, and promptly executed the seven men who were detained there. They deserved the fate that befell them; they had been amongst the promoters of the Confederation of Targovitsa, they had been agents of Russia. Kosciuszko condemned this bloody justice, and insisted on the punishment of the rioters, but at the same time hastened the trial of the guilty prisoners.

General Zaïontchek had been defeated in the battle of Golkof by the Russians, and the Prussians were marching on the Vistula. The King of Prussia had quitted his army on the Rhine in order to direct the siege and bombardment of Warsaw. Catherine affected to be indignant at this abandonment of the holy war which was to put down the Revolution and to help the common cause of kings and religion. The pretensions of Prussia in respect to Krakof disturbed the good understanding between the three powers of the North, disquieted Austria, and threatened to break the coalition formed against France. Frederic William, greatly disgusted with his Russian ally, General Krushtchof, countermanded the order for assault, and raised the siege, being recalled to his own dominions by an insurrection in Great Poland.

The Poles had hardly time to congratulate themselves on this success. The Russians were again in possession of Vilna; the Austrians had entered Lublin. Still more threatening was the fact that the Russian general, Fersen, had crossed to the right bank of the Vistula in spite of Poninski, and was advancing to meet Suvorof, who was coming up with the army of the Ukraina, and had already beaten Siérakovski at Kruptchitsé and at Brest-Litovski. If the two Russian armies, each of which was superior to the whole Polish force, managed to effect a junction, the insurrection was crushed.

Kosciuszko, who had hastened to reinforce Siérakovski, speedily returned to take up a position at Matsiovitsui on the Vistula, equidistant from Warsaw and Lublin, where he meant to oppose Fersen. Around him were gathered his bravest lieutenants, — Pototski, Kaminski, Kolontaï, Niemtsevitch, the patriotic poet and general. The evening before the battle Kaminski pointed out to Niemtsevitch the crows that were flying on their right. "Remember your Livy," he said; "it is a bad omen." "A bad omen for the Romans, not for us," replied the brave poet. On the tenth of October, seventeen hundred and ninety-four, Krushtchof attacked the van of the Poles, while Fersen ordered Denisof to lead the assault on the right, and Tormasof on the left. The Polish army, shaken by a violent cannonade, could not resist the charge of the bayonets. They gave way, and twenty-one guns and two thousand seven hundred prisoners remained in the hands of the Russians. All the generals were captured; Kosciuszko was carried off half dead by the hetman Denisof, but there is absolutely no truth in the commonly repeated story that he exclaimed, "Finis Poloniæ." The Russian generals treated their prisoners well, and the officers tried to console the wounded Niemtsevitch by complimenting him on the "Return from the other World," a poem in manuscript which they found in his pocket.

Warsaw was horror-stricken by this calamity. Vavrzhevski took the place of Kosciuszko, but proved no adequate substitute for the popular hero who had been the soul of the revolt. Suvorof was already before Praga, and the whole Russian army occupied its positions to the sound of drums and music. The impetuous general at once divided his army into seven columns. The Russian soldiers, on the eve of the assault, put on white shirts, as if for a wedding, and the holy images were placed at the head of the columns. At three o'clock on the morning of the fourth of November the signal was given, and in an instant the fosses were filled and the ramparts scaled. "The Poles," says a Russian witness, "defended themselves like heroes, with desperate recklessness." Praga suffered all the horrors of a capture by assault. In vain Suvorof renewed his orders "to spare the inhabitants, to give quarter to the vanquished, not to slay without a motive." The soldiers were too much exasperated against the Poles, whom they believed to be republicans, atheists, accomplices of the French Jacobins, murderers of their comrades, disarmed in the revolt of the seventeenth of April. The dead numbered twelve hundred, the prisoners only a thousand. "The streets are covered with corpses; blood flows in torrents," says the first despatch of Suvorof. The massacre of Praga terrified Warsaw, which was ill protected by only the width of the Vistula from the Russian bullets. Suvorof refused to treat with Pototski and the men of the seventeenth of April, and King Stanislas had to act as mediator. Suvorof guaranteed to the inhabitants their property, a pardon, and offered passports to all persons who were compromised. He made his entrance into Warsaw, and was created field-marshal by the Empress. The King was sent to Grodno. The third treaty of partition, forced on the Empress by the importunity of Prussia, and in which Austria also took part, was put in execution in seventeen hundred and ninety-five. Russia took the rest of Lithuania as far as the Niemen, including Vilna, Grodno, Kovno, Novogrodek, Slonim, and the rest of Volhynia to the Bug, including Vladimir, Lutsk, and Kremenets. It thus attained the extreme limit of the countries formerly governed by the princely descendants of Rurik, except in the case of Gallicia, for the Empress, whose policy had abandoned Poland to the Germans, allowed Austria to take Red Russia after the first partition. Besides the Russian territory, Russia also annexed the old Lithuania of the Iagelos, and finally acquired Kurland and Samogitia.

Prussia now possessed all Eastern Poland, with Warsaw; Austria had Krakof, Sandomir, Lublin, and Shelm. Its possessions extended towards the north, almost to the vicinity of Warsaw.

The Polish army of Vavrzhevski had refused to be included in the capitulation of Warsaw, but, agitated by the quarrels of its leaders, and weakened by want of discipline and desertion, it was obliged to accept an honorable convention at Radoshuitsé. The officers kept their swords, and obtained passports for foreign travel. The prisoners made at Matsiovitsui had been divided amongst the governments which had seized the places of their birth. Madalinski was sent to

Prussia; Kolontaï and Zaïontchek to Austria; Kosciuszko, Kapostas, Kilinski, Pototski, and Vavrzhevski to Saint Petersburg. Poland was not yet dead: out of the remains of the army dispersed at Radoshuitsé, Dombrovski was to form the famous Polish legions, for twenty years inseparable from the banners of the French Republic and the Empire. We shall find Dombrovski in Egypt, Iosiph Poniatovski at Borodino. The Poles, defeated at Matsiovitsui, will meet their conquerors on all the battle-fields in Europe, — in Italy, in Switzerland, in Austria, in Prussia, in Poland, in Lithuania. Napoleon will satiate their vengeance against the robber powers, and, two hundred years after Vladislas, will lead the Polish troops into the holy city of Moscow.

CATHERINE THE SECOND AND THE FRENCH REVOLUTION. — WAR WITH PERSIA.

Just before the breaking out of the Revolution the two governments of Louis the Sixteenth and Catherine the Second entered into negotiations for the purpose of forming a quadruple alliance, including Russia, Austria, and both houses of Bourbon, which was destined to keep in check the naval pretensions of England and the encroachments of Prussia. After the taking of the Bastile, Catherine understood that she could no longer look to France, which was then occupied with its internal transformation, for support. She followed events in Paris, however, with much anxiety, showed the most lively antipathy to the new principles, was one of those who advised Louis the Sixteenth to take refuge in Varennes, and fell ill at the news of the execution of the King on the twenty-first of January. The correspondent of Voltaire and Diderot allowed herself to be carried away by terror into the opposite of liberalism. She had the bust of Voltaire taken down and cast among the rubbish of a lumber-room. She caused Russians suspected of liberal ideas to be watched, and their letters to be inspected; she mutilated Kniazhnin's tragedy of " Vadim at

Novgorod," and spoke of having it burned by the executioner; Radishtchef, the author of the "Journey from Saint Petersburg to Moscow," a curious book, with many reflections on serfage, was dismissed and sent to Siberia; Novikof was arrested and confined in Schlüsselburg, his publishing-houses and his printing-press closed, and all his enterprises ruined. She dismissed Genest, the French ambassador, and refused to recognize, first the Constitution of seventeen hundred and ninety-one, and then the Republic; put forth an edict announcing the rupture of diplomatic relations with France; forbade the tricolor flag to enter the Russian ports; expelled all French subjects who refused to swear fidelity to the monarchic principle; received the émigrés with open arms, and hastened to acknowledge Louis the Eighteenth.

In seventeen hundred and ninety-two she wrote the celebrated note on the restoration of the royal power and aristocratic privileges in France, assuring every one that ten thousand men would be sufficient to operate a counter-revolution. She encouraged Gustavus the Third, who was shortly afterwards assassinated by his nobility, at a masked ball, on March sixteenth, seventeen hundred and ninety-two, to put himself at the head of the crusade against democracy; urged England to aid the Count of Artois in a scheme for a descent on France; and stimulated the zeal of Austria and Prussia. In spite of all this, though she had many times consented to negotiate treaties of subsidies and promised troops, she took care never to engage in a war with the West. "My position is taken," she said, "my part assigned; it is my duty to watch the Turks, the Poles, and Sweden." The latter became reconciled with France after the death of Gustavus the Third. The punishment of the Jacobins of Warsaw and Turkey was indeed more easy and certainly more lucrative work. Perhaps we must also take into account an admission that she made, in seventeen hundred and ninety-one, to her Vice-Chancellor Ostermann: "Am I wrong? For reasons that I cannot give to the Courts of Berlin and Vienna, I wish to involve them in these affairs, so that I may have elbow-room. Many of my enterprises are still unfinished, and they must be occupied so as to leave me unfettered." She excused herself for not taking part in the anti-revolutionary contest, alleging the war with Turkey; and when obliged to hasten the Peace of Iassy on account of the revolution of the third of May, she made the Polish war another excuse. When the war was ended, she pretended to excite the zeal of Suvorof and his soldiers against the "atheists" of the West, but in reality only dreamed of forwarding her schemes in the East. Mohammed, the new king of Persia, had invaded Georgia and burnt Tiflis, the capital of Irakli, Catherine's protégé. The Empress sent for an exiled brother of Mohammed to her court, and ordered Valerian Zubof to conquer Persia.

In reality Catherine had been, against her will, more useful to France than to the coalition. By her intervention in Poland and her projects against the East, she had raised the jealousy and suspicions of Prussia and Austria. She took care to play off one against the other; made the second partition with Frederic William in spite of Austria; and with Francis the Second the third partition, which disgusted Prussia. She contributed indirectly to agitate and dissolve the coalition, whilst the Polish insurrection, encouraged by France, prevented her from joining it. She died on the sixth (or more properly the seventeenth) of November, seventeen hundred and ninety-six, aged sixty-seven years. No sovereign since Ivan the Terrible had extended the frontiers of the empire by such vast conquests. She had given Russia for boundaries the Niemen, the Dniester, and the Black Sea.

CHAPTER XII.

PAUL THE FIRST.

1796–1801.

PEACE POLICY: ACCESSION TO THE SECOND COALITION. — CAMPAIGNS OF THE IONIAN ISLANDS, ITALY, SWITZERLAND, HOLLAND, AND NAPLES. — ALLIANCE WITH BONAPARTE: THE LEAGUE OF THE NEUTRALS AND THE GREAT SCHEME AGAINST INDIA.

PEACE POLICY: ACCESSION TO THE SECOND COALITION.

PAVEL, or Paul the First, was forty-two years of age when he ascended the throne. He was intelligent, and had some natural gifts, but his character was soured by the close dependence in which he had been held by his mother, who had even deprived him of the education of his children, and forbade him to appear before the army, by the humiliations forced on him by the favorites, and by the isolation to which he was abandoned by the courtiers, who always took pains to pay court to the powers of the moment. The mystery surrounding his father's death troubled and disquieted him. There was a touch of Hamlet in Paul the First. Like Peter the Third, he had a taste for military minutiæ which amounted to a mania. He had a high idea of his authority, and was born a despot. He is supposed to have uttered the famous saying, "Know that the only person of consideration in Russia is the person whom I address, and only during the time that I am addressing him." He hated the Revolution with a blind hate, such as even Catherine could not feel. Many of his eccentricities of conduct may be explained by his desire always to take a course directly in opposition to his mother, whom he secretly accused of having usurped his crown. Without being cruel, he caused much unhappiness, since he was as prompt to chastise as to pardon, as prodigal of exiles to Siberia as of unexpected favors.

He began by abolishing the edict of Peter the Third about the succession, and re-established the monarchic principle of inheritance by primogeniture, from male to male in the direct line. He took advantage of his mother's obsequies to cause his father's remains to be exhumed, and to render the same honors to both sovereigns in the Church of the Fortress. Alexis Orlof had to march in procession by the coffin of his father, and to carry his crown. He did not punish his mother's favorites, but removed them from about his own person, giving his confidence to Rostoptchin and the austere Araktchéef. Bezborodko he confirmed in his place as Minister of Foreign Affairs.

To re-establish the principle of authority, which he thought had been shaken in Russia, he revived the old rude manners, compelled the carriages of his subjects to halt when he passed, and made women as well as men salute him by throwing themselves on their knees in the mud or snow. He issued decrees full of minute provisions, forbidding the wearing of round hats, frock-coats, waistcoats, high collars, large neckties, and everything which savored of Jacobinism. He banished from the official language the words "society," "citizen," and other terms which his mother had delighted to honor. He made the censorship of the theatre and the press more rigorous than ever, forbade the importation of European books and music, forced the Russians who were travelling or studying abroad to return, and refused to allow any Frenchman to enter his territory, unless he were provided with a passport signed by the princes of the house of Bourbon.

In Catherine's last years grave abuses must have crept into

the army, and no one but an emperor with a genius for war could accomplish the reforms which were necessary if Russia were to keep pace with Western improvements in tactics and in arms. Paul unfortunately took up the reforms in his usual narrow spirit. He had a craze for Prussian methods, and abolished the Russian national uniform, convenient, soldier-like, and well suited to the climate as it was. The Russians did not recognize themselves in their Prussian costume, with pigtails, powder, shoe-buckles, shoes, gaiters, heavy caps, and uncomfortable hats. Old Suvorof shook his head and said, " Wig-powder is not gun-powder; curls are not cannon; a pigtail is not a sabre; I am not a Prussian, but a Russian born." This epigram, a roughly rhymed quatrain in the original, was punished by the exile of the martial humorist to his village of Kutchevskoé. There he could bestride a cane and play horse with the small boys of the district, ring the church bells, read the epistle, and play the organ to his heart's content. Paul showed more method and common-sense when he tried to reform the finances, which had been impaired in the last years of Catherine by endless wars, the dishonesty of officials, the luxury of the court, and the prodigal gifts bestowed on favorites.

As to foreign affairs, Paul's early policy was peaceful. He discontinued the levying of recruits in the way that his mother had been accustomed to do — that is, in the proportion of three men to every five hundred souls. He withdrew his forces from Persia, and left Georgia to take care of its own destiny. To the Poles he even showed some pity, recalled prisoners from Siberia, transferred King Stanislas from Grodno to Saint Petersburg, visited Kosciuszko at Schlüsselburg, and set him, with the other captives, at liberty. He bade Koluitchef, Envoy Extraordinary at Berlin, tell the King of Prussia that he was neither for conquest nor aggrandizement. He dictated to Ostermann a circular which was to be communicated to foreign powers, in which he declared that Russia, and Russia alone, had not ceased from waging war since seventeen hundred and fifty-six; that these forty years of war had exhausted the nation; that the Emperor's humanity did not allow him to refuse his beloved subjects the peace for which they were longing; that though for these reasons the Russian army would take no part in the contest with France, nevertheless, "the Emperor would remain as closely as ever united with his allies, and oppose by all possible means the progress of the mad French republic, which threatened Europe with total ruin, by the destruction of its laws, privileges, property, religion, and manners." He refused all armed assistance to Austria, then alarmed by Bonaparte's victories in Italy; he recalled the vessels sent by Catherine to join the English fleet in blockading the coasts of France and Holland. He even received the overtures made by Caillard, the French envoy in Prussia, to the Russian envoy Kolnitchef, and caused the latter to observe "that the Emperor did not consider himself at war with the French, that he had done nothing to harm them, that he was disposed to live in peace with them, and that he would persuade his allies to finish the war, offering to this end the mediation of Russia."

But difficulties soon arose between France and Russia. The treaty of Campo Formio had given the Ionian Islands to the French, who thus acquired a position threatening to the East, and a greater influence over the Divan. The Directorate authorized Dombrovski to organize Polish legions in Italy. Panin at Berlin intercepted a letter from the Directorate to the French envoy, in which there was a question of the restoration of Poland, under a prince of Brandenburg. Paul, on his side, took into his pay the corps of the Prince of Condé, and stationed ten thousand émigrés in Volhynia and Podolia. He offered an asylum to Louis the Eighteenth, who was expelled from Brunswick, established him in the ducal palace of Mitava, and gave him a pension of two hundred thousand rubles. The news that a French expedition was being mysteriously organized at Toulon caused him to tremble for the security of the coasts of the Black Sea, which were immediately put into a state of defence. The capture of Zagurski, Russian Consul at Corfu; the reduction of Malta by Bonaparte, and the arrival at Saint Petersburg of the banished knights, who offered Paul the protectorate of their order, with the title of Grand Master; the invasion of the Swiss territory by the Directorate; the expulsion of the Pope and the proclamation of the Roman Republic, — all precipitated the rupture.

Paul further concluded an alliance with Turkey, which was irritated at the invasion of Egypt, and also with England, Austria, and the kingdom of Naples. It was thus that, owing to Bonaparte's double aggression against Malta and Egypt, Russia and Turkey were forced, contrary to all traditions, to make common cause. Paul undertook that his fleet should join the Turkish and English squadrons, to furnish a body of troops to make a descent upon Holland, and another to conquer the Ionian Islands, besides a great auxiliary army for the campaigns in Switzerland and Italy.

CAMPAIGNS OF THE IONIAN ISLANDS, ITALY, SWITZERLAND, HOLLAND, AND NAPLES.

In the autumn of seventeen hundred and ninety-eight a Turco-Russian fleet captured the French garrisons of the Ionian Islands. Among the powers opposed to France, Naples was the first to take the field. The unlucky Colonel Mack was summoned from Vienna to organize the wretched army which the Queen had managed to collect. Championnet was the commander of the French forces stationed in the vicinity of Rome. On the twenty-fifth of November the Neapolitan army suddenly invaded the territory of the Roman republic in five divisions. The strongest column, consisting of thirty thousand men, under the command of the King, directed its course upon Rome, which Championnet immediately evacuated so as to unite his forces farther to the North. Although Ferdinand entered the Holy City with all possible pomp, when he found that the French had closed in on every side of him, he took his favorite, the Duca d'Ascoli, and, exchanging clothes with him, secretly deserted his army and returned to Naples on the tenth of December. Seventeen days after the Neapolitan army had entered Rome the French returned in the full glory of conquest. Meanwhile in Naples cowardice had shown itself everywhere, but nowhere more strikingly than in the King. He ordered all his ships of war to be burnt, and hastened himself to Palermo. The lower classes, seeing the fearful conflagration, suspected treachery in the generals, and a tumult broke out which threatened Mack and his officers with destruction. The King then fled under Nelson's protection to Sicily, and appointed as Viceroy Prince Pignatelli, one of the Queen's favorites, a man of the lowest qualities. When the people heard that Pignatelli had sent a messenger to Championnet without asking permission of the city authorities, that Capua had been evacuated by Mack, and that the French had gained all the approaches to the town without striking a blow, they immediately formed into a kind of assembly, and strengthened themselves by a choice of officers from the nobility and middle classes, so that they were ready to act against not only Mack and the Viceroy, but also the French. Mack and Pignatelli had persuaded the French to agree to a truce of two months on the condition that certain strongholds should be evacuated and that the city of Naples should pay the French ten million francs. But when the French delegates came to collect the first half of this impost, a great tumult arose, and thousands of the lazzaroni stormed Castel Nuovo, or the New Port, and collecting arms at the arsenal, hastened against Pignatelli's palace. The Viceroy then followed the King's example, and fled to Sicily, where he was confined in prison for desertion. Mack, in January, seventeen hundred and ninety-nine, resigned his position as Neapolitan general, and in the uniform of an Austrian took refuge with Championnet, who received him with kindness.

The uproar increased in the city, and finally every one, not a lazzarone or priest, who was found on the street was ruthlessly murdered. Championnet, on the twentieth of January, divided his army into four columns, and endeavored to penetrate the city by four different gates. Every step was bought with blood; every house was transformed into a castle, and though the skill of the French and their well-directed artillery did great execution, and though the natives fought without officers, yet it was only on the third day that the bloody conflict came to an end. Before the thousand Frenchmen and three thousand Neapolitans who had lost their lives were buried, the new republic was declared. The French made a triumphal entry, Championnet took up his abode in the King's palace, and the Philosopher of Southern Italy, Maria Pagano, was summoned to prepare the constitution of the new state, which was called the Parthenopean Republic, after the old name of Naples.

The Russian army in Holland was put under the orders of Hermann, that of Switzerland under those of Rimski-Korsakof, while, at the request of Austria and the suggestion of England, the victor of Fokshany and Ruimnik was appointed to the Austro-Russian army of Upper Italy. Paul the First, flattered by this mark of deference, recalled Suvorof from his village exile. "Suvorof has no need of laurels," wrote the Tsar, "but the country has need of Suvorof."

The Directorate, taken by surprise, having not only France to protect, but likewise the Batavian, Helvetian, Cisalpine, Ligurian, Roman, and Neapolitan republics, — that is to say, the vast line of country that extends from the Zuyder Zee to the Gulf of Taranto, — had very inferior numbers to oppose to those of the coalition: in Holland twenty thousand men, under Brune, against forty thousand Anglo-Russians, under

York and Hermann; on the Rhine, fifty thousand, under Bernadotte and Jourdan, against the seventy thousand of the Archduke Charles; in Switzerland, thirty thousand, under Masséna, against Hotze and Bellegarde, who had seventy thousand Austrians in the Vorarlberg and the Tyrol; in Upper Italy, fifty thousand, under Scherer, against the sixty thousand Austrians of Kray; at Naples, thirty thousand, under Macdonald, against thirty thousand English, Russians, and Sicilians.

At last the Russians arrived in Switzerland, forty thousand in number, under Rimski-Korsakof; in Italy, to the number of forty thousand, divided into two corps, that of Rosenberg and that of Rebinder, with Suvorof in chief command. Consequently the French had only one hundred and eighty thousand to oppose to three hundred and fifty thousand allies.

When Suvorof passed through Vienna, and was offered the position of Austrian field-marshal, he took it on the condition that he should be subject only to the Emperor, not to the Hof-Kriegsrath, the Aulic council of war. He therefore refused to communicate his schemes to Thugut, the acting minister. When the Austrians questioned him as to his plan of campaign, he showed a blank paper signed by the Emperor Paul. His object, he declared, was Paris, where he would restore the throne and the altar. To his soldiers he repeated the formulæ of his military catechism: "A sudden glance, rapidity, impetuosity! The van of the army is not to wait for the rear! Musket-balls are fools; bayonets are the fine fellows! The French beat the Austrians in columns, and we will beat them in columns." He scoffed at the slowness and pedantry of the Hof-Kriegsrath. "Parades, manœuvres! too much confidence in their talents! To know how to conquer, well; but to be always beaten is not smart! The Emperor of Germany desires that, when I have to give battle to-morrow, I should first address myself to the Court of Vienna. The accidents of war change rapidly; one cannot be tied down to a fixed plan. Fortune flies like the lightning: one must seize opportunity by the forelock; it will never come back."

The Austrians had already defeated Jourdan at Stokach, March twenty-ninth, seventeen hundred and ninety-nine, and Scherer at Magnano, April ninth. Masséna, although victorious at the first battle of Zurich, had been obliged to retreat behind the Limmat and the Linth, on the heights of the Albis. On the twenty-eighth of April, Austria, believing that where the French were concerned it might violate with impunity the law of nations, assassinated their plenipotentiaries at Rastadt. Suvorof, on his arrival at Verona, took the command of the allied forces.

The Austro-Russian army numbered about ninety thousand; the French, under Moreau, no more than thirty thousand, which included the Italian legions and three or four thousand men of the Polish legions. These Poles represented the Slav element in the French army, as the Russians did in that of the coalition. This quarrel of kinsmen, which began at Matsiovitsui and Warsaw, was to be continued on the bank of the Adda. Suvorof surprised the passage of this river at Cassano, on April twenty-eighth, penetrated the centre of Moreau's division, and surrounded the right wing; Serrurier and about three thousand men were made prisoners.

Moreau retired into Piedmont; imperilled next by the loss of Ceva and of Turin, he was forced to take refuge in the Alps. Suvorof made his entry into Milan amidst the acclamations of the nobles, the priests, the excited populace, of all the enemies of the Revolution, and abolished the Cisalpine Republic. But, harassed by the advice of the Hof-Kriegsrath, instead of attacking the fifteen thousand men who remained with Moreau, he amused himself by laying siege to Mantua, Alessandria, and the citadel of Turin.

Macdonald hastened from the end of the Peninsula with the army of Naples. After having opened communications with Moreau, he conceived the project of throwing himself between Alessandria and Mantua, and separating the two principal bodies of the allied army. He defeated the Austrians on the Tidona, but came up with Suvorof on the Trebbia. The battle lasted three days, from the seventeenth to the nineteenth of June: the ferocity of the French, Russians, and Poles rendered it extremely bloody. On the seventeenth the French amounted to only twenty-eight thousand against forty thousand; the next day twenty-four thousand against thirty-six thousand: numbers were sure to tell. Each army lost from ten to twelve thousand men, and Macdonald hastened to rejoin Moreau in the gorges of the Alps. Mantua had capitulated. In the South the Anglo-Russians, allied with the banditti of Cardinal Ruffo and of the brigand Michael Pezza whom the people called Fra Diavolo, expelled the French garrisons from Neapolitan territory. A frightful reaction flooded the streets of Naples with blood, and two thousand houses were burned by the bandits and lazzaroni in July, seventeen hundred and ninety-nine.

The Directorate made a last effort to reconquer Italy. The army of the Alps, increased by new reinforcements to forty thousand men, was placed under the command of General Joubert, who had said to his young wife, " You will see me either dead or victorious." Joubert wished to relieve Alessandria, and to prevent this Suvorof marched quickly up with seventy thousand men, and gave him battle at Novi on August fifteenth. Joubert was killed at the beginning of the action. The two armies each lost eight thousand men, and the remains of the Polo-French troops fell back into the mountains of Genoa. Italy was lost to France; the Cisalpine, Roman, and Neapolitan republics were extinguished.

The Russians and Austrians separated after the victory. The German generals could not endure the vanity of Suvorof, who had been given the additional title of Kniaz Italiiski. Thugut was even more disturbed by his peculiar views of policy. Italiiski imagined that he had fought for the restoration of sovereigns, and not for the private ambition of the house of Austria. He wished therefore to establish a national government in Piedmont, and to reorganize the Piedmontese army under its own standard. But Thugut cared nothing about the restoration of Victor-Amadeus, or of the Pope. The misunderstanding increased; it was decided that Suvorof should abandon Italy, and join Rimski-Korsakof in Switzerland, so as to defend the snowy mountains of Helvetia with a purely Russian army. Suvorof, who already saw himself in Franche-Comté and on the route to Paris, accepted the work.

In Switzerland, after the first battle of Zürich, Masséna had retired to the heights of the Albis, behind the line formed by the Linth, the lake of Zürich, and the Limmat. He had been opposed in his movements by the Archduke Charles, with twenty-five thousand men; by Korsakof, with twenty-eight thousand Russians; and by Hotze, with twenty-seven thousand Austrians. The Archduke was about to evacuate Switzerland and lay siege to Philippsburg, and he was to be replaced by Suvorof with twenty thousand men. It would be a critical moment for the allies when the Archduke should have evacuated Switzerland and Suvorof should not yet have arrived, and this was the moment eagerly awaited by Masséna. He had now sixty thousand men against fifty-five thousand, which the army of Suvorof, Prince of Italy, would increase to seventy-five thousand. On the twenty-fifth of September Masséna surprised the passage of the Limmat near Diétikon, and cut the Russian army in two. The Russian grenadiers who defended Diétikon fought till their powder was exhausted, refused to surrender, and died in their ranks. The other corps were defeated one after the other. Korsakof, forced back upon Zürich, caused the gates to be closed. In the night Masséna sent him envoys, who were captured or repulsed by musketry. On the twenty-sixth of September Korsakof formed an immense square of fifteen thousand men, and attacked the French. "This dense and impenetrable mass," says Major Masson, "had always driven the enemy before it at every point." But this system of tactics, which had been successful against the Poles and the Turks, was certain to fail against the French. Decimated by the sharpshooters and light artillery, shaken by a general charge of cavalry, and infantry with bayonets, the Russians had to fall back into Zürich, leaving the field of battle covered with dead, and with wounded, who pressed holy images and relics to their breasts. They had lost six thousand men, their guns, the army treasure, the official papers, and sacred plate. Korsakof fled to Eglisau. Then Masséna made Udinot attack Zürich and the Swiss legion, and took all the Russian stores and baggage. It was here that the celebrated Lavater perished, killed by a drunken Swiss soldier. On the twenty-fifth Soult, on his side, had crossed the Linth, and defeated Hotze, who was killed. The allies retreated in disorder on Schaffhausen, with a loss of ten thousand prisoners, twenty Austrian cannons, and nearly all the Russian artillery.

Such was the victory of Zürich. "Bonaparte," says M. Duruy, "has no more glorious battle, for the victories which insure the salvation of a country are worth more than those which only add to its power or the glory of its chiefs."

Suvorof, however, had arrived, by dint of forced marches, at Taverno, near Bellinzona. The Austrian administration had neglected to gather together a sufficient number of sumpter mules for the passage of the Alps, and Suvorof lost four precious days, which were spent in impressing them from the surrounding country. He reached only as far as the Saint Gothard on the twenty-first, and crossed it under immense difficulties, after a sharp skirmish with some French detachments stationed on the mountains. He plunged at once into the narrow valley of the Reuss, enclosed between mountains so precipitous that the road many times crosses the torrent, notably at the Pont du Diable.

"In this kingdom of terrors," writes Suvorof in his despatch to Paul, "abysses open beside us at every step, like tombs awaiting our arrival. Nights spent among the clouds, thunder that never ceases, rain, fog, the noise of cataracts, the crashing of avalanches, enormous masses of rocks and ice which fall from the heights, torrents which sometimes carry men and horses down the precipices, the Saint Gothard, that colossus which sees the mists pass under it, — we have surmounted all, and in these inaccessible spots the enemy has been forced to give way before us. Words fail to describe the horrors we have seen, and in the midst of which Providence has preserved us." The impression produced on the natives of the great Russian plains by the grandeur of the Swiss Alps is graphically sketched in the curious "Narrative of an Old Soldier," the memoirs of an eyewitness who was a companion of Suvorof.

The tenacious Lecourbe, charged by Masséna to retard the Russian advance, had only eleven thousand men, but with them he expected to "crush Suvorof in the mountains." At Hospital he disputed the passage of the Reuss, cannonaded the Russians till his ammunition was exhausted, threw his artillery into the stream, went down to defend the Pont du Diable, which he blew up, and finally fell back on Seedorf, where he broke down the bridge. Suvorof crossed the precipitous chain of Schachenthal, and only reached Altdorf and Multenthal on the twenty-sixth, having lost two thousand men on the way. It was here that he heard of the disaster of Zürich and the flight of Korsakof, and that he grasped the full horror of his situation; lost in the heart of the mountains, betrayed by the carelessness of his allies, enclosed in Multenthal as it were in a mouse-trap, surrounded on all sides by a victorious army, with numbers superior to his own. On his rear Gudin had again occupied the Upper Reuss; on the road to Stanz Lecourbe had taken up a position at Seedorf; on the road to Schwitz Masséna had concentrated the corps of Mortier;

on the road to Glarus Molitor was posted, whom Soult was about to reinforce. This was the most splendid moment of Suvorof's life. His heroic retreat is more glorious than his victories in Italy, which were gained with superior forces; no general in such a desperate situation ever showed more indomitable energy than this little man, now nearly seventy years old. He resolved to cross Mont Bragel, though the snow was sixty-five centimeters deep, and to cut a way by the Kleinthal and the route to Glarus. His rearguard, left in the Multenthal, resisted for three days the assaults of Masséna, thus protecting the retreat of the army, while the vanguard took Glarus, and forced Molitor back on Naefels. There Molitor checked the Russians, who were obliged to retire on the Rindskopff, on whose glaciers many hundreds of men perished. Thence they succeeded in gaining Illanz, Coire, and Feldkirch. Suvorof, with the gallant remnant of his army, took up his winter-quarters between the Iller and the Lech.

On the twenty-seventh of August the Anglo-Russians had disembarked on the Texel, and captured the Dutch fleet, but the Batavian populations remained faithful to the cause of liberty, and on the nineteenth of September Brune, reinforced, defeated the allies at Bergen. He then fought them in four other battles, besieged them in Zyp, and made Alkmaer and the Duke of York capitulate on October eighteenth. The Anglo-Russian army obtained leave to march out. The remains of the Russian forces re-embarked; but being coldly received in England, they were, so to speak, "interned" in the islands of Jersey and Guernsey.

Masséna and Brune had saved the frontiers of the republic, prepared the ruin of the coalition, and deprived the coup-d'état of Brumaire of all excuse.

ALLIANCE WITH BONAPARTE: THE LEAGUE OF THE NEUTRALS, AND THE GREAT SCHEME AGAINST INDIA.

Paul the First, Suvorof, and all Russia accused Austria of treason. The Emperor Francis, by the advice of England, humbly consented to explain the misunderstanding which had lost Korsakof, and almost lost Suvorof. The Tsar, a little softened, suspended the retreat of the Russian army, but insisted in return on the recall of Thugut, and the restoration of the Italian princes to their reconquered States. Austria could not relish this disinterested policy, or renounce its plans. Thugut, threatened with the loss of his post, labored to complete the rupture. It was insinuated to the Russian Emperor that the maintenance of his troops in Bohemia constituted a heavy charge for the hereditary States. The irritable Tsar learned in addition that a conflict had taken place at the siege of Ancona. This maritime station was being besieged by the Austrians, Russians, and Turks; the Austrian general secretly concluded a capitulation with the French, stipulated that his soldiers alone should be admitted into the fortress, and caused the Turkish and Russian flags, which had been fixed on the ramparts beside his own, to be removed. This insult to his banner completed Paul's exasperation.

Similar diplomatic results followed after the defeat at Bergen; a quarrel with England, which was likewise accused of treason, soon succeeded to the dispute with Austria. Bonaparte, who promptly destroyed at Marengo all the fruits of Suvorof's victories, who appeared to the Russians almost as an avenger against the perfidy of the Austrians, — Bonaparte, whose despotic principles reassured the Tsar, and whose glory blinded him, cleverly turned to account Paul's irritation. He began by declaring that he returned, without exchange, all the Russian prisoners, newly equipped at the expense of France. Paul was the more touched by this action, as Austria and England had refused to exchange the Russian soldiers for the French prisoners whom they held. Negotiations were opened by means of Berlin, and the French and Russian agents at Hamburg. Bonaparte took care to attack the Tsar on his weak sides, his easily offended dignity and his affectation of chivalrous disinterestedness. He offered to indemnify the King of Sardinia, to re-establish the Pope in Rome, and to recognize Paul as Grand Master of Malta, and owner of the island. Malta was at that time blockaded by the English, who in September, eighteen hundred, made themselves masters of it. Their refusal to relinquish this important post to Paul the First greatly irritated him. Disturbed by the maritime tyranny of Great Britain, which had declared the ports of France and its allies in a state of siege, and had begun once more the system of vexations against the neutral ships, Paul renewed the famous Act of Armed Neutrality, and sought the support of Prussia, Sweden, and Denmark. Bonaparte hastened to express his assent to the Russian principles. During this time General Sprengtporten, who, under pretext of taking command of the Russian prisoners in Paris, had been sent on a secret mission, was followed there by Koluitchef, charged with more precise instructions. Koluitchef was particularly to persuade Bonaparte to take the title of King himself, and to make it hereditary in his family, as the only means "of changing the revolutionary principles which have armed all Europe against France." On this point the First Consul was only too well disposed. Negotiations began on the following bases : France was to respect the integrity of Naples and Würtemberg, to re-establish the King of Sardinia in Piedmont, while reserving Savoy for itself, and to retain the left bank of the Rhine, subject to an understanding with Russia, for the indemnification of the depossessed princes. It was under the Franco-Russian mediation that secularization was to take place in Germany.

Paul, with his usual impetuosity, was possessed by a daily increasing passion for Bonaparte ; he surrounded himself with his portraits, drank his health publicly, and abruptly ordered Louis the Eighteenth to quit Mitava.

It was then that the two sovereigns arranged together the great scheme that had for its object the complete overthrow of the English rule in India. France still occupied Egypt; it was authorized to keep garrisons in the southern ports of the kingdom of Naples; the French agents traversed Arabia and the Indian States. Paul on his side, to secure himself a basis of operations, ordered his troops to the Caucasus, and, at the request of the son of Irakli, pronounced Gruzia, or Georgia, to be united to the empire. The expedition against English India was to be made by two different routes; the command of a Russian army, destined for the Upper Indus by way of Khiva and Bokhara, was given to Knorring. In January, Orlof-Denisof, Ataman of the Don Cossacks, received letters from Paul, desiring him to begin his movement on Orenburg. "The English are preparing for an attack by land and sea against me and my allies, the Swedes and the Danes; I am ready to receive them. But it is necessary to be beforehand with them, and to attack them on their most vulnerable point, and on the side where they least expect it. It is three months' march from Orenburg to Hindostan, and it takes another month to get from the encampments of the Don to Orenburg, making in all four months. To you and your army I confide this expedition. Assemble therefore your men, and begin your march to Orenburg; thence, by whichever of the three routes you prefer, or by all, you will go straight with your artillery to Bokhara, Khiva, the river Indus, and the English settlements in India. The troops of the country are light troops, like yours; you will therefore have over them all the advantage of your artillery. Prepare everything for this campaign. Send your scouts to reconnoitre and repair the roads. All the treasures of the Indies shall be your recompense. . . . . Such an enterprise will cover you with immortal glory, will secure you my good-will in proportion to your services, will load you with riches, give an opening to our commerce, and strike the enemy a mortal blow." . . . .

"India, to which I send you, is governed by a supreme head, called the Great Mogul, and a number of small sovereigns. The English possess commercial establishments there, which they have acquired by means of money, or conquered by force of arms. The object of this campaign is to ruin these establishments, to free the oppressed sovereigns, to put them with regard to Russia in the same state of dependence that they now are with regard to the English, and finally to secure for ourselves the commerce of those regions. . . . . Be sure to remember that you are only at war with the English, and the friend of all who do not give them help. On your march you will assure men of the friendship of Russia. From the Indus you will go to the Ganges. On the way you will occupy Bokhara, to prevent the natives from going over to China. At Khiva you will deliver some thousands of my subjects who are kept prisoners there. If you need infantry, I will send it to follow in your footsteps. There is no other way, but it will be best if you can be sufficient for yourselves." In February he wrote: "The expedition is urgent; the earlier the better."

Such were the instructions, a little premature and inconsequent, that Paul sent daily with incomplete maps to Orlof-Denisof. These letters abound in contradictions. He promises his Cossacks all the wealth of the Indies, and forbids them to attack princes who remain neutral; in the same line he enjoins them to free the princes, and to place them under the sovereignty of Russia. To go from the Don to the Volga, from the Ural to the Indus, from the Indus to the Ganges, is far from being an easy undertaking, and he intrusts the Ataman, besides, with missions to Khiva and Bokhara. These letters of Paul, published by the Russkaïa Starina, made some noise in the Russian press at the beginning of the present quarrels with England.

This plan really began to be executed, as we see by the "Memoirs of the Ataman Denisof," nephew of the late Ataman, published in the same collection. He assembled eleven regiments of Cossacks, and succeeded in crossing the Volga on the floating ice, in the midst of unheard-of difficulties. This vanguard of the great Cossack army had reached the left bank of the river, when in March, eighteen hundred and one, its chief suddenly received the news of the death of the Emperor, and the order to return.

The other expedition was to be composed of thirty-five thousand French and thirty-five thousand Russians, at whose head Paul, with noble and chivalrous feeling, insisted on placing the victor of Zürich, Masséna. The thirty-five thousand French were to start from the banks of the Rhine, descend the Danube in ships furnished them by the Austrian government, embark at the mouth in Russian ships, which would transport them to Taganrog, then go up the Don as far as Piati-Isbanskaïa, cross the Volga at Tsaritsuin, drop down as far as Astrakhan, and thence, navigating the Caspian in Russian vessels, arrive at Asterabad on the Persian shore, where the thirty-five thousand Russians would await them. The combined army was then to march by way of Herat, Ferah, and Kandahar to the Upper Indus, and begin the war against the English. This project, on the margin of which are scrawled the criticisms of Bonaparte and the reply by the Emperor of Russia, enters into the most minute details. Twenty days were reckoned to descend the Danube, fifty-five days to reach Asterabad, and forty-five to arrive at the Indus, or one hundred and twenty days in all, from the Rhine to Scinde. Aërosticians, artificers, and a body of savants such as went to Egypt, were to accompany the expedition. The French government was to send precious objects, the produce of the national industry.

"Distributed with tact among the princes of these countries, and offered with the grace and courtesy natural to the

French," says the Russian note, " these gifts will enable these races to form the highest idea of the magnificence of French industry and power, and will in consequence open an important branch of commerce." To inspire the people with the most exalted conception of France and Russia, brilliant fêtes were to be given, accompanied by such military evolutions " as celebrate in Paris great events and memorable epochs." Paul the First seemed to be reconciled to the anniversaries of the Revolution.

It does not appear that Paul ever doubted the success of this hazardous expedition. Bonaparte naturally made this objection : " Supposing the combined army to be reunited at Asterabad, how do you propose that it should get to India through countries almost barbarous, and without any resources, having to march a distance of three hundred leagues, from Asterabad to the frontiers of Hindostan ? " The Tsar replied that these countries were neither barbarous nor arid, that caravans traversed them every year and made the journey in thirty-five or forty days, and that in seventeen hundred and thirty-nine and seventeen hundred and forty Nadir Shah had marched through the reverse way, from Delhi to the Caspian. Paul ended by saying : " The French and Russian armies are eager for glory ; they are brave, patient, and unwearied ; their courage, their perseverance, and the wisdom of their leaders will know how to surmount all obstacles. . . . . What a really Asiatic army did in seventeen hundred and thirty-nine and seventeen hundred and forty, we cannot doubt that an army of French and Russians can do to-day ! "

On the Continent, Paul did his best to make Prussia declare against England. The League of Neutrality made the British government so uneasy, that, notwithstanding the peace, Admirals Parker and Nelson seized the Danish fleet in the naval battle of Copenhagen, on the second of April, eighteen hundred and one. An event still more extraordinary broke up the coalition.

On the night of the twenty-third of March, eighteen hundred and one, the Emperor was assassinated. For some time Paul's capricious wilfulness and his violent acts of authority had tended to alienate those who were associated with him. There was no one who felt safe about himself or his friends. The Russian nobility secretly disapproved of his eager desire for war, first with France, and afterwards with England, the rupture of friendly relations with which, by putting a stop to the export of corn, hemp, and other raw products, affected most seriously the income of the landed proprietors. Many times Paul had used threatening language against his wife and his oldest son, Alexander, and he was charged with the intention of annulling his edict of inheritance, and of changing the order of succession. The Court became accustomed to the notion of a revolution which should result in depriving him of his crown, though not of his life, and of calling Alexander to the throne. Count Panin, at one time minister at Berlin, often discussed this project with Alexander, and gradually overcame his scruples. He soon found the man who was needful for the execution of his design. Count Pahlen, a Livonian noble, became the soul of the conspiracy, and took advantage of his position as governor of the capital, and chief of the police, to conceal the development of it. The bold frankness of his answers calmed whatever suspicions the Tsar might feel. One day Paul asked him point-blank if he remembered what took place in seventeen hundred and sixty-two. "Yes, sire, I was sergeant of the guard at that time." "They seem to be going to begin again to-day," said the Emperor, handing him a note which revealed some particulars of the plot. "Sire, I was aware of the fact, and in order better to find out who were your enemies, I have felt it my duty myself to play the part of a conspirator." According to Sablukof's account, Pahlen's mode of action was rigorously to execute the Emperor's most absurd orders, so as to increase the number of his enemies. If he heard any one complain of Paul, he looked him straight in the eye, and said simply, "The —— —— speaks, the wise man acts." He fanned Alexander's suspicions against his father and Paul's hatred of his son. He won Taluizin, Colonel of the Preobrazhenski, and many young officers of the guard; moreover, in this conspiracy against Paul were several names famous in the conspiracy against Peter the Third; they were the children of the first regicides, the "Epigonoi" of seventeen hundred and sixty-two. Pahlen associated with him the Hanoverian Bennigsen, a man of remarkable boldness and energy. One day Pahlen was asked what would be the result if the Emperor refused to abdicate : " You must break your eggs when you want to make an omelet," was his reply. Unworthy elements also were mingled in this conspiracy: Platon Zubof, Catherine's last favorite, his brother Nikolai, their sister, who was hand and glove with the English party, and on terms of familiarity with the British embassy, together with courtiers who had grown wealthy on the spoils of Poland during the preceding reign, and feared that Paul would make them reimburse the Poles, whose property they had. Paul had just disgraced Rostoptchin and banished Araktchéef, both of them devotedly attached to him. When he reconsidered his sentence and wrote them to return, it was too late; he was already in the power of his enemies. On the twenty-third of March Paul sent an order to his minister in Berlin to put a stop to the indecision of Prussia by threatening the King with war, and Pahlen had the boldness to add the following postscript in his own handwriting : " His imperial majesty is not well to-day; his illness may have important results." That evening the palace was under the guard of the Semenovski, many of whose officers had been won over to the plot. While the conspirators went to the Emperor's chamber, Pahlen was on the watch, ready, it is said by some narrators, himself to hand them over to Paul should the plot fail. Bennigsen, sword in hand, presented Paul an act of abdication to sign; a struggle ensued, the lamp which lighted the room fell, and in the darkness Paul the First was thrown to the floor by Nikolai Zubof or by Prince Iashvil, and strangled with an officer's scarf. On the twenty-fourth of March Alexander, who had not expected this terrible event, was proclaimed Emperor.

England could not help being satisfied by the simultaneous news of the destruction of the Danish fleet and the terrible death of the Tsar, who was the soul of the coalition. In France the consternation was great. Bonaparte, who saw the downfall of his vast projects, could not contain himself. He caused the following lines, full of rage and hate against England, to be printed in the *Moniteur*, making himself the mouthpiece of an absurd suspicion : "It is for history to clear up the secret of this tragic death, and to say what national policy was interested in provoking such a catastrophe."

CHAPTER XIII.

ALEXANDER THE FIRST: FOREIGN AFFAIRS.

1801-1825.

First War with Napoleon: Austerlitz, Eylau, Friedland, and Treaty of Tilsit.—Interview at Erfürt: Wars with England, Sweden, Austria, Turkey, and Persia.—Grand Duchy of Warsaw: Causes of the Second War with Napoleon.—The "Patriotic War": Battle of Borodino; Burning of Moscow; Destruction of the Grand Army.—Campaigns of Germany and France: Treaties of Vienna and Paris.—Kingdom of Poland: Congresses at Aix-la-Chapelle, Carlsbad, Laybach, and Verona.

FIRST WAR WITH NAPOLEON: AUSTERLITZ, EYLAU, FRIEDLAND, AND TREATY OF TILSIT.

THE Emperor Alexander, who was now about twenty-five years old, was warmly welcomed to the throne. He was distinguished for his liberal ideas, but at the same time indecision of character was his prevailing weakness. Soon after his accession Count Pahlen, who tried to treat Alexander as an inferior, was disgraced, and his dismissal was soon followed by that of Zubof and Panin, the conspirators who had murdered Paul. Alexander then took three young men into his especial confidence, — Paul Strogonof, Novosiltsof, and Adam Tchartoruiski, whom Paul had sent as minister to Sardinia, fearing his influence upon his son. These three were all filled with generosity, and perhaps even with illusions. Associated with them was Prince Kotchubey, an older man, who had seen more of the world, and was well calculated to temper their impetuosity by his cooler reason. With the new reign, therefore, began a new foreign policy. Immediately after his accession Alexander addressed a letter of reconciliation to George the Third. He ordered the embargo on English vessels to be raised, and the sailors who had been captured to be set at liberty; he also entreated Admiral Parker to cease hostilities against Denmark. Those acts announced the dissolution of the League of Neutrality. On the seventeenth of July, eighteen hundred and one, a compromise was agreed upon by which England consented to define more strictly what articles should be understood to be contraband in war, admitted that a blockade must be effective before it could be considered binding, and gave up boarding foreign men-of-war.

The concessions made by Russia were of a much graver kind. They consisted in the abandonment of the principles of the armed neutrality, and the disavowal of the naval policy of Catherine the Second and Paul the First. Alexander allowed that the flag was not to cover merchandise; vessels of war were not to have the right to hinder the inspection, nor even the seizure of the merchant ships that they convoyed. England restored the islands taken from the Swedes and Danes. Denmark and Sweden, considering the common cause betrayed, confined themselves to making peace with Great Britain without touching the disputed points.

Alexander affected, nevertheless, a desire to remain on good terms with France, and instructed Count Markof to continue at Paris the negotiations begun by Koluitchef. Affairs had gone on so rapidly under Paul, that the two States had arranged an offensive alliance without ever having concluded a formal treaty of peace. The First Consul was greatly irritated at the abrupt change in the Russian policy. On the other hand, the instructions given by Alexander to Markof breathed defiance towards Bonaparte, who, "by flattering the deceased Emperor, had chiefly in view the use of him as a weapon against England, and who doubtless only thought of gaining time."

Bonaparte, however, sent Duroc to represent him at Alexander's coronation. He received Count Markof courteously, assuring him of his esteem for Alexander, but he made him understand that the situation was no longer the same, and that Russia had not the right to exact so much from France. "My obligations towards the Emperor Paul, whose great and magnanimous ideas corresponded perfectly with the views of France, were such that I should not have hesitated to become the lieutenant of Paul the First." He complained that Russia insisted on such unimportant trifles as that of the "little kinglet" of Sardinia, and that it wished to treat France "like the republic of Lucca."

In his demands in favor of the King of Sardinia, Alexander felt that he had not the support of England, which, while negotiating for peace, had advised Cornwallis "not to embarrass himself with questions foreign to purely British interests." On the eighth of October, then, a treaty was signed between France and Russia, and on the eleventh of October there was a secret convention, of which the seven principal articles were as follow : —

The common mediation of the two powers for the Germanic indemnities stipulated by the Peace of Lunéville; an agreement about Italian affairs; the mediation of Russia for the establishment of a peace between France and Turkey; the independence of Naples, and the evacuation of its territory by the French, after the latter had evacuated Egypt; an indemnity to the King of Sardinia "according to present circumstances"; a suitable indemnity to the sovereigns of Bavaria, Würtemberg, and Baden; independence and neutrality of the Ionian Isles.

The two parties also bound themselves to do all that lay in their power to strengthen the general peace, to re-establish the equilibrium of the different parts of the world, and to insure liberty of navigation.

The treaty of the eighth of October followed that of Lunéville between France and Austria, and led to that of Amiens with England. It secured the dictatorship of France and Russia in the regulation of continental affairs. Common mediation for the indemnities, and joint action in Italian affairs, — these were the principles that the late Tsar would have wished to see prevail; but circumstances were changed. Out of regard for Paul the First, Bonaparte might have renounced Piedmont, Naples, and Italy, but Paul the First fought for the liberty of the seas, threatened England in the Baltic and India, and assured the revenge of the French against Great Britain. The first act of Alexander had been, on the contrary, to desert his allies, and seek a reconciliation with England.

In the regulation of German affairs the will of France naturally preponderated. If Bonaparte increased the dominions of the houses of Bavaria, Würtemberg, Baden, and Darmstadt, which were related to the imperial family of Russia, it was doubtless partly with a view to pleasing Alexander, but above all because he wished to recompense their fidelity to the French alliance. It was the influence of France, and not that of Russia, that was increased on the left bank of the Rhine. This was plainly to be seen in eighteen hundred and five, when all these princes hastened to conclude separate treaties with France, which already announced the Confederation of the Rhine. For the moment it was the self-esteem of Alexander that was specially wounded; he saw that everything was worked from Paris, that Bonaparte was all-powerful, and that his envoy, Markof, was sought by the German princes only after they had paid court to Talleyrand.

In Italy the question of the indemnity to the King of Sardinia dragged on slowly. On the eleventh of September, eighteen hundred and two, Bonaparte announced the union of Piedmont to France, but he always declined to fix the equivalent which he promised to give. He at first suggested Parma and Piacenza, then had given them to an Infanta of Spain. He no longer offered anything beyond Siena, Orbitello, and a pension of five hundred thousand livres, saying, "As much money as you like, but nothing more"; and again, "This affair ought not to interest the Emperor Alexander more than the affairs of Persia interest me, the First Consul."

In Switzerland, in that Helvetia through which Suvorof had hoped to march as victor, it was Bonaparte who laid down the law, accepting the title of mediator, and occupying cantons troubled by intestine discords. It is true that in the Ionian Islands, ceaselessly agitated by small civil wars, it was a Russian plenipotentiary who arrived to appease the popular excitement, while the Emperor of Russia guaranteed the constitution.

The Peace of Amiens was on the eve of being broken, and, to hinder the rupture between France and England, Russia would have wished to offer its mediation. It feared above everything the French occupation of Naples and Hanover. The occupation of Naples meant the humiliation of another Italian client of Russia; the occupation of Hanover would bring the French very near to the Elbe and Hamburg. The fears of Alexander were realized. In a war against England, Bonaparte could not neglect such important points. Gouvion Saint Cyr occupied Tarento, Otranto, and Brindisi; Mortier invaded Hanover and got a loan from Hamburg; Holland and Tuscany were also garrisoned with French troops in June and July, eighteen hundred and three.

The choice of Markof as the Russian representative at Paris had not been happy. Like almost all the Russian aristocracy, he alike hated new France, the Revolution, and Bonaparte. He was the declared friend of the émigrés at the very moment when the royalist plots were putting the life of the First Consul in danger. His Austrian sympathies were notorious.

He proved to be proud, excessively obstinate, and even impertinent. When the consular court and all the diplomatic body went into mourning on the death of General Leclerc, Bonaparte's brother-in-law, he alone declined to wear it. He was compromised by the seizure of some pamphlets published against the government, his name being found at the head of the list of subscribers. He had the audacity to say, "The Emperor of Russia has his will, but the people also have theirs." The Russian government refused to recall him, in spite of Talleyrand's declaration that since the renewal of the war with England "the presence of so ill-disposed a man was more than unpleasant to the First Consul." Bonaparte complained also of some French émigrés whose intrigues were protected by Russia: of Christin, formerly secretary to Calonne, at Paris, of Vernègues at Rome, of D'Entraigues at Dresden. At last, after an angry scene in which Napoleon entirely forgot his dignity, Markof appeared no more at the Tuileries, and was finally recalled. The French were, however, no better contented with D'Oubril, who remained at Paris as chargé d'affaires.

The seizure and execution of the Duc d'Enghien in March, eighteen hundred and four, increased the misunderstanding between the two cabinets. The news of this murder reached Saint Petersburg on the eve of a diplomatic reception; when the reception itself took place, the Emperor and all his court were in mourning. Alexander passed General Hédouville, the French ambassador, without speaking to him. D'Oubril presented to the French government a note protesting against the violation of the law of nations and of neutral territory. Alexander, in his character as Guarantee of the German Empire, a title which had been conferred on the Russian Emperor at the Treaty of Teschen, caused a similar note to be laid before the Diet at Ratisbon, which Sweden and England hastened to ratify, but which terribly embarrassed the Diet and all the Germanic body. Bonaparte replied by recalling "

Hédouville. He replied officially to D'Oubril's note by complaining of the unfriendly acts of the Russian government towards him, of the ill-will of all its agents, of the embarrassing situation which it sought to create for France by everywhere patronizing the émigrés; he contested the right of Russia to interfere in the affairs of Germany, and declared that in the affair of Ettenheim the government had acted only in self-defence. "The complaint made by Russia to-day compels us to ask if, when England meditated the assassination of Paul the First, men had been aware that the authors of the conspiracy were lurking within a league from the frontiers, they would not have hastened to capture them?" After such an interchange of letters, the chargés d'affaires themselves were recalled, and all diplomatic relations broken.

Napoleon had just been crowned Emperor; he had taken at Milan the crown of Italy, united Genoa to the French territory, and modified the constitution of Holland. From the camp at Boulogne he threatened England, but a coalition was already formed against him. Novosiltsof, one of Alexander's favorite ministers, in September, eighteen hundred and four, left for London with special instructions drawn up by the Emperor; we find in them all kinds of Utopian schemes, sometimes generous, often incoherent, which he still cherished at this epoch. He proposes to wrest from the French, who gave themselves out as the champions of liberty, this illusion, which was a dangerous weapon of propaganda; to give to the troubled world a good example by restoring the King of Sardinia; to render back to Switzerland and Holland the liberty to choose their own rulers; to declare to the French, who would gladly welcome the allies, that the war was directed, not against them, but against their government, from which they suffered as severely as the rest of Europe. In this note Alexander renewed the question of the reconstitution of Europe: taking count of natural frontiers, of crests of mountains, of groups of nationalities, he added a scheme for the partition of the Ottoman Empire, in the case of its existence becoming incompatible with the present state of Europe. The British Cabinet received these communications somewhat coldly, but on the eleventh of April, eighteen hundred and five, concluded a treaty in which it was agreed to drive the French from Northern Germany, to declare Holland and Switzerland independent, and bring about a state of things which would secure universal peace. England, moreover, promised a yearly subsidy in the proportion of six hundred and twenty-five thousand pounds for every one hundred thousand men put under arms by Russia.

Sweden and Naples entered the coalition; Austria was already attacking Bavaria, the ally of Napoleon. Alexander wished to assure himself also of Frederic William the Third, who was always constantly vacillating between France and Russia, and who had undertaken engagements towards both. He went to Berlin so as to use his personal influence, and thought to gain Frederic by announcing that his army was about to cross Silesia and Pomerania; but the King of Prussia instantly mobilized his troops, to cause his neutrality to be respected. The violation of the territories of Anspach and Baireuth by the French soon changed the course of his ideas. During his visit Alexander had his famous interview, near the tomb of Frederic the Great, with the King and Queen of Prussia. They went by torchlight into the vault where the coffin lay, and knelt before it. Alexander was moved to tears, and clasping his friend to his bosom promised never to desert him. By the Treaty of Potsdam Prussia undertook to furnish eighty thousand men to the coalition if Napoleon did not accept its ultimatum. The ultimatum stipulated for the independence of Germany and Italy, and the indemnity to the King of Sardinia. Baron Haugwitz was ordered to carry it to Napoleon.

During these negotiations the Russian army was put in motion. Behind the three great Austrian armies, led by the

Archduke Charles in Italy, the Archduke John in the Tyrol, and Mack with the Archduke Ferdinand against Bavaria, were ranged the Russian troops. Besides the twenty thousand men under Tolstoï, who were to join the Swedes and disembark at Stralsund, and the twenty thousand under Admiral Seniavin, who were to join the English and disembark at Naples, there were the troops who guarded the frontiers of Turkey and Prussia, and the great German army. The latter had as its vanguard Kutuzof, who, with forty-five thousand men, hastened to the Inn to unite with Mack. In Moravia, where the Emperor was in person, strong forces were gathering under the orders of Buxhœvden. Alexander had with him his three ministers, — Tchartoruiski, Novosiltsof, and Strogonof. All the Imperial Guard was there, — the Horse Guards, the Knights, the Preobrazhenski, the Semenovski, the Ismaïlovski, the Pavlovski, and the flower of the army.

Kutuzof had already reached Braunau on the Inn, where he learned the capitulation of Ulm, and the annihilation of Mack's army, on the nineteenth of October, eighteen hundred and five. He found his own position very critical, being at a great distance from the main body. He had under him excellent troops, and three admirable lieutenants : Prince Bagration, one of the heroes of the campaign of seventeen hundred and ninety-nine, the favorite pupil of old Suvorof; Dokturof, the intrepid leader of the grenadiers; Miloradovitch, surnamed the Murat of the Russian army, and of whom it was said, " Whoever wishes to follow Miloradovitch must have a spare life." To escape being cut off on the right bank of the Danube by Murat's cavalry, by Oudinot and by Lannes, and on the left bank by the corps of Mortier, Kutuzof retreated, giving battle to Oudinot at Lambach and at Amstetten in November, eighteen hundred and five. He then crossed the Danube at Krems, fought the battle of Dirnstein with Mortier, and marched to the north to join the great Russian army. The surprise of the bridge of Vienna by Lannes and Murat endangered him on his left flank during his retreat into Moravia. To save his army, he had to sacrifice his rear-guard. The tenacious Bagration was charged to check the pursuit of the French. He intrenched himself at Hollabrunn and Schöngraben. Murat came up first, and desired to gain time in order to allow Lannes to join him; Bagration wished to give Kutuzof time to escape. He received Murat's envoy favorably, and sent to propose an armistice in the name of the Tsar. Ten hours passed while they awaited the answer of Napoleon. The latter, furious at Murat's credulity, sent orders that he was to attack immediately. Bagration's ten thousand men fought desperately during twelve hours. At night Bagration retreated, having lost two thousand men and all his guns. Kutuzof, who had been saved by his devotion, embraced him, and exclaimed, " You live, and that is enough for me."

The junction of Kutuzof, Buxhœvden, and the Austrians took place at Olmütz, and Napoleon was concentrating his forces at Brünn. He had collected about seventy thousand men, the Emperors of Russia and Austria about eighty thousand. The greatest exultation reigned in the Russian headquarters. The young Emperor and his young officers, proud of the splendid battles fought by Kutuzof and Bagration, spoke with profound contempt of the Austrians, who had allowed themselves to be so easily trapped at Ulm; they had only hatred and disdain for " Buonaparte the Corsican," who owed his victories to the imbecility of his adversaries. A small success of the vanguard at Wischau, the apparent timidity of Napoleon, and the arrival of General Savary as envoy, completely turned their heads. Alexander sent the young Prince Dolgoruki to the French headquarters, with a note addressed to the " head of the French nation." It was necessary, said the Prince to Napoleon, that the French should abandon Italy, if they wanted immediate peace. If they were vanquished, they would have to lose not only the Rhine, but Piedmont, Savoy, and Belgium, which would be formed into barriers against them. "What! Brussels also?" exclaimed Napoleon, and coldly dismissed him. "These people are mad," he said. "What would they do with France if I were defeated!"

"It is difficult," relates a Russian eyewitness, Zhirkiévitch, the lieutenant of artillery, " to picture the enthusiasm that animated us all, and the strange and ridiculous infatuation that accompanied this noble sentiment. It seemed to us that we were going straight to Paris. No one spoke of anything but Dolgoruki, a young man of twenty-five, who presented himself to Napoleon with a letter from the Emperor, and all admired the cleverness of the superscription, in which the imperial title of Napoleon had been so skilfully avoided. It was even added that when Dolgoruki gave the letter to Napoleon, as the latter remained covered, Dolgoruki replaced his hat. A few days passed, and our ideas became greatly changed." One scheme, conceived by Weirother the Austrian, and approved by Alexander, was that Bagration on the right should keep Lannes in check; the two Imperial guards would be sufficient to watch the plateau of Pratzen; Dokturof, Langeron, Przhébishevski, even Kutuzof and Miloradovitch, were to descend into the valley of Goldbach to meet Napoleon, cut him off from the Danube, and force him back on the mountains of Bohemia.

The evening before the battle it was still believed that Napoleon would retreat. Dolgoruki recommended his soldiers " to watch well which way the French retired." On the morning of the second of December, eighteen hundred and five, the valley of Goldbach was covered by a fog, from the waves of which emerged, as from the bosom of a milky sea, the mountain heights which were gilded by the early rays of the sun; on the west lay the peaks of Schlapanitz, where Napoleon had taken up his position; on the east, the hills of Pratzen, where the allied emperors were encamped. Napoleon distinctly saw the Russian columns descend the plateau of Pratzen, and disappear in the fog; and from the side of Lakes Sokolnitz, Satchan, and Menitz — that is to say, to his right — he heard the noise of their artillery carriages. He was therefore certain that, as he had foreseen, the allies intended to attack this wing. When the plateau of Pratzen, the centre of the Russian army, seemed to him sufficiently bare, he gave the signal. In twenty minutes the corps of Soult scaled the slopes in heavy masses, and attacked Kutuzof and Miloradovitch, whose divisions alone remained on the plateau. There a desperate battle was fought. The Emperor of Russia found himself under fire, his men were dispersed, and he himself was obliged to retire at a gallop, attended only by his doctor, a single orderly, and two Cossacks. A little to the right of the plateau the Grand Duke Konstantin, the Emperor's brother, with the guards, tried to oppose the cavalry of Murat and the French guards. It was an epic struggle, where fought on one side the famous Russian regiments of the foot guards, the horse guards, the flower of the Russian nobility, the uhlans, the chasseurs of the guard, the Cossacks, and the cuirassiers of Lichtenstein; on the other, the Mamelukes of Rapp, the mounted grenadiers of Bessières, the light cavalry of Kellermann, the cuirassiers of Hautpoul and of Nansouty. At the extreme right of the Russians, Bagration could easily beat a retreat before Lannes; but on their left, the columns of Dokturof, Langeron, and Przhébishevski, entangled in the network of lakes, engaged since morning by the corps of Davoust, and suddenly attacked in their rear by the victorious troops returning from the plateau of Pratzen, found themselves in a frightful situation: Buxhœvden was hard pressed near a frozen lake which some of the infantry tried to cross. The French broke the ice with their artillery and many Russians perished. The French at first reported the number drowned to be twenty thousand, but afterwards it was reduced to two thousand. Dokturof protected the retreat. Tchartoruiski wrote the Tsar, "The feeling throughout the whole army at this moment was not of the need of avenging the insult it had received, but rather a desire to go away as soon as possible and consider the war at an end."

Such was "the battle of the three emperors." The Russians fell back on Austerlitz. Without reckoning the Austrian loss, their own amounted to twenty-one thousand men, two hundred cannons, and thirty flags. They were furious against their allies. As happened after the battle of Zürich, they accused them of incapacity, and even of treason. It was the Austrians who had sketched the plan of the battle; and, fighting in their own country, on ground which they had studied at leisure in their manœuvres on parade, they had not succeeded in either arranging their troops to advantage or in providing forage and ammunition. Dolgoruki, in a report to the Emperor, remarks: "They conducted your majesty's army rather in a way to deliver it to the enemy than to fight; and what puts the finishing touch to this infamy is, that the disposition of our forces was known to the enemy, a fact of which we have certain proof." Rostoptchin, in a letter to Prince Tsitsianof, echoes him: "The plan had been treacherously communicated to Bonaparte; forty-eight hours before we were ready, the latter began the attack at break of day. From the beginning, half of the Austrians took up arms; the other half crossed over to the enemy, and some even fired on us."

On the fourth of December the Emperor Francis of Austria had an interview with Napoleon, and obtained for the Russian army, which was greatly imperilled after its disaster, and was closely pressed by Davoust, leave to retire, on condition that it should evacuate Hungary and Moravia within a fortnight, and Gallicia within a month. On the twenty-sixth the Treaty of Presburg was signed, which deprived Francis the Second of Venice, the Tyrol, and Austrian Suabia; he was likewise to give up the title of Emperor. This new intervention of the Russians in Europe ended in a formidable growth of French power. On the fifteenth of March, eighteen hundred and six, Napoleon appointed his brother-in-law, General Joachim Murat, Grand Duke of Cleves and Berg. On the thirty-first the King of Naples was dethroned and replaced by Joseph Bonaparte; the kingdom of Italy was increased by Venice; the sovereigns of Bavaria, Würtemberg, and Baden, strengthened by the spoils of Austria, decorated with the titles of king and grand duke, declaring themselves independent of the German Empire, formed, with the new Prince-Primate Charles of Dalberg, the Grand Duke of Hesse-Darmstadt, and fifteen other sovereign princes, the Confederation of the Rhine, the Rheinbund. There was no longer reason for Russian interference in Germany. Already Napoleon's family was contracting matrimonial alliances with those of Bavaria, Würtemberg, and Baden. The German vassals of the successor of Charles the Great, of the new Emperor of the West, could add to his army from one hundred thousand to one hundred and fifty thousand men. Haugwitz, who had been ordered to inform Napoleon of the ultimatum stipulated by the Treaty of Potsdam, found himself at Schönbrunn in the presence of a defiant and invincible conqueror; he was forced to sign a treaty which obliged Prussia to accept Hanover, in exchange for Auspach and Baireuth, and irrevocably brought on a war with England. The coalition was therefore beaten in the field and dissolved in the cabinet. Russia, isolated by the ruin of Naples, the desertion of Austria, and the defection of Prussia, found itself almost alone on the Continent.

It is well known how from this same Treaty of Schönbrunn, which appeared to attach Prussia to Napoleon, sprang a new war. The coalition was renewed between Russia, England, Sweden, and Prussia. The Prussians showed in eighteen hundred and six the same precipitation as the Austrians in eighteen hundred and five; like them, they did not allow time for the Russians to join them; and when Alexander found himself able to undertake a second campaign, he learned the twofold catastrophe of Jena and Auerstädt, on the fourteenth of October, as he had formerly learned that of Ulm. For the second time his principal ally was beaten, and the whole weight of the war fell upon Russia. On this occasion the disaster was even greater, for the Prussian monarchy ceased to exist. The French occupied Berlin, and took the fortresses on the Oder and the Vistula. Nothing remained to Frederic William in the North but three fortresses, Dantzig, Königsberg, and Memel, and a small body of fourteen thousand men under Lestocq.

These events had followed one another with a rapidity so startling that Alexander found himself taken unawares. After Austerlitz he had tried to negotiate with Napoleon, and sent D'Oubril to Paris; but D'Oubril, who had consented to the evacuation of Cattaro and the Ionian Isles, and the recognition of the principle of Ottoman integrity, had been disavowed at Saint Petersburg, like Haugwitz at Berlin. Russia found itself in a terrible plight; and it had in addition the prospect of a double war against Persia and Turkey. Tchartoruiski, Minister of Foreign Affairs, addressed a memorial to the Emperor, counselling peace. He showed that Russia had two vulnerable points, — Poland, and the serfage of the peasants. Invasion must be avoided at all costs, for the invader would not fail to proclaim the re-establishment of Poland, and the freedom of the serfs. It was of little consequence that Germany was subject to Napoleon, if the latter would consent not to pass the Weser or even the Elbe. It was necessary to consent to the evacuation of Cattaro and the Ionian Isles, to guarantee only Sicily to the King of Naples, and to obtain some sort of an indemnity to the King of Sardinia. It would be better to secure the co-operation of Napoleon for regulating the affairs of Turkey. Only one thing was important, the safety of the empire.

But Alexander, secure of Prussia, which was at this moment still intact, inclined to war. He commanded a new conscription of one man in every hundred, lowered the regulation height one inch, ordered muskets even from private manufacturers and foreigners, created new regiments, summoned students and young nobles, promising them the grade of officer after six months' service, for the fight at Pratzen had made terrible havoc with the guards. A plan of organizing militia was talked of, which would have given them six hundred and twelve thousand men. The priests were ordered to proclaim everywhere that war was made, "not for vainglory, but for the salvation of the country." England was asked for a loan of six million sterling. An appeal was once more made to Austria. When Prussia was crushed, the fourteen thousand Prussians of Lestocq were sent for.

Buxhœvden had twenty-eight thousand men; another army of sixty thousand men was confided to Bennigsen, a learned man of boundless energy, who had been one of the conspirators of eighteen hundred and one, and had a considerable genius for tactics. He has, however, been reproached with indecision at the critical moment, with neglecting discipline, and not being able to repress pillage; the marauders did not respect even his headquarters or his own house. These defects were, however, partially atoned for by a tenacity which astonished Napoleon. The old field-marshal Kamenski, nominated generalissimo, had concentrated all his forces on the Vistula. When his infirmities obliged him to resign his command, Bennigsen succeeded him.

Murat, Davoust, and Lannes had entered Warsaw, which was then a Prussian possession, and had established themselves on the Bug, forming the right of the Grand Army. Soult and Augereau crossed the Vistula at Modlin, and formed the centre; on the left Ney and Bernadotte occupied Thorn and Elbing. In the rear Mortier acted in Pomerania against the Swedes; Lefèbvre besieged Dantzig; and Jerome Bonaparte, with Vandamme, finished the conquest of Silesia. Pressed by the Grand Army, Bennigsen was obliged to evacuate Poland, after some severe fighting, especially at Pultusk on December twenty-six, and retired by way of Ostrolenka, leaving in the mud of Poland eighty field-pieces and nearly ten thousand men; he stopped on the Alle to cover Königsberg.

Winter was at hand: the Grand Army was reposing in camp, when Bennigsen conceived the audacious project of moving his left wing, passing between the two forces of Bernadotte and Ney, crushing Bernadotte, and forcing Ney into the sea; of relieving Dantzig and carrying the war into Brandenburg on the rear of Napoleon. Bernadotte, however, resisted so stubbornly at Mohrungen and Osterode, that Napoleon had time to come up, and Bennigsen himself was on the point of having his left wing turned, and seeing his lines of communication cut. An intercepted despatch warned him of the risk he ran; it was necessary to sound a retreat, and Bagration was again called on to protect it. As at Schöngraben, he covered himself with glory, and allowed himself to be sacrificed for the salvation of the army; his "incomparable regiment of Kostroma" was almost annihilated, and he himself severely wounded. During this time Bennigsen marched to Eylau and took up a position to the east of the town, on a line of heights which extended from Schloditten to Serpallen; behind his centre lay the village of Sansgarten; his front was covered by two hundred and fifty pieces of cannon.

When Napoleon arrived at Eylau, which was taken on the seventh of February, he had with him only Soult, Augereau, Murat, and the guard; Davoust, who was to form his right wing, and Ney, who was to form his left wing, and who had been delayed by his pursuit of Lestocq, were still wanting. Bennigsen, on his side, awaited Lestocq, who was to compose his right wing. The battle, however, began on February eighth, eighteen hundred and seven, and was one of the bloodiest of the century. A thick snow was falling, which ever and anon hid the battle-field from sight; the sky was of a livid gray; the landscape was as gloomy as the result of the action. The battle began by a formidable cannonade, which lasted all day. The French, sheltered by the buildings of the town of Eylau, and disposed in thin lines, suffered from it less than the Russians, who had little cover, and were ranged in compact masses. The corps of Augereau and the division of Saint Hilaire, intrusted with the attack on the Russian left wing, went astray, blinded by a squall of snow; when the sky cleared, the two divisions of Augereau found themselves opposite the Russian centre, forty paces from a battery of seventy-two guns; mown down at the cannon's mouth, they lost in a few minutes five thousand two hundred men. Augereau and his two generals of division were wounded. At the same moment an enormous mass of cavalry, uhlans, and cuirassiers dashed themselves against Saint Hilaire's infantry, upsetting everything in their passage. The infantry of the Russian centre advanced almost to the cemetery of Eylau, where Napoleon was standing. Then Murat, in his turn, assembled eighty squadrons, and led against this infantry the most frightful charge mentioned in the annals of these wars; solid squares were broken by his cuirassiers. The two armies continued to watch and to fire at each other, but the battle made little progress till Davoust at last joined the right wing of the French army, turned the Russian left and threw it back upon the centre, and reached Sausgarten on their rear. The Prussians of Lestocq arrived in their turn at the other extremity of the line, but they were followed by Ney, who in the darkness of night, at half past nine o'clock, began to break Bennigsen's right wing. The Russians now ran the risk of being surrounded. They had suffered cruel losses: one of their divisions, that of Count Ostermann Tolstoï, counted no more than twenty-five hundred men. "The general in chief," says M. Bogdanovitch, "trembled as he read the reports of the generals of divisions." They had not thirty thousand men under arms; twenty-six thousand were killed or wounded; among the latter were Barclay de Tolly, Dokturof, and seven other generals. He profited by the darkness to beat a retreat, and did not hesitate to claim as a victory what in reality had only been a glorious resistance. Bennigsen boldly ordered the Te Deum to be sung.

The French had more right to call themselves victorious, as they remained masters of the field of battle. Unlike the Russians, some of their troops were still intact, such as Ney's corps and the Foot Guards, but they had likewise suffered terribly, and a gloomy sadness hung over the survivors. Such efforts, so much blood shed, so few trophies! This melancholy impression is reflected even in Napoleon's despatch, where he allows himself to describe the funereal aspect of the battle-field, the thousands of heaped-up corpses, the gunners killed on their pieces, "all thrown into relief by a background of snow." Ney shrugged his shoulders on seeing the carnage. "What a massacre," he said, "and without result!" They suffered hunger and cold; the immense spaces, the broken roads, the marshy plains, the stoical resistance of the Russians, had disconcerted the calculations of Napoleon. Eylau gave him a foretaste of eighteen hundred and twelve; the delay of Ney a foretaste of Waterloo. Fortune took care to warn him that she would not always be punctual to her rendezvous. The effect produced on Europe was unlucky for France; in Paris the Funds fell.

In order to confirm his victory, reorganize his army, reassure France, re-establish the opinion of Europe, encourage the Polish insurrection, and to curb the ill-will of Germany and Austria, Napoleon remained a week at Eylau. He negotiated: on one side he caused Talleyrand to write to Zastrow, the Prussian foreign minister, to propose peace and his alliance; he sent Bertrand to Memel to offer to re-establish the King of Prussia, on the condition of no foreign intervention. He also tried to negotiate with Bennigsen; to which the latter made answer "that his master had charged him to fight, and not negotiate." After some hesitation, Prussia ended by joining its fortunes to those of Russia. By the convention of Bartenstein, of the twenty-fifth of April, eighteen hundred and seven, the two sovereigns came to terms on the following points : —

The re-establishment of Prussia within the limits of eighteen hundred and five ; the dissolution of the Confederation of the Rhine ; the restitution to Austria of the Tyrol and Venice ; the accession of England to the coalition, and the aggrandizement of Hanover ; the co-operation of Sweden ; the restoration of the house of Orange, and indemnities to the kings of Naples and Sardinia. This document is important; its conditions are almost the same as those offered to Napoleon at the Congress of Prague, in eighteen hundred and thirteen.

Russia and Prussia proposed then to make a more pressing appeal to Austria, Sweden, and England; but the Emperor Francis was naturally undecided, and the Archduke Charles, alleging the state of the finances and the army, strongly advised him against any new intervention. Sweden was too weak ; and notwithstanding his fury against Napoleon, Gustavus the Third had just been forced to treat with Mortier. The English ministry, consisting of the Duke of Portland with Canning and Castlereagh, showed a remarkable inability to conceive the situation ; they refused to guarantee the new Russian loan of a hundred and fifty millions, and would lend themselves to no maritime diversion.

Napoleon showed the greatest diplomatic activity. The Sultan Selim the Third declared war against Russia ; General Sebastiani, the envoy at Constantinople, put the Bosphorus in a state of defence, and repulsed the English fleet; General Gardane left for Ispahan, with a mission to cause a Persian outbreak in the Caucasus. Dantzig had capitulated, and Lefèbvre's forty thousand men were therefore ready for service. Masséna took thirty-six thousand from Italy.

In the spring Bennigsen, who had been reinforced by ten

thousand regular troops, six thousand Cossacks, and the Imperial Guard, being now at the head of one hundred and ten thousand men, took the offensive; Gortchakof commanding the right and Bagration the left. He tried, as in the preceding year, to seize Ney's division; but the latter fought, as he retired, two bloody fights, at Gutstadt and Ankendorff. Bennigsen, again in danger of being surrounded, retired on Heilsberg, where, on the tenth of June, he defended himself bravely; but the French, extending their line on his right, marched on Eylau, so as to cut him off from Königsberg. The Russian generalissimo retreated; but, being pressed, he had to draw up at Friedland, on the Alle.

The position he had taken up was most dangerous. All his army was enclosed in an angle of the Alle, with the steep bed of the river at their backs, which in case of misfortune left them only one means of retreat, over the three bridges of Friedland. The French vanguard arrived at two in the morning of June fourteenth, eighteen hundred and seven, filled the woods of Posthenen with sharpshooters, and held the Russians in check till the Emperor's arrival. The Russian army was almost entirely hidden in the ravine of the Alle. "Where are the Russians concealed?" asked Napoleon when he came up. When he had noted their situation, he exclaimed: "No, it is not every day that an enemy is surprised in such a blunder." He placed Lannes and Victor in reserve, ordered Mortier to hold Gortchakof in check on the left and to remain still, as "the movement to be made by the right wing would turn upon the left." As to Ney, he was to cope with Bagration on the right, he was to drive like a wedge among the Russians who were shut in by the angle of the river; he was to meet them in hand-to-hand conflict, without taking any thought of his own safety. Ney led this charge with irresistible fury; the Russians were riddled by his artillery at one hundred and fifty paces. He successively crushed the chasseurs of the Russian guard, the Ismaïlovski regiment, and the horse guards; he burnt Friedland with his shells, and cannonaded the bridges, which was their only way of retreat. In a quarter of an hour the Ismaïlovski lost four hundred men out of five hundred and twenty. Bagration, surrounded by the grenadiers of Moscow, was obliged to cut his way through; his lieutenants, Raievski, Iermolof, and Baggovut, wasted their strength in vain efforts. The Russian left wing was almost thrown into the river. Bagration, with the Semenovski and other troops, was hardly able to cover the defeat on the Russian right; Gortchakof, who had advanced to attack the immovable Mortier, had time only to reach the Alle, which he had to ford; Count Lambert retired with twenty-nine guns along the left bank; the rest fled by the right bank, closely pursued by the cavalry. Meanwhile Murat, Davoust, and Soult, who had taken no part in the battle, arrived before Königsberg. Lestocq, with twenty-five thousand men, tried to defend it, but on learning the disaster of Friedland he hastily evacuated it. Only one fortress now remained to Frederic William, — the little town of Memel. The Russians lost at Friedland from fifteen thousand to twenty thousand men, besides eighty guns.

Alexander, who was established at Jurburg, received a report from Bennigsen merely announcing that he had been obliged to evacuate the banks of the Alle, and that he would wait in a more advantageous position till Lobanof-Rostovski brought him reinforcements. But Lobanof had only a few thousand Kalmuiki, and it was to these badly armed savages that they looked for the salvation of Russia. More explicit accounts reached Alexander from the Tsarévitch Konstantin and other officers. The situation was desperate: Alexander had no longer an army. Only one man, Barclay de Tolly, proposed to continue the war; but in order to do this it would be necessary to re-enter Russia, to penetrate into the very heart of the empire, to burn everything on the way, and present only a desert to the enemy. Alexander hoped to get off more cheaply. He wrote a severe letter to Bennigsen, and gave him powers to treat. Prince Lobanof left for the headquarters of Napoleon, who sent in his turn the Captain de Talleyrand-Périgord. Alexander had at that time a common sentiment with Napoleon, — hatred of the English. He did not pardon them either for their refusal to guarantee a Russian loan, or for the calculated insufficiency of their diversions, or for their mercantile selfishness.

On June twenty-fifth the interview on the raft at Tilsit took place. Alexander and Napoleon conversed for nearly two hours. The King of Prussia was not admitted to a conference on which the fate of his dynasty depended. On horseback on the shore, urging his horse even into the water, he waited the result with his eyes fixed on the fateful raft. Even the personal graces of the Queen of Prussia could not soften the severity of the treaty. It was from "respect for the Emperor of all the Russias and desire to unite the two nations in a bond of eternal friendship," that Napoleon "consented" to restore to Frederic William the Third, Old Prussia, Pomerania, Brandenburg, and Silesia.

These articles of the treaty of July eighth, eighteen hundred and seven, completed the fall of Prussia. On the west Napoleon took from it all the possessions between the Rhine and the Elbe, with Magdeburg; he destroyed the thrones of the allied States of Brunswick and Hesse-Cassel. On the east he confiscated all Poland. He thus broke the two wings of the Prussian Eagle. On its right he established the kingdom of Westphalia, on its left the grand duchy of Warsaw. Dantzig was declared a free town. The district Bielostok, with one hundred and eighty-four thousand inhabitants, a part of the dismembered Black Russia, again became Russian soil. The estates of the Princes of Mecklenburg and Oldenburg were restored to them; but they had to suffer the occupation of their territory for the carrying out of the Continental blockade, and like Saxony, the States of Thuringia and all the small princes of Germany, they were obliged to accede to the

Confederation of the Rhine. The King of Prussia adhered to the Continental blockade. His possessions were not to be given back to him till after full payment of a war indemnity.

Besides the conditions relative to Prussia, the Treaty of Tilsit established: Russian mediation between France and England; French mediation between England and Turkey; the recognition by Alexander, and likewise by Frederic William the Third, of Napoleon's brother Joseph as king of Naples, Louis as king of Holland, Jerome of Westphalia, as well as the recognition of the Confederation of the Rhine, and of all States founded by Napoleon; and lastly, reciprocal guarantees for the integrity of the present possessions of Russia and France.

A second treaty, with secret articles, stipulated that Cattaro should be restored to France; that France should have the Ionian Isles in perpetuity; that if Ferdinand were deprived of Sicily, he should have no other equivalent than the Balearic Isles, or Cyprus and Candia; that in this case Joseph should be acknowledged King of the Two Sicilies; that an amnesty should be accorded to the Montenegrins, Herzegovinians, and other peoples who had revolted at the call of Russia; that if Hanover were united to the kingdom of Westphalia, Prussia should receive in exchange a territory on the left bank of the Elbe, with three hundred thousand or four hundred thousand inhabitants.

A third treaty, offensive and defensive, provided that an ultimatum should be addressed to England on the first of November, and that if it had no results war should be declared by Russia on the first of December; that unless Turkey should make peace with the Tsar within three months, then "the two high contracting powers should come to an understanding to withdraw all the Ottoman provinces in Europe, with the exception of Constantinople and Rumelia, from the yoke and tyranny of the Turks"; that Sweden should be summoned to break with England, and if it refused Denmark was to be invited to take part in the war against it, and Finland was to be annexed to Russia; that Austria should be invited to accede to the system of continental blockade at the same time with Sweden, Denmark, and Portugal.

In certain respects this peace deserved the name of "the treacherous peace," which the English agent, Wilson, applied to it in his disappointment. Turkey was abandoned, delivered over by its old friend France, though it is true that Napoleon alleged in excuse the revolution which had just overthrown his friend the Sultan Selim. He acted the same way in regard to Sweden, another old ally. He made all these sacrifices so as to have the right of executing his Machiavelian designs against Spain, whose troops were fighting loyally under his banners. Alexander in no small degree sacrificed his honor and interest to these new combinations. He abruptly consented to go to war with his former ally, England; he renounced the principle of the integrity of Prussia, and even accepted as his share in its spoliation the province of Bielostok; he did not hesitate to wrest Finland from his brother-in-law, his ally Gustavus the Fourth. He consented to see under the euphemism of the grand duchy of Warsaw a nucleus of Poland formed on his frontier. This strange treaty might, however, have satisfied the two States, had it been faithfully executed. The part played by Russia was more brilliant, on the whole, than Napoleon's; while France was about to become exhausted in a fruitless war with Spain, splendid vistas for Alexander's ambition were opening in the East and on the Danube. Thanks to the French alliance, he could follow in this direction the glorious steps of Sviatoslaf, of Peter the Great, and of his grandmother Catherine. For several days, at least, Alexander seemed enthusiastic about his ally. They interchanged the ribbons of their orders; each decorated one of the bravest soldiers of the other army; the grenadier Lazaref received the cross of the Legion of Honor; a battalion of the Imperial guard offered a fraternal banquet to the Preobrazhenski.

INTERVIEW AT ERFÜRT: WARS WITH ENGLAND, SWEDEN, AUSTRIA, TURKEY, AND PERSIA.

The change in the foreign policy was to bring with it a change in the composition of the government. Alexander's early companions, who had entered upon the task of government with no experience, but with lofty aims and with keen expectations of success, had been disappointed. Corruption still was rampant, disorders increased, the chances for culture, which were at the disposal of the upper classes, were neglected; the provincial nobility failed to throng the halls of the new universities. This failure in his hopes led Alexander to distrust his counsellors; such wide-spread disaffection, perhaps, sprung from the personality of his ministers. Most thoroughly was he estranged from Novosiltsof, who had been his most intimate friend. Devoted to England as he was, the announcement that Alexander had accepted the cross of the Legion of Honor caused him at Tilsit to demand his dismissal. Napoleon could have no confidence in Alexander's promises so long as his enemy, Novosiltsof, was at the head of foreign affairs. But Alexander did not "chase him out," but simply neglected him until Novosiltsof made some cutting remarks about the rupture with England and the Russian subservice to France. Then he was ordered to travel abroad, and when he returned, several years after, he was merely appointed senator. Count Kotchubey also was allowed, in November, eighteen hundred and seven, to go abroad to recuperate his failing health, and Stroganof was removed from the immediate presence of the Emperor, with the title of major-general in the army. He had distinguished himself for his bravery in the field of battle, and was made a Knight of the Order of Saint George. Prince Adam Tchartoruiski was now living in Warsaw, charged with the direction of the University of Vilna and the Lithuanian Department of Instruction. Although he was playing a double game, Alexander failed to discover it, and saw in him only the man by whose means, sooner or later, he should become king of Poland. Tchartoruiski took pains to further the illusion, and showed himself almost unscrupulous in the way that he deceived the Emperor with an appearance of straightforwardness. Baron Budberg, who had taken Tchartoruiski's place as minister of foreign affairs, and was well known as an enemy of Napoleon, was also dismissed. The minister of finance, Vasilief, died about this time; so that of the former ministers only three were left. The chief in importance was Rumiantsof, who was made Chancellor, but had in reality only a small influence on the Emperor. Golubzof was appointed minister of finance, and Kurakin, who was distinguished for the Oriental number of his children, took Kotchubey's place in the department of the Interior. At the same time appeared two men who were destined to exert a great influence upon Russian affairs, Araktchéef and Speranski. Araktchéef was supposed to be a skilful artillerist, and in May, eighteen hundred and three, the Emperor appointed him inspector-general of that service. He managed to use the knowledge of a French émigré, named de Barbiche, who was thoroughly grounded in the use of guns, and by a scrupulous observance of details so deceived Alexander, that in eighteen hundred and five he appointed him to a command in the field, which he hastened to decline. Afterwards the Emperor made him war minister, and he set to work to get rid of all those who stood in his way. As long, however, as the Emperor remained firm in his liberal views, Araktchéef was kept in the background. He was especially overshadowed by Mikhail Speranski.

Mikhail Mikhailof was the son of a poor priest who, like other peasants, had no distinctive family name. He was destined for the priesthood, and was sent to the seminary at Vladimir, where he was put under the special protection of a relative, who, conceiving great hopes of him, allowed him to take the name of Speranski. He soon won distinction, and was advanced to the higher seminary in Saint Petersburg. The Metropolitan of Moscow selected him as a candidate for the highest office of the church, but Speranski found that the priesthood was not his calling, so he became instructor of mathematics, and later of philosophy, in the seminary of the Petersburg Monastery. He reached the highest point of honor in this profession when he was made Prefect of the Seminary, at the age of thirty-two. During the latter years of Catherine's reign Prince Kurakin, finding himself in need of a private secretary, took Speranski into his pay at the recommendation of the Metropolitan, and afterwards, when the prince was summoned by Paul to the senate, Speranski entered the service of the State. In three months he was raised to the eighth degree of the Tchin, which gives hereditary nobility, and in spite of the successive changes which ensued in Paul's administration, he kept his position, and shortly before the Emperor was assassinated was presented with a large domain in the government of Saratof, and became a Knight of the Order of Malta. Under Alexander he was made Secretary of State, and having won Kotchubey's favor, he was brought especially to the Emperor's notice. He took Novosiltsof's place after the Peace of Tilsit, and became even more necessary to Alexander than the former had been. He had the gift of expressing the Emperor's ideas in pleasing language, and of accomplishing rapidly and successfully whatever there was to be done. But Speranski's position was by no means enviable. His rapid rise had brought him many enemies, who looked upon him as an interloper. Araktchéef was watching with envious eyes for an opportunity to destroy him. Unpopular as the war had been, the peace was still more so, and Speranski did not conceal his admiration for the genius of the French Emperor, for the principles born of the

Revolution, and embodied in the Civil Code. He seriously desired the maintenance of the French alliance; and M. Pogodin, one of the Slavophils of our time, has not the courage to condemn this policy. "It proves, on the contrary," he says, "his perspicacity as a statesman. The conditions imposed by Napoleon the First would certainly have been more easy to bear than those imposed by Napoleon the Third at Sevastopol. The future of Europe would have been different. Sevastopol would still have shone on the shores of the Black Sea, and the Continent would not lately have been inundated with blood by two cruel wars." "The Eastern question," says another Slavophil, M. Oreste Müller, "would in this case have probably been settled, and English preponderance would have been extinguished in the Levant."

We must recognize the fact that in eighteen hundred and seven Russian aristocracy was not yet reconciled to the state of things to which the Revolution had given rise. The Empress-mother surrounded herself with French émigrés; her court was the centre of the English and Austrian party. It was not only the sudden abandonment of the ancient alliances which was blamed, but it was also the partial restoration of the hereditary enemy, Poland; and yet the question of the grand duchy of Warsaw seemed secondary, — it was considered as a consequence of the subjection to Napoleon. The dismissal of Louis the Eighteenth, who was obliged to leave Mitava for England, and the plot at Bayonne against the Bourbons of Spain still further inflamed the passions of men.

Savary, Napoleon's ambassador, had to endure the brunt of these bitter feelings. The choice of him was by no means a fortunate one, as Savary was supposed to have been more or less concerned in the affair of the Duc d'Enghien. "Feeling against the French ran so high," says Savary, "that no hotel would take me as a lodger. The general reception of myself and my companion was in inverse proportion to the kindness of the Emperor Alexander. During the first six weeks of my stay here I could not get a single door opened to me. The Emperor of Russia saw all this, and wished it had been otherwise. At the moment of my arrival at Saint Petersburg prayers were publicly offered in the churches against us, and particularly against the Emperor Napoleon." The bookstores were full of pamphlets against France, against Napoleon, and against the French ambassador. "Nothing," continues Savary, "was equal to the irreverence with which the Russian youth dared to express itself about its sovereign. For some time I was much disturbed at the consequences this license might have in a country where revolutions in the palace were only too common." Napoleon's envoy thought it even his duty to place in Alexander's hands a correspondence lately seized, in which the writer sent letters of this kind from Prussia to his friends in the interior: "Have you no longer any Pahlens, any Zubofs, any Bennigsens?"

Stedingk, the Swedish ambassador, also wrote to Gustavus the Fourth: "The discontent against the Emperor Alexander increases daily, and things are said at this moment which are frightful to hear. The partisans of the Emperor are in despair, but there is no one among them who dares to remedy the evil, or to reveal to him the full danger of the situation. A change of government is spoken of, not only in private conversations, but in public meetings." Some echo of the public discontent reached Alexander's ears, however. Admiral Mordvinof wrote to him: "Though the days of glory may be passed, those in which Russia laid down the law; though it may have lost the bright hopes which it cherished in our youth, the sons of Russia are ready to shed the last drop of their blood rather than bow ignominiously before the sword of him whose only advantage over them is that he has known how to use weakness, treachery, and incapacity." The historian Karamsin was already preparing for the Emperor his work on "Ancient and Modern Russia."

In general, the literature of this epoch has a very pronounced anti-French character. The national tragedies of Kriukovski and Ozérof; the patriotic odes of Zhukovski; even the comedies and fables of "diédushka" Kruilof, the "little grandfather," as he was affectionately called; the productions of the press, represented by Glinka, Gretch, Batiushkof, and Shishkof, — all breathe hatred against Napoleon and aversion for that new France which the Russians, accustomed as they were to admire and imitate the old France of Versailles, looked upon with the eyes of the émigrés themselves. The most impetuous of the Gallophobes of this epoch was Count Rostoptchin. About eighteen hundred and seven he published his new satire, " O, the French ! " and a comedy entitled " The News," or " The Living-Dead," in which he sharply attacked the alarmists and the extravagant partisans of Western customs. In his " Spoken Thoughts on the Red Staircase," in eighteen hundred and seven, he exclaims: " How long shall we go on imitating monkeys ? As soon as a Frenchman arrives who has escaped the gallows, we fly to welcome him. And he sets the fashions, he represents himself as a prince or a gentleman who has lost his fortune for faith or loyalty, when in reality he is only a lackey or a shopkeeper, or a tax collector, or a suspended priest who has fled his country in fear. What are children taught to-day ? To pronounce French properly, to turn their toes out, and to frizz their hair. He alone is a wit whom a Frenchman will take for his countryman. But how can men love their country when they do not even know their native language ? Is it not a shame ? In every country French is taught to children, but only that they may understand it, and not in order that it may take the place of their mother tongue." He continues with violent invectives against French ambition, and invokes the brave soldiers of Eylau: " Glory to thee, victorious Russian army, bearing the sword in the name of Christ ! Glory to our Emperor, and to our mother Russia ! Hail to you, Russian heroes, Tolstoï, Kozhin, Galitsuin, Dokturof, Volkonski, Dolgoruki ! Eternal peace to you in heaven, young and gallant Galitsuin! Triumph, Russian Empire! the enemy of the human race recoils before thee; he cannot struggle against thy invincible strength. He came as a savage lion, thinking to devour everything; he flies like a hungry wolf, grinding his teeth."

By a contradiction, explained by his education, it is chiefly in his correspondence, and his works written in French, that Rostoptchin attacks the nation so bitterly; it is in French that the Russian nobles, pupils of the French of the eighteenth century, curse France. Miss Wilmot, writing about eighteen hundred and five, with an obvious intention of disparaging both nations, scoffs "at the absurdity of Bruin the bear when he gambols with a monkey on his shoulders." "In the midst of this adoption of French manners, habits, and language, there is something stupidly puerile in declamation against Bonaparte and the French, when the Russians cannot dine without a French cook to make ready their repast; when they cannot bring up their children without the help of adventurers come from Paris, under the names of tutors and governors; in a word, when all their notions of fashion, luxury, and elegance are borrowed from France. What arrant folly!"

Such was Russian society after Tilsit. On account of these evil dispositions towards France, the indignation raised by the abominable attempt of England against Denmark, and the bombardment of Copenhagen in a time of peace in September, eighteen hundred and seven, made a diversion of only short duration. At one moment we might almost believe that the Peace of Tilsit had but three partisans in Russia, — the Emperor, the Chancellor Rumiantsof, and Speranski. Yet Alexander began to find one illusion after another disappear: all the acts of his ally wounded his convictions. After the exile of the kings of Sardinia and Naples, he had to see the expulsion of the house of Braganza, the dethronement of the Bourbons of Spain, the forced flight of the Pope of Rome. The Confederation of the Rhine, increasing beyond all measure, now extended across the Elbe, and had reached the Baltic by means of Lübeck and Mecklenburg; on the Vistula, the grand duchy of Warsaw was being organized with formidable power. Peter Tolstoï, who certainly had done nothing to make himself liked at Paris, who was involved in a quarrel with Ney, and had entered into relations with the legitimists of the Faubourg Saint-Germain, was unable in any way to soften the lot of Frederic William the Third, or to obtain the promised evacuation of the Prussian States. Scanty, indeed, was the compensation for all these sacrifices. The first campaign against Sweden had been far from brilliant. The naval war with England was causing the ruin of Russian commerce. At Constantinople, General Guillémor, Napoleon's ambassador, had managed on the twenty-fourth of August, eighteen hundred and seven, to conclude an armistice between Turkey and Russia, in virtue of which the latter had to evacuate the Danubian principalities within thirty-five days; but as none of the conditions were fulfilled, the Russian troops still remained in Moldavia and Valakhia. There was no longer any likelihood of the partition of the Ottoman Empire, that brilliant vision which had led astray Alexander's lively imagination.

The famous Franco-Russian alliance was shaken. Napoleon, who wanted to make Spain and Portugal domains of his family, and had exiled the Spanish reigning family to Bayonne, had on his hands a terrible revolt to quiet, and he saw rising above the horizon another war with Austria. He therefore felt that he must give his ally some satisfaction. The interview at Erfürt took place on the seventeenth of September, eighteen hundred and eight, and lasted four weeks. Alexander was accompanied by his brother Konstantin, the ministers, Rumiantsof, Speranski, Prince Alexander Galitsnin, and two Frenchmen, the ambassador Caulaincourt, and Marshal Lannes, whom he had found at Bromberg, in Poland, on his visit to the King of Prussia, and had taken him into his favor. Napoleon brought with him Berthier, the diplomatists Talleyrand, Champagny, Maret, and the Russian ambassador Tolstoï. There was also another court, formed by his German vassals: the Prince-Primate of the Rheinbund; the kings of Saxony, Bavaria, Würtemberg, and Westphalia; the grand dukes of Baden, Darmstadt, Oldenburg, and Mecklenburg; and the sovereigns of Thuringia. Prussia was represented by Prince William, who came to plead for the interests of his brother; Austria by Baron Vincent, charged to salute the two emperors in the name of his master. The Russians, with wounded pride, did not fail to take notice of the superior influence of the French. "I seem to see my country degraded in the person of its sovereign," says Nikolai Turgénief, with passionate exaggeration. "There was no need to know what was passing in European cabinets; you could tell at a glance which of the two emperors was master at Erfürt and in Europe." Napoleon certainly wished to receive the Tsar in a town that was his own property, at Erfürt; it was certainly around him that this assemblage of sovereigns specially pressed, and these appearances really answered to a superiority of power. But though Napoleon neglected nothing to make the young Emperor forget all that was unequal in their respective situations, he could not undo the fact that Alexander had not been the victor at Friedland. Nor was he always wise in his overweening pride. He had a hare-hunt on the battle-field of Jena, and invited Prince William of Prussia. He decorated French soldiers with the cross of the Legion of Honor, bringing into special notice their glorious deeds in battle with the Russians, the cannon they had captured, the standards they had taken from the fleeing regiments of the Tsar. Such a scene was not calculated to soothe the Russian Emperor's irritation. The Grand Duke Konstantin was unable to endure it, and withdrew. But Alexander in no way showed his sensitiveness, and when the French players acted Voltaire's Œdipe, Alexander repeated the celebrated line, "A great man's friendship is the noblest gift the gods can give," applying it to himself and Napoleon.

In the midst of fêtes, banquets, balls, theatrical representations, and hunting-parties, serious interests were discussed between the two sovereigns and their ministers. On the twelfth of October, eighteen hundred and eight, Champagny and Rumiantsof signed the following convention, which was to remain secret: The emperors of France and Russia renewed their alliance with all solemnity, and engaged to make peace or war in common; they were to communicate to each other all proposals which might be made to them; they were to propose an immediate peace to England in a manner as public and conspicuous as possible, so as to render refusal on the part of the British Cabinet more difficult. This proposition took the form of a letter addressed to the King of England, and signed by the two emperors. They agreed, moreover, to negotiate on the basis of Uti possidetis: France was to consent only to such a peace as secured to Russia, Finland, Valakhia, and Moldavia; Russia, only to a peace which should confirm France in all its actual possessions, and give to Joseph Bonaparte the crown of Spain and the Indies. Russia might set about immediately to obtain the Danubian provinces from Turkey, whether by peace or by war; but the French and Russian ambassadors should come to an understanding about the language to be used, "so as not to compromise the existing friendship between France and the Porte." And if Russia by the acquisition of the Danubian provinces, or France about its Italian or Spanish affairs, found themselves exposed to a rupture with Austria, the two allies were to make war in common. Napoleon had now fully determined to separate from Josephine. Talleyrand was trusted to treat of the question of Napoleon's marriage with Ekaterina Pavlovna, Alexander's sister. The recall of Tolstoï was demanded, and his place was filled by Prince Kurakin. Prussia obtained a remission of twenty million francs of its war indemnity of one hundred and forty millions, and the evacuation of its territory on condition that its army should be reduced to forty-two thousand men. To recapitulate: Alexander guaranteed to Napoleon the tranquillity of the continent during his operations in Spain, while Napoleon ratified the seizure of Finland and the Danubian provinces. Napoleon accompanied Alexander a considerable way on the road from Erfürt to Weimar; they then once more bade each other farewell, and separated on the fourteenth of October. It was the last time that they met.

The alliance formed at Tilsit and confirmed at Erfürt involved Russia in three wars, — with England, with Sweden, and afterwards with Austria. Moreover, hostilities had been going on with Turkey since eighteen hundred and six, and with Persia and the tribes of the Caucasus ever since Alexander's accession to the throne.

The war with England is notable for only one fact of importance: The Russian fleet of the Archipelago, commanded by Admiral Seniavin, on its way to the Atlantic, as it sought harbor in the Tangas, on September eighth, eighteen hundred and eight, was obliged to surrender to Admiral Cotton, according to the Treaty of Cintra, signed by the French General, Junot. It was conveyed to England. The officers and the crews were treated with perfect courtesy, and sent back to Russia at English expense. Five years later Russia recovered the ships. The embargo was still in force against English shipping, and Russia to a certain degree fell in with the system of the continental blockade.

Gustavus the Fourth, King of Sweden, was not well regulated in mind; his hatred of Napoleon only equalled his inability to do him injury. Being a firm believer in the Bible, he saw in the Emperor of the French the veritable Beast of the Apocalypse. He caused a wretched pamphlet, called the "Nights of Saint Cloud," to be translated into Swedish. After concluding an armistice with Mortier, in eighteen hundred and six, he broke it at the very time the negotiations were pending at Tilsit, just in time to lose his last possessions in Pomerania. He was able to live in peace neither with England, which he defied, nor with Prussia, which in misfortunes he insulted, nor with his brother-in-law Alexander. He alone of the European sovereigns applauded the bombardment of Copenhagen, and he regaled Admirals Gambier and Jackson at Helsingfors. When Alexander had to make him the first overtures relative to the peace with France and the adoption of the continental system, Gustavus the Fourth impertinently returned the ribbon of Saint Vladimir. On the eighteenth of February, eighteen hundred and eight, he signed a treaty with England. Then sixty thousand Russians, under Buxhœvden, crossed the Kiümen, which had been, since the time of Elisabeth, the boundary between the two States. A proclamation was addressed to the Finns, advising them not to resist "their friends, their protectors," and to appoint deputies for the diet which Alexander intended to assemble. The Swedish troops were dispersed, and retreated to the north; Finland was almost conquered in March, eighteen hundred and eight; Helsingfors, the impregnable Svéaborg, Abo, and the Isles of Aland fell into the hands of the Russians. Fortune seemed for one moment to hesitate when Klingspor gained two important successes over the Russians, but he was immediately after obliged to retire into the deserts of Bothnia. Another proclamation was issued to the Finnish soldiers serving in the Swedish army, inviting them to desert with arms and baggage, promising them two rubles for every gun, one ruble for a sabre, and six for a horse. During the winter the Russians fortified themselves in the Isles of Aland; and three corps, commanded by Kulner, Bagration, and Barclay de Tolly, crossed the Gulf of Bothnia on the ice, and carried the war into the Swedish country. A military revolution broke out in Stockholm on the thirteenth of March, eighteen hundred and nine. No blood was shed, but Gustavus the Fourth was arrested, and confined at Drottingholm with his family. Later he was set at liberty, and travelled in Europe under the name of Colonel Gustaffson. His uncle, the Duke of Sudermania, assumed the crown under the title of Charles the Thirteenth. He signed the Peace of Fredericksham, which ceded Finland as far as the river Tornea. In eighteen hundred and ten, when Christian Augustus of Holstein-Augustenburg, the prince royal elected by the States, died, Bernadotte, marshal of France, was chosen to fill his place. Napoleon had little sympathy with this proceeding; he would have preferred a Danish prince, whose accession would have brought about a Scandinavian union. The success of the war with Sweden caused little enthusiasm in Saint Petersburg, though the capital was secured from hostile attack, though the Swedish fleet was henceforth banished from the Gulf of Finland. "Poor Sweden! poor Swedes!" said the people. Finland, coveted for so long, had lost its value in the eyes of the Russians; it seemed too much a gift of Napoleon. According to his promise, Alexander had convoked the Diet of Finland, and guaranteed to the "grand duchy" its privileges, its university, and its constitution.

In April, eighteen hundred and nine, began the war of Napoleon and the fifth coalition against Austria. Alexander, whom the Treaty of Erfürt obliged to furnish a contingent, had done all he could to prevent this war. He had warned the Cabinet of Vienna that he was in alliance with Napoleon, and offered, on the part of himself and his ally, to guarantee the integrity of the Austrian possessions. Forced to put a contingent under arms, he gave the command of thirty thousand men to Prince Sergi Galitsuin, to act in concert with Poniatovski and Dombrovski, generals of the grand duchy of Warsaw, against the Archduke Ferdinand. This war of the Russians against the Austrians was a comedy; they detested their Polish allies, and feared their success in Gallicia above everything. In the whole campaign there were only two encounters between the Russians and Austrians : at the battle of Ulanovka, on June fifteenth, there was only one killed and two wounded, and the Austrian major sent excuses to Galitsuin, saying he thought he was attacking the Poles; at the battle of Podgurzhe, near Krakof, there were two killed and two wounded.

The conflicts between the Russians and Poles were much more frequent. Galitsuin allowed Sandomir to be taken by the Austrians under his very eyes, and Poniatovski in vain denounced to Alexander this "traitorous conduct." On the other hand, the Russians entered Lemberg when the Poles had already taken it, and attempted to prevent the people swearing allegiance to Napoleon. At Krakof, the Russian and the Polish armies almost came to blows. The Poles were uneasy at seeing the Muscovites in Gallicia, and the Russians attributed all kinds of dangerous projects to the Poles. "Our allies disturb me more than the Austrians," writes Galitsuin to his master. He complains that Poniatovski, after having taken the title of commandant of the "Warsaw troops," or of "the ninth corps of the Grand Army," appropriated that of "commandant of the Polish army." "There is no Polish army," he said; "there is only an army of Warsaw." "The Emperor of the French is at liberty to give what names he chooses to the corps which are under his orders," replied Poniatovski.

Galitsuin announced that Poniatovski had reinforced his army with Polish soldiers, deserters from Austrian regiments, and Lithuanian nobles, subjects of Russia. In the theatres of the Gallician towns the King of Poland was represented leaving his tomb, the Dwina and the Dnieper forming the frontiers of new Poland. Galitsuin counselled Alexander to take from the French this weapon of Polish propaganda, by proclaiming himself restorer of Poland. The Tsar refused, alleging the inconstancy of the Poles, and the necessity of preserving the Lithuanian provinces from all contagion.

At the Congress of Schönbrunn, on October fourteenth, eighteen hundred and nine, which preceded the Treaty of Vienna, the Emperor of Russia declined to have himself represented. He did not intend to sanction the results, but by so doing he left Austria unsupported, and in consequence it was obliged to cede its Illyrian provinces, and all Gallicia. Napoleon added Western Gallicia, with fifteen hundred thousand souls, to the grand duchy of Warsaw, while he gave Eastern Gallicia, and a population of four hundred thousand, to Russia. This gift was not, however, sufficient to compensate Alexander for the danger of an aggrandized Poland.

The war with Turkey had already been going on for many years. In eighteen hundred and four Russia proposed to the Divan an alliance against France, but demanded at the same time that the subjects of the Sultan professing the orthodox religion should be placed under the immediate protection of the Russian diplomatic agents. Selim the Third repelled a proposal that threatened the very integrity of his empire. He tried to make advances to France, applauded the victories of Napoleon, and after Austerlitz acknowledged his imperial title and sent an envoy to Paris with presents, in spite of the efforts of the Russian ambassador Italinski. After Jena an Ottoman ambassador left for Berlin, to strengthen the alliance with the padishah of the French. Ypsilanti and Morusi, hospodars of Valakhia and Moldavia, who were devoted to Russia, were stripped of their dominions. This was a breach of the Peace of Iassy with Catherine the Second.

About this time began the troubles of Serbia. The Janissaries of this country formed a turbulent militia, like that of Egypt and Algiers, oppressed the Christian populations, entered into a contest with the Pasha of Belgrad, the spahis, or noble cavalry, and other Mussulmans, and even trod under foot the authority of the Sultan. They would obey only their chiefs, four in number, who were called dakhić, or deys.

Several times the Sultan, Selim the Third, resolved to suppress this dangerous element, and at last the Janissaries of Serbia, in order to anticipate any attempt to do away with their privileges, decided to massacre the princes of the Christian population, which was hostile to them. This massacre took place during the month of February, eighteen hundred and four. Those who escaped joined the Haiduki, — powerful bands of Serbians who had fled from their homes and taken refuge in the forests. Thoroughly aroused by the murder of their countrymen, the Haiduki rose against the Janissaries, and put at their head Iuri Petrovitch, who was called Kara-Iuri, or George the Black. He was a rich pork-merchant, but having been involved in a previous revolt, and obliged to flee to Austria, he had in a fit of indignation killed his father, who was anxious for him to return and submit to the Turks. He returned to Serbia, however, and began a war of extermination with the Janissaries. The Haiduki expelled the Mussulmans and deys from Belgrad, Shabatch, and Ushitza, affecting all the time to be only executing the orders of the Sultan. When Selim wished to recall them to obedience and demanded the restitution of the strong places, they broke with the Sultan himself, and declared themselves independent. They would have been crushed by the superior forces of the neighboring pashas, if the Russians had not taken up arms in eighteen hundred and six, which freed the frontiers. Alexander sent them an auxiliary corps under Colonel Bala.

The Russian ambassador protested against the deposition of Ypsilanti and Morusi, and against the violation of the Treaty of Iassy. The English ambassador almost induced the Divan to yield on October seventeenth, eighteen hundred and six, when without a declaration of war the Russian general Michelson crossed the frontier, invaded Moldavia with thirty-five thousand men, took Khotin and Bender, entered Bukarest, and advanced towards the Danube. The British ambassador wished to act as mediator, but he was not listened to, and so he demonstratively withdrew from Constantinople.

In February, eighteen hundred and seven, the English fleet under Admiral Duckworth passed the Dardanelles, burnt a part of the Turkish fleet in the Sea of Marmora, and appeared at the entrance of the Bosphorus, blockading Constantinople for a few days. This demonstration failed before the firmness of the Sultan Selim and the military preparations of the French ambassador Sebastiani. Engineer and artillery officers hastened from the French army of Dalmatia. The English vessels returned to Malta, and the Turkish fleet, crossing the Dardanelles in its turn, gave battle to the Russian Admiral Seniavin, in the waters of Tenedos. It was beaten. A short time after, in May, Selim the Third was deposed in consequence of a revolt of the Janissaries, who claimed that he insulted the faith of Islam by introducing reforms into the army and the empire. Napoleon used his fall as a pretext for sacrificing Turkey at Tilsit.

Guilleminot, Sebastiani's successor, received an order to aid the Russians "in everything, not officially, but effectively." In spite of the armistice concluded by his exertions, the Russian troops continued to occupy the principalities, whose administration was confided to a divan composed of Russians and Rumanian boyars. After Erfürt, the Sultan having refused to subscribe to the dismemberment of his empire, the war began anew. The campaign of eighteen hundred and nine was partially successful; the Russians conquered nearly all the fortresses on the Danube, but were defeated in Bulgaria by the Grand Vizier. In eighteen hundred and ten Field-Marshal Kamenski reconquered Bulgaria as far as the Balkans, and gained a brilliant victory at Batinia, near Rushtchuk. In eighteen hundred and eleven his successor, Kutuzof, managed to draw the Grand Vizier to the left bank of the Danube, and crushed him at Slobodzei, but the imminence of a rupture with France forced the Tsar to withdraw five divisions of the army of the Danube. A congress assembled at Bukarest in eighteen hundred and twelve, in which Russia gave up Moldavia and Valakhia, but kept Bessarabia, a Rumanian district, with the fortresses of Khotin and Bender. The Pruth and the Lower Danube, where Russia acquired Ismail and Kilia, formed the limit of the two empires. It was agreed that the hospodars of Valakhia and Moldavia should be restored, and all the ancient privileges of those countries confirmed. The eighth article stipulated for an amnesty in favor of the Serbians, who were to remain subjects of the Sultan, but to be governed by Iuri Petrovitch, assisted by the *skupshtchina*, or national assembly. Turkey took no part in the wars of eighteen hundred and twelve and eighteen hundred and thirteen; but it profited by them to violate the eighth article, and demand that the Serbians should deliver over all their arms and accoutrements, and receive Turkish garrisons into all the cities of the principality. The Serbians had an army of twenty thousand men, and one hundred and fifty cannon. George the Black refused to listen to these demands, and in the spring of eighteen hundred and thirteen three Ottoman armies invaded the country, and re-established the ancient order of things. George the Black, and the greater part of the Serbian voïevodui, fled to Austrian soil; others were put to death; one alone remained in the country, and managed to gain the respect and even confidence of the Turks. This was Milosh Obrénovitch. When the oppression became too intolerable, he gave the signal for a new insurrection in the spring of eighteen hundred and fifteen, and reconquered the independence of his country. The Turks, having been defeated at Ertari and Mashva, withdrew from the country, and George the Black hastened to return. Milosh, however, caused him to be assassinated just as he crossed the border, and, being now free from a dangerous rival, he entered into negotiations with the Turks, and made the Porte accept a treaty in November, eighteen hundred and seventeen, which recognized the autonomy of Serbia, under the sceptre of the Sultan, with a national government composed of Milosh as hereditary prince, and a *skupshtchina*, but with the principal fortresses occupied by Ottoman garrisons. This system lasted till eighteen hundred and sixty-seven.

At the same time as the Turkish war, hostilities began in eighteen hundred and six against Persia, which wished to regain its authority over Georgia, and against the tribes of the Caucasus. Prince Tsitsianof, Count Gudovitch, Tormasof, and Kotliarevski all distinguished themselves in this campaign. In eighteen hundred and three Tsitsianof had caused Maria, the Tsaritsa-mother of Georgia, to be transported to Saint Petersburg, as she refused to recognize the legitimacy of the cession made by her eldest son to Paul the First. He subdued the Shirvan, but was treacherously assassinated by the khan Hussein-Kuli, under the walls of Baku. Glasénop punished Ali-Khan, an accomplice in the crime, by depriving him of Derbend. Persia attempted to come to the aid of the Caucasian tribes, and Prince Abbas-Mirza passed the Araxes with twenty thousand men, but was defeated. This laborious war lasted till eighteen hundred and thirteen. But a more serious struggle was already beginning to absorb all the attention and forces of Russia.

GRAND DUCHY OF WARSAW: CAUSES OF THE SECOND WAR WITH NAPOLEON.

The misunderstanding between Alexander and Napoleon became more bitter day by day. The most important of the causes leading to it were the following: The growth of the grand duchy of Warsaw; the discontent of Napoleon at the conduct of the Russians in the campaign of eighteen hundred and nine; the abandonment of the project of a Russian marriage, and the substitution of an Austrian marriage; the increasing rivalry of the two States at Constantinople and on the Danube; the Napoleonic encroachments of eighteen hundred and ten in Northern Germany; irritation produced by the continental blockade; and the mistrust occasioned by the respective armaments.

At the Treaty of Tilsit, Napoleon had formed the grand duchy of Warsaw out of the Prussian provinces of Warsaw, Posnania, and Bromberg, with a population of two million five hundred thousand. At the Treaty of Vienna he had increased it by Western Gallicia, including Krakof, Radom, Lublin, and Sandomir, inhabited by fifteen hundred thousand people. He had reserved to himself all the means for reconstituting Poland; he had given Dantzig to no one, and had declared it a free city; the Illyrian provinces of Austria might in his hands soon be exchanged for the rest of Gallicia; and the treaty of eighteen hundred and twelve with the Emperor Francis was to realize this calculation. There was no need even to take away the acquisitions of the third partitioner, Russia, for at that time Russia possessed only Lithuania and White Russia, provinces which, as we know, are not Polish. It sufficed to take back what he had himself ceded to Alexander out of the spoils of Prussia and Austria, — Bielostok and Western Gallicia, the latter being still in great part Little Russian. The name of Poland was not pronounced officially, but in fact it already existed. To be sure, it had a foreigner, the King of Saxony, for its sovereign, but the ancestors of Frederic Augustus had reigned over Poland, and it was to the house of Saxony that the patriots of the third of May, seventeen hundred and ninety-one, had wished to secure the succession after Stanislas Poniatovski.

The Constitution of eighteen hundred and seven, compiled by a Polish commission, and approved by Napoleon, was almost that of the third of May, seventeen hundred and ninety-one. Napoleon had advised the King of Saxony to dismiss the Prussian officials, and to govern Poland with the Poles. The executive power belonged to the king, who was assisted by a council of responsible ministers with a president at their head. The legislative power was divided between the king, the senate, and the legislative body. The senate was composed of six bishops, six palatines, and six castellans;

the legislative body, of sixty deputies elected in the districts from the nobility, and forty deputies from the towns; their chief work lay in the imposition of taxes and the compilation of the laws. After the annexation of Western Gallicia the number of members of parliament was increased. Napoleon could boast, as Bignon says, of having " raised a tribune in the midst of the silent atmosphere of the neighboring governments." The Zamok, the old royal castle in which the Parliament sat, was the centre of the Polands still disunited. Napoleon gave the grand duchy his Civil Code, which did not express the actual social state of the country, but on which the social state was to model itself. He proclaimed the freedom of the serfs, while preserving to their former masters the right of property over the lands. With regard to this, the present Russian government has proceeded in a more radical fashion. Napoleon created parliamentary Poland, — a Poland whose liberty was based on greater equality than in former times.

The army of the grand duchy was raised to thirty thousand men after eighteen hundred and seven, to fifty thousand after eighteen hundred and nine; at its head was Iosiph Poniatovski, nephew of the last king, the man who was vanquished at Ziélentsé, the hero of many a Napoleonic battle. Under him served Dombrovski, a soldier of the campaign of seventeen hundred and ninety-nine; Zaïontchek, who had fought with the French in Egypt; and Khlopitski, the intrepid leader of the Polish legions in Spain. The sentiments which animated the army are still reflected in the recently published " Memoirs of a Polish Officer," written by General Brandt.

In a country where every peasant is born a horseman, the cavalry was always admirable; the infantry had lately been improved; the artillery had been organized by the Frenchmen Bontemps and Pelletier; the fortresses of Plotsk, Modlin, Thorn, and Zamosts had been restored by Haxo and Alix.

The army, where the former serf was shoulder to shoulder with the gentleman, was a school of equality. The famous legions of the Vistula, made use of by Napoleon for his own private ends, acquired an imperishable glory in the wars of Prussia, Austria, and Russia.

The ministers of the grand duchy — Stanislas Pototski, president of the council, Iosiph Poniatovski, minister of war, Lubienski, of justice, Matushevitch, of finance, Sobolevski, of police, and others — were upright and intelligent men. Bignon, Napoleon's representative, a man of clear understanding and admirable qualifications, was full of devotion to Poland. Unfortunately, he was recalled, on the eve of the supreme crisis, and the Archbishop of Malines, Abbé de Pradt, a noisy and vain character, made still more disagreeable by literary vanity, was sent to Warsaw to play the part of a mighty and luxurious lord, and a large sum of money was put at his disposition, to enable him to entertain the Polish gentry. He was instructed to do all in his power to induce the Poles, in case war broke out between France and Russia, to join their army with the French. But Napoleon soon had reason to repent of his choice of the Archbishop, who, meddling with despatches and debates, seriously compromised him, when he wished at present to remain neutral. Finally, he was obliged to tell the enthusiastic Poles that he could not see it in his power to do anything toward re-establishing Poland on its old footing. It is true, Warsaw had its parties. The Tchartoruiski had with reason made up their minds, in case of need, to have recourse to Alexander's generosity. Nevertheless, in eighteen hundred and eleven, when the guns of Warsaw announced the birth of the King of Rome, all thought themselves in safety under the protectorate of France. Never had the lively and witty Polish society been so brilliant. The growth of the Warsaw army, which was in reality the vanguard of the Grand Army of the Vistula, was always an object of disquietude for Alexander and anger for the Russians. The "mixed subjects" — that is, the nobles who held lands in the grand duchy and in Lithuania, and who passed from one service to the other — were the pretext for perpetual diplomatic intrigues. Alexander remarked bitterly that "the spectre of Poland" was being worked on the untrustworthy frontier of Lithuania.

Napoleon had not hesitated to complain to Kurakin of the way in which the Gallician campaign had been conducted. "You were lukewarm," he said; "you never drew the sword once."

The projected marriage with Anna Pavlovna, Alexander's sister, met with difficulties in more than one direction. The Empress-mother, Mary of Würtemberg, by the will of Paul, which was kept at the Assumption in the Kreml, had been invested with absolute power to dispose of her daughters in marriage. But she alleged that the laws of the orthodox church did not allow marriage with a man who had been divorced. Anna was already betrothed to the Prince of Saxe-Coburg, while her sister Ekaterina, perhaps with a view of escaping a request of this nature, had been married to the Grand Duke Peter of Oldenburg. Napoleon's first marriage had been barren, and he might a second time repudiate his wife. The difference of religion was another barrier. Anna could not embrace Catholicism, and the idea of seeing a Russian priest and chapel at the Tuileries was repugnant to Napoleon. Alexander took little pains to press the negotiation; he complicated it by another negotiation for a formal promise that Poland should never be re-established. Napoleon lost all patience, and, as the house of Hapsburg seemed to be ready to meet his wishes, the Austrian marriage was concluded.

Alexander felt both anger and regret. A closer alliance between France and Austria was prejudicial to the essential interests of Russia in the East and on the Danube. In eighteen hundred and nine Talleyrand submitted to Napoleon a project which consisted in indemnifying Austria by putting it in possession of the Rumanian principalities, and of the Slav provinces of Turkey, which would have created a permanent conflict of interests between Russia and Austria. The former, driven from the Danube, would have been forced to turn towards Central Asia, towards Hindostan. In this emergency it would in turn have found itself at perpetual war with England, and all germ of coalition against the French Empire would by this means have been extinguished. In the same year Duroc laid before Napoleon another memorial, in which he showed: that the alliance with Russia was contrary to French traditional policy; that the French possessions in Italy and Dalmatia were threatened by the action of Russia in Serbia and Greece; that Russia defended Prussia only because it reckoned on the use of the Prussian army if needed; that it favored the Spanish enterprise, in the hope of seeing two hundred thousand Frenchmen perish in the Peninsula; that the interest of the Napoleonic dynasty demanded that Russia should be pushed as far as possible to the East; that the dismemberment of Poland had been the shame of the old dynasty; and lastly, that the re-establishment of it was necessary to the greatness of France and the security of Europe. Prince Kurakin managed to procure a copy of this memorial, and sent it to the Emperor Alexander in March, eighteen hundred and nine, pointing out "how dangerous it was for Russia to permit the ruin of Austria." Alexander remembered this in the campaign of eighteen hundred and nine.

In eighteen hundred and ten the Senatus Consultum of July pronounced the union of the whole of Holland to the French Empire; that of December, the reunion with France of three Hanse towns, besides Oldenburg, and other German territories. It was not a simple occupation for the purpose of securing the execution of the continental blockade; it was an annexation. In the law of nations, as understood by

Napoleon, these decisions of the senate were to replace treaties. Where were these encroachments to stop? Hamburg, Bremen, and Lübeck, free towns, whose existence was an object of interest to the commerce of the whole world, and especially to Russia, were now French. By means of Lübeck, the French Empire would strengthen its hold on the Baltic, on that "Varing Sea," where the Russians, since Peter the First, had been disputing the preponderance of the Scandinavians. Another of these annexations, that of Oldenburg, wounded Alexander yet more deeply. He saw his sister Ekaterina and her husband, robbed of their crowns, taking refuge in Saint Petersburg. The wrong to his interests and his affections was yet further increased by the want of respect towards him. He had neither been consulted nor informed of the step. Like the rest of the world, Alexander heard of this conquest, in the height of peace, through the *Moniteur*. It is true, that since that time many other German allies of the imperial house have been deprived of their crowns or their essential prerogatives, without any remonstrance from Russia.

Kurakin was charged to draw the attention of Champagny to the twelfth article of the Peace of Tilsit, which expressly declared that Oldenburg was to be under Russian auspices. Champagny talked of the necessity of the step, and assured him that the Grand Duke should receive an indemnity, but that he must become a French subject if he wished to remain in Oldenburg. Alexander sent a note to all the other cabinets, in which, while affirming the maintenance of his alliance with Napoleon, he protested against the annexation of Oldenburg. The conqueror was deeply irritated at the publicity of this note, as well as at the remarks accompanying the protest.

As to the continental blockade, although it was observed by Russia less strictly than by France, yet it suffered cruelly from it. The commerce with England was stopped. The

Russian aristocracy made a plot to reopen the sea to their hemp, their grains, and the other natural productions of the country. The paper ruble, which was worth sixty-seven silver kopecks in Paul's reign, and which, during Alexander's early years, had risen as high as eighty, was not worth more than twenty-five in eighteen hundred and ten. In December of this same year Alexander promulgated an edict which, with the apparent design of preventing specie from leaving the country, proscribed the importation of objects of luxury from whatever country they came, particularly of silks, ribbons, embroideries, bronzes, and porcelains; and wines were heavily taxed. This struck chiefly at French commerce. The forbidden goods were ordered to be burnt. Napoleon was exasperated, and said, "I would rather have received a blow on the cheek."

For some time Kurakin, the Russian envoy at Paris, while recognizing the fact that Russia could not cope with Napoleon, had been advising a policy of intimidation by collecting great armaments. Accordingly five divisions of the army of the Danube were recalled; a levy of four men in every five hundred was ordered to be raised, and the fortresses of the Dwina and the Dnieper were put in a state of defence. A new fortress, Bobruisk, was built in Lithuania, which seemed likely to be the theatre of the war. These preparations provoked similar measures by Napoleon. Such an emulation in threatening precautions naturally led to a rupture. As soon as the "army of Warsaw" was put on a warlike footing, the army of occupation in Northern Germany was reinforced; Napoleon summoned some regiments from Spain, and notably the Polish legions; the army of Naples advanced towards Upper Italy, the army of Italy towards Bavaria; in the vast military establishment known as the Grand Army, which covered the entire Continent, from Madrid to Dantzig, a general movement from the West to the East was felt. The grievances of the two emperors against each other were brought forward in some lively interviews of Napoleon, first with the ambassador Kurakin, and then with the aide-de-camp Tchernishef, Alexander's envoy extraordinary, who was twice sent to Paris with autograph letters. Napoleon received Tchernishef in a friendly way, and even pinched his ear, but passionately discussed all the questions relative to Poland, to the Danubian principalities, to Oldenburg, to the continental blockade, to the ukas of December, to Alexander's threatening preparations. He at once rejected the idea of giving the whole or even a part of the grand duchy of Warsaw as an indemnity for Oldenburg. "Expect nothing from Poland," said Napoleon, in an interview on his birthday in August; "I will not give you a village or a mill from that country." The mission of Tchernishef was unsuccessful, but in February and March, eighteen hundred and twelve, he was again sent to Napoleon, and thought to have accomplished great things, but he compromised himself seriously; Michiels, an employé of the War Minister, was shot for allowing himself to be bribed, and for having delivered to him the estimates of the Grand Army, which proved, however, to be of very slight value. It was about this period that Napoleon ordered the publication in the newspapers of a series of articles wherein it was shown "that Europe was sure to become the prey of Russia," and declared that "the invasion must be checked, the universal domination must be extinguished." About this time also Lesur published the famous book, entitled "Of the Progress of the Russian Power," in which we meet for the first time with the apocryphal document called the "Will of Peter the Great."

Napoleon recalled Caulaincourt, whom he thought too Russian, and who, being conciliatory, was much embarrassed with the part he had to play. He replaced him by General Lauriston, who could not reckon on the confidence of Alexander. Everything showed that war was inevitable. Alexander, like Napoleon, was negotiating only in order to gain time and finish his preparations. The rupture of the alliance was patent to all. At Murat's court the French envoy, Durand, fought a duel with the Russian envoy, Dolgoruki. Alexander suddenly disgraced Speranski, the friend of France, whom Araktchéef and other of his enemies had finally succeeded in traducing. He was summoned to the Emperor's cabinet on the evening of the twenty-ninth of March, and after a two hours' interview left the palace in tears. When he reached his home, the police were already occupied in sealing his papers. A kibitka stood at the door, and without even taking leave of his only daughter, he was driven to Nijni Novgorod, where he was kept under the closest surveillance. The Emperor mourned as for the loss of a right hand, but placed in his position Admiral Shishkof, a moderately talented man, who prayed much and fasted more, and confined himself to simply accompanying the Emperor on his journeys. Alexander sent for Stein, the great German patriot, Napoleon's mortal foe, who was then, at Napoleon's instigation, under the ban of the Confederation. Russia hastened to conclude peace with Turkey, and negotiated with Sweden for an alliance, with England for a treaty of subsidies. Napoleon, on his side, signed two conventions with Prussia and Austria, which assured him the help of twenty thousand Prussians and thirty thousand Austrians in the projected expedition. Sweden and Turkey would have been more certain allies, but the treaties of Tilsit and Erfürt had alienated them from the French; Sweden had suffered, like Russia, from the continental blockade, and the Prince-Royal Bernadotte had not pardoned Napoleon for his refusal to give him Norway, and for having occupied Swedish Pomerania. On the ninth of May, eighteen hundred and twelve, Napoleon left Paris for Dresden, for the centre of his army. The ambassadors, Kurakin and Lauriston, demanded their passports.

THE "PATRIOTIC WAR": BATTLE OF BORODINO; BURNING OF MOSCOW; DESTRUCTION OF THE GRAND ARMY.

With the military resources of France, which then counted one hundred and thirty departments, with the contingents furnished by his Italian kingdoms, by the Confederation of the Rhine, by the grand duchy of Warsaw, and with the auxiliary forces of Prussia and Austria, Napoleon could bring a formidable army into the field. On the first of June the Grand Army amounted to six hundred and seventy-eight thousand men, three hundred and fifty-six thousand of whom were French, and three hundred and twenty-two thousand foreigners. Reckoning the reserves, it amounted to eleven hundred thousand men. It included not only Belgians, Dutchmen, Hanoverians, Hanseats, Piedmontese, and Romans, then confounded under the name of Frenchmen, but also the Italian army, the Neapolitan army, the Spanish regiments, natives of Germany and Baden, Würtembergers, Bavarians, Darmstadt Hessians, Jerome's Westphalians, soldiers of the half-French grand duchies of Berg and Frankfort, Saxons, Thuringians, and Mecklenburgers. Besides Napoleon's marshals, it had at its head Eugène, Viceroy of Italy; Murat, King of Naples; Jerome, King of Westphalia; the princes royal, and heirs of nearly all the houses in Europe. The Poles alone in this war, which recalled to them that of sixteen hundred and twelve, mustered sixty thousand men under their standards. Other Slavs from the Illyrian provinces, Karinthians, Dalmatians, and Kroats, were led to assault the great Slav empire. It was indeed the "army of twenty nations," as it is still called by the Russian people.

Napoleon swept all the races of the West against the East by a movement similar to that of the great invasions, and Russia seemed likely to be overwhelmed by a human avalanche.

When the Grand Army prepared to cross the Niemen, it

was arranged thus: To the left, before Tilsit, Macdonald with ten thousand French, and twenty thousand Prussians under General York of Wartenburg; before Kovno, Napoleon with the troops of Davoust, Oudinot, Ney, the guard commanded by Bessières, the immense reserve cavalry under Murat, — in all a total of one hundred and eighty thousand men; before Pilony, Eugène with fifty thousand Italians and Bavarians; before Grodno, Jerome Bonaparte, with sixty thousand Poles, Westphalians, Saxons, and others. We must add to these the thirty thousand Austrians of Schwartzenberg, who would fight in Gallicia as mildly against the Russians as the Russians had fought against the Austrians in eighteen hundred and nine. Victor guarded the Vistula and the Oder with thirty thousand men; Augereau, the Elbe with fifty thousand. Without reckoning the divisions of Macdonald, Schwartzenberg, Victor, and Augereau, it was with about two hundred and ninety thousand men, half of whom were French, that Napoleon marched to cross the Niemen and threaten the centre of Russia.

Alexander had collected on the Niemen ninety thousand men, commanded by Bagration; on the Bug, tributary to the Vistula, sixty thousand men, commanded by Barclay de Tolly: those were what were called the Northern army and the army of the South. On the extreme right, Wittgenstein with thirty thousand men was to oppose Macdonald almost throughout the campaign; on the extreme left, to occupy the Austrian Schwartzenberg as harmlessly as possible, Tormasof was placed with forty thousand. Later this latter army, reinforced by fifty thousand men from the Danube, became formidable, and was destined, under Admiral Tchitchagof, seriously to embarrass the retreat of the French. In the rear of all these forces was a reserve of eighty thousand men, — Cossacks, and the militia. Only a few contingents of the militia, brave muzhiki with long beards, were to figure in the campaign, but its imposing total of six hundred and twelve thousand men could hardly have existed except on paper. In reality, to the two hundred and ninety thousand men Napoleon had mustered under his hand, the Emperor of Russia could oppose only the one hundred and fifty thousand of Bagration and Barclay de Tolly. He counted on the devotion of the nation. "O that the enemy," says a proclamation of the Tsar, "may encounter in each noble a Pozharski, in each ecclesiastic a Palitsuin, in each citizen a Minin. Rise, all of you! With the cross in your hearts and arms in your hands, no human force can prevail against you."

At the opening of the campaign the headquarters of Alexander were at Vilna. Besides his generals, he had there his brother Konstantin, his ministers Araktchéef, Balashef, Kotchubey, and Volkonski, the chiefs of the Lithuanian nobility, Princes Sulkovski and Lubetski, and others. There were collected also refugees of all nations, — Stein from among the Germans, the generals Wolzogen and Pfühl, the Piedmontese Michaux, the Swede Armfelt, and the Italian Paulucci. They deliberated and argued much. To attack Napoleon was to furnish him with the opportunity he wished; to retire into the interior leaving a desert behind them, as Barclay had advised in eighteen hundred and seven, seemed hard and humiliating. A middle course was sought by adopting the scheme of Pfühl, — to establish an intrenched camp at Drissa, on the Dwina, and to make it a Russian Torres Vedras. The events in the Peninsula filled all minds. Pfühl desired to act like Wellington at Torres Vedras. Others proposed a guerilla warfare like that of Spain. But while they were wasting their time in vain deliberations, the French army crossed the Niemen and surprised Vilna. Barclay had to fall back on the Dwina, and Bagration on the Dnieper.

Napoleon made his entry into Vilna, the ancient capital of the Lithuanian Gedimin. He had said in his second proclamation, "The second Polish war has begun!" The Diet of Warsaw had pronounced the re-establishment of the kingdom of Poland, and sent a deputation to Vilna to demand the adhesion of Lithuania, and to obtain the Emperor's protection. We can understand with what ardor the Lithuanian nobility crowded around Napoleon. The decision of the Polish diet was solemnly accepted by the Lithuanians. "This ceremony," relates Fezensac, "took place in the cathedral of Vilna, where all the nobility had assembled together. The men were dressed in the ancient Polish costume, the women adorned with red and violet ribbons, the national colors." As to the Poles, properly so called, although Napoleon, by dispersing the army of sixty thousand men among the divisions, had rendered it invisible, nothing could equal their enthusiasm; boundless hope filled all hearts. The work begun at Tilsit at the expense of Prussia, continued at Vienna at the expense of Austria, was to be finished at the expense of Russia! At last they were to taste the revenge which France had prepared for eighteen years for the faithful legions of Dombrovski! This was the splendid gift with which the Emperor was going to reward the zeal of his Grognards, his old soldiers of the Vistula! "The young officers had recovered their confidence in the star of Napoleon," says Brandt. "Our elders might well laugh at our enthusiasm, and call us mad and possessed; we dreamed only of battles and victories; we feared only one thing, a too great anxiety for peace on the part of the Russians. .... We had in our ranks numerous descendants of the Lithuanians who had fought a hundred years before, under the banners of Charles the Twelfth, — Radzivils, Sapichas, Tysenhauses, and Khodskos." However, the enormous incapacity of Pradt at Warsaw, and the somewhat reserved answers of Napoleon at Vilna, caused a little hesitation. This was his reply to the deputation from Warsaw: "If I had reigned during the partitions of Poland, I should have armed all my subjects to support you. I applaud all that you have done; I authorize the efforts that you wish to make; all that depends on me to second your resolutions, I will do. But I have guaranteed to the Emperor of Austria the integrity of his States. Let Lithuania, Samogitia, Volhynia, the Ukraina, and Podolia be animated by the same spirit that I have seen in Great Poland, and Providence will crown with success the sanctity of your cause." In Lithuania the movement could not be truly national, since the people were not Poles. Napoleon, either with the design of pleasing Austria, of preserving the possibility of peace with Russia, or because he was afraid to make Poland too strong, took only half-measures. He gave Lithuania an administration distinct from that of Poland; assembled a commission, which voted the creation of a Lithuanian army, formed of four regiments of infantry and five of cavalry; and spent four hundred thousand francs in aid of their equipment. A national guard — composed of infantry for the towns, of horse for the country — was to watch over the security of the provision trains, and to help the French soldiers to maintain discipline. A last attempt to negotiate a peace failed. To gain time, Alexander sent General Balashof to Vilna, demanding that the whole French army should recross the Niemen before any negotiations could be begun. And on his side Napoleon proposed two unacceptable conditions: the abandonment of Lithuania, and the declaration of war against Great Britain. If Napoleon, instead of plunging into Russia, had contented himself with organizing and defending the ancient principality of Lithuania, no power on earth could have prevented the reestablishment of the Polish-Lithuanian State within its former limits. The destinies of France and Europe would have been changed.

The road which led to Vilna passed through a sort of natural pass, due to the configuration of the Dwina and the Dnieper, the one making an angle near Vitepsk, the other near Orsha, thereby ceasing to bar the way to the invader. To be sure, there were the raised works at Drissa on the Dwina, the Torres Vedras of the learned Pfühl; but the place of the camp was so badly chosen, with the river at the back, and only four bridges in case of retreat, and was so easily outflanked by way of Vitepsk, that it was resolved to abandon it. There existed in the army immense irritation against Pfühl, against the Germans, against the multiplicity of commands. It seemed out of place for the Tsar to be with the army; they remembered Austerlitz. The Russian nobles made up their minds to induce him to depart; Araktchéef himself, and Balashof, the Minister of Police, respectfully represented to him that his presence would be more useful at Smolensk, at Moscow, or at Saint Petersburg, where he could convoke the orders of the State, demand sacrifices both in men and money, and keep up the patriotic enthusiasm. From that time Barclay and Bagration commanded their armies alone.

Napoleon feared to penetrate into the interior; he would have liked to gain some brilliant success not far from the Lithuanian frontier, and overwhelm one of the two Russian armies, but the vast spaces, the bad roads, the misunderstandings, the growing disorganization of the army, caused all his movements to fail. Barclay de Tolly, after having given battle at Ostrovno and Vitepsk, fell back on Smolensk; Bagration fought at Mohilef and Orsha, and in order to rejoin Barclay retreated to Smolensk. There the two Russian generals held council. Their troops were exasperated by this continual retreat, and Barclay, a good tactician, with a clear and methodical mind, did not agree with Bagration, who was impetuous, like a true pupil of Suvorof. The one held firmly for a retreat, in which the Russian army would become stronger and stronger, and the French army weaker and weaker, as they advanced into the interior; the other wished to act on the offensive, full of risk as it was. The army was on the side of Bagration, and Barclay, a German of the Baltic provinces, was suspected, and all but insulted. He consented to take the initiative against Murat, who had arrived at Krasnoé, and a bloody battle was fought on August fourteenth.

On the sixteenth, seventeenth, and eighteenth of August another desperate fight took place at Smolensk, in which the town was burnt, and twenty thousand men perished. Barclay still retired, drawing with him Bagration. In his retreat Bagration fought Ney at Valutina; it was Eylau on a smaller scale: fifteen thousand men of both armies remained on the field of battle.

Napoleon felt that he was being enticed into the interior of Russia. The Russians still retreated, laying waste all behind them. "Tell us only when the moment is come, we will set fire to our dwellings," said the peasants to the soldiers. Smolensk caused a loss of three days; but the Russians on their side were astonished that the ancient fortress, which had sustained so many lengthy sieges in the sixteenth and seventeenth centuries, had resisted Napoleon only that length of time. The Grand Army was melting away before their very eyes. From the Niemen to Vilna, without ever having seen the enemy, it had lost fifty thousand men from sickness, desertion, and stragglers; from Vilna to Mohilef, nearly one hundred thousand. Ney was reduced from thirty-six thousand men to twenty-two thousand; Oudinot from thirty-eight thousand to twenty-three thousand; Murat from twenty-two thousand to fourteen thousand; the Bavarians, attacked by dysentery, from twenty-seven thousand to thirteen thousand; the Italian division Pino from eleven thousand to five thousand; the Italian guard, the Westphalians, the Poles, the Saxons, and the Kroats had not suffered less. The "ignoble and dangerous crowds of stragglers," as they were called by Brandt, encumbered all the roads, pillaged the convoys and the magazines, with open violence plundered the villages and towns, and did not even respect their officers when they found them alone. They had devoured Poland and Lithuania in their passage through them. At Minsk, whilst the Te Deum was being chanted for the deliverance of Lithuania, cuirassiers had broken into the shops. In this march against the enemy the miseries of the retreat might be clearly foreseen. Napoleon did what he could to fill the voids which were already so sensible. He ordered Victor's army to advance into Lithuania, Augereau to pass the Elbe and the Oder, and the hundred cohorts of the national guards to make themselves ready to cross the Rhine. In the north Macdonald repulsed Wittgenstein, took Polotsk after a battle on the eighteenth of August, occupied Dünaburg, threatened to invest Riga, and disquieted Saint Petersburg; but in the south, Tormasof obtained some success over Reynier and Schwartzenberg.

In the Russian army the discontent grew with the retreating movement; they were always retiring, now on Dorogobuzh, now on Viasma; they began to murmur as much against Bagration as against Barclay. Then Alexander, yielding to the common feeling, united the two armies under the supreme command of Kutuzof, of whom, indeed, he had a very low opinion. But Kutuzof had on his side the reminiscences of Amstetten, Krems, and Dirnstein; it was not to him that Austerlitz was imputed. He was a true Russian of the old school, indolent and sleepy in appearance, but very judicious and very patriotic. No one understood better than he did the Russian soldier and the national character. Men needed hope above all things. His appointment excited general enthusiasm; the rumor immediately spread in the army that "Kutuzof had come to beat the French." Happy sayings raised his popularity to the skies. Passing his regiments in review, "With such soldiers," he exclaimed, "who would think of beating a retreat?" He ordered, however, a retrograde movement; but "all felt that in retiring they were marching against the French." They recoiled, but only to reinforce themselves, to await the troops that Miloradovitch was to bring them, the Cossacks that Platof was to recruit on the Don, the bearded militia that had risen at the voice of the Tsar, the famous drujina of Moscow, promised by the Governor Rostoptchin.

Kutuzof halted at the village of Borodino. He had then seventy-two thousand infantry, eighteen thousand regular cavalry, seven thousand Cossacks, ten thousand militiamen, and six hundred and forty guns served by fourteen thousand artillerymen or pioneers; in all, one hundred and twenty-one thousand men. Napoleon had been able to concentrate only eighty-six thousand infantry, twenty-eight thousand cavalry, and five hundred and eighty-seven guns, served by sixteen thousand pioneers or artillerymen. This was about equal to the effective force of the Russians; but his army, now tempered by the long march of hundreds of kilometers, was still the most admirable of modern times. On the fifth of September the French took the redoubt of Shevardino; the seventh was the day of the great battle, one of the bloodiest of modern times: this was known as the battle of Borodino among the Russians, while it was called the battle of the Moskova in the bulletins of Napoleon, though the Moskova flows at some distance from the field of carnage.

The front of the Russian army was bounded on the right by the village of Borodino on the Kolotcha; on the centre by the Red Mountain, where rose what the French called the Great Redoubt, and the Russians the Raïevski battery, on the spot where now stands the memorial column; and on the left by three little redoubts or outworks of Bagration's, on the site of the monastery since founded by Madame Tutchkof. Between the Red Mountain and Bagration's outworks ran the ravine of Semenovskoé, with the village of the same name. During the battle Napoleon remained near the redoubt of Shevardino; Kutuzof, at the village of Gorki. Barclay de Tolly commanded on the right; he occupied Borodino, with the forces of Miloradovitch, and Gorki, with those of Dokturof. Bagration commanded the left; he occupied the Red Mountain with the troops of Raïevski and Semenovskoé, and the three redoubts with those of Borosdin. Napoleon had placed Eugène, with the army of Italy and the Bavarians, opposite the great redoubt; Ney, with Junot and the Würtembergers, opposite the three small ones; Davoust with the Poles and Saxons, and Murat with his numerous cavalry, were to turn the Russians by their left. On the extreme right Poniatovski was to clear the woods of Utitsa. In the rear the division of Friant and the guard formed an imposing reserve.

Profound silence reigned in the Russian camp on the eve of the battle; religious fervor and patriotic fire inflamed all hearts; they passed the night confessing and communicating; they put on white shirts as if for a wedding. In the morning one hundred thousand men, on their knees, were blessed and sprinkled with holy water by the priests; the wonderworking Virgin of Vladimir was carried in procession round the front of the troops, in the midst of sobs and enthusiasm; an eagle hovered over the head of Kutuzof, and a loud "hurrah" saluted this happy omen. The battle began by a terrible cannonade of twelve hundred guns, which was heard one hundred kilometers around. Then the French, with an irresistible charge, took Borodino on one side, and the redoubts on the other; Ney and Murat crossed the ravine of Semenovskoé, and cut the Russian army nearly in two. At ten o'clock the battle seemed won, but Napoleon refused to carry out his first success by employing the reserve, and the Russian generals had time to bring up new troops in line. They recaptured the great redoubt, and Platof, the Cossack, made a sudden attack on the rear of the Italian army; a stubborn fight took place at the outworks. At last Napoleon made his reserve troops advance; again Murat's cavalry swept the ravine; Caulaincourt's cuirassiers assaulted the great redoubt from behind, and flung themselves on it like a tempest, while Eugène of Italy scaled the ramparts. Again the Russians lost their outworks. Then Kutuzof gave the signal to retreat, and collected his troops on Psarévo. Napoleon refused to hazard his last reserves against these desperate men, and to "have his guard demolished." He contented himself with crushing them with artillery until night. The French lost thirty thousand men, the Russians forty thousand; the former had forty-nine generals and thirty-seven colonels killed and wounded, the Russians almost as many, and they numbered Bagration, Count Kutaïsof, and the two Tutchkof brothers, among their dead. Napoleon still concentrated one hundred thousand men in his immediate vicinity, Kutuzof only fifty thousand; but Napoleon's losses were irreparable at this distance; the Grand Army was condemned to gain nothing by its victories. The novelist Tolstoï uses this expression, " The beast is mortally wounded." " Napoleon," says Brandt, the Pole, " had gained the victory, but at what a price ! The great redoubt and its surroundings offered a spectacle which surpassed the worst horrors that could be dreamed of. The ditches, the fosses, the very interior of the outwork, was buried beneath an artificial hill of dead or dying, six or eight men deep, heaped one upon the other." Alexander, in spite of this defeat, named Kutuzof field-marshal, and in the churches solemn services were performed as though a success had been obtained.

Kutuzof retired in good order, announcing to Alexander that they had made a steady resistance, but were retreating to protect Moscow. He called a council of war at Fily, on one of the hills which overhang Moscow; and the sight of the great and holy city extended at their feet, condemned perhaps to perish, caused inexpressible emotion to the Russian generals. The only question was this, Was it necessary to sacrifice the last army of Russia in order to save Moscow? Barclay declared that "when it became a matter of the salvation of Russia and of Europe, Moscow was only a city like any other." Others said, like the artillery officer Grabbe, " It would be glorious to die under Moscow, but it is not a question of glory." " But," said Prince Eugène of Würtemberg, "many feel that they are held by honor to stop all retrograde movements: just as the tomb is the end of man's journey on earth, so Moscow ought to be the goal, the tomb of the Russian warrior; beyond it another world already begins." Bennigsen, Iermolof, and Ostermann were in favor of a last battle. Kutuzof listened to all, and then said, " Here my head, be it good or bad, must decide for itself," and ordered a retreat beyond the town. Yet he felt that Moscow was not " only a city like any other." He would not enter it, and passed through the suburbs weeping. For the retreat also there were two alternative paths. Barclay advised that of Vladimir, which allowed Saint Petersburg to be covered. Kutuzof preferred that of Riazan, by which he could place himself on Napoleon's right flank, receive reinforcements from the south, and keep the French from the route to the most fertile provinces of the empire. The event proved that he was right.

Up to this time Alexander had raised the militia in only sixteen governments: those of Moscow, Tver, Iaroslavl, Vladimir, Riazan, Tula, Kaluga, and Smolensk were to furnish one hundred and twenty-three thousand men; Saint Petersburg and Novgorod twenty-five thousand. At Tula seven thousand muskets of a new pattern were being manufactured every month. Alexander had said to Michaux, " We will make of Russia a new Spain." The Metropolitan of Moscow and all the priests were calling men to arms against the " impious Frenchman, the bold Goliath," who was to be thrown to the earth by the sling of a new David.

Alexander had appointed Count Rostoptchin Governor of Moscow, and when he left the city he gave him absolute power. This noble, who possessed a Frenchman's wit, was well acquainted with all classes of people, but affected the picturesque language of the peasants, and understood, as he said, " how to throw dust in men's eyes." The patriot Glinka compared him to Napoleon. His correspondence with Semen Vorontsof, his. proclamation of eighteen hundred and twelve, his Memoirs written in eighteen hundred and twenty-three, his pamphlet of the same year, entitled " The Truth about the Burning of Moscow," may be counted amongst the most curious documents of Russian history. "I do everything," he writes to the Emperor, "to gain the good-will of every one. My two visits to the Mother of God at Iberia, the free access of all towards myself, the verification of the weights and measures, fifty blows with a stick applied in my presence to a sub-officer who, when charged with the sale of salt, caused the muzhiki to wait too long, have won me the confidence of your devoted and faithful subjects." " I resolved," he says, " at every disagreeable piece of news to raise doubts as to its truth; by this means I weakened the first impression, and before there was time to verify it others came which needed to be examined." He organized a regular system of spies to watch over the propagators of false news, the Martinists, the Freemasons, and the Liberals. He was jealous of Glinka, who nevertheless admired him, and who in the " Russian Messenger " " unchained the furies of the patriotic war." When Alexander came to Moscow and convoked the three orders at the Kreml, Rostoptchin caused kibitki to be prepared to carry into Siberia any who might ask the Emperor indiscreet questions. These precautions were unnecessary. The nobles gave their peasants, the merchants their money; the reading of the imperial manifesto was received with enthusiasm. " At first," relates Rostoptchin, " they listened with the greatest attention, then they gave some signs of anger and impatience; when they came to the phrase which declared that the enemy came with " flattery on their lips and irons in their hands," the general indignation burst forth. They beat their heads, they tore their hair, they wrung their hands, and tears of rage fell down their faces, which recalled those of the ancients. I saw one man gnashing his teeth." At bottom, the government mistrusted the people, who, being serfs, might allow themselves to be tempted by the proclamations of liberty put forth by the invader. It was for this reason that Rostoptchin placed three hundred thousand rubles at the disposal of Glinka, the popular writer. There was no need of the money, and Glinka restored the three hundred thousand rubles.

Rostoptchin invented good news; one day he posted up "Great Victory of Ostermann," another day "Great Victory of Wittgenstein." Sensible men ended by never believing him, but his bulletins had always firm hold on the people. "Fear nothing," he said: "a storm has come; we will dissipate it; the grain will be ground, and become meal. Only beware of drunkards and fools; they have large ears, and whisper ridiculous things one to the other. Some believe that Napoleon comes for our good, while in reality he only thinks of flaying us. He makes the soldiers expect to get the field-marshal's staff, he makes beggars expect mountains of gold, and while they are waiting he takes every one by the collar and sends him to his death. And for this reason I beg you, if any of our countrymen or foreigners begin to praise him, and to promise this or that in his name, seize him, whoever he may be, and take him before the police. As to the culprit, I shall know how to bring him to his senses, were he a giant." "I will answer with my head that the scoundrel does not enter Moscow. And see on what I base my prophecy. . . . . If that is not enough, then I shall say, 'Forward, drujina of Moscow! let us also march. And we shall be one hundred thousand men of war. Let us take with us the image of the Mother of God, one hundred and fifty guns, and we shall finish the affair together.'" After Borodino he again puts forth this proclamation: "Brothers, we are many, and ready to sacrifice our lives for the salvation of the country and to prevent that wretch from entering Moscow; but you must help me. Moscow is our mother; she has suckled us, nourished us, enriched us. In the name of the Mother of God I invite you to the defence of the temples of the Lord, of Moscow, of Russia! Arm yourselves in any way you can, on foot or on horseback; take only enough bread for three days, go with the cross, preceded by the banners that you will take from the churches, and assemble at once on the three mountains. I shall be with you, and together we will exterminate the invaders. Glory in heaven for those who go there! Eternal peace to those who die! Punishment in the last judgment to those who draw back!" The majority of the people did not think of the possibility of abandoning the holy city to the enemy without striking a blow. They all armed themselves as best they could. The arsenals were thrown open to them, and with steadfast courage they waited the command to go out against their foe.

Meanwhile forty Frenchmen or foreigners who were settled at Moscow were transferred to Kazan. Domergue, the director of the French theatre at Moscow, describes their sad journey. Rostoptchin made a certain Leppich or Schmidt work secretly at a wonderful balloon, which would cover with fire the whole French army. He removed all the archives and the treasures of the churches and palaces to Vladimir. When the Russian army left Moscow, he also quitted it, after cruelly slaying Vereshtchaghin, who was accused of having spread Napoleon's proclamations. He caused the prisons to be opened, took away the fire-engines, and ordered Voronenko to set on fire the stores of brandy, and the boats loaded with alcohol. The burning of Moscow no doubt arose from this. By his own confession it was "an event which he had prepared, but which he was far from executing." He contented himself with "inflaming the spirits of men." Already the gates of the capital were crowded with vehicles of all sorts; every one emigrated who could leave the town.

The people who remained at Moscow steadily nursed their illusions. When the first soldiers of the Grand Army appeared, they thought that it was the Swedes or English who had come to their help. The pillage of the deserted houses began, and the populace rivalled the zeal of the invaders. Napoleon arrived, and tried to quell the disorder; he appointed Mortier governor of the town. "Above all, no pillage!" he said; "you will answer for it with your head." On September fourteenth, eighteen hundred and twelve, the troops defiled through the streets of Biélui-gorod and Kitaï-gorod, singing the Marseillaise. Napoleon ascended the Red Staircase, and established himself in the ancient palace of the Tsars. Almost immediately the fires broke out in many places. The night of the fifteenth of September was especially terrible. The Kreml itself, with the artillery wagons of the guard, was in danger. Napoleon had to leave it, and force his way through the flames; he almost perished on the road, and finally reached the Petrovski park. The courts-martial condemned about four hundred incendiaries, real or suspected, to death. All was over with the French conquest; only a fifth of the houses and churches remained standing. From that time it was impossible to prevent the plunder of the cellars, and of the buildings which were intact. The German allies were, according to the Muscovites, incomparably more greedy than the true Frenchmen. They deserved the name of "the merciless army," which was given them by the common people who suffered at their hands.

During the thirty-five days that the troops remained at Moscow their disorganization was brought to a climax, and probably ten or twelve thousand men perished from hunger. The troops began to eat the horses. Napoleon, however, got together a company of comedians in the house of Posniakof, held concerts in the Kreml, and sent down the decree from Moscow regulating the Théâtre Français of Paris; but in spite of all this he was a prey to disquietude. The plan of a march to Saint Petersburg on the approach of winter was rejected as impracticable. He sent General Lauriston to offer terms of peace, but all attempts to open negotiations with Alexander were unsuccessful. He thought of declaring himself King of Poland, of re-establishing the principality of Smolensk, and of dismembering Western Russia; he studied papers relative to the attempt of seventeen hundred and thirty, to see if he could not seduce the nobles by the bait of a constitution, and dreamed of decreeing the liberty of the serfs and of raising the Tatars on the Volga, but he was powerless, without means of action, without news, almost blockaded in Moscow. To the south the way was barred by Kutuzof, who, having led seventy-five thousand men, wearied with long marches and incessant fighting, into his camp of Tarutino, was continually becoming reinforced by volunteers from all parts of the empire. In three weeks his army had increased by more than thirty thousand. The Ataman of the Don Cossacks, Platof, enrolled twenty-six regiments and came to his aid. As the result of the victorious battle which Kutuzof fought with Murat near the village of Vinkovo, on the eighteenth of October, the road to Riazan was shut; by the battle of Malo-Iaroslavets on the twenty-third and twenty-fourth of October, the way to Kaluga was blocked, leaving free only the road to Smolensk, which had been laid waste. Even this was no longer safe. The war of guerillas, the war of peasants, the Cossack war, had begun. Herasim Kurin, a peasant of the village of Pavlovo, assembled fifty-eight hundred men "to fight for the country and the holy temple of the mother of God against an enemy who threatened to burn all the villages, and to take the skin off all the inhabitants."

The muzhiki fell on foraging parties and marauders; they killed them by blows with pitchforks; they hung them; they drowned them. Wilson the Englishman relates that they buried men alive. In the single district of Borovsk thirty-five hundred soldiers were killed or taken. The guerilla chiefs, Figner, Seslavin, Davuidof, Benkendorff, and Prince Kurakin, captured the provision wagons on the road to Smolensk. Dorokhof, with a band of twenty-five hundred men and a party of Cossacks, took Vercïa by assault. The peasant Vasilisa and Sudaruina Nadezhda Durova gave warlike examples to the Russian women. Cossacks already appeared disguised in Moscow.

On the thirteenth of October, in the first snow, Napoleon made the ambulances and the first convoys quit Moscow. From the eighteenth to the twenty-third, ninety thousand combatants left the city. They took with them six hundred guns, two thousand artillery wagons, and fifty thousand non-combatants, — invalids, workmen, women, and inhabitants of the town who feared the first excesses of the Cossacks. Mortier was the last to leave Moscow, after having sprung mines under the Kreml. Elisabeth's palace was blown up; the gate of the Saviour, that of the Trinity, and the tower of Ivan the Great were cracked by the explosions; there were many gaps in the Kreml walls. It was a cruel, useless revenge, which was likely to call down horrible reprisals on the wounded, of whom twelve hundred were left behind.

The only road to Smolensk was opened by the battle of Viasma on the third of November, where Ney and Eugène, cut off from Davoust by Miloradovitch, defeated forty thousand Russians, but themselves lost several thousand men. Until the sixth and seventh of November the cold was endurable, but the snow and ice made the roads almost impassable for the horses. The Emperor himself reached Smolensk on the ninth, but it was several days before the whole army was reunited. At Smolensk they found the shops plundered and deserted. The orders which Napoleon had given for collecting provisions had been neglected. Hunger and the terrible cold began to decimate the remains of the Grand Army. Marshal Ney, who commanded the rear-guard, left Smolensk on the seventeenth, blowing up the walls and towers. The appearance of Platof's Cossacks alone saved the rest of the city. At Krasnoé Napoleon was obliged to return with the guard to the assistance of Davoust, who was in great danger of being cut off. Ney was reduced to such extremities that he was believed to be entirely lost, but on the nineteenth of November, having given battle to sixty thousand Russians with a body of only six thousand fighting men and as many stragglers, he crossed the Dnieper on the ice and unexpectedly joined the rest of the army at Orsha. From Smolensk to Krasnoé twenty-six thousand stragglers and wounded, two hundred and eight cannon, and five thousand carriages fell into the hands of Kutuzof.

Zherkievitch, in his "Memoirs," tells us how the old general, who had collected all these trophies almost without a blow, triumphed in his success. They brought him a French flag, where amidst the names of immortal battles he read that of Austerlitz. "What have we there?" he asked. "Austerlitz! It is true it was hot work at Austerlitz. But I wash my hands of it before the whole army. They are innocent of Austerlitz." Again at the camp of the Semenovski, one of his officers exclaimed, "Hurrah for the Savior of Russia!" "No," said Kutuzof; "listen, my friends! It is not to me that the honor belongs, but to the Russian soldier." And, throwing his cap into the air, he cried with all his strength, "Hurrah! hurrah for the brave Russian soldier!" Then, made communicative by the joy of success, he said to his officers, "Where will the son of a dog lie this night? I know already that he will not sleep quietly at Liadui: Seslavin has given me his word of honor. Listen, gentlemen, to a pretty fable that Kruilof the good story-teller has sent me. A wolf entered into a kennel and tormented the dogs. As to his entrance, he had managed that very well; but it was quite another affair to get out! All the dogs were after him, and he was driven into a corner with his hairs standing on end, and saying, 'What is the matter, my friends? What is your grievance against me? I came simply to see what you were doing, and now I am going away.' The huntsman by this time had hastened to the spot, and replied, 'No, friend Wolf, you will not impose upon us! It is true you are an old rascal with gray hair, but I am also gray, and not more stupid than you.'" And, taking off his cap and showing his gray locks, Kutuzof continued, "You shall not go as you have come, for I have set my dogs at your heels."

The situation of the French army was critical. In the north, Saint Cyr, after a bloody battle at Polotsk on the nineteenth of October, evacuated the line of the Dwina. Macdonald was therefore left without support, expecting the desertion of some of his Prussians. In the south, Schwartzenberg had retreated on Warsaw, being more occupied with Poland than with the safety of Napoleon. Thus, Wittgenstein on the north, and Tchitchagof on the south, could hang on the flanks of the Grand Army; both hoped to come up with it at the passage of the Berezina, and to enclose it between themselves and Kutuzof. Kutuzof himself reckoned on this, and restrained the ardor of the most impatient of the Cossacks, and of Wilson the Englishman, who said, "What a shame to let all these ghosts roam from their graves!" They all believed that a breath would scatter what had been the Grand Army, but Kutuzof would not hazard what he had gained in a battle; he left it to time, to hunger, and to winter. The cold was destined to reach twenty-six degrees. A witty Russian said that the French were conquered in this retreat by Marshal Morozof, corresponding to our General Jack Frost.

In spite of Kutuzof, in spite of Wittgenstein, in spite of Tchitchagof, the ice, and the breaking down of the bridges, the French army crossed the Berezina near Studianka from the twenty-sixth to the twenty-ninth of November. The world knows what a price the passage cost, but still it was a great success, a victory of the desperate. Surrounded by one hundred and forty thousand Russians, these forty thousand men with the Emperor managed to cross. A third of them were Poles. They continued their journey. Arriving at Smorgoni on the fifth of December, Napoleon, accompanied by only Caulaincourt, Duroc, and Mouton, quitted the army to hasten to Paris, leaving the command to Murat. Three days later the army reached Vilna, where some months previously splendid fêtes had received the restorer of Poland, the liberator of Lithuania. The starving soldiers rushed eagerly into the houses. Suddenly the cannons sounded on three sides: it was the three Russian armies which had come up. Ney, with his four thousand "braves," protected the flight of this tumultuous crowd. After his departure there happened in Vilna a scene more frightful, perhaps, than the passage of the Berezina. The city was filled with sick and wounded French; nearly every house was crowded with them. The Jews, who were very numerous in this town, through fear of the Russians and hatred of the French and Polish conscriptions, threw these unhappy wretches out of the windows. The Jewish women could easily kick to death the men who had only lately taken the bridge of Friedland or the great redoubt of Borodino. The Cossacks, first to enter the town, fell furiously upon the defenceless camp-followers, on the women and the sutlers. Then a frightful carnage took place. Thirty thousand corpses were burned on piles. The remains of the army, always protected by the intrepid Ney, at last recrossed the Niemen. They left behind them three hundred and thirty thousand French and allies, dead or prisoners.

CAMPAIGNS OF GERMANY AND FRANCE: TREATIES OF PARIS AND VIENNA.

After the extinction of the Grand Army, Kutuzof and the Chancellor Rumiantsof were agreed not to tempt fortune, but simply to take the eastern provinces of Prussia and Poland, to make the Vistula the frontier of Russia, and to conclude a peace with Napoleon.

"But," says M. Bogdanovitch, "they did not reflect that Napoleon could easily repair his losses, thanks to the strong concentration of France in a confined space, to the rapidity with which French conscripts were taught, to the great supplies of war material, and to the vast financial resources. We, on the contrary, had to assemble our recruits over immense spaces, and our finances were in great disorder. Consequences proved that even with the help of Prussia, then exerting all its strength, we could not make head against Napoleon in the battles of Lützen and Bautzen. What, then, would have happened if the Prussians, irritated at our pretensions, had allied themselves with France? Obviously Napoleon, reinforced by Prussian armies and the Polish contingents, would have reappeared on the Dwina, and, profiting by the lesson of eighteen hundred and twelve, would have acted with more precaution and perhaps with more success." Alexander, therefore, resolved to find in the nations which were said to be oppressed by Napoleon the forces necessary to vanquish him, to make the security of Russia rest on the "liberation" of the whole of Europe; and following the example of Napoleon, who had provoked a general movement from West to East against Russia, to raise the nations from East to West against France. The burning of his palace and his capital rendered him inaccessible to all proposals of peace; Stein and the other German refugees did not allow him to forget his vengeance.

While the Russian troops were invading Poland, and giving battle to the remnants of the Grand Army at Elbing and Kalish; while Tchartoruiski was entreating the Tsar to re-establish Poland, under the sceptre of the Grand Duke Mikhail, Alexander opened negotiations with Prussia. Frederick William negotiated at once both with him and Napoleon. He disavowed General York of Wartenburg, whose defection from the French at Tauroggen had given the signal for the Germanic movement, and who was raising Eastern Prussia. He sent, however, Knesebeck, disguised as a merchant, to the headquarters of the Tsar. Alexander in his turn sent him Stein and Anslett, who induced him to sign the Treaty of Kalish on February twenty-eighth, eighteen hundred and thirteen, by which the two princes formed an offensive and defensive alliance, "for the re-establishment of the Prussian monarchy within limits which may assure the tranquillity of the two States." Russia furnished one hundred and fifty thousand men, Prussia eighty thousand; they were not to treat with Napoleon except in concert, and Russia was to try to obtain for Prussia a subsidy from England. It was only on the seventeenth of March, when Wittgenstein had made his entry into Berlin, that the King of Prussia declared war against Napoleon, and put forth proclamations "To my people! to my army!" On the nineteenth of March, when Blücher entered Saxony, the two princes concluded the convention of Breslau: they decided to summon all the princes and all the people of Germany to hasten to set free their common country; the princes who refused within a specified time were to be deprived of their territories. The Confederation of the Rhine was broken up: a central council of government was created to administer the countries which were to be reconquered, from Saxony to Holland, to collect the revenues assigned from that time to the allied Powers, and everywhere to organize levies.

Meanwhile Napoleon had been displaying his usual activity; he had set on foot four hundred and fifty thousand men with more than twelve hundred cannon; his good cities of Paris, Lyons, Rome, Amsterdam, and Hamburg had made him patriotic presents of thousands of horses. The Confederation of the Rhine, with the exception of Saxony, which was at that time being invaded, prepared contingents. It was with one hundred and eighty thousand men and three hundred and fifty guns that Napoleon reappeared on the line of the Elbe, and he might well count on crossing it, for in his strong places on the Vistula and the Oder — Dantzig, Thorn, Polotsk, Modlin, Küstrin, Glogau, Stettin, and Stralsund — he had left garrisons amounting to nearly an equal number. The weak point of this new army was the great number of conscripts, the youth of the soldiers, and the feebleness of the cavalry. The veterans, the innumerable squadrons of Murat, were buried beneath the snows of Russia.

On the second of May, at the city of Lützen, and on the twentieth of May at Bautzen, Napoleon gained two hard-fought and brilliant victories over the allied kings who were present, but he captured neither cannon nor prisoners, nor could he pursue the vanquished for want of cavalry. He entered Dresden, and re-established his ally the King of Saxony; even Silesia was reduced to subjection. In the north Davoust recaptured Hamburg and Lübeck, which an insurrection had lost to the French; the guerillas who had shown themselves in Westphalia and Hanover were driven back.

The King of Prussia was singularly discouraged. Never able to put aside the recollections of eighteen hundred and six, he remarked after Lützen, " It is just as it was at Auerstadt." "The loss of these two battles," says M. Bogdanovitch, " loosened the bonds of the alliance. The Prussian generals complained that their country was ravaged by the Russians as well as by the French. The ideas of Barclay de Tolly and most of the Russian leaders did not agree with those of Blücher and his officers. In proportion as the Russians increased the distance from their country, did they find it difficult to get ammunition, and even food. In all the space included between the Elbe and the Vistula there were as yet no store-houses. The soldiers were badly clothed and badly shod. The habitual discipline of the troops was becoming lax. The condition of the Prussian army was no better." Alexander and especially the King of Prussia had reason to say to themselves that they were playing for heavy stakes.

In June the Emperor Francis interfered and persuaded his son-in-law to sign the armistice of Pleischwitz, of which Napoleon said, " If the allies do not really wish for peace, this truce may be fatal to us." During this time the Russian army was in fact reinforced and reorganized; Prussia created its Landwehr; the two powers concluded their treaties with England; the Prince of Sweden became a member of the Coalition, being attracted by the promise of Norway; Moreau, another Frenchman, brought his talents to the help of the allies; Dantzig, Stettin, Küstrin, and Glogau were besieged. A piece of exciting news reached Germany. Wellington had gained the battle of Vittoria on June twenty-first, Spain was lost to Napoleon, and the English threatened to cross the Bidassoa into France itself. As to Austria, its tendency to defection showed itself more and more; after Lützen, Stadion had been sent to Alexander, and at the same time Bubna to Napoleon. Negotiations were prolonged, and Napoleon, discontented with the state of affairs, tried in vain to approach Alexander; Caulaincourt was not received.

Austria at last transmitted to Napoleon the conditions of the allies, which were: the destruction of the grand duchy of Warsaw, and the partition of Poland between the three courts of the North; the re-establishment of Prussia, as far as possible, within the limits of eighteen hundred and five; restitution to Austria of its Illyrian provinces, together with Trieste; restoration of the Hanse Towns; and the dissolution of the Confederation of the Rhine, though the latter was not made an absolute condition. Napoleon manifested the most lively irritation; he had the celebrated interview with Prince Metternich in Dresden, in which he even charged him with accepting bribes from England; nevertheless, he consented that a congress should assemble at Prague to discuss the conditions. How unimportant he considered the congress, however, is seen from the fact that he sent Caulaincourt without authority, and with the simple instruction to wait for Count Narbonne, who arrived only a few days before the truce had expired. To punish Austria's disloyalty, he determined that "not one single village" should be ceded to it; with Russia he wished for a glorious peace, but on the condition that their possessions should be the same as before the war. Pretensions so opposite could not be reconciled, and the allies increased their claims still further, by demanding that the Italian provinces should be restored to Austria, and Holland abandoned. When Napoleon, on the fifteenth of August, eighteen hundred and thirteen, finally consented to sacrifice the grand duchy of Warsaw and the Illyrian provinces, Austria declared that it was too late, and that it had entered into the Coalition.

The allies had now three armies in Germany: that of the North, under Bernadotte, encamped on the Havel, with one hundred and thirty thousand Russians, Swedes, and Prussians; that of Silesia, under Blücher, posted on the Oder, numbering two hundred thousand Russians and Prussians; that of Bohemia, under Schwartzenberg, consisting of one hundred and thirty thousand Austrians and Russians, which had taken up its position in the neighborhood of Prague. Thus of the three commanders-in-chief not one was Russian. The Grand Duke Konstantin, Barclay, Ostermann, and Iermolof served under Schwartzenberg, Sacken under Blücher, and Wintzingerode under Bernadotte. The old Kutuzof had left the army and died at Buntzlau during the summer campaign.

On the other hand, the Emperor of Russia, before whom the pale sovereigns of Austria and Prussia were eclipsed, seemed to direct the armies and the diplomacy of the Coalition. It was he who to the end was to be the firmest against Napoleon, the most thoroughly convinced of the necessity of his downfall, and who, after having transported the war from Russia to Germany, would transport it from Germany to France.

To all these forces Napoleon opposed the thirty thousand men of Davoust who occupied Hamburg, seventy thousand under Oudinot at Wittenberg, and the one hundred and eighty thousand which he had concentrated under his own command from Dresden to Liegnitz, with Vandamme, Saint Cyr, Ney, Macdonald, Mortier, and Murat. He fought a great battle with the army of Bohemia in the very suburbs of Dresden, on the twenty-sixth and twenty-seventh of August, in which the latter was forced to fall back in disorder on Bohemia, with the loss of forty thousand men and two hundred guns. The allies henceforth resolved to avoid all encounters with Napoleon, and to fight his lieutenants only.

Napoleon had posted Vandamme, with twenty-five thousand men, in the defiles of Peterswald, to bar the way to the fugitives, and in the events which followed forgot to recall him. Vandamme descended as far as Töplitz, to cut off the allies, but on the twenty-ninth he came up with the Russian guard, which made a desperate resistance; even the musicians, the drummers, and the clerks demanded muskets. Ostermann lost six hundred men, and was so severely wounded in one arm that it had to be amputated. Vandamme, still without orders, retreated to Kulm. He there found himself attacked and surrounded by forces four times as numerous as his own, and on the thirtieth of August was taken with more than half of his corps. Kulm was almost entirely a Russian victory, due above all to Barclay, Ostermann, and Iermolof. It cost dear, for the Russians lost six thousand men, twenty-eight hundred of whom belonged to the guard. In his joy Alexander covered the Preobrazhenski, the Ismaïlovski, the sailors, and the chasseurs of the guard with decorations, and caused Saint George's cross to be attached to their standards. The Coalition had at last gained a success which did much to encourage the army after the terrible defeat at the Saxon capital. About the same time Macdonald was defeated by Blücher on the Katzbach, Oudinot at Gross-Beeren, and Ney at Dennewitz, by Bernadotte. At the battle of Dennewitz the French lost fifteen thousand men and eighty cannon; it also cost the Prussians dear. The Cossacks threw themselves into Westphalia, and Tchernishef took Cassel and the archives of King Jerome.

From that time the three armies pressed in a closer circle

around Napoleon. Bennigsen had just brought the Russian army a reinforcement of sixty thousand men. The French army, reduced to one hundred and sixty thousand men, found itself face to face with three hundred thousand allies and twelve hundred guns, which formed a half-circle round it, and left free only the way to the West. Then Napoleon, whose army divisions were stationed at each gate of Leipzig, so as to command all the roads, fought the celebrated "battle of nations," which lasted four days. Alexander showed great personal bravery, remaining almost under the fire of the French batteries, and hastening the arrival of reinforcements on the most threatened places. On the sixteenth of October the French still maintained their position, on the seventeenth the two armies watched each other, and meanwhile the allies reached their maximum of concentration. On the eighteenth the battle began with renewed fury: the cannonade was more terrible than that of Borodino, says Miloradovitch; it was on this day that thirty-five hundred Saxons deserted. On the nineteenth the French army began to retreat towards the west, Victor and Augereau at the head; Ney, Marmont, the guard, and Napoleon in the centre, while Lauriston, Macdonald, and Poniatovski formed the rear-guard, which was destroyed by the premature explosion of the one narrow bridge over the Elster. Macdonald saved himself by swimming; Lauriston was captured with thirty thousand men and one hundred and fifty guns; Poniatovski was drowned. With him perished the hope of the regeneration of Poland by the hand of Napoleon: intrepid, disinterested, and patriotic, Poniatovski did not care for the staff of a marshal of France; he wished only to remain "the chief of the Poles."

The Prussians, who detested Saxony, were anxious to take the town of Leipzig by assault. Alexander was obliged to interfere, and managed to negotiate a capitulation with the remains of the French troops. As to the King of Saxony, a prisoner in his own palace, Alexander received him coldly;

he refused to treat with him under the pretext that he had rejected the appeal made by the Coalition to the German princes, and had persisted in his devotion to Napoleon. Perhaps he also wished to punish in him the last Saxon prince who had reigned over Poland. We shall see, besides, that the schemes of Alexander with regard to this part of Europe did not allow him to hold out any hopes to the King of Saxony.

The battle of Leipzig was the overthrow of the French rule in Germany; there remained, as evidence of what they had lost, only one hundred and fifty thousand men, as garrisons scattered among the fortresses of the Vistula, the Oder, and the Elbe. Each success of the allies had been marked by the desertion of one of the peoples that had furnished its contingent to the Grand Army of eighteen hundred and twelve: after Prussia, Austria; at Leipzig the Saxons; the French had not been able to regain the Rhine except by passing over the bodies of the Bavarians at Hanau. Baden, Würtemberg, Hesse, and Darmstadt declared their defection at nearly the same time; the sovereigns were still hesitating whether to separate themselves from Napoleon, when their people and regiments, worked upon by the German patriots, had already passed into the allied camp. Jerome Bonaparte again quitted Cassel; Denmark found itself forced to adhere to the Coalition.

Napoleon had retired to the left bank of the Rhine. Would Alexander cross this natural frontier of revolutionary France? "Convinced," says M. Bogdanovitch, "by the experience of many years, that neither losses inflicted on Napoleon, nor treaties concluded with him, could check his insatiable ambition, Alexander was not willing simply to set free the involuntary allies of France, but he resolved to pursue the war till he had overthrown his enemy." The allied sovereigns came together again at Frankfort, and an immediate march to Paris was discussed. Alexander, Stein,

Blücher, Gneisenau, and all the Prussians were on the side of decisive action. The Emperor Francis and Metternich desired Napoleon to be only weakened, as his downfall would expose Austria to another danger, the preponderance of Russia on the Continent. Bernadotte insisted on Napoleon's dethronement, with the ridiculous design of appropriating the crown of France, traitor as he was to its cause. England would have preferred a solid and immediate peace to a war which would demand exhausting subsidies, and increase its already enormous debt. These divergences, these hesitations, gave Napoleon time to strengthen his position. After Hanau, in the opinion of Ney, "the allies might have counted their stages to Paris."

Napoleon then reopened the negotiations. The relinquishment of Italy, though Murat on his side was negotiating for the preservation of his kingdom of Naples, the relinquishment of Holland, of Germany, and of Spain, and the confinement of France between its natural boundaries of the Rhine and the Alps, — such were the "Conditions of Frankfort." Napoleon sent an answer to Metternich, "that he consented to the opening of a congress at Mannheim; that the conclusion of a peace which would insure the independence both on land and sea, of all the nations of the earth, had always been the aim of his policy and of his desires." This reply seems evasive, but could the proposals of the allies have been serious? Encouraged by disloyal Frenchmen, they published the declaration of Frankfort, by which they affirmed "that they did not make war with France, but against the preponderance which, to the misfortune of Europe and of France, Napoleon had too long exercised beyond the limits of his empire." Deceitful assurance, too obvious snare, which could take in only a nation weary of war, enervated by twenty-two years of sterile victories, and at the end of its resources! During this time Alexander, with the deputies of the Helvetian Diet summoned at Frankfort, was discussing the basis of a new Swiss Confederation.

Holland was already raised by the partisans of the house of Orange, and entered by the Prussians. The campaign of France now began.

Alexander issued at Freiburg a proclamation to his troops: "Your heroism has led you from the banks of the Oka to those of the Rhine; it will conduct you still farther; we will cross the Rhine, we will penetrate to the territory of the people against whom we have sustained such a fierce and bloody struggle. Already we have saved and glorified our country; we have given back to Europe its liberty and its independence. O that peace and tranquillity may reign over the whole earth! that each State may prosper under its own government and its own laws! By invading our empire, the enemy has done us much harm, and has therefore been subjected to a terrible chastisement. The anger of God has overthrown him. Do not let us imitate him. The merciful God does not love cruel and inhuman men. Let us forget the evil he has wrought; let us carry to our foes, not vengeance and hate, but friendship, and a hand extended in peace. The glory of Russia is to hurl its armed foe to the earth, but to load with benefits its disarmed enemy and the peaceful populations." He refused to receive Caulaincourt at Freiburg, declaring that he would treat only in France. "Let us spare the French negotiator the trouble of the journey," he said to Metternich. "It does not seem to me a matter of indifference to the allied sovereigns, whether the peace with France is signed on this side of the Rhine, or on the other, in the very heart of France. Such an historical event is well worth a change of quarters."

Without counting the armies of Italy and the Pyrenees, Napoleon had now a mere handful of troops, eighty thousand men, spread from Nimeguen to Bâle, to resist five hundred thousand allies. The army of the North under Wintzingerode invaded Holland, Belgium, and the Rhenish provinces; the army of Silesia under Blücher crossed the Rhine between

Mannheim and Coblentz, and entered Nancy; the army of Bohemia under Schwartzenberg passed through Switzerland, and advanced on Troyes, where the Royalists demanded the restoration of the Bourbons. Napoleon was still able to bar for some time the way to his capital. He first attacked the army of Silesia; he defeated the vanguard, the Russians of Sacken, at Saint Didier, and Blücher at Brienne; but at La Rothière he encountered the formidable masses of the Silesian and Bohemian armies, and after a fierce battle on the first of February, eighteen hundred and fourteen, had to fall back on Troyes. After this victory had secured their junction, the two armies separated again, the one to go down the Marne, the other the Seine, with the intention of reuniting at Paris. Napoleon profited by this mistake. He threw himself on the left flank of the army of Silesia, near Champeaubert, where he dispersed the troops of Olsufief and Poltaratski, inflicted on them a loss of twenty-five hundred men, and took the generals prisoners. At Montmirail, on the eleventh of February, in spite of the heroism of Zigrot and Lapukhin, he defeated Sacken; the Russians alone lost twenty-eight hundred men and five guns. At Château Thierry he defeated Sacken and York reunited, and again the Russians lost fifteen hundred men and five guns. At Vauchamp it was Blücher's turn, who lost two thousand Russians, four thousand Prussians, and fifteen guns. The army of Silesia was in terrible disorder. Bogdanovitch describes how "the peasants, exasperated by the disorder inseparable from a retreat, and excited by exaggerated rumors of French successes, took up arms, and refused supplies. The soldiers suffered both from cold and hunger, Champagne affording no wood for bivouac fires. When the weather became milder, their shoes wore out, and the men, obliged to make forced marches with bare feet, were carried by hundreds into the hospitals of the country."

Whilst the army of Silesia was retreating in disorder on the army of the North, Napoleon, with fifty thousand soldiers full of enthusiasm, turned on that of Bohemia, crushed the Bavarians and Russians at Mormans, the Würtembergers at Montereau, the Prussians at Méry: these Prussians made part of the army of Blücher, who had detached a corps to hang on the rear of Napoleon. This campaign made a profound impression on the allies. Castlereagh expressed, in Alexander's presence, the opinion that peace should be made before they were driven across the Rhine. The military chiefs began to feel uneasy. Seslavin sent news from Joigny that Napoleon had one hundred and eighty thousand men at Troyes. A general insurrection of the eastern provinces was expected in the rear of the allies.

It was the firmness of Alexander which maintained the Coalition, it was the military energy of Blücher which saved it. Soon after his disasters he received reinforcements from the army of the North, and took the offensive against the marshals; then, hearing of the arrival of Napoleon at La Ferté Gaucher, he retreated in great haste, finding an unexpected refuge at Soissons, which had just been taken by the army of the North. At Craonne, on March seventh, and at Laon from the tenth to the twelfth of March, with one hundred thousand men against thirty thousand, and with strong positions, he managed to repulse all the attacks of Napoleon. At Craonne, however, which was one of the fiercest battles of the whole army, the Russian loss amounted to five thousand men, the third of their effective force; Lanskoï and Ushakof were killed, and four other generals were wounded. The battle of Laon cost them four thousand men. Meanwhile De Saint Priest, a general in Alexander's service, had taken Rheims by assault on the thirteenth of March, but was dislodged by Napoleon after a fierce struggle, where the émigré commander was badly wounded, and four thousand of his men were killed.

The Congress of Châtillon-sur-Seine was opened on the fifth of February. Russia was represented by Razumovski and

Nesselrode, Napoleon by Caulaincourt, Austria by Stadion and Metternich. The conditions proposed to Napoleon were the reduction of France to its frontiers of seventeen hundred and ninety-two, and the right of the allies to dispose of the reconquered countries without reference to him. Germany was to be a confederation of independent Provinces, Italy to be divided into free States, Spain to be restored to Ferdinand, and Holland to the house of Orange. "Leave France smaller than I found it? Never!" said Napoleon. Alexander and the Prussians would not hear of a peace which left Napoleon on the throne. Still, however, they negotiated. Austria and England were both agreed not to push him to extremities, and many times proposed to treat. After Napoleon's great success against Blücher, Castlereagh declared for peace. "It would not be a peace," cried the Emperor of Russia; "it would be a truce which would not allow us to disarm one moment. I cannot come four hundred leagues every day to your assistance. No peace, as long as Napoleon is on the throne." Napoleon, in his turn, intoxicated by his success, enjoined Caulaincourt only to treat on the basis of Frankfort, — natural frontiers. After Montereau he forbade him to treat at all without authority. At this time he addressed a letter to his father-in-law, the Emperor of Austria, trying to make him ashamed of his alliance with the "Tatars of the desert, who scarcely deserve the name of men," and tempting him by the offer of a separate and advantageous peace. He afterwards again permitted Caulaincourt to treat, but only on the basis of Frankfort. Caulaincourt likewise demanded that Eugène should be maintained in Italy, Elisa Borghese at Lucca, the sons of Louis Napoleon at Berg, and the King of Saxony at Warsaw. These conditions proved unacceptable; and, as fortune returned to the allies, the congress was dissolved on the nineteenth of March. The Bourbon princes were already in France; Louis the Eighteenth was on the point of being proclaimed at Bordeaux.

Alexander, tired of seeing the armies of Bohemia and Silesia fly in turn before thirty or forty thousand French, caused the allies to adopt the fatal plan of a march on Paris, which was executed in eight days. Blücher and Schwartzenberg united, with two hundred thousand men, were to bear down all opposition on their passage. The first act in the drama was on the twentieth, at the battle of Arcis-sur-Aube, where both armies suffered great loss in men, but neither could claim a decisive victory, though the Russians took six guns from Napoleon. The latter conceived a bold scheme, which perhaps might have saved him if Paris could have resisted, but which was his ruin. He threw himself on the rear of the allied army, abandoning to them the route to Paris, but reckoning on raising Eastern France, and cutting off their retreat to the Rhine. The allies, uneasy for one moment, were reassured by an intercepted letter of Napoleon to the Empress, and by the letters of the Parisian royalists, which revealed to them the weakness of the capital. "Dare all!" writes Talleyrand to them. They, in their turn, deceived Napoleon by causing him to be followed by a troop of cavalry, about ten thousand in number, continued their march, defeated Marmont and Mortier, crushed the National Guards of Pacthod in the battle of La Fère-Champenoise, and arrived in sight of Paris.

Barclay de Tolly, forming the centre, first attacked the plateau of Romainville, defended by Marmont; on his left, the Prince of Würtemberg threatened Vincennes; and on his right, Blücher deployed before Montmartre, which was defended by Mortier. The heights of Chaumont and those of Montmartre, which were not defended by a single battery, were taken; Marmont and Mortier with Moncey were thrown back on the ramparts. Marmont obtained an armistice from Colonel Orlof, to treat for the capitulation of Paris. King Joseph, the Empress Marie-Louise, and all the imperial government, with an escort of three thousand of the best troops, had already fled to the Loire. Paris was recommended "to the generosity of the allied monarch"; the army could retire on the road to Orleans. Such was the battle of Paris on the thirtieth of March, eighteen hundred and fourteen, which, according to M. Bogdanovitch, cost eighty-four hundred men to the allies, and four thousand to the French.

In the morning of the thirty-first Alexander received the deputies of Paris. He promised that the allied armies should behave with the utmost propriety in Paris, that the security of the capital should be confided to the National Guards, and that the inhabitants should be asked for provisions only. He made his entry with great pomp between the King of Prussia and Schwartzenberg, the Emperor of Austria being absent at Lyons; but the Parisians had eyes for him only, the one question being, "Which is the Emperor Alexander?" The allied troops maintained a strict discipline, and were not quartered on the inhabitants. Alexander had not come to play the part of a friend to the Bourbons; Napoleon's fiercest enemy was least bitter against the French; he intended to leave them the choice of their government. He had not favored any of the intrigues of the émigrés, and he scornfully remarked to Jomini, "What are the Bourbons to me?" He reproved by a witty speech the baseness of a Royalist: "We have waited for your Majesty a long while." "I should have come earlier if I had not been prevented by the bravery of your soldiers," said Alexander. He sent a detachment of the Semenovski to protect the column of the Grand Army against the attempts of the émigré Maubreuil. He repeated in the senate that he did not make war on France, that he was the friend of the French, and that he would protect the freedom of discussion, which tended to the establishment of liberal and lasting institutions, in accordance with the progress of the century. He yielded when Talleyrand assured him that "the republic was an impossibility, the regency and Bernadotte an intrigue, the Bourbons alone a principle." On the second of April the senate proclaimed the dethronement of Napoleon; on the eleventh he wrote in almost illegible characters and signed the act of unconditional abdication at Fontainebleau. Alexander had promised Caulaincourt to defend the interests of his old ally of Tilsit; he chiefly contributed to secure him the sovereignty of the Isle of Elba. Count Shuvalof was ordered to accompany the fallen Emperor to this place of exile. "I confide to you," said Alexander, "a great mission; you will answer to me with your head for a single hair which falls from that of Napoleon." He confessed to Caulaincourt that the imbecile conduct of the Royalists did not seem to him less dangerous for the peace of Europe than the unreasonable wars of the Empire.

Every one knows what the French lost by the first Treaty of Paris, in which the boundary of France was reduced to that of the first of January, seventeen hundred and ninety-two. On the third of May, Louis the Eighteenth made his entry into the Louvre. He affected, even with Alexander, the lofty ceremonial of the ancient court; gave him only a chair, while he seated himself on a throne; preceded his guests, the King of Prussia and the Emperor of Russia, to the dining-hall, and, seated in the place of honor, caused himself to be helped before them. Alexander paid no attention to these points. Like his ancestor, Peter the Great, he inspected with interest the monuments and great institutions of the capital. It was at Vienna that the destinies of Europe were to be regulated.

At the Congress of Vienna Alexander was represented by Razumovski, Nesselrode, Capo d'Istria, and Stackelberg; he had confided the discussion of Polish affairs to Tchartoruiski and Anslett. On one point he and his ally, the King of Prussia, were agreed; the latter asked only to get rid of his Polish provinces, and Alexander desired to unite the whole of Poland under his own sceptre, and to fulfil the promise he had made to Tchartoruiski and to the gallant remnant of the legions of the Vistula. In exchange, Prussia demanded Saxony, whose king was to receive an indemnity elsewhere. We cannot see what interest the Bourbon king could have secured by sacrificing Poland to the King of Saxony, and by opposing a combination which, by establishing this prince on the left bank of the Rhine, would have given France a neighbor infinitely less dangerous than Prussia. Talleyrand, however, used the influence that he had acquired in the congress only to combat the views of Russia and Prussia, and to support the resistance of England and Austria. On the twenty-first of October Alexander took a decisive step: he ordered Prince Repnin, Governor of Saxony, to hand over that country to the Prussian government, and to announce its incorporation with the territories of Frederick William the Third. By his orders the Grand Duke Konstantin entered Poland, assembled an army of seventy thousand men, and summoned Poland to the defence of the national integrity. Then Talleyrand, with the consent of Castlereagh, concocted a scheme of alliance between France, Austria, and England. This convention was signed January third, eighteen hundred and fifteen, but remained secret. Discord reigned in the Congress of Vienna: Europe was on the eve of another general war. In one way or another France was bound to regain its place in Europe; but it was a question whether its interests were to be found on the side of England and Austria, now that Razumovski had formally proposed to establish the King of Saxony in its Rhenish provinces.

At last the storm rolled away; Alexander declared that he would content himself with only a part of Poland, and Prussia that it would be satisfied with only a third of Saxony, with seven hundred thousand inhabitants. The other decisions of the Congress of Vienna — the organization of the Germanic Confederation, of Italy, and the kingdoms of the Low Countries — belong to general history. Nevertheless, the formation of Germany into a confederation in which the clients of Russia, the allies of the imperial house, enjoyed an independent existence, and a considerable influence on the diet, was far more advantageous to Russian power and security than the state of things resulting from the war of eighteen hundred and seventy. Poland was again divided between Russia, Prussia, and Austria: this was the fourth partition. The treaties of Vienna, however, provided that "the Poles, the subjects of Russia, Austria, and Prussia respectively, should be given a representation and national institutions; whose political existence was to be regulated in the way that the governments to which they each belonged should judge the most suitable." Krakof was pronounced free and independent. In all these treaties Russia gained only three millions of souls belonging to the kingdom of Poland, while Prussia obtained five million three hundred and sixty-two thousand in Western Poland, Saxony, Swedish Pomerania, Westphalia, and the Rhenish provinces, and Austria ten millions in Gallicia, Germany, and Italy. The power which had struck hardest for the "freedom of Europe" was the most poorly recompensed.

The event which had suddenly smoothed the difficulties of the Saxo-Polish conflict, and hastened the signing of the treaties, was the news of the return of Napoleon to Paris. The bad government of the Bourbons had realized Alexander's unfavorable predictions. The sovereigns and plenipotentiaries at Vienna did not hesitate for a moment; Alexander was resolved to pursue the common enemy to his fall, if he had to spend "his last man and his last ruble." Bonaparte's couriers, the bearers of pacific assurances, were arrested on the French frontier, and were prevented from reaching the sovereigns. In vain did Napoleon try to sow mistrust between the allies, and to win over Alexander by sending him a copy of the convention signed between Talleyrand, England, and Austria on the subject of the Saxo-Polish affair. As Albert Sorel says: "The only result of this movement was to irritate Alexander a little more against the Bourbons and Talleyrand. Napoleon did not profit by it, and France suffered." Out of the eight hundred thousand men that the Coalition had prepared to march against France, the Russian contingent amounted to one hundred and sixty-seven thousand: Barclay de Tolly, field-marshal since the battle of Paris, was commander-in-chief; under him were Dokturof, Raievski, Sacken, Langeron, Sabanéef, Iermolof, Wintzingerode, and Pahlen. In spite of the news of the battle of Waterloo, on June sixteenth, eighteen hundred and fifteen, and the second abdication of Napoleon, the Russians still continued their invasion of France. When Alexander reached Paris, he found Blücher already established there, treating it as a conquered city, exacting a tribute of a hundred millions, and preparing to blow up the bridge of Jena. Alexander was hailed as a deliverer by the inhabitants, who were terrified by the Prussian violence. He protested against the outrageous demands of the Germans, and found support in the wise policy of Wellington. Both felt that to restore the Bourbons to a greatly weakened France would be to render this unlucky dynasty still more powerless. They could not this time prevent the pillage of the museums, but the exactions of Russia and England were relatively the most moderate. There was a reason for this: these two sovereigns understood that in the regulation of European affairs, and especially of the affairs of the East, France would be an ally in the future, an obstacle to the exaggerated pretensions of either side, at once "a menace and a protection"; it was essential to the equilibrium of Europe. On the other hand, Alexander did not care to obtain for Germany the "territorial guarantees" which it demanded. "He wished," says Sybel, "to allow some danger to exist on this side, so that Germany, having need of Russia, might thus remain dependent." "A Russian diplomat," says Pertz, "avowed ingenuously that it was not the policy of Russia to give Germany secure frontiers against France." Capo d'Istria said openly to Stein that it was Russia's interest to strengthen France, so that the other powers should not employ all their forces against Russia. If

Stein used all his influence with Alexander to cause the claims of the Russian patriots to prevail, other influences were at work to oppose him. First, there was the Duc de Richelieu, who had been the governor of New Russia, the founder of Odessa, and whom Alexander desired to see replace the wily Talleyrand in the cabinet of Louis the Eighteenth. Then came Capo d'Istria, Pozzo di Borgo, and his Greek advisers, who, seeing the Eastern question appearing on the horizon, wished to secure for the Hellenic interest an alliance with Russia against the narrow policy of Austria and England. Last came Madame de Krüdener, the widow of a Russian diplomat, in her youth distinguished for her beauty, who placed before Alexander her mystic and religious ideas of absolute justice, of greatness of soul, of forgiveness for offences, of universal brotherhood, and who in her drawing-room, one of the most brilliant in Paris, surrounded the emperor with every one France could boast who was brilliant and seductive,— Chateaubriand, Benjamin Constant, Madame Récamier, and the Duchesses de Duras and d'Escar.

It is an incontestable fact, that of all the allies Russia showed itself the least grasping. Here is the table of propositions made officially by each member of the Coalition : Russia, temporary occupation of France, and a war indemnity ; England, the same conditions, and the return of the frontiers to those of seventeen hundred and ninety ; Austria, the same, together with the dismantling of the fortresses of Flanders, Lorraine, and Alsace ; Prussia, occupation, indemnity, return to the frontier of seventeen hundred and ninety, cession of the fortresses of Flanders, Lorraine, and Alsace. The secondary states of Germany and the Low Countries demanded the cession of Flanders, Lorraine, Alsace, and Savoy. "Such," says M. Sorel, "were the official propositions; the oral demands were quite another thing." "Look here, my dear Duke," said Alexander to Richelieu in eighteen hundred and eighteen, "this is France as my allies wished to make it; they wanted only my signature, and that, I promise you, they shall want always." The map that he showed the Duke presented a line of frontiers which would have deprived France of Flanders, Metz, Alsace, and the east of Franche-Comté, which was even more than was allowed by Carlovitz, who proposed to Stein that France should be divided into Langue d'Oc and Langue d'Oïl, after being robbed of its Flemish and German speaking provinces, or by the demoniacs who clamored for Burgundy and the ancient kingdom of Arles.

Richelieu had just succeeded Talleyrand as Minister of Foreign Affairs. He found himself in the presence of a collective ultimatum of the powers, demanding the cession of Savoy, Condé, Philippeville, Marienburg, Givet, Charlemont, Landau, Fort-Joux, Fort-l'Ecluse, the demolition of Huningue, the payment of eight hundred million francs, and the occupation of the north and east for seven years. He discussed this ultimatum point by point. "The Russians," writes Gagern, "without openly opposing them, are working secretly for the modification of the articles." Richelieu finally succeeded in saving Condé, Givet, Charlemont, the forts of Joux and l'Ecluse, and obtained the reduction of the indemnity to seven hundred millions, of the occupation to five years, with the addition of this clause, that "at the end of three years the sovereigns reserved to themselves the power to cut short the term of occupation, if the state of France permitted it." This was the treaty of November twentieth, eighteen hundred and fifteen. Alexander left Paris. In the army of occupation Champagne and Lorraine were intrusted to Russia; Vorontsof commanded twenty-seven thousand men and eighty-four guns; Alopeus had charge of the political affairs, and both lived at Nancy. Nikolai Turgénief, a member of the official staff, has given us some curious details about the Russians in Lorraine.

KINGDOM OF POLAND: CONGRESSES AT AIX-LA-CHAPELLE, CARLSBAD, LAYBACH, AND VERONA.

With regard to Poland, Alexander accomplished more loyally and more completely than the two other co-partitioners the somewhat vague obligations imposed on them by the Treaty of Vienna. After the farewells of Fontainebleau, Dombrovski, commander-in-chief of the legions of the Vistula, placed his troops at the disposal of the Emperor Alexander, from whom the Poles hoped for the restoration of their country. The Tsar assigned Poznania as their place of assembly, and gave them his brother Konstantin as head. On the eleventh of December, eighteen hundred and fourteen, the Grand Duke addressed them a proclamation in French: "Gather around your banners; arm yourselves to defend your country and to maintain your political existence. While this august monarch is preparing the happy future of your country, show yourselves ready to second his noble efforts, even at the price of your blood. The same chiefs who for twenty years have led you on the path of glory will know how to bring you back to it. The Emperor appreciates your courage. In the midst of the disasters of a fatal war he has watched your honor survive events for which you were not responsible. Great feats of arms have distinguished you in a struggle whose cause was often not your own. Now that your efforts are consecrated to your country, you will be invincible. . . . . Thus you will reach that happy position which others may promise, but the Emperor alone can secure to you." This proclamation, by which Russia adopted all the glories of the ancient army of Warsaw, was the most magnificent of amnesties. In a letter of Alexander to Oginski, President of the Polish Senate, dated the thirtieth of April, eighteen hundred and fifteen, he takes the title of King of Poland, and speaks of the efforts he had made to "soften the rigors of separation, and even to obtain for the Poles all possible enjoyment of their national institutions."

On the twenty-first of June, eighteen hundred and fifteen, the cannon at Warsaw announced the restoration of Poland. As a delicate attention to Polish loyalty, the act of abdication of the King of Saxony was published, as well as the manifesto of the new King of Poland. The army, assembled in the plain of Vola, took the oath of allegiance. The warlike blazon of the kingdom was wedded to the arms of Russia. The new constitution was almost the reproduction of that of the Napoleonic grand duchy. It contained a senate and a chamber of deputies; the senate was composed of bishops, voïevodui, castellans, nominated as life members by the king; the chamber, of seventy-seven noble deputies and fifty-one deputies from the towns. The necessary qualification was property taxed at fifteen rubles for the deputies, and at three hundred for a senator; the former must have reached the age of thirty, the latter that of thirty-five. The electors of the deputies were proprietors above the age of twenty-one, priests, professors, learned men, and artists. The diet was to meet every two years, and to sit thirty days. Laws had to be passed by both chambers, and sanctioned by the king. The constitution declared the liberty of the press, with the exception of one law which restrained its abuses. Amongst the responsible ministers, we find some men of the former régime. Sobolevski was Minister of Finance, Matuszevitch of the Interior, Stanislas Pototski of Education, Vavrzhevski of Justice, Viélćhorski of War. The namiestnik, or viceroy, was Zaïontchek, a veteran of the Napoleonic wars. Konstantin, the Emperor's brother, was commander-in-chief of the Polish army; Novosiltsof, imperial commissioner. They had thus taken the places of Poniatovski, leader of the Poles, and of Bignon, the envoy of Napoleon. The ministers formed the council of government, and, united to the principal dignitaries, they formed the general council of the kingdom. Tchartoruiski could not console himself for not having been chosen namiestnik.

Alexander's mystic notions soon, however, began to obscure

his liberal ideas. At the time of the burning of Moscow he had turned for comfort to the companion of his youth, Prince Alexander Galitsuin, who was inclined to mysticism, and directed him to the Bible as the only source of strength, comfort, and peace. Henceforth the religious notions of the Emperor were changed, and a sort of Protestant mysticism began to claim his attention. Madame de Krüdener, who had written a novel somewhat in the style of " Werther," having outlived her beauty, was now devoted to religion, and felt that she was a prophetess. The Empress Elisabeth, Alexander's wife, spent the summer of eighteen hundred and fourteen with her brother, the Duke of Baden. There Madame de Krüdener became the firm friend of one of the court ladies, the Princess Roxandra Sturdza. In the letters which she afterwards wrote her new friend, she says: " You wish you could only express to me the many profoundly beautiful characteristics of the Emperor's soul. I think that I already know a great deal about him. I have been sure for a long time that the Lord will give me the joy of seeing him. I have immeasurable things to communicate to him, for I have suffered much on account of him; the Lord alone can prepare his heart to receive them." And again, " Although the Prince of darkness do his utmost to prevent it and to keep at a distance from him those who can speak to him of things divine, yet the Eternal will be victorious." These letters were shown to the Emperor, and interested him deeply. Madame de Krüdener followed the Emperor to Paris, and we saw with what associates she surrounded him. Franz Bader, however, was the originator of the idea of the Holy Alliance. He was a man of unusual power and of very peculiar views. Philosophy in his eyes was better understood by the mystics of the Middle Ages than by such skeptics as Kant, upon whom he looked with unmeasured contempt. In eighteen hundred and fourteen he addressed from Münich a letter to the Emperors of Russia and Austria and the King of Prussia, suggesting the idea of a

Christian Alliance founded on universal brotherhood and love. Many things conspired to make Bader's plan bear fruit in Alexander's heart. In Paris Madame de Krüdener kept urging him to perform mighty Christian deeds, and it was under the influence of this adventuress, and a magnetizing quack by the name of Bergasse, that the Emperor wrote the first draught of the Holy Alliance, by which the sovereigns were to agree to consider all men as brothers, and to remain in a bond of perpetual fraternity, giving each other comfort and assistance, and looking upon their armies and subjects as children, at the same time protecting religion, peace, and righteousness. They then agreed to become the members of one and the same nation in Christ, ruling in accordance with the power intrusted them by God in his three essences, and finally allowing all other powers to join the Alliance on the condition of recognizing these axioms. Inoffensive though it was, it made a great noise in Europe, and is a singular monument and a curious proof of his temper at this period. Without doubt he meant it to be a mystic bond, and hence would allow none but the sovereigns to sign their names; but Francis declared that Metternich must become a party to it, and Alexander finally consented. The King of Prussia signed it willingly, but, as Madame de Krüdener afterwards bitterly complained, without laying weight to it, the Emperor of Austria without knowing why, Louis the Eighteenth surely with a smile; Castlereagh refused his signature "to a simple declaration of biblical principles, which would have carried England back to the epoch of the Saints, of Cromwell, and the Roundheads." Later, all the princes of Europe were invited to sign, except the Sultan and the Pope, against whom the Emperor had acquired a deeply rooted prejudice. Nevertheless, Russia had then in Europe a preponderating influence, out of proportion to its real strength and the number of its army. But it was Alexander who had given the signal for the struggle against Napoleon, and had shown the most perseverance in pursuit of the common end. Alone, he could never have crushed the man of destiny, the black angel, as Madame de Krüdener called him, but without his example the States of Europe would never have dreamed of arming against him. His skilful leniency towards France finished the work begun by the war. Alexander was incontestably the head of the European areopagus. Nicholas had to commit many faults before Russia lost this place, which prestige and public opinion had given it.

Alexander's influence showed itself in the congresses in which the European States tried to arrange together the affairs of the Continent. The first in date after the Congress of Vienna is that of Aix-la-Chapelle in eighteen hundred and eighteen, which regulated the relations of Europe with France; this country appeared sufficiently quiet for the occupation to cease. This was not the fault of the Court of Artois and of the "pavillon de Marsan"; but their famous secret note made Alexander only indignant. In a visit which he paid to Louis the Eighteenth, he said, "If any of my subjects had committed a similar crime, I should have put him to death." But Richelieu gained his object, the entrance of France once more into the European assembly.

The second congress was that of Carlsbad in eighteen hundred and nineteen, where the tone of mind prevalent in Germany was discussed. The disloyalty of the German princes, who had forgotten the promises of liberty made in eighteen hundred and thirteen; that of Frederick William the Third, who had caused himself to be absolved from his engagements by the Prussian bishop Eylert; and the reactionary influence of Metternich on the Diet of Ratisbon, had provoked a general stir in German public opinion. The young men and university professors, the liberal writers, and the former members of the Tugenbund demanded the promised constitutions. The ecstatic demonstrations of the German students, and the murder of Kotzebue by Maurice Sand, shook all the cabinets.

From this moment Alexander's character seems to change: the liberator of Europe, the champion of liberal ideas, submits in his turn to the influence of Metternich; he subscribes to measures which have for their aim to deprive Germany of the liberties which he himself had promised in eighteen hundred and thirteen. The press is subjected to a rigorous censure; the universities are closely watched and the liberal professors expelled; and the patriots of the war of independence, and Alexander's companions in arms, are obliged to seek refuge in the France they had despoiled.

Soon the stir in men's minds spread through Europe. Spain rose and imposed a constitution on its king; this constitution became an object of envy to the neighboring peoples; then broke out the revolutions of Portugal, Naples, and Piedmont. As champion of divine right Alexander now defended the contemptible petty kings of the South, Ferdinand the Seventh of Spain and Ferdinand the Fourth of Naples, who had perjured themselves to their people. He who had wished to give Poland a constitution, and to guarantee that of France, opposed to the utmost the constitutional measures of Spain and Italy. By an aberration similar to that which Paul the First had experienced, he thought himself obliged to interfere, in these remote regions, about questions foreign to the interests of Russia. He convoked a congress at Troppau in eighteen hundred and twenty, then transferred it to Laybach, so that the King of Naples might more easily be present at it, be absolved from his constitutional oath, and provoke vengeance against his too credulous subjects. Alexander was on the point of sending an army to Naples under the command of Iermolof, the hero of Borodino and of Kulm; but Austria, always uneasy at Russian interference in Italy, hastily despatched Frimont, who put an end to the Neapolitan and Piedmontese constitutions. The Russian flag thus escaped the doubtful honor of protecting, as in seventeen hundred and ninety-nine, the bloody Neapolitan reaction, and of sanctioning the vengeance of Austria against Pellico, Pallavicini, and Maroncelli. Iermolof rejoiced at it. "There is no example," he writes, "of a general appointed to command an expedition being so delighted as I am that there is no war. It is by no means advantageous to one's reputation to appear in Italy after Suvorof and Bonaparte, who will be the admiration of future centuries."

In eighteen hundred and twenty-two the Congress of Verona took place. Russia sent, like the other powers, a threatening note to the constitutional cabinet of Madrid. The latter returned a proud answer; it was the French army which was intrusted to carry out the wishes of Europe beyond the Pyrenees.

Still graver events were at hand in the East. The Balkan peninsula, almost entirely peopled by the co-religionists of the Russians, began to be in thorough commotion. The Ottoman yoke bore heavily on all. The Valakhians and Moldavians complained of the violations of the Treaty of Bukarest. The Serbians, whose independence Alexander had guaranteed, and who had been crushed by the Porte while the eyes of Europe were turned another way, had taken up arms under Milosh Obrenovitch. A young Greek by the name of Rigas conceived the idea of freeing his native land, and founded the hetaireia; this secret brotherhood was spreading in all the provinces, in all the isles of Greece; it counted already one martyr, its founder, Rigas, who was arrested at Trieste, delivered up by the Austrians, and executed by the Turks. What was Alexander to do in the presence of this awakening universe? Would he burn with something of that crusading ardor which hurried Peter the Great to the banks of the Pruth? Would he act here "according to the principles and after the heart of Catherine," as he said in his manifesto at his accession? Would Serbia find in him the liberator of eighteen hundred and thirteen, or the president of the Congress of Carlsbad, the man believing in legitimacy at all costs, the champion of absolute monarchical rights, the theorist of the passive obedience of subjects? This seemed so impossible to the nations, that the Greeks refused to believe Capo d'Istria when he asserted that they would not be supported. Ypsilanti could not imagine that the Emperor would seriously disavow him; he crossed the Pruth, raised the Rumanian populations, and succumbed at Ruimnik, which had witnessed the triumph of Suvorof. Alexander might multiply his disavowals, but the Peloponnesos rose under Kolokotroni, and the Mainotes under Mavromichalis. The war of extermination had already begun by the Mussulman riot at Constantinople. At the feast of Easter, eighteen hundred and twenty-one, the Greek population were assaulted, and, as if the better to insult the orthodox religion, the Patriarch was seized at the altar, and hung at the doors of the church in his sacerdotal robes. The Grand Vizier amused himself for an hour by seeing his corpse ill-treated by the Turkish populace, and dragged through the mud by the Jews. Three metropolitans, eight bishops, thirty thousand Greeks, men, women, and children, were slain. Russia trembled with indignation. Dibitch drew up an admirable plan of campaign, which still deserves to be studied, and which he executed in the following reign. Alexander exchanged diplomatic notes with the Porte, and allowed himself to be lulled to sleep by England and Austria, which did not desire intervention. The massacres continued. Alexander occupied himself about them at Verona, at the same time as the affairs of Spain. The Russian people were astounded, and attributed to the wrath of God, angry at the impunity accorded to the assassins of the Greek patriarch, first the terrible inundation of Saint Petersburg, and soon the premature and mysterious death of Alexander.

CHAPTER XIV.

ALEXANDER THE FIRST: INTERNAL AFFAIRS.

1801–1825.

EARLY YEARS: THE TRIUMVIRATE; LIBERAL MEASURES; THE MINISTERS; PUBLIC INSTRUCTION.—SPERANSKI: COUNCIL OF THE EMPIRE; PROJECTED CIVIL CODE; IDEAS OF SOCIAL REFORM.—ARAKTCHÉEF: POLITICAL AND UNIVERSITY REACTION; MILITARY COLONIES.—SECRET SOCIETIES: POLAND.—LITERARY AND SCIENTIFIC MOVEMENT.

EARLY YEARS: THE TRIUMVIRATE; LIBERAL MEASURES; THE MINISTERS; PUBLIC INSTRUCTION.

IN the home affairs of the empire, the early years of Alexander's reign, succeeding to the hard rule of Paul the First, had been a period of emancipation, of generous ideas, and liberal reforms. The Emperor had announced in his manifesto on his accession that he would govern "according to the principles and after the heart of Catherine the Second." When he managed to free himself from the guardianship of the conspirators of the twenty-fourth of March, eighteen hundred and one, he surrounded himself either with his grandmother's ministers, or with new men, young like himself, who shared his great hopes and his schemes of regeneration. Like him, they brought to the regulation of affairs much inexperience, but immense good-will. Those who at that time most influenced Alexander were Prince Adam Tchartoruiski, Novosiltsof, Strogonof, and Kotchubey. The first three were closely united, and were known by the name of the triumvirate. They knew Western Europe better than Russia; the English constitution was their ideal; Tchartoruiski, a great Polish lord, whose family had given kings to Poland, cherished a dream of the reorganization of his native country, under the sceptre of the Emperor of Russia. He profited by his situation as guardian of the academic department of Vilna, to favor the teaching of the Polish language in White Russia. As Minister of Foreign Affairs, or intimate adviser of Alexander, he never lost sight of the interests of his nation, at whose head he hoped one day to place himself, in the capacity of viceroy or namiestnik of the Emperor.

The tyrannical measures of the preceding reign were reversed; the Russians were again permitted to travel abroad freely, and foreigners were allowed to penetrate into Russia. European books and papers entered the country freely, the censorship was mitigated, and new instructions ordered the doubtful passages of a book to be interpreted in the sense most favorable to the innocence of the author. The "secret expedition," another form of the secret court of police, or of the State inquisition, was abolished, and its functions handed over to the senate. Priests and deacons, gentlemen and citizens belonging to the guilds, were declared exempt from corporal punishments.

Grander designs were brought forward in the council of the young sovereign. As an introduction to the code of the empire, a sort of constitutional scheme was discussed, in which the privileges of the supreme power were defined, its obligations spoken of, and where the rights of subjects, and of the four orders of the State, were in question. A sort of civil list was established, under the name of "his Majesty's cabinet." The emancipation of the serfs, as in the brightest period of the reign of Catherine the Second, was the topic of the day. The situation of the Crown peasants, who were much more free and happy than those belonging to individuals, was assured by the resolution taken by the Emperor to make no more donations of "souls." They even went so far as to devote a million of rubles yearly to the acquisition of land with serfs for the Crown. While waiting for a more general measure, Alexander put forth the edict of February, eighteen hundred and three, which legalized contracts of freedom voluntarily entered into between the owners and their slaves; the individuals or the communes who thus acquired liberty while they kept their land, formed in Russia a new class, the "free cultivators," who, with the ancient freeholders, became the nucleus of a rural third estate. The German nobility of Esthonia in eighteen hundred and sixteen, that of Kurland in eighteen hundred and seventeen, and that of Livonia in eighteen hundred and nineteen, resolved to anticipate the needs of the new century, so as not to be obliged to submit to them entirely; they took the initiative in the emancipation of Lett or Tchud serfs, in order that they might consult their own interests in the operation. "All the serfs of these provinces," says M. Bogdanovitch, "were gradually to pass in an interval of fourteen years to the condition of free persons. It was forbidden to sell them with or without land, individually or by families, to give them away, to hire them out, or to make them slaves by any means whatever. Their right to acquire land, houses, and other property was recognized. In civil cases they were in the first two instances amenable to judges elected by themselves and partly drawn from among them. Thus they had now only civil relations with their former masters; but as the latter had distributed no lands among them, the serfs were kept in a burdensome state of dependence upon them." Formerly they were slaves body and soul, but possessed lands; now they were free, but forced for their livelihood to continue to cultivate for others, as farmers or day-laborers, the soil which had belonged to their warlike ancestors.

The prohibitions of the former reigns against the sale of slaves at auctions, and the separation of the members of one family, were renewed. The abuse, however, still continued, and Nikolai Turgénief assures us that there was a public slave-market almost under the windows of the imperial palace.

Alexander also gave evidence of his good intentions towards the raskolniki. "Reason and experience," says the edict, "have for a long while proved that the spiritual errors of the people, which official sermons cause to take only deeper root, cannot be cured and dispelled except by forgiveness, good examples, and tolerance. Does it become a government to employ violence and cruelty to bring back these wandering sheep to the fold of the Church?" These inoffensive sects were protected rather than persecuted; Alexander visited their settlements more than once in the course of his travels. A sect of dancing raskolniki were allowed to celebrate their rites in the Mikhail Palace, and Prince Galitsuin, Minister of Public Worship, was seen honoring with his presence the absurdities of the priestess Tatarinof, and the sacred dances of her adherents.

In political institutions two great innovations took place in eighteen hundred and two. The collegiate organization of the branches of the administration was set aside; the colleges of Peter the Great, which had succeeded the prikazui of the ancient Tsars, were now replaced by ministers, after the European custom. Here is a list of the first ministry of Alexander the First: War, General Viasmiatinof; Marine, Admiral Mordvinof, a bold patriot and distinguished administrator; Foreign Affairs, the Chancellor Alexander Vorontsof, nephew of Elisabeth's great Chancellor; Home Office, Count Kotchubey; Justice, Derzhavin, the poet; Finance, Count Vasilief; Commerce, Count Rumiantsof, celebrated for his patronage of arts and sciences; Public Education, Count Zavadovski. The number and functions of the ministers were more than once modified. Ministers of domains, of the Crown, of general control, of roads and bridges, and of the Emperor's household, were afterwards created.

The second innovation bore upon another great institution

of Peter the First, the senate, whose importance had been lessened by the formation of an imperial council, presided over by the Emperor or by an appointed minister. Ministers and the general council lacked, however, one essential thing, — responsibility. Autocracy abdicated none of its rights. On one occasion one of the councillors of Alexander put this question: "Sire, if a minister refused to sign an edict of your Majesty, would the edict be binding without this formality?" "Certainly," replied Alexander; "an edict must be executed under all circumstances."

Alexander and his young fellow-laborers undertook a vast reorganization of public education. The empire was divided into six scholastic circles. That of Saint Petersburg included eight governments; that of Moscow, eleven; that of Dorpat, the three German provinces; that of Kharkof, sixteen, with the Caucasus and Bessarabia; that of Kazan, twelve, including Siberia; that of Vilna, six in White Russia. At the head of each circle was placed a popetchitel, or guardian, ordinarily a considerable personage, like Novosiltsof, Pototski, or Adam Tchartoruiski, charged with the protection of the schools and their general direction.

For the instruction of the clergy, ecclesiastical schools were founded, whose revenues were obtained from the exclusive sale of tapers in the churches. Above these schools were seminaries; next the ecclesiastical academies of Moscow, Saint Petersburg, Kazan, and Kief. The laity were to be instructed in parish and district schools, and gymnasia; to furnish masters, the pedagogic institutes of Moscow and Saint Petersburg were established. The universities of Moscow, Vilna, and Dorpat were reorganized; those of Kazan and Kharkof, and, later, that of Saint Petersburg, were founded. There was a plan of establishing two at Tobolsk and Ustiug. Fifteen government schools, or corps of cadets, were also founded, where the young nobles could receive a military education. The Alexander Lyceum at Tsarskoć-Selo, afterwards transferred to Kamennui-Ostrof, was built for the same purpose. From this epoch also dates the lyceum of commerce, or Gymnasium Richelieu, at Odessa, and the Lazaref Institute, or school for Oriental languages.

SPERANSKI: COUNCIL OF THE EMPIRE; SCHEME OF THE CIVIL CODE; IDEAS OF SOCIAL REFORM.

From eighteen hundred and six to eighteen hundred and twelve the preponderating influence over Alexander was that of Speranski. The son of a village priest, educated at a seminary, then mathematical and philosophical professor at the school of Alexander Nevski, preceptor to the children of Alexis Kurakin, by whose means he quitted the ecclesiastical career for the civil service, he became secretary to Troshtchinski, who was at that time chancellor of the imperial council. Later, when director of the department of the Interior under Prince Kotchubey, Speranski succeeded to the post of Secretary of State, and began to enjoy the absolute confidence of the Emperor. The favorites of the preceding period were all imbued with English ideas; Speranski, on the contrary, loved France, had imbibed the principles of the Revolution, and entertained a deep admiration for Napoleon. These French sympathies, then shared by Alexander the First, formed a fresh bond between the prince and the minister, — a bond which was severed by the rupture between the Emperor and Napoleon. "Besides," says M. Bogdanovitch, "we know the inclinations of Alexander for representative forms and constitutional governments, which could not fail to seduce the former disciple of Laharpe; but this taste resembled that of a dilettante who goes into ecstasies over a beautiful picture. Alexander had promptly convinced himself that neither the vast extent of Russia, nor the constitution of civil society, allowed this dream to be realized. He therefore deferred the execution of his Utopia from day to day, but delighted to hold conversations with his friends about his projected constitution and the disadvantages of absolutism. Speranski, to please the Emperor, showed himself the ardent defender of the principles of liberty, and thereby was exposed to accusations of entertaining anarchical ideas, and scheming against the institutions consecrated by time and manners." Hard-working, well-educated, both patriotic and humane, he would have been the man to realize all that was practicable in Alexander's Utopian schemes.

Speranski presented a systematic plan of reforms to his sovereign. The Council of the Empire received still more extensive privileges. Composed of the chief dignitaries of the State, it became in some measure the legislative power; it had to examine all the new laws, the extraordinary measures, the relations of the ministers. It was a kind of sketch of a representative government. The Council of the Empire was divided into four departments: war, law, political economy, civil and ecclesiastical affairs. Alexander solemnly opened this parliament of officials on the thirteenth of January, eighteen hundred and ten. Speranski was nominated secretary of the Council of the Empire. All affairs passed through his hands: he became in a manner the Prime Minister. To his mind, the Council of the Empire being at the head of the legislation, and the ministers at the head of the administration, the Senate ought to occupy the same rank in the judicial order. As the legislative power had been reorganized by the reform of the council, and the administrative power by the reform of the ministry, so the judicial power, in its turn, ought to undergo a complete change. The tribunals, in his opinion, ought to be composed of judges partly nominated by the monarch, partly elected by the nobles. It was plain that Speranski had studied the laws of the French assemblies, the system of Siéyès and the Constitution of the year eight. The judicial was to be followed by a financial reform. Already, by the edict of the fourteenth of February, eighteen hundred and ten, the assignats were recognized as part of the national debt, and were to be guaranteed by the imposition of new taxes; the emission of paper money was to be restrained; the budget was to be published, and a fund for the redemption of the bonds to be created. Speranski, in short, had in his mind something like the French Grand Livre of the public debt and the budget of the Western States. As a minor task he had undertaken to codify the laws. To him the Code Napoléon — that legacy of the French Revolution, which had at that time been adopted by Holland, Italy, the Bund, and the grand duchy of Warsaw — seemed the very model of all progressive legislation. After the interview at Erfürt, where Napoleon showed him particular attention, Speranski had been exchanging letters with the French legal writers, — Locré, Legras, Dupont de Nemours, and had made them correspondents of the legislative commission of the Council of the Empire. The Code Napoléon could suit only a homogeneous nation, free from personal and feudal servitude, where every one enjoyed a certain equality before the law. Thus Speranski looked on the emancipation of the serfs as the corner-stone of his building; he dreamed of forming a middle class, of limiting the numbers of the privileged classes, and of forming an aristocracy of great families like the English peerage. As early as eighteen hundred and nine he had decided that persons holding university degrees should enjoy certain advantages over others, when aspiring to the degrees of the Tchin. Thus a doctor would be on a level with the eighth rank, a master of arts with the ninth, a man of master's standing who had not taken his degree with the tenth, a bachelor of arts with the twelfth.

Speranski, like Turgot, the minister of Louis the Eighteenth, and like Stein, the Prussian reformer, set every one in arms against him. The nobles of the court and of the antechamber, — the "sweepers of the parquets," as Alexander called them, — and the young officials who wished to owe their promotion solely to favor, were exasperated by the edict of eighteen hundred and nine. The proprietors were alarmed at Speranski's schemes for the emancipation of the serfs; the senators were irritated by his plan of reorganization, which reduced the first order of the empire to the position of a supreme court of justice; the high aristocracy were indignant at the boldness of a man of low extraction, the son of a village priest. The people themselves murmured at the increase of the taxes. All these injured interests leagued themselves against him. The minister was accused of despising the institutions of Muscovy, of daring to present to the Russians the Code Napoléon as a model, the country being at that time on the eve of a war with France. The ministers Balashef, Armfelt, Gurief, Count Rostoptchin, and the Grand Duchess Ekaterina Pavlovna, the Emperor's sister, influenced Alexander against him. The historian Karamsin addressed to his sovereign his enthusiastic essay on New and Ancient Russia, in which he made himself the champion of serfage, of the old laws, and of autocracy. They went the length of denouncing Speranski as a traitor and accomplice of France. In March, eighteen hundred and twelve, he suddenly vanished from the capital and went as governor to Nijni-Novgorod, but was shortly afterwards deprived of his post, and subjected to a close surveillance. In eighteen hundred and nineteen, when passions had calmed down, he was nominated governor of Siberia, where he was able to render important services. In eighteen hundred and twenty-one he returned to Saint Petersburg, but without recovering his former position.

ARAKTCHÉEF: POLITICAL AND UNIVERSITY REACTION; MILITARY COLONIES.

Another period, another season, had begun. The enemies of Speranski — Armfelt, Shishkof, and Rostoptchin — were in places of the highest trust; but the favorite above all was Araktchéef, the rough " corporal of Gatchina," the instrument of Paul's tyranny, the born enemy of all new ideas and all thoughts of reform, the apostle of absolute power and passive obedience. He first gained the confidence of Alexander by his devotion to the memory of Paul; next by his punctuality, his prompt obedience, his disinterestedness and habits of work, and by the naïve admiration which he showed for the "genius of the Emperor." He was the safest of servants, the most imperious of superiors, and the instrument best fitted for a reaction. His influence was not at first exclusive. After having conquered Napoleon, Alexander liked to think himself the liberator of nations. He had freed Germany; he spared France, and obtained for it a charter; he granted a constitution to Poland, and meant to extend its benefit to Russia. If the censorship of the press had become more severe, and forbade the Viestnik Slovesnosti, the Courier of Belle Letters, to criticise "his Majesty's servants," Alexander had not yet renounced all his utopias. To the French influence succeeded the Protestant and English influence. The French theatres were shut, and Bible Societies opened. The British and Foreign Bible Society established itself in the capital, received subscriptions amounting to three hundred thousand rubles, and published five hundred thousand volumes in fifty different languages. The Russian Bible Society, with its offshoot, the Cossack Bible Society at Tcherkask, published hundreds of thousands of copies of the holy books. It was at this time that the influence of Madame de Krüdener, and a revival of the terrible memories of March, eighteen hundred and one, made Alexander a dreamy mystic. He received a deputation of Quakers, prayed and wept with them, and kissed the hand of old Allen. Notwithstanding, the first epoch of the ministry of Araktchéef was an epoch of sterility. If at present there were no reaction, everything had at least come to a standstill. The war of eighteen hundred and twelve had interrupted the reforms which had been begun, and they were not resumed. There was an end of the Code of Speranski, and the efforts to compile another more suitable to the Russian traditions came to nothing.

The character of Alexander soon sadly changed. He grew

gloomy and suspicious. His last illusions had flown, his last liberal ideas were dissipated. After the congresses of Aix-la-Chapelle and Troppau, he was no longer the same man. It was at Troppau that Metternich announced to him, with calculated exaggeration, the mutiny of the Semenovski, his favorite regiment of guards. From that time he considered himself the dupe of his generous ideas, and the victim of universal ingratitude. He had wished to liberate Germany, and German opinion turned against him: his pensioner, Kotzebue, had been assassinated by Maurice Sand. He had sought the sympathy of vanquished France, and at Aix-la-Chapelle a French plot was discovered against him. He had longed to restore Poland, and Poland desired only to be completely free, while Russia demanded an explanation from Alexander of the new danger he had created on his frontier, by the reconstruction of the Lekhite kingdom. It was at this moment that the Holy Alliance of the sovereigns became an alliance against popular liberty; at Carlsbad, at Laybach, and at Verona, Alexander was already the leader of the European reaction. In the East he disavowed Ypsilanti; in Russia he owned the influence of Araktchéef and the Obscurants. The Araktchéevtchina had begun.

Remonstrated with by Archbishop Serafim, Alexander broke with the Bible Societies, and forced his old friend, Prince Galitsuin, the liberal and tolerant Minister of Public Instruction, to resign. Galitsuin was replaced by Shishkof. The censorship became daily more strict. The Jesuits, who had been expelled from St. Petersburg, were banished from the whole empire, as a punishment for their proselytism; and they really were unnecessary in Russia, for the orthodox guardians of the Russian universities could rival them in the art of stifling independent thought. The popetchitel of Kazan University was Magnitski, who proposed to organize the teaching in accordance with the "act of the Holy Alliance." He dismissed eleven of the professors; struck out of the list of honorary members Abbé Grégoire, a Frenchman and "a regicide," and excluded all suspicious books from the library, notably the work of Grotius on International Law. He forbade the geological theories of Buffon and the systems of Copernicus and Newton to be taught, as contrary to the text of Scripture. The professor of history was obliged to become inspired with the ideas of Bossuet as expressed in his "Histoire Universelle." The science of medicine ought to be a Christian science; hence dissection was almost entirely forbidden, as incompatible with the respect due to the dead. The professor of political economy was enjoined to insist principally on the virtues that turned material goods into spiritual possessions, "thus uniting the lower and contingent economy with the true and superior economy, and by this means forming the real science, in a politico-moral sense." Nikolski, professor of geometry, already demonstrated in the triangle the symbol of the Trinity; and in unity, that is to say, the number *one*, the divine Unity. At Kharkof, the Professors Schad and Ossipovski, and at Saint Petersburg the professors of philosophy, history, and statistics were expelled from the universities. Galitch, Hermann, Arsenius, and Raupach were summoned by the popetchitel Runitch before a university commission. The first was accused of impiety, because he had taught the philosophy of Schelling; the others of Maratism and of Robespierrism, for having expounded the theories of Schlœtzer, the protégé of Catherine the Second, or criticised agricultural serfage, and the extent to which the issue of paper money had been carried. It was forbidden in future to employ professors who had studied in the West, and it was forbidden to send thither Russian students.

The most salient feature of Araktchéef's administration, of which the initiative proceeded from the gentle Alexander, was the creation of military colonies, — a system borrowed from Austria, which consisted of the settlement of soldiers among the peasants, in a certain number of districts. If these soldiers were married, their wives also were brought to the village; if they were not, they were married to the daughters of the peasants. A village was therefore composed, in the first place, of the military settlers, the soldiers, and, secondly, of colonized peasants, the natives. The soldiers assisted the peasant in his field-work; the children of both were destined for military service. The colonized districts were removed from the jurisdiction of the civil authorities, and subjected to military administration and government. At the end of ten years, according to Schnitzler, the total in these military districts in the governments of Novgorod, Kharkof, Mohilef, Ekaterinoslaf, and Kherson amounted to sixty thousand men and thirty thousand horse, in the midst of a population of four hundred thousand male peasants. This system appeared to have certain advantages, which gained over Speranski himself. It was argued that it secured regular recruits, lightened the burden on the rest of the population, raised the morals of the soldier by keeping him with his family, guaranteed him an asylum in his old age, restored to agriculture the labor of which the army had formerly deprived it, diminished for the government the expenses of the army and for the people the cost of lodging the troops and paying requisitions, and finally created a military nation on the frontier of the empire. And although the colonization was a heavy weight upon the natives, they were compensated by various advantages. The government augmented their lots of land, secured them personal liberty like that of the Crown peasants, repaired their houses, and dowered their daughters.

The country people did not understand it thus. Subjected at their hearths to an interference more annoying than that of their former masters and their stewards, forced into a twofold servitude as laborers and as soldiers, their habits and traditions all invaded, they cursed Araktchéef's ingenious idea, which official circles extolled. Revolts broke out, and Araktchéef, blaming the gross ignorance and ingratitude of the muzhik, repressed them with implacable severity.

SECRET SOCIETIES: POLAND.

Other elements of trouble fermented in Russia. We are no longer in the time of Catherine the Second, when the gravest social questions could be discussed with impunity, before an inattentive or indifferent nation. The noble efforts of Alexander's early years now found a decided support in public opinion. Unfortunately the sovereign and his people were at variance. While a party among the nation had become enthusiastic for liberal ideas, Alexander had grown cold about them: formerly his courageous initiative was hardly appreciated; at present it was the backsliding spirit of the government which irritated the country. A transformation had taken place; it was not in vain that the Russian officers had seen Paris, had dwelt on French soil. Those revolutionary principles of which under Catherine the Second men had caught only a glimpse across the prism of their prejudices, they had found realized in the States of the West, and had been forced to remark the coincidence of their triumph with the rapid development of a new prosperity. "From the time that the Russian armies returned to their country," writes Nikolai Turgénief, "liberal ideas, as they were then called, began to propagate themselves in Russia. Independently of the regular troops, great masses of militiamen had also seen foreign places. These militiamen of various ranks recrossed the frontier; went back to their homes, and related all that they had seen in Europe. Facts had spoken louder than any human voice. This was the true propaganda." Pestel, one of the conspirators of eighteen hundred and twenty-five, acknowledged that the restoration of the Bourbons had made an epoch in the history of his ideas and political convictions. He says: "I then saw that though the greater number of the institutions necessary to the well-being of a State were brought in by the Revolution, they were continued after the re-establishment of the monarchy as conducive to the public welfare, while formerly we all, myself among the earliest, rose against this Revolution. From this I concluded that apparently it was not so bad as we represented to ourselves, and even contained much good. I was confirmed in my idea by observing that the States in which no revolution had taken place continued to lack many rights and privileges."

People read not only Montesquieu, Raynal, Jean-Jacques Rousseau, as in the time of Catherine the Second, but Bignon, Lacretelle, De Tracy, and Benjamin Constant; and the eloquent voices of the French tribune found an echo in the young Russian nobility and part of the middle class. Politeness, the spirit of justice, and respect for the human person had made great progress. European culture no longer lay only on the surface, but it penetrated deeply into hearts and consciences. Many declared, like Wilhelm Küchelbecker: "At the thought of all the brilliant qualities with which God has endowed the Russian people, — that people which is the foremost of all in power and in glorious actions, that people whose language, so sonorous, so rich and strong, is without a rival in Europe, whose national character is a mixture of good-nature, of tenderness, of lively intelligence, and a generous disposition to pardon offences; — at the thought that all this was stifled, and would wither and perhaps perish before having produced any fruit in the moral world, my heart nearly broke." To these noble souls it was absolute suffering to see despotism hold its sway through all the grades of Russian society, in all the relations of the autocrat with the nation, of the officials with those they governed, of the officers with their soldiers, and of the proprietors with the peasants. They were indignant at beholding the Russian people alone in Europe dishonored by the serfage of the soil, and by domestic servitude, that shameful legacy of ancient Slav barbarism and the Tatar yoke, that Asiatic ignominy which continued to defile a Christian people; at the sight of the Russian soldier, the conqueror of Napoleon, the liberator of Europe, submitting to the degradation of corporal punishment. They did not believe that the inconstant will of an autocrat with even the best intentions, that the noble plans of an Alexander — that " happy accident," as he called himself to Madame de Staël — could make up for the want of laws and liberal institutions.

In spite of the watchfulness of suspicious police, freemasonry, forbidden since the time of Catherine the Second and Paul, was reorganized and spread over Russia, the kingdom of Poland, and the Baltic provinces. Societies of a more warlike character, and with a definite object, whose existence for a long while remained a secret, were also established at certain points. It was in eighteen hundred and eighteen that the Society for the Public Advantage, an imitation of the Germanic Tugenbund, was formed at Moscow, and reckoned among its members Prince Trubetskoï, Alexander and Nikita Muravief, Matvei and Sergi Muravief-Apostol, Nikolai Turgénief, Feodor Glinka, Mikhail Orlof, the two brothers Fon-Vizin, Iakushkin, Lunin, the princes Feodor Shakovskoï and Obolenski, and many others. The members of this association were not agreed as to the form of government they wished to give to Russia, some clinging to the idea of a constitutional monarchy, others to that of a republic, which Novikof had been one of the first to suggest. This society was dissolved in eighteen hundred and twenty-two, and gave rise to two others, — the Society of the North, or of Saint Petersburg, which had constitutional aims, and the Society of the South, which recruited its associates chiefly among the officers of the garrisons of the Ukraina-or of Little Russia, where Colonel Pestel preached republicanism. A third and less important society, that of the United Slavs, dreamed of a confederacy of the Slav races, and tried to form ramifications in Bohemia, Serbia, and Bulgaria. About eighteen hundred and twenty-three the Russian societies entered into relations with the Patriotic Society of Poland, then preparing for an insurrection, and, in order to secure the help of the Poles, engaged to do all in their power to favor the restoration of the country. The most ardent members of the Russian associations were at that time Colonel Pestel and Ruileef, the one a son of a former director of posts, the other of the head of police under Catherine the Second. By the warmth of their republican convictions, they seemed to wish to expiate the servility of their fathers. At the period of the meetings at Kief in eighteen hundred and twenty-three, Pestel read a scheme of a republican constitution and of an equalizing code. As the chief obstacle to the realization of his projects seemed to him to be the existence of the Romanof dynasty, it was decided not to shrink from the murder of the Emperor, and the extermination of the imperial family. In the bosom of the Society of the South, a still closer and more secret association had been formed, with the end of regicide in view. They were to profit by the first opportunity that presented itself, which would be a review in which Alexander was to inspect the troops of the Ukraina, in eighteen hundred and twenty-four. An active propaganda was set on foot among the soldiers of the garrisons, and common soldiers were gained over by promising them the liberty of the peasants, and the mitigation of the military régime.

LITERARY AND SCIENTIFIC MOVEMENT.

The awakening of the Russian mind did not show itself in political schemes alone. In science, in letters, and in arts, the reign of Alexander was an epoch of magnificent blossom. The intellectual, like the liberal movement had not the exotic and superficial character of the reign of Catherine. It penetrated deeply into the heart of the nation, gained in power and in extent, carried away the middle classes, and was propagated in the most distant provinces. The impulse given in eighteen hundred and one had not stopped, although the government at once tried to quell the spirit it had excited, and Alexander, imbittered and cured of his illusions, had become mistrustful of all manifestations of private thought.

Though the severity of the censorship increased, the number of secret societies was not at all diminished, and reviews and literary journals continued to multiply.

The Besiéda was now formed, the literary club at which Kruilof read his fables and Derzhavin his odes, and which represented classical tendencies; whilst the Arzamas was founded by the romantic school, — Zhukovski, Dashkof, Uvarof, Pushkin, Bludof, and Prince Viazemski. At Saint Petersburg the Society of the Friends of Science, Literature, and Arts; that of the Friends of Russian Literature at Moscow, which published an important collection of its "transactions"; that of the History of Russian Antiquities, and the Society of Patriotic Literature, at Kazan; that of the Friends of Science at Kharkof, and many others of less importance, devoted themselves to letters, archæology, and the mathematical, natural, and physical sciences. At Saint Petersburg appeared the *Northern Post*, the *Saint Petersburg Messenger*, the *Northern Mercury*, the *Messenger of Sion*, an organ of the mystic party, the *Beehive*, and the *Democrat*, in which Kropotof declaimed against the influence of French ideas and manners, and in the "Funeral Oration of my Dog, Balabas," congratulated this worthy animal, among other things, on having studied at no university, on having never occupied himself with politics, and on having never read Voltaire. Literary activity was, as ever, still greater at Moscow. Karamsin was the editor of a review entitled the European Messenger, which had a brilliant career, and published the masterpieces of the poets and authors of the time; Makarof edited the Moscow Mercury; Sergi Glinka established the Russian Messenger, in which he tried to excite a national feeling, now putting the people on their guard against any foreign influence, moral or intellectual, now arming them against Napoleon, "teaching the people to sacrifice themselves to their country," and letting loose the furies of the "patriotic war." With the victory of Russia over the invader his task ended, and the Russian Messenger disappeared, but his work was taken up by Gretch in his "Son of the Soil," who continued beyond the frontier the war with Napoleon, whom he taunted as a "murderer" and an "infamous tyrant," and against his companions in arms, whom he called "brigands." "Taste beforehand," he cries to the conqueror, "the immortality which you deserve. Know from this time how posterity will curse your name! You are seated on your throne amidst thunder and flames, like Satan in the midst of hell, encircled with death, with devastation, fury, and fire." The Invalide Russe was founded in eighteen hundred and thirteen, for the benefit of wounded or infirm soldiers. Even when the warlike fever calmed down, and men's minds were occupied with other things less hostile to French influence, this great literary movement still continued.

Almost all the writers of this period took their part in the crusade against the Gallomania and the influence of Napoleon. Some had fought in person in the war with France. Zhukovski was present at Borodino; Batiushkof had marched in the campaigns of eighteen hundred and seven and eighteen hundred and thirteen, and had been wounded at Heilsberg; Petin was killed at Leipzig; the Princes Viazemski and Shakovskoï had served among the Cossacks; Glinka in the militia, in which Karamsin, in spite of his age, had wished to enroll himself. Their writings bear the stamp of their patriotic passions. Kruilof, besides his fables, which place him not far from La Fontaine, wrote comedies, the "School for Young Ladies" and the "Milliner's Shop," in which he turned into ridicule the exaggerated taste for everything French. Amongst several classical tragedies, such as "Œdipus at Athens," "Fingal," "Polyxena," Ozérof wrote that of "Dmitri Donskoi," which recalled the struggles of Russia against the Tatars, and seemed to predict the approaching contest with another invader. The tragedy of "Pozharski," the hero of sixteen hundred and twelve, by Kriukovski, contains allusions of the same sort. In eighteen hundred and six the poet Zhukovski sang the exploits of the Russians against Napoleon, in the "Song of the Bard on the Graves of the Victorious Slavs," and in eighteen hundred and twelve in the "Bard in the Camp of the Russian Warriors." Rostoptchin, the enemy of the French, did not even await the grand crisis to empty the vials of his wrath upon them.

In general the literature of the time of Alexander marks the transition from the imitation of the ancients, or of classic French writers, to the imitation of the German or English masterpieces. The Bésiéda and the Arzamas clubs formed, as it were, the headquarters of the two rival armies, which fought in Russia the same battle as the French romantic and classic schools at Paris. Schiller, Goethe, Bürger, Byron, and Shakspere were as fashionable as in France, because they were strange, and because they created a kind of literary scandal. If Ozérof, Batiushkof, and Derzhavin kept up the traditions of the old school, Zhukovski translated Schiller's "Joan of Arc " and Byron's " Prisoner of Chillon "; Pushkin contributed "Ruslan and Liudmila," the "Prisoner of the Caucasus," the " Fountain of Bakhtchi-Seraï," and the *Tsuiganui*, or the " Gypsies," and began his romance in verse of " Evgeni Oniégin " and the drama of " Boris Godunof " published in eighteen hundred and twenty-nine.

As in France the romantic movement had been accompanied by a brilliant renaissance of historical studies, so in Russia the dramatists and novelists were inspired with a taste for national subjects by Karamsin's " History of Russia," — a work uncritical in its methods, and indiscriminating in its appreciation of historical events, but remarkable for the brilliance and eloquence of its style, as well as the charm of its narrative. Schlœtzer had just edited Nestor, the old Kievan annalist, the father of Russian history.

Science enjoyed a certain amount of protection in this reign. In eighteen hundred and three the Captains Krusenstern and Lisianski, accompanied by Tilesius of Leipzig and

Horner of Hamburg, accomplished the first Russian voyage round the world, in the Nadézhda and the Neva, and opened relations with the United States and with Japan. In eighteen hundred and fifteen Captain Kotzebue explored the Southern Ocean, and afterwards the icy ocean to the north, and sought by Behring's Straits a communication with the Atlantic, that is, the Northwest passage; others surveyed the coasts of Siberia, and it was ascertained that Asia was not joined to America, as the Englishman Burney had asserted.

In eighteen hundred and fourteen the imperial library of Saint Petersburg was solemnly thrown open to the public. It then contained two hundred and forty-two thousand volumes and ten thousand manuscripts. The nucleus had been formed by the victories of Suvorof, who had sent to Russia the library of the kings of Poland.

In spite of the expenses of the war, the Russian cities received embellishments. At Saint Petersburg the better-paved streets and the granite quays gave evidence of the care of the government. Thomont built the palace of the Bourse, Rosser the new Mikhail Palace, and Montferrand began the vast and splendid cathedral of Saint Isaac. Saint Peter's at Rome served as a model for Our Lady of Kazan, before which the bronze statues of Barclay de Tolly and Kutuzof were afterwards erected. In eighteen hundred and one a statue was erected to Suvorof. Poltava had its monument in honor of the victory of Peter the Great; Kief that of Vladimir the Baptist; Moscow those of Minin and Pozharski, erected in eighteen hundred and eighteen; but the plan of raising on the Hill of Sparrows at Moscow a colossal church dedicated to the Saviour, in memory of the deliverance, failed through the inexperience of the architect. The plan was carried out, though in another place, during the present reign.

Alexander, stifling the benevolent impulses which were natural to him, and listening only to the voice of foreign statecraft, had resisted the wishes of his people, and refused to come to the assistance of the persecuted Greeks. The Russians therefore considered the misfortunes which clouded the last years of his life as the punishment from Heaven for this culpable indifference toward their co-religionists of the East.

The most striking of these misfortunes was the frightful flood which happened at Saint Petersburg in November, eighteen hundred and twenty-five. The Neva is a sort of continuation of Lake Ladoga. Saint Petersburg is, in large measure, situated upon low, marshy islands, formed by the different branches of the river and by the artificial canals which were constructed for the purpose of drainage or communication. The mouth of the Neva faces the west, and is exposed to the storms which often rage over the Gulf of Finland. In such times the waters of the gulf make a sort of tide in the Neva, and are forced back between the low banks which confine them. Solid granite quays line these water-courses, and, as a general thing, prevent the catastrophes which threaten. The story is told that Peter the Great was informed by a Finnish peasant of the danger of floods when he laid the foundations of his new city; but he disregarded the warning, and cut down the girdled tree which marked the height to which the river rose two years before Sophia became regent. Since that time five or six such inundations had been recorded, but none so terrible as that which occurred the year before Alexander's death. The wind blew violently from the northwest, and the Neva rose four meters above its ordinary level. Nearly the whole of Saint Petersburg was overwhelmed. The number of lives lost was reckoned at more than five hundred, and millions of dollars' worth of property was destroyed. The Emperor, who had just returned from a long journey to the Kirghiz Steppes, assisted in rescuing the unfortunate inhabitants, whose wooden houses were carried away by the waves, and he contributed munificently to the subscriptions started to relieve the distress, which was aggravated by the sudden approach of winter. Alexander's moody melancholy was increased by this calamity; his deafness was growing upon him; erysipelas, causing symptoms of insanity, attacked him; he became suspicious of his own immediate family.

The people of Europe cordially detested the Holy Alliance, which was opposed to the notions of popular liberty; secret societies, supported by the young spirits of all nations, were everywhere in process of formation; the universities were hotbeds of radicalism, and the students were anxious to strike at the tyranny of kings. Poland was thoroughly turbulent, and caused Alexander constant anxiety. In spite of the arrest of Lukasinski and other members of the Polish revolutionary societies, in eighteen hundred and twenty-three, the movement still continued with ceaseless activity. The peasants in the neighborhood of Novgorod, and in other localities, feeling that their burdens were too heavy to be borne, were inclined to insurrection, and severe measures of repression had to be taken. The military colonies were unsuccessful; both soldiers and serfs complained bitterly of their unhappy lot.

Through the communications of the young officer, Sherwood, Alexander knew something of the plot which was to involve his assassination. He gave up the plan which he had conceived of abdicating the throne, in order that it might not be said that fear of losing his life influenced him.

A still more cruel grief was added to his cup of bitterness. Alexander had been married at the age of sixteen to Louisa Maria Augusta, of Baden, who, upon her baptism into the Orthodox Greek Church, took the name Elisaveta Alexcïovna. But in the early years of their married life there was a lack of sympathy between them. Their two daughters died young, and Alexander formed an attachment with the Countess Naruishkin, by whom he had three illegitimate children, only one of whom survived. This daughter, Sophia Naruishkin, was soon to be married to a young Russian; the wedding preparations were partly made, when she suddenly died. Alexander felt that this affliction was a chastisement for his faithlessness, and from this time he began to recognize the true worth of Elisabeth.

During the last years of his life the Emperor made extensive journeys to visit the distant parts of his empire. As the health of the Empress was delicate, her physicians ordered her to have a change of climate. She refused to go to Baden, asserting that if she was destined not to live, it was fitting for a Russian empress to die on Russian soil. Alexander decided, therefore, that she should try the milder climate of Southern Russia, and, having settled upon the port of Taganrog as preferable to the Crimea, he announced his determination to accompany her thither.

At the moment of his departure he seems to have been shaken by gloomy presentiments; in everything connected with his journey he saw prognostications of his approaching death. He left Saint Petersburg on the thirteenth of September, eighteen hundred and twenty-five, and ordered a requiem mass to be said at the monastery of Alexander Nevski, where his two infant daughters and many members of the imperial family lay buried. In broad daylight burning tapers were left in his room.

After a journey of nearly two weeks Alexander reached Taganrog. He spent the week before the arrival of the Empress in making arrangement for her comfort, and not until her health showed signs of improvement did he venture to make various excursions in the southern part of the empire. He then visited the shores of the Sea of Azof, ascended the Don for a considerable distance, and visited the capital of the Don Cossacks. It was his intention to defer his expedition to the Crimea until the following spring; but as the fine weather continued he accepted the invitation of Prince Mikhail Vorontsof, governor-general of New Russia, and, in November, left Taganrog for the Crimea. He visited the German colonists and Simferopol on his way, and also stopped at Vorontsof's romantic and beautiful palace at

Alupka. Finally he reached Sevastopol, where he reviewed the fleet, and inspected the fortifications and arsenals. In this journey he overexerted himself, and neglected the precautions which his physician advised him to take. When he reached Taganrog again, the fever of the Crimea was fixed upon him. On the anniversary of the great flood at Saint Petersburg it began to increase in violence. It was impossible to keep the Emperor from receiving from General De Witt circumstantial accounts as to the conspiracy of the South and the traitorous conduct of Colonel Pestel. "Ah! the monsters, the ungrateful monsters; I intended nothing but their happiness," he repeated over and over. Cruel recollections of his father's assassination, and the way by which he came to the throne, may have mingled with his melancholy. He thought sadly of the terrible embarrassments which he was about to bequeath to his successor; he thought of his lost illusions; of his liberal sympathies of former days, which in Poland, as well as in Russia, had ended in reaction; he thought of his broken purposes and changed life. In the Crimea he was heard to repeat, "They may say of me what they will; but I have lived and shall die republican." But what a strange Republic is the system preserved in the memory of the people under the name of "Araktchéevtchina"!

On the first of December, eighteen hundred and twenty-five, the Emperor expired in the arms of the Empress Elisabeth.

In the judgment of his contemporaries Alexander possessed many amiable qualities. "He was courteous and affable in his deportment; in his temper mild and placable; and in his habits active and temperate. His education had raised his mind above the baneful prejudices which haunt the courts of absolute sovereigns, and gave to him sympathies in the welfare of the humblest of his subjects." "As a private citizen, Alexander united all the qualities necessary to win love; as emperor, the events which occupied his cares are known to all the world. The history of Europe is epitomized in his life. For a dozen years he ruled the destinies of the continent. Party spirit may dispute the services which he has rendered, but the Russian people will not hesitate to place him in the list of its greatest sovereigns. In this empire, already so vast, he incorporated, by victory or by treaty, the grand duchy of Finland, Bessarabia, the country of Persia as far as the Araxes and the Kur, the province of Biélostok, and the kingdom of Poland. He did more. By means of wisely-endowed institutions he has introduced the elements of civilization into his realm. He has prepared for the general abolition of serfdom. He has secured the good fortune of his people; he has increased their power and military glory."

We shall now see how Russia celebrated the obsequies of Alexander the Magnanimous.

COMPARATIVE TABLE OF THE RUSSIAN TCHIN, OR ORDER OF RANK.

	Civil Service.	Army.	Navy.	Court.	Church.	
1	Chancellor of the Empire.	Field-Marshal.	Chief Admiral.	Ober Kammerherr (Grand Chamberlain), Lord Steward.	Metropolitan. Archbishop.	The first and second class have the title of Vuisoko-prevoskhoditelstvo, or High Excellency. The third and fourth, the title of Prevoskhoditelstvo, or Excellency. The Councillor of State is called High born. The sixth, seventh, and eighth classes have the title Vuisokoblagorodié, High well-born. The rest have the title of Well-born or Your Honor. These titles are given only to those who have no others. Russian nobles are addressed as Siatelstvo, or Your Excellence, and the
2	Privy Councillor (Actual).	General-in-Chief.	Admiral.		
3	Privy Councillor.	Lieutenant-General.	Vice-Admiral.	Hofmeister, Hofmarshal, Master of the Chace.	Bishop.
4	Councillor of State (Actual).	Major-General.	Rear-Admiral.		Archimandrite.
5	Councillor of State.				Abbot.
6	Councillor of the College.	*Staff Officers.* Polkovnik, or Colonel.	*Staff Officers.* Captain, 1st rank.	Quartermaster.	Protopope.
7	Councillor of the Court.	Lieutenant Colonel.	Captain, 2d rank.		Priest or Rector.
8	Assessor of the College.	Major.	First Lieutenant.		Archdeacon.
9	Titular Councillor.	Captain.	Lieutenant.	Harbinger of the Household.	Deacon.
10	Secretary of the College.	Second Captain.			
11	Secretary of the Navy.				
12	Secretary of the Government.	Porutchik, or Lieutenant.	Midshipman.	Tafeldecker.	
13	Registers of the Senate, Synod, and Cabinet.	Sub-Lieutenant. Ensign (Infantry).			
14	Register of the College.	Cornet (Cavalry).			

Princes of the Empire as Sviétlost, or Your Serene Highness. In the military and marine hierarchies the fourteenth up to the seventh grades give a life-title. Hereditary nobility belongs to the six higher classes. In the civil and court hierarchies personal nobility belongs from the ninth to the fourth, and hereditary to the four higher classes.

www.ingramcontent.com/pod-product-compliance
Lightning Source LLC
Chambersburg PA
CBHW032013220426
43664CB00006B/229